SKILL PRACTICE

PRACTICE

GRADE  5

IncentivePublications
BY WORLD BOOK

Many thanks to Leland Graham, Frankie Long, Charlotte Poulos, Sheri Preskenis, and Diana Standing, whose adapted exercises are included in this book.

Written by Imogene Forte and Marjorie Frank
Illustrated by Kathleen Bullock
Cover by Brenda Tropinski

Print Edition ISBN 978-1-62950-488-9
E-book Edition ISBN 978-1-62950-489-6 (PDF)

World Book, Inc.
180 North LaSalle Street
Suite 900
Chicago, Illinois 60601
USA

For information about World Book and Incentive Publications products, call **1-800-967-5325**, or visit our websites at **www.worldbook.com** and **www.incentivepublications.com**.

Printed in the United States of America by Sheridan Books, Inc.
Chelsea, Michigan
1st printing June 2016

TABLE OF CONTENTS

INTRODUCTION 12

SKILLS CHECKLISTS

    Reading Comprehension Skills Checklist 16

    Words & Vocabulary and Spelling Skills Checklist 17

    Writing Skills Checklist 18

    Grammar & Usage Skills Checklist 19

    U.S. History, Government, & Citizenship Skills Checklist 110

    Map Skills & Geography Checklist 111

    Science Skills Checklist.. 172

    Problem Solving Skills Checklist 202

    Computation & Numbers Skills Checklist 203

    Geometry & Measurement Skills Checklist 204

    Graphing, Statistics, & Probability Skills Checklist 205

LANGUAGE ARTS 15

Reading Comprehension Skills Exercises

    Adventures, Unlimited! . . . (Context • Synonyms & Antonyms) 20

    Lights Required . . . (Context • Prediction) 22

    No License Necessary . . . (Context • Generalization) 23

    Space Mission . . . (Fact & Opinion) 24

    Tricks on the Slopes . . . (Captions)... 25

    The Mysterious Atlantis . . . (Main Idea) 26

    Bring Your Axe! . . . (Read for Details • Draw Conclusions) 27

    Strange Disappearances . . . (Literary Techniques • Figurative Language) 28

    Rock into the Past . . . (Read for Details) 29

    Tracking Down Clues . . . (Predictions • Inference) 30

    A Stomach Dropper . . . (Evaluation) 31

    Here Comes the Judge . . . (Evaluation) 32

    Bring a Mask . . . (Character Analysis • Conclusions) 33

    Meet the Man of La Mancha . . . (Summarize • Conclusions) 34

    Welcome to Camelot . . . (Information from Illustrations • Incorrect Details) 35

    Golden Recipes . . . (Sequence • Read for Details) 36

    It's Great to be Queen . . . (Follow Directions) 37

    A Sweet Record . . . (Follow Directions) 38

    The Greatest Cowboy . . . (Personal Response) 39

Spelling Skills Exercises

    Words That Confuse . . . (Commonly Misspelled Words) 40

    Who's Right? . . . (Identify Correct Spelling) 41

    The Outstanding, Outrageous O . . . (Words with the Letter O) 42

Quartets, Quicksand, & Queens . . . (Words with the Letter Q) 43

Wily Words . . . (Words with the Letter Y) 44

Extraordinary Words . . . (Words with the Letter X) 45

Look-Alike Words . . . (Similar Words) 46

Words with Pizzaz . . . (Words with the Letter Z) 47

Additions to the Beginning . . . (Words with Prefixes) 48

Additions to the End . . . (Words with Suffixes) 49

Words & Vocabulary Skills Exercises

Bon Voyage! . . . (Denotation & Connotation) 50

Words with a Past . . . (Word Histories) 51

Little Shop of Opposites . . . (Antonyms) 52

Wild Surf . . . (Synonyms) 53

Unforgettable! . . . (Roots) 54

Stars on the Beach . . . (Multiple Meanings) 55

After Dark . . . (Learning New Words) 56

Ho, Hum! . . . (Figurative Language) 57

Writing Skills Exercises

Writing with a Spark . . . (Effective Words) 58

Feature Yourself . . . (Effective Sentences) 60

Weathered Words . . . (Effective Words & Phrases • Visual Images) 61

Better Beginnings . . . (Good Beginnings) 62

Good Questions . . . (Effective Questions) 63

What Characters! . . . (Characterization) 64

Cliff-Hangers . . . (Imaginative Writing) 66

Convince Me! . . . (Persuasive Writing) 67

Strange Disappearances . . . (Adapt Writing for Audience) 68

Coming Alive! . . . (Personification).. 69

Quite by Accident . . . (Sentence Sequence) 70

Unsolved Mysteries . . . (Vary Sentence Length) 71

Courtroom Impostors . . . (Unrelated Details) 72

Lost Headlines . . . (Good Titles) 74

Wrapping It Up . . . (Strong Endings) 76

Great Choices . . . (Supporting Details) 78

Terrible Choices . . . (Supporting Details) 79

Grammar & Usage Skills Exercises

Where Is Camp Lookout? . . . (Kinds of Sentences) 80

Step by Step . . . (Subjects & Predicates) 81

Camper Carl's Compound Problem . . . (Simple & Compound Sentences) 82

Running Out of Control . . . (Fragments & Run-on Sentences) 83

The Greenhorns Camp Out . . . (Singular & Plural Nouns) 84

A Grand Mess in the Mess Hall . . . (Singular & Plural Nouns) 85

Picture the Owner . . . (Singular Possessive Nouns) 86

Lost & Found . . . (Plural Possessive Nouns) 87

Pack Rats . . . (Subject Pronouns) 88

Getting There . . . (Object Pronouns) 89

Bear Creek . . . (Future Tense Verbs) 90

Irregular Beings . . . (Irregular Verbs) 91

Ghost Story . . . (Action Verbs) 92

Survival Training . . . (Helping Verbs) 93

Wet, Wetter, Wettest . . . (Comparing with Adjectives) 94

Camp Field Day . . . (Comparing with Adjectives) 95

Meet Billy B. Good . . . (Comparing with Adverbs) 96

Getting Nowhere . . . (Negatives) 97

Go Fish . . . (Direct Objects) 98

Taken by Storm . . . (Homophones) 99

Getting the Picture . . . (Homophones) 100

Campside Capers . . . (Quotation Marks) 102

A Counselor's Midnight Hike . . . (Editing: Punctuation) 103

Hello Mother, Hello Father . . . (Editing: Punctuation & Capitalization) 104

Treasure Hunt . . . (Editing: Spelling, Punctuation, & Capitalization) 106

SOCIAL STUDIES

SOCIAL STUDIES 109

U.S. History, Government, & Citizenship Skills Exercises

Skating into the Past . . . (Overview of Historical Events) 112

They Were Here First! . . . (First Americans) 114

The Great Explorers . . . (European Explorations) 116

Settling Down . . . (Colonization) 117

An Important Piece of Paper . . . (Declaration of Independence) 118

"The British Are Coming!" . . . (American Revolution) 119

Powerful Words . . . (The Preamble) 120

The Main Document . . . (U.S. Constitution) 121

Checks and Balances . . . (U.S. Government Structure) 122

A Congressional Maze . . . (Legislative Branch) 123

"I Do Solemnly Swear" . . . (Executive Branch) 124

Order in the Court! . . . (Judicial Branch) 125

The Road from Bills to Laws . . . (Bills & Laws) 126

13 Originals . . . (Thirteen Colonies) 127

10 Bold Statements . . . (Bill of Rights) 128

Such a Bargain! . . . (Louisiana Purchase) 130

Secrets of the West . . . (Explorers of the West) 131

The Big Argument . . . (Slavery & Abolition) 132

A Nation Divided . . . (Civil War) 133

Carpetbaggers & Scalawags . . . (Reconstruction) 134

The Golden Spike . . . (Transcontinental Railroad) 135

Machines Replace Muscles . . . (Industrial Revolution) 136

The Old West . . . (The Old West) 137

Coming to America . . . (Immigrants) 138

Into the Recent Past . . . (20th Century Events) 140

The Big Chill . . . (Cold War • Space Race) 141

Cruising the Capital . . . (Washington, D.C.) 142

Where Did It Happen? . . . (Historical Landmarks) 144

When Did It Happen? . . . (Timeline of Major Events) 146

Back to the Present . . . (Current Government) 148

Mystery VIPs . . . (Famous Americans) 149

Map & Geography Skills Exercises

We Deliver! . . . (Map Tools & Resources) 150

Anything! Anywhere! . . . (Map Tools & Resources) 151

Muddy Map Disaster . . . (Map Titles & Labels) 152

Watch Out for Ghosts! . . . (Map Key) 153

A Sundae Delivery . . . (Scale) 154

Business Is Booming . . . (Hemispheres) 155

Dentist's Nightmare . . . (United States) 156

Help Wanted! . . . (Geographic Terms) 158

Off to Saddlesore Acres . . . (Using a Grid) 159

Ups & Downs . . . (Latitude) 160

Where's the Tea? . . . (Longitude) 161

Worldwide Pizza Party . . . (Latitude & Longitude) 162

For Animals Only . . . (Find Locations) 164

Hazards of the Job . . . (Find Information) 165

It's About Time! . . . (Time Zone Map) 166

The Weirdest Delivery . . . (Make a Map) 168

SCIENCE

SCIENCE 171

Science Skills Exercises

Fitness Search . . . (Health & Fitness) 173

Attack of the "Germ"-inators . . . (Body Defenses) 174

Hanging Together . . . (Compounds) 176

A Changeable Day . . . (Physical & Chemical Changes) 178

A-mazing Matter . . . (States of Matter) 179

A Hot Joke . . . (Heat) 180

An Electrifying Topic . . . (Electricity) 181

A Light Study . . . (Properties of Light) 182

Snow Problems . . . (Energy, Force, & Motion) 183

It's Out of This World . . . (Solar System) 184

Strange Encounters . . . (Space Features) 186

A Vacation Paradise? . . . (Earth Processes) 188

A Rocky Business . . . (Rocks) 189

Everybody Talks About It! . . . (Weather Patterns) 190

Ocean Snooping . . . (Oceans) 192

Where Would You Find It? . . . (Earth & Space Science Vocabulary) 193

Science Challenge . . . (Science Facts) 194

Super Science Challenge . . . (Science Facts) 195

Definitely Not Trivial . . . (Earth & Space Science Facts) 196

Such Odd Stuff . . . (Earth's Features) 197

Science Terms 198

MATH 201

Problem Solving Skills Exercises

Something's Missing! . . . (Too Little Information) 206

More Than Enough . . . (Too Much Information) 207

Wild Whitewater Whirl . . . (Choose Correct Equation) 208

Sink That Basket . . . (Write Equations to Solve Problems) 209

A Slippery Slope . . . (Solve Problems Using a Chart) 210

Goal or Not? . . . (Solve Problems Using a Graph) 211

Just in Case . . . (Solve Problems with U.S. Customary Measurements) 212

Amazing Feet . . . (Solve Problems with Metric Measurements) 213

Bruno's Burly Brew . . . (Fractions & Mixed Numerals) 214

"Figuring" Out Decimals . . . (Solve Problems with Decimals) 215

Where's the Food? . . . (Solve Problems with Money) 216

Bumps, Bruises, & Breaks . . . (Choose Correct Operation) 217

Beach Bag Jumble . . . (Use Formulas to Solve Problems) 218

Diamonds, Rings, & Courts . . . (Use Formulas to Solve Problems) 219

Hang Ten Percent . . . (Solve Problems with Percent & Fractions) 220

"But Coach, Can We Rest Now?" . . . (Solve Problems with Percent) 221

Time Out . . . (Solve Problems with Time) 222

Rack Up the Savings . . . (Solve Problems with Taxes & Discounts) 223

Chill Out . . . (Estimate Problem Solutions) 224

Fantastic Finishes . . . (Create Diagrams to Solve Problems) 225

Criss-Cross Bike Race . . . (Mental Math) 226

Hitting the Bricks . . . (Trial and Error) 227

Locker Room Logic . . . (Solve Problems with Logic) 228

Logical Lineup . . . (Solve Problems with Logic) 229

Gridiron Solutions . . . (Find More Than One Solution) 230

Just Hanging Around . . . (Choose a Problem-Solving Strategy) 232

Practice Makes Perfect . . . (Choose a Problem-Solving Strategy) 233

Submerged Solutions . . . (Explain Problem Solutions) 234

Hitting Their Stride . . . (Determine Accuracy of Solutions) 236

Computation & Numbers Skills Exercises

Athletes on Parade . . . (Read & Write Numbers) 237

En Guard! . . . (Add & Subtract Whole Numbers) 239

The Big Winners . . . (Whole Number Operations) 240

Explosive Speeds . . . (Factors) 241

No Brakes! . . . (Greatest Common Factors) 242

May the Best Sailor Win . . . (Multiply Whole Numbers) 243

Fans by the Thousands . . . (Divide Whole Numbers) 244

Making It over Hurdles . . . (Whole Number Operations) 245

Tourist Attractions . . . (Choose Operations) 246

The Right Properties . . . (Properties) 247

Watch That Puck! . . . (Fractions as Parts of Sets) 248

Over the Net . . . (Compare & Order Fractions) 249

Lost! . . . (Compare Fractions) 250

Winter Olympic Trivia . . . (Equivalent Fractions) 251

The Longest Jumps . . . (Improper Fractions & Mixed Numerals) 252

Getting to Venues . . . (Improper Fractions & Mixed Numerals) 253

The #1 Sport . . . (Add & Subtract Fractions) 254

Through Wild Waters . . . (Divide Fractions) 255

A Huge Obstacle Course . . . (Round Decimals) 256

Who Wears the Medals? . . . (Add Decimals) 257

What's the Cost? . . . (Multiply & Divide Decimals) 258

Over the Top . . . (Fractions & Decimals) 259

The Dream Team . . . (Fractions & Percents) 260

Temperature Counts . . . (Integers) 261

Geometry Skills Exercises

Signs from the Crowd . . . (Identify Points, Lines, Angles, Rays, & Planes) 262

A Plane Mess . . . (Identify Plane Figures) 263

Duffel Bag Jumble . . . (Use Formulas to Find Perimeter, Area, and Volume) 264

The Longest Practices . . . (Measure Time) 265

The Great Shape Match-Up . . . (Identify Kinds of Polygons) 266

Keeping Busy . . . (Identify Kinds of Quadrilaterals) 267

Mirror Images . . . (Identify Symmetrical Figures) 268

Out of Order . . . (Recognize Transformations of Plane Figures) 269

More or Less? . . . (Compare and Convert U.S. Customary Units) 270

Climbing the Wall . . . (Use Metric Units to Measure Length) 271

Circles Everywhere You Look . . . (Find Circumference of Circles) 272

Sky-High Measurements . . . (Area of Plane Figures) 273

Pep Rally Measurements . . . (Find Area and Perimeter) 274

Hungry Fans . . . (Find Volume with Metric Units) 275

Uniform Confusion . . . (Find Volume with U.S. Customary Units) 276

Graphing Skills Exercises

Spectacular Bubbles . . . (Read & Interpret a Frequency Graph) 278

Wonderful Walls . . . (Create a Frequency Graph from Statistical Data) 279

Enormous Edibles . . . (Find Median, Mode, & Range in Data) 280

Incredible Creations . . . (Use Tables of Statistics to Solve Problems) 281

Studying to Set Records . . . (Use Graph Information to Solve Problems) 282

Dozens of Dancers . . . (Find Locations on a Coordinate Grid) 283

Piggy Bank Probabilities . . . (Find Probability of an Event) 284

Lots & Lots of Litter . . . (Find Probability of an Event) 285

Walking Tall for New Records . . . (Find Probability of an Event) 286

Will There Be Light? . . . (Find Odds of an Event) 287

The Biggest Drop . . . (Describe Outcomes of Two Events) 288

Carefully Balanced Eggs . . . (Identify Combinations of Sets within a Set) 290

A Puzzling Record . . . (Use Sampling to Make Predictions) 291

Barrow Racing for Dollars . . . (Use Probability to Solve Problems) 292

APPENDIX 293

Language Arts Skills Test 294

    Part One: Reading Comprehension 294

    Part Two: Words & Vocabulary 297

    Part Three: Spelling 301

    Part Four: Grammar & Usage 304

    Part Five: Writing 307

Social Studies Skills Test 310

    Part One: U.S. History, Government, & Citizenship 310

    Part Two: Map Skills & Geography 314

Science Skills Test 317

Math Skills Test 320

    Part One: Problem Solving 320

    Part Two: Computation & Numbers 322

    Part Three: Geometry & Measurement 324

    Part Four: Graphing, Statistics, & Probability 326

Skills Test Answer Key 330

Skills Exercises Answer Key 334

INTRODUCTION

Do basic skills have to be boring? Absolutely not! Mastery of basic skills provides the foundation for exciting learning opportunities for students. Content relevant to their everyday life is fascinating stuff! Kids love learning about topics such as galaxies and glaciers, thunderstorms and timelines, continents and chemicals, tarantulas and tornadoes, poems and plateaus, elephants and encyclopedias, mixtures and mummies, antonyms and Antarctica, and more. Using these topics and carefully-designed practice they develop basic skills which enable them to ponder, process, grow, and achieve school success.

Acquiring, polishing, and using basic skills and content is a cause for celebration—not an exercise in drudgery. *Skill Practice: Grade 5* invites students to sharpen their abilities in the essentials of language arts, social studies, science, and mathematics.

As you examine *Skill Practice: Grade 5,* you will see that it is filled with attractive age-appropriate student exercises. These pages are no ordinary worksheets! *Skill Practice: Grade 5* contains hundreds of inventive and inviting ready-to-use lessons based on a captivating theme that invites the student to join an adventure, solve a puzzle, pursue a mystery, or tackle a problem. Additionally, each illustrated exercise provides diverse tools for reinforcement and extension of basic and higher-order thinking skills.

Skill Practice: Grade 5 contains the following components:

- **A clear, sequential list of skills for eleven different content areas**
  Checklists of skills begin each content section. These lists correlate with the exercises, identifying page numbers where specific skills can be practiced. Students can chart their progress by checking off each skill as it is mastered.

- **Over 300 pages of student exercises**
  Each exercise page:
  > . . . addresses a specific basic skill or content area.
  > . . . presents tasks that grab the attention and curiosity of students.
  > . . . contains clear directions to the student.
  > . . . asks students to use, remember, and practice a basic skill.
  > . . . challenges students to think creatively and analytically.
  > . . . requires students to apply the skill to real situations or content.
  > . . . takes students on learning adventures with a variety of delightful characters!

- **A ready-to-use assessment tool**
  Four skills tests follow the skills exercises. The tests are presented in parts corresponding to the skills lists. Designed to be used as pre- or post-tests, individual parts of these tests can be given to students at separate times, if needed.

- **Complete answer keys**
  Easy-to-find-and-use answer keys for all exercises and skills tests follow each section.

HOW TO USE THIS BOOK:

The exercises contained in *Skill Practice: Grade 5* are to be used with adult assistance. The adult may serve as a guide to ensure the student understands the directions and questions.

Skill Practice: Grade 5 is designed to be used in many diverse ways. Its use will vary according to the needs of the students and the structure of the learning environment.

The skills checklists may be used as:
> . . . record-keeping tools to track individual skills mastery;
> . . . planning guides for instruction; and
> . . . a place for students to proudly check off accomplishments.

Each exercise page may be used as:
> . . . a pre-test or check to see how well a student has mastered a skill;
> . . . one of many resources or exercises for teaching a skill;
> . . . a way to practice or polish a skill that has been taught;
> . . . a review of a skill taught earlier;
> . . . reinforcement of a single basic skill, skills cluster, or content base;
> . . . a preview to help identify instructional needs; and
> . . . an assessment for a skill that a student has practiced.

The exercises are flexibly designed for presentation in many formats and settings. They are useful for individual instruction or independent work. They can also be used under the direction of an adult with small groups.

The skills tests may be used as:
> . . . pre-tests to gauge instructional or placement needs;
> . . . information sources to help adjust instruction; and
> . . . post-tests to review student mastery of skills and content areas.

Skill Practice: Grade 5 is not intended to be a complete curriculum or textbook. It is a collection of inventive exercises to sharpen skills and provide students and parents with tools for reinforcing concepts and skills, and for identifying areas that need additional attention. This book offers a delightful assortment of tasks that give students just the practice they need—and to get that practice in a manner that is not boring.

As students take on the challenges of the enticing adventures in this book, they will increase their comfort level with the use of fundamental reading, writing, and language skills and concepts. Watching your student check off the sharpened skills is cause for celebration!

LANGUAGE ARTS

Skills Exercises

Grade Five

SKILLS CHECKLIST
READING COMPREHENSION

✔	SKILL	PAGE(S)
	Recognize and use synonyms	20–23
	Determine word meaning from context	20–23
	Recognize and use antonyms	21
	Distinguish between facts and opinions	24
	Read to find details and information	24–39
	Gain information from reading captions	25
	Read to find answers to questions	25–27, 29–33, 35–39
	Identify literal and implied main ideas	26
	Identify supporting details	27, 29
	Identify figurative language; describe its effect on the writing	28
	Identify literary techniques used to enhance written pieces	28
	Predict future actions or outcomes	30
	Use information gained from text to make inferences	30
	Evaluate ideas, conclusions, or opinions from a text	31, 32
	Analyze characters described in written pieces	33
	Draw logical conclusions from written material	33, 34
	Paraphrase or summarize a written text	34
	Identify incorrect details in a passage	35
	Supply missing information for a passage	35
	Make use of illustrations or graphics to understand a text	35–38
	Determine sequence of events	36
	Interpret and make graphs	37
	Read to follow directions	37, 38
	Explain personal responses to written material	39

SKILLS CHECKLIST
WORDS & VOCABULARY and SPELLING

✔	SKILL	PAGE(S)
	Correctly spell commonly misspelled words	40
	Identify words that are spelled correctly	40, 41, 46, 49
	Correctly spell words that contain the letter *o*	42
	Identify words that are spelled incorrectly	42
	Correctly spell words that contain special letters: *q, s, x, y, z*	43–47
	Correctly spell and distinguish among words that look or sound similar	46
	Correctly spell words with prefixes	48
	Correctly spell words with suffixes	49
	Distinguish between denotation and connotation	50
	Give the denotation and connotation of words	50
	Explore the history and origin of words	51
	Use a dictionary to find information about word history and origin	51
	Recognize and use antonyms	52
	Recognize and use synonyms	53
	Identify the meanings of common root words	54
	Recognize and use roots to determine meanings of words	54
	Identify and define multiple meanings of a word	55
	Learn and use new words	56
	Learn new words in a variety of categories	56
	Use a dictionary to find word meanings	56
	Identify and use figurative language	57

SKILLS CHECKLIST
WRITING

✔	SKILL	PAGE(S)
	Recognize and replace overused or ordinary words and phrases	58
	Recognize and use effective words (specific, unusual, colorful, active, etc.)	58–61
	Infuse personal flavor into a selection	60
	Recognize and write clear, interesting sentences	60, 62, 63, 76
	Recognize and create fluent sentences and paragraphs	60, 62, 63, 76
	Identify poetry; use writing skills to write poetry	61
	Recognize and choose words that produce strong visual images	61
	Recognize and include sensory appeal in writing	61
	Recognize and create strong beginnings	62
	Recognize and write clear questions	63
	Recognize characterization; use writing skills to write a characterization	64
	Recognize a clear main idea; create pieces that clearly reveal the main idea	64, 66–67, 69
	Recognize and write selections that have a clear beginning, middle, and end	64, 66–67, 69
	Recognize imaginative writing; use writing skills to write an imaginative selection	66
	Recognize persuasive selections; use writing skills to write a persuasive selection	67
	Recognize and include literary techniques to make writing effective	68
	Adapt form and content for a specific audience	68
	Recognize and include personification in writing	69
	Recognize and arrange sentences for proper sequence and interesting sound	70, 71
	Recognize and write sentences of varied length and structure	71
	Recognize and eliminate excess or unrelated details	72
	Recognize and eliminate repetitive or unnecessary words, phrases, or sentences	72
	Recognize and use enough examples to support the main idea well	72, 78–79
	Recognize and create strong titles	74
	Recognize and create strong endings	76
	Recognize and show clear organization within a written piece	78, 79
	Recognize and supply plenty of interesting, relevant details to a written idea	78, 79
	Recognize and include details that are surprising, unusual, or extraordinary	79

SKILLS CHECKLIST
GRAMMAR & USAGE

✔	SKILL	PAGE(S)
	Identify and write declarative, interrogative, imperative, and exclamatory sentences	80
	Find simple subjects and simple predicates	81
	Identify and write simple and compound sentences	82
	Identify and correct sentence fragments and run-on sentences	83
	Identify and use singular and plural nouns	84–87
	Distinguish among parts of speech	84–96
	Identify, form, and use singular possessive nouns	86
	Identify, form, and use plural possessive nouns	87
	Identify and use subject and object pronouns	88, 89
	Identify and use verb tenses: past, present, and future	90, 91
	Identify and use irregular verbs	91
	Identify and use action verbs	92
	Identify and use helping verbs	93
	Identify and use adjectives	94, 95
	Identify and use comparative and superlative adjectives	94, 95
	Identify and use adverbs	96
	Identify and use comparative and superlative adverbs	96
	Use negatives correctly; correct double negatives	97
	Identify and use direct objects	98
	Identify and distinguish among homophones	99, 100
	Use quotation marks properly in dialogue	102
	Use proper capitalization in a variety of situations	102, 104–106
	Properly use a variety of punctuation marks	102–106
	Make corrections in improper capitalization	106
	Use proper capitalization	104, 106
	Correct spelling in a variety of situations	106

ADVENTURES, UNLIMITED!

Let us take you on the adventure of your dreams! **Adventures, Unlimited** is the one stop when you are shopping for travel anywhere, anytime. We have special trips to real and fantasy locations in the past, present, and future! Choose your adventure—and start packing!

Find a word on the adventure posters that matches each direction below.
Look on both pages (pages 20 and 21).

Find a word that is a synonym for . . .

1. adventure   Question

2. fly   Soar

3. tricks   Magic

4. socialize   entertain

5. examine   Study

6. try   Attempt

7. travel   Expedition

Use with page 21.

Find 2 synonyms for *search*

8. _____
   Explore

Find a word or phrase that means . . .

9. make-believe   fake

10. grand   formal

11. having to do with food   hungry

12. climb

Name _____

Space MOUNTAIN DREAM

Fabulous

OUTRAGEOUS EXPEDITIONS
Take off on an escapade to the International Space Station. Camp alone in the dark, foreboding forest. Endeavor to climb the Empire State Building.

Creature Escapades!
Catch an elusive Leprechaun.
Face the fiercest bull.
Search for a mythical mermaid.

REAL EXCITEMENT IN REAL PLACES

Probe the world's deepest cavern.
Spend a month at Clown College.
Learn downhill antics from Olympic Champions.
Scale the great Denali Mountain.
Sail the highest, wildest seas.
Compete in the Iditarod.
Helicopter to ski the remote Alps.
Engage a ride on the Orient Express.

IMAGINE EXUBERANCE

GREAT

Modern

BARGAIN ADVENTURES
Rule the court for a day.
Learn to soar through the air on a pole.
Eat your way to a culinary world record.

mother nature
perfect

GREAT MYSTERY ADVENTURES
Search for the lost city of Atlantis.
Venture into the Bermuda Triangle, if you dare.
Meet the unfathomable Loch Ness Monster.

Holy Cow!

vacation

QUEST Echoes

Find a word on the adventure posters that matches each direction below.

Write a word that is an antonym for . . .

13. safe _dangerous_

14. real _fake_

15. modern _old school_

16. pleasant _dreadful_

17. small _big_

18. plain & simple _fancy, colorful_

19. believable _unbelievable_

20. past _future_

Write a word that is a synonym for . . .

21. hard to catch_____

22. famous_____

23. wreck_____

24. a good price _____

25. hire_____

26. a look_____

27. far away_____

28. scariest_____

Use with page 20.

Name

LIGHTS REQUIRED

ADVENTURE #1 Explore the Réseau Jean Bernard Cave, one of the deepest caves in the world. Bring a hard hat, wear a raincoat, and don't forget the lights!

Decide what the words below the dialogue balloons mean in the context of the conversation. Write the meaning.

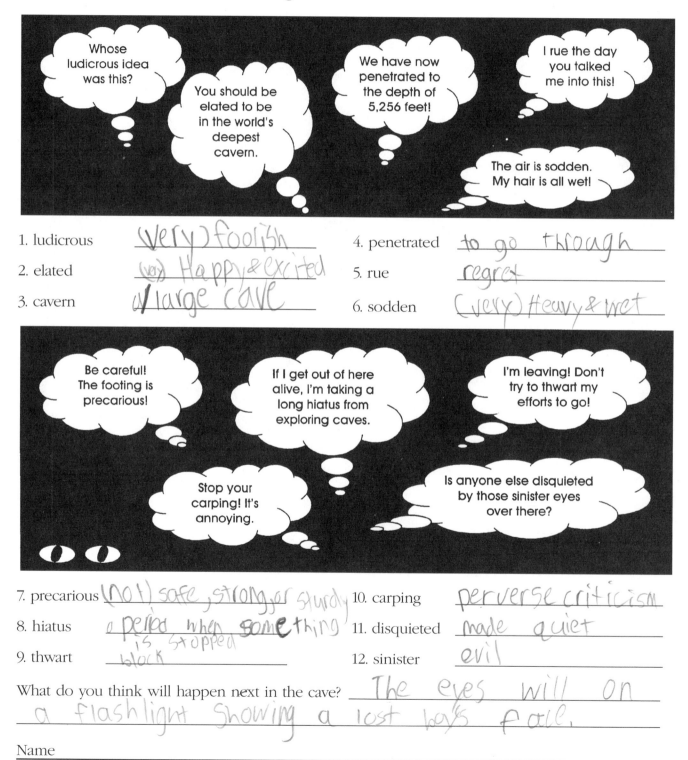

1. ludicrous (very) foolish

2. elated (very) Happy & excited

3. cavern a large cave

4. penetrated to go through

5. rue regret

6. sodden (very) Heavy & wet

7. precarious (not) safe, strong, or sturdy

8. hiatus a period when something is stopped

9. thwart block

10. carping perverse criticism

11. disquieted made quiet

12. sinister evil

What do you think will happen next in the cave? The eyes will on a flashlight showing a lost boys face.

Name

NO LICENSE NECESSARY

ADVENTURE #2 We'll sneak you into the secret showroom of one of the top car companies to see some cars of the future. Then you can hop right into the car of your choice and take it for a test drive!

Read the rules for test-driving this awesome vehicle. Tell what each word listed below means. Decide its meaning from seeing how it is used in the Rules for Test Drivers.

RULES for TEST DRIVERS

#1 Drivers must certify that they are over age 10.

#2 Never render body safety restraints inoperable.

#3 Submit to all instructions given by the computer.

#4 Do not deploy parachutes at speeds under 70 mph.

#5 No ingesting of liquids at speeds over 200 mph.

#6 Do not eat pizza or other lardaceous foods in the car.

#7 Do not deposit or throw refuse in the car.

#8 Drivers are precluded from watching the movie system.

#9 Attend to information disseminated by the computer.

#10 This model is banned from the monorail systems.

#11 Do not tamper with automatic speed control devices.

#12 Drivers showing excessive aggression will be chastened.

#13 Any traffic citations will be charged to the driver.

#14 This car must be promptly returned at termination of drive.

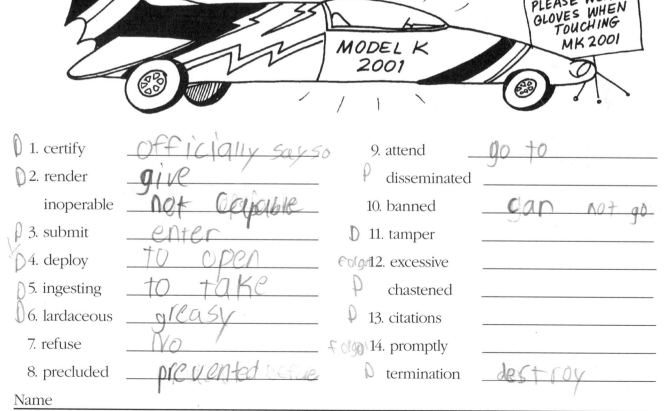

PLEASE WEAR GLOVES WHEN TOUCHING MK 2001

MODEL K 2001

1. certify ___officially says so___

2. render ___give___

inoperable ___not capable___

3. submit ___enter___

4. deploy ___to open___

5. ingesting ___to take___

6. lardaceous ___greasy___

7. refuse ___No___

8. precluded ___prevented___

9. attend ___go to___

disseminated ___

10. banned ___can not go___

11. tamper ___

12. excessive ___

chastened ___

13. citations ___

14. promptly ___

termination ___destroy___

Name ___

SPACE MISSION

ADVENTURE #3 Fly a shuttle through space to visit the International Space Station. This is the place where astronaut Scott Kelly set an American record for longest consecutive time in space in 2016. You don't have to stay as long as he did!

Read the travel brochure for the station. Use red to circle all statements that are facts. Use blue to circle all statements that are opinions.

You'll be so glad you did this!!

VISIT
INTERNATIONAL SPACE STATION

Travel to the station by space shuttle

- Orbit Earth and see fantastic sights!
- Astronauts will enjoy your visit!
- See Dextre, the space station's robot.
- Explore the living and working spaces.
- Get fitted with your own space suit.
- Walk in space.
- All food and equipment are provided.
- You'll love the food!
- You'll have fun feeling weightless!
- No dangers or accidents will occur.

All astronauts & cosmonauts want a chance to live on the International Space Station!

Must be at least 25 years of age.

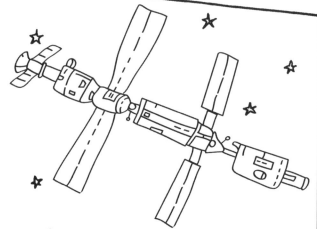

WE PROVIDE TRAINING!

STAY 5, 10, or 15 days

We won't keep you as long as we kept Cosmonaut Valeri Polyakov. He stayed 438 days!

The first module of the International Space Station was launched in 1998.

Schedule
TRAINING	January 1
LAUNCH	December 5
RETURN FLIGHTS	December 9
	December 14
	December 19

Adventures, Unlimited

You can afford it!
See your Adventure Company Representative

Health examination required.

Name

TRICKS ON THE SLOPES

ADVENTURE #4 Learn downhill tricks from the champions! All kinds of fantastic antics happen on the slopes in the Winter Olympic Games. Here's your chance to learn some tricks from the best athletes!

Read the caption beside each picture. Then answer the questions. If the captions do not supply an answer, write NA (for not applicable).

1. In the halfpipe event, snowboarders zip up and down the steep sides of a halfpipe. It is a U-shaped structure covered in ice and snow. Halfpipe competitors do wild tricks with crazy names like Ollies, Stale Fish, McTwist, and Fakies.

3. Aerial skiing contests are great fun! Daring skiers perform flips and twists in the air off a 66-yard-long ramp. Judges give them a score that is based 20% on the takeoff, 50% on the flight in the air, and 30% on the landing.

2. USA's Lindsey Vonn became the first American woman to win a gold medal in downhill racing at the 2010 Olympics. Then she broke her knee in 2013 and her ankle in 2014. Vonn came back to win the World Cup in downhill racing in 2016.

4. Ski jumpers fly through the air with their ski tips spread apart in a V-style. This V gives them greater lift from the air as the air flows beneath the skis. This helps the skiers fly farther. Anders Fannemel of Norway is one of the best ski jumpers ever.

1. In which three sports are athletes jumping into the air? _____
2. Why do ski jumpers use a V-style in the air? _It gives greater lift._
3. Which sport has a trick named Stale Fish? _The ha_
4. How much of an aerial skier's score is based on the landing? _30% of it._
5. For what event did Lindsey Vonn win a medal in 2010? _In downhill racing_
6. What is the sport of Norway's Anders Fannemel? _It is ski jumping_
7. In which two sports shown do athletes do twists? _In, halfpipe and Aerial skiing._
8. How high in the air do aerial skiers perform? _Over 66 yards._
9. When did Lindsey Vonn break her knee? _In 2013._
10. What is a halfpipe? _Snow boarders zip up & down steep sides of a halfpipe_
11. How long is the ramp for aerial skiing? _66 yards long._

Name _____

THE MYSTERIOUS ATLANTIS

ADVENTURE #5 Climb aboard a submarine to search the oceans for the lost continent of Atlantis. People wonder if Atlantis really existed. You can help to solve the mystery once and for all!

1.

Atlantis was a mythical continent in the Atlantic Ocean. Plato, a writer in ancient Greece, wrote a tale about this continent. The tale told of a great empire that existed on Atlantis. In the tale, earthquakes, floods, and great storms shook the whole continent. During the great storms, Atlantis sank into the sea.

The main idea of this paragraph is

a) Plato was a great writer.

b) Atlantis is a mythical continent that disappeared into the sea.

c) Many tales have been told about Atlantis.

d) Earthquakes have destroyed many continents in the ocean.

2.

For centuries, people were fascinated with Plato's tales about Atlantis. Many wondered where it was and how it sank. Many wondered if it was a real place or just another Greek myth. Perhaps it really existed at one time. Over the years, many stories and fantasies have been told about a great continent that lies beneath the ocean. Some think that it is still inhabited by sea creatures such as mermaids and mermen. Some scientists think the tales were inspired by a real island, the island of Thira in the Aegean Sea. This island was destroyed by a volcanic eruption in 1500 B.C.

The main idea of this paragraph is

a) There are many questions and theories about the existence and fate of Atlantis.

b) Many people think sea creatures still live in Atlantis.

c) Atlantis was destroyed by a volcano.

3.

The great mythical empire of Atlantis was built on a continent in the Atlantic Ocean. Atlantis had powerful armies which planned to conquer all of the lands in the Mediterranean area. They had success in parts of Europe and North Africa, but the armies of Athens defeated them and drove them away.

The main idea of this paragraph is

a) Atlantis had powerful armies.

b) Athens had powerful armies.

c) Armies of Atlantis tried to conquer other lands.

Name

(handwritten math in top margin:)
112
×8
———
96
+1 1
———
10 7

BRING YOUR AXE!

ADVENTURE #6

Are all those stories about Paul Bunyan really true? Head off into the forest and meet him for yourself. Maybe he'll teach you how to swing an axe or how to eat 37 pancakes at one sitting!

JOB APPLICATION
Position: LUMBERJACK

Name	Paul Bunyan
Age	22
Place of Birth	Maine
Height	8 feet 11 inches
Weight	344 pounds
Physical Condition	EXCELLENT
Shoe Size	200
Experience	Woodsplitting, tree felling, lumberjack work across the nation
Abilities & Qualities That Make You Fit for the Job	*great strength and endurance *can fell two trees at one blow *can swing axe 16 hours without stopping *created the Great Lakes with my footprints *5 years experience
Special Requirements	I need to eat 20,000 calories a day.
Preferred Working Conditions and Why	I prefer to work with my great blue ox, Babe. The spread of his horns is the length of 42 axe handles. He can haul great quantities of wood.

1. How tall was Paul in inches? _107"_

2. Whom did Paul prefer for a working partner? _Babe_

3. If Paul worked as a lumberjack for 25 years after he got this job, how old was he when he quit? _47_

4. Would you hire Paul for this job? _Yes_

5. Why or why not? _He is expirienced_

6. Which quality do you think best qualified him for this job? _Great strength and endurance._

7. What characteristic might make an employer hesitate to hire Paul? _I is his hieght and weight._

8. If you were the employer, what question would you like to ask Paul in an interview? _Do you have diabetes._

9. Write a one-sentence description of Paul. _Very fit and tall._

Name

STRANGE DISAPPEARANCES

ADVENTURE #7 Take a trip to the Bermuda Triangle—if you dare! Many ships and airplanes have supposedly disappeared in this area of the Atlantic Ocean off the coast of Bermuda. Scientists are baffled. Do you want to try it?

Writers sometimes use figurative language to describe things like the Bermuda Triangle. Similes and metaphors compare things which are not usually thought of as having anything in common. Read the similes and metaphors here. Then try writing some of your own!

Your room is the Bermuda Triangle.
Your room is a black hole,
(Things that go into it are never seen again!)
Kate B., Gr.5

What's It Like?
by Laura A., Gr. 6

Life is like a flower
that is blooming.
The sky is like
a never ending story,
Life is like a dark pool of water—
You never know what's in it.

Finish these:

My room is like ___Mad house   library,_____.

Life is like ___1 cheater   and   1 honest   guy_____.

My friend is like ___A   baby   bottle.   Me: baby._____.

_____ is like _____.

_____ is as _____ as _____.

Life is Like
by Camille M., Gr.5

Life is Like
A gift waiting to be opened
Counting to infinity and beyond
Walking somewhere you've never been
(You never know what's around the corner)
Unsolved mysteries
A never ending road (just keep on driving)
An everlasting gob-stopper

Name _____

ROCK INTO THE PAST

ADVENTURE #8 Attend the very first rock concert! Take an awesome time machine into the Stone Age and get ready to rock!

1. Who performs *My Cave's on Fire?*
   The Paleo-Lyths

2. What is the closing song?
   Till the Volcano blows

3. What follows the intermission?
   Be a little boulder honey

4. What song does Mick Jagged & the Rolling Boulders perform?
   I Dino if I love you anymore.

5. Which song is sung by the Smashing Marbles?
   Your as cuddly as a wooly mammoth

6. Who sings with Bronto?
   The cave dudes

7. What do the Limestone Lovers perform?
   I've cried pebbles over you.

8. Who is the lead singer with the Hot Rocks?
   Terri Dactyl

9. Who performs *The Gravel Pit Rock?*
   The cro-magnon crooners

10. Who sings about a brontosaurus?
    The Petro cliff Trio

11. Where is the concert held?
    Graniteville music Fest

12. How many groups perform before the intermission? 5

13. Who performs *Dancin' at the Quarry?*
    Tommy shale

14. When does the concert begin?
    After dark

15. Who sings about granite?
    The Standing stones.

Name

GRANITEVILLE MUSIC FEST
Place: Hard Rock Arena
Time: After Dark

PROGRAM

I Dino If I Love You Anymore
Mick Jagged & the Rolling Boulders

I Feel Like a Brontosaurus Stomped on my Head
The Petro Cliff Trio

Your Love Is Like a Sabre-Tooth Tiger
Terri Dactyl & the Hot Rocks

Sha-boom, Sha-boom, Sha-Rock
The Lava-Ettes

You're as Cuddly as a Woolly Mammoth
The Smashing Marbles

INTERMISSION

Be a Little Boulder, Honey
Curt McCave

The Gravel Pit Rock
The Cro-Magnon Crooners

Please Don't Take Me for Granite, Baby
The Standing Stones

My Cave's on Fire
The Paleo-Lyths

Your Heart's Made of Stone
Bronto & the Cave Dudes

Dancin' at the Quarry
Tommy Shale

I've Cried Pebbles over You
The Limestone Lovers

Till the Volcano Blows
The Square Wheels

TRACKING DOWN CLUES

ADVENTURE #9 Track down clues and crimes with the world's most famous detective, Sherlock Holmes.

You can snoop around Sherlock's Detective Log and see what cases he's working on. After you read the notes on each page, you can write your prediction to help solve the case.

Case #1   Mrs. McCurty's Missing Jewels

Jewels are stolen at 8 P.M. Friday from dresser drawer.

Suspects:

Nanny Opal: did not come to work Saturday
  Her sister and doctor say she is sick.

Grandma Ruby: stays locked in her room
  She has taken the jewels before.

The Butler: has bulging pockets
  He is angry at his employer for refusing a pay raise.

Neighbor, Professor Gem: recently put a large sum into his bank account
  He is really Simon Topaz, previously arrested for jewel theft.

Predict: Who will be arrested? _The Butler_

Why do you think so? _Angry, bulging pockets_

Case #2   The Missing Raw Meat

Butcher reports 22 pounds raw meat missing, Saturday midnight.

Suspects:

Count Janson's cat: has an extended belly

Butcher's dog: has stolen meat several times before.
  Has a satisfied look on his face on Sunday, raw meat on his paws.

Cook at La Mancha Hotel: served beef rolls Sunday, was out of town
  until Sunday morning at 6 A.M.

Garbage Collector: seen digging through Butcher's trash

Predict: Who will be arrested? _Garbage Collector_

Why do you think so? _animals won't be arrested, cook out of town._

Case #3   Broken Lamppost on Canterbury Lane

• Yellow paint found on bent lamppost Wednesday night;
  broken glass on ground from burst lamp
• Talked to all homeowners in the area
• Checked all carriage repair shops
• Checked with shops selling yellow paint
• Found names of owners of 7 yellow carriages

What should Sherlock do next? _Look for some fingerprints._

Name

Copyright © 2016 World Book, Inc./
Incentive Publications, Chicago, IL

A STOMACH DROPPER

ADVENTURE #10 Be the first person to ride the Heartstopper, the world's newest and biggest and most terrifying roller coaster. Don't choose this adventure unless you have a stomach of iron!

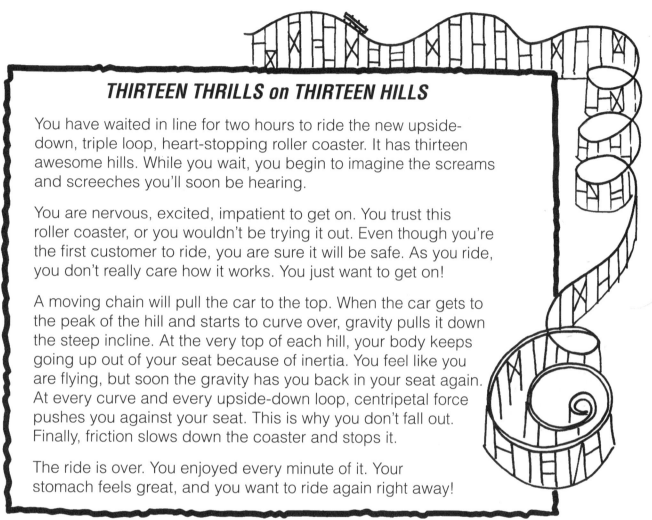

THIRTEEN THRILLS on THIRTEEN HILLS

You have waited in line for two hours to ride the new upside-down, triple loop, heart-stopping roller coaster. It has thirteen awesome hills. While you wait, you begin to imagine the screams and screeches you'll soon be hearing.

You are nervous, excited, impatient to get on. You trust this roller coaster, or you wouldn't be trying it out. Even though you're the first customer to ride, you are sure it will be safe. As you ride, you don't really care how it works. You just want to get on!

A moving chain will pull the car to the top. When the car gets to the peak of the hill and starts to curve over, gravity pulls it down the steep incline. At the very top of each hill, your body keeps going up out of your seat because of inertia. You feel like you are flying, but soon the gravity has you back in your seat again. At every curve and every upside-down loop, centripetal force pushes you against your seat. This is why you don't fall out. Finally, friction slows down the coaster and stops it.

The ride is over. You enjoyed every minute of it. Your stomach feels great, and you want to ride again right away!

1. The author makes some assumptions about the way the rider feels or will feel. Underline these with a red pen or marker.

2. What do you think of the writer's approach of telling the reader how he or she will feel about the ride? _I think it will be very fun_

3. Did the writer have good reasons to claim that the rider enjoyed the ride? _Yes_

4. Evaluate how well the writer explained the workings of the roller coaster. _____

_____

_____

_____

Name _____

HERE COMES THE JUDGE

ADVENTURE #11 Just what you've always wanted! This week, you get to be the judge. Take over Judge Weary's courtroom and decide the cases yourself. The black robe and gavel will be provided.

Read the facts you have been provided for each case. Then write your judgment. Tell what you will order to settle the question.

CASE #1   The Naughty Dog

Miss LaGrady claims that her neighbor's dog dug up all her flowers. She found a hole under the fence between her neighbor's yard and her own. She saw the neighbor's dog with dirt and flower bits on its front paws and muzzle. Should Mr. Clam pay for new plants for Miss LaGrady's garden?

Your judgment _No, because dogs are animals_

I'll be the judge of that.

CASE #2   Neighbors vs The Magenta Family

The entire neighborhood association is suing the Magenta Family for disrupting the neighborhood. They claim that the purple spots that the Magentas painted on their house are an eyesore. They say the awful color drives home buyers away. They have asked that the Magentas be forced to repaint their house and pay each neighbor a sum of $1,000.

Your judgment _No, because it is the owners opinion and choice_

CASE #3   The Potato Chip Deceit

Mr. Port claims that the Crunchy Potato Chip Company is responsible for his gain of 100 pounds. He points out that the potato chip bag says that the chips contain 200 calories. He thought that meant 200 calories per bag, so he ate a bag every day for two years. When he gained so much weight, he became suspicious of the chips and had them analyzed. The truth is, the chips contain 200 calories per serving. That adds up to 2,000 calories per bag. Should the company pay Mr. Port $3,000 to go to a weight loss program?

Your judgment _No, because that is his fault._

Name _____

BRING A MASK

ADVENTURE #12 Find yourself a great costume and a wonderful mask. You're invited to be the guest of King Louis XIV at the great palace of Versailles!

Read about each guest at the ball. Then write a question you would ask that character in order to find out more about her or him.

Count Pompous is strutting about the great hall with a fancy hat and his high-heeled boots. He will probably keep his nose in the air the entire evening.

What is your hobby

Countess Dainté dances lightly across the ballroom floor. She seems to float around the room with a light step. Everything about her seems soft, sweet, and sincere.

Can you do a split

Lady Columbine is busy showing off her beauty and grace. She just knows that everyone is looking at her and no one else. If you are not a young, handsome, wealthy prince, she won't want to waste her time on you!

How old are you

What a jolly fellow is the friendly Jacques Joli! It's a pleasure to have his company. He has a clever, happy word for every guest.

Can you do a flip

Little Prince Mischief just loves these parties, too! He is so small, that guests hardly notice him. He lurks around under tables and behind curtains, having loads of fun!

What is your ambition

There's Dowager La-de-da! How honored you should be to come into the presence of this rich old dame. Be sure you do not say anything rowdy or improper in her presence. She has no time for foolishness.

How heavy are you

Judge d'Éclaire is a very important man. He loves these parties because of the plentiful food. Oh, how he loves to eat! If you stop to visit with him, do bring him a pastry or two.

Do you like animals

Name _____

MEET THE MAN OF LA MANCHA

ADVENTURE #13 Ride with the outlandish, mythical knight, Don Quixote, Man of La Mancha! See what fun he had on his outlandish adventures!

DRAGONS, WINDMILLS, & FIERCE ARMIES TO CONQUER

An unusual young man spent years reading wonderful tales about knighthood. His fantasies were filled with all the battles and quarrels, loves, adventures, dragons, and enchantments of the lives of knights. He read so much that his brain dried up and he got a little crazy. He decided to become a knight and do everything he had read about. He thought up an excellent, knightly name for himself: Don Quixote, Man of La Mancha.

The new knight got some old armor of his grandfather's and saddled up his weak old horse. He took Sancho, a simple neighbor, along as his squire. Off he went to have the adventures of a knight.

It's a four-armed giant!

Soon he came upon a gang of more than thirty giants. Sancho pointed out that these were windmills, not giants, but Don Quixote rode forward bravely to fight the giants, waving his sword wildly. He broke his sword and was thrown from his horse, but he still believed he had fought giants.

Next he saw two huge armies and decided to join one and lead it to defeat the other. The armies were two flocks of sheep, but Don Quixote did not seem to notice. Waving and whirling his sword, he charged into the midst of the sheep. The shepherds thought he was crazy. They threw stones at him to drive him off. He was sure he had been wounded by the swords of the enemy in battle.

Write a short summary of the story of Don Quixote.

Don Quixote was crazy
about knights. He became
crazy. He thought
windmills are giants and
sheep are soldiers.

Name _____

WELCOME TO CAMELOT

ADVENTURE #14 Meet King Arthur! Visit Camelot! Get your very own suit of mail! Learn to fight a dragon, if you wish! Many have dreamed of this adventure. You can actually live it!

Sir Prance-a-lot is caught in the depths of a terrible dungeon, fighting a fire-breathing dragon. The dragon has wrapped itself around the knight, and it seems he will have no chance of escape. Sir Prance-a-lot is a brave and skilled warrior, so perhaps he will defeat this wingless dragon yet!

Meanwhile, back inside the castle, a worried damsel is chained to a pillar. She is waiting for Sir Prance-a-lot to slay the dragon and rescue her. She does not have to wait long! Here comes the dashing knight to the rescue! How fortunate she is to have such a brave friend to save her from peril.

What is wrong with this story? Rewrite the story, using correct information supplied by the picture.

_____

_____

_____

_____

_____

_____

Name

GOLDEN RECIPES

ADVENTURE #15

Search for gold with the Forty-Niners! Travel back to 1849 when the Gold Rush was in full swing in Northern California. Maybe you'll be one of the fortunate adventurers and end up with a pan full of golden nuggets!

Gus Grubb is the camp cook for the prospectors. He needs to get some supper ready fast, but his recipe directions are all out of order! Straighten them out for Gus by numbering the sentences in the correct order in each recipe.

GOLDEN NUGGET STEW

___ Then cook them in hot chicken fat in a big kettle.
___ First, cut up 5 chickens into small nuggets.
___ Sprinkle with red pepper flakes before serving.
___ Cook for 1 more hour.
___ Roll the nuggets in flour mixed with salt and mustard powder.
___ When the chicken is tender, throw in many handfuls of cut up carrots, turnips, onions, and potatoes.

HEARTY CORN BREAD

___ Add 5 cups of whole wheat flour to the starter.
___ Finally, stir in some chunks of cheese.
___ Toss 1 cup of baking powder into the flour and cornmeal mixture.
___ Next, mix 5 cups of cornmeal in with the flour and starter.
___ Bake over a hot fire until it's brown on top.
___ Start with ⅓ cup of sourdough starter.
___ Sprinkle kernels of corn on top of the pan.
___ Pour the mixture into a pan.

My number one secret ingredient is....

Catsup!

GREAT CAMPOUT GRUB

___ Boil the hambone in 2 gallons of water for 3 hours.
___ After the beans, add your favorite spices.
___ Serve with hot corn bread.
___ Start with a big old hambone.
___ The second ingredient is 10 cans of beans— loads of fat, white beans.
___ Cook for 1 hour over a hot camp fire.
___ During the last 20 minutes of cooking, add 2 cups of sliced carrots.

Name _____

IT'S GREAT TO BE QUEEN

ADVENTURE #16 Hop aboard the time machine and travel all the way back to A.D. 593 and visit with the world's 10 longest-reigning queens along the way. Spend a day sharing a throne with each one. Bring dressy clothes. We'll loan you a crown!

Follow the directions below to complete the graph.

Reign, in Years 30 35 40 45 50 55 60 65 70

WORLD'S LONGEST-REIGNING QUEENS

QUEEN

Write each queen's name on the graph as you read about her. Color a bar to show how long she reigned.

1. Queen Isabella II of Spain reigned from 1833 to 1868.

2. Queen Maria Theresa of Austria reigned from 1740 to 1780.

3. Queen Wu Chao of China reigned from 655 to 705.

4. Queen Victoria of the United Kingdom reigned from 1837 to 1901.

5. Queen Salote Tubou of Tonga reigned from 1918 to 1965.

6. Queen Suiko Tenno of Japan reigned from 593 to 628.

7. Queen Elizabeth I of the United Kingdom reigned from 1558 to 1603.

8. Queen Elizabeth II of the United Kingdom still reigns. Her reign began in 1952.

9. Queen Joanna I of Italy reigned from 1343 to 1382.

10. Queen Maria I of Portugal reigned from 1777 to 1816.

11. Queen Wilhelmina of the Netherlands reigned from 1890 to 1948.

Name

A SWEET RECORD

ADVENTURE #17 Get yourself in the Guinness Book of World Records—with a little help from our company. We'll teach you the secret tricks to help you eat the largest ice cream sundae of all time. You like ice cream, we hope!

Follow the directions below to draw the sundae. You'll need markers or crayons.

1. Draw seven large scoops of bubble gum–raisin ice cream on the bottom layer.
2. Draw eight long slices of banana around the edges of this layer.
3. Draw six large scoops of peppermint-fudge ice cream on the next layer.
4. Draw five large scoops of lemon chiffon sherbet on the next layer.
5. Draw a layer of crushed chocolate cookies on top of the lemon sherbet.
6. Draw four large scoops of blueberry-marshmallow ice cream on the next layer.
7. Draw strawberry sauce on top of this layer.
8. Draw three huge scoops of pumpkin pie ice cream on the next layer.
9. Draw caramel sauce on top of this layer.
10. Draw two huge scoops of chocolate chunk ice cream on top of this.
11. Draw sticky hot fudge running all over the sundae.
12. Draw fluffy squirts of whipped cream all over the sundae.
13. Draw loads of nuts sprinkled on the sundae.
14. Draw one huge cherry on the top.

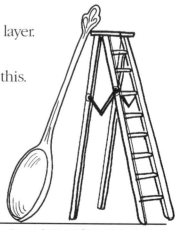

Name _____

THE GREATEST COWBOY

ADVENTURE #18 Join the wild escapades of the great cowboy hero, Pecos Bill! Ride a cyclone, tame rattlesnakes, and learn to lasso a speeding train!

A TALL COWBOY TALE

Pecos Bill was the greatest cowboy of all—a hero to all cowboys. When he was a baby, he fell out of his family's wagon and was left behind along the Pecos River. A family of coyotes adopted him, and he thought he was a coyote for many years.

Some cowboys found him and took him in. They taught him cowboy skills. He grew to be so big and strong and brave, that he could do far more than the other cowboys.

Bill was eight feet tall and carried seven guns and nine knives in his belt. He could ride the biggest, most powerful horses. No horse could throw him. He could ride anything—no matter how wild. One time he rode a mountain lion, using a rattlesnake as a whip. Another time, he rode a wild cyclone!

One day, two rattlesnakes bothered Bill. He grabbed one in each hand and shook the daylights out of them. Then he tied their tails together and hung them in a tree.

Pecos Bill could lasso whole herds of cattle at one time. He could lasso anything! The best trick he ever did happened the day he spied a runaway train. Bill just grabbed his lasso, and lassoed that train!

Yes, Pecos Bill is still talked about in cowboy country. If you go to the Arizona desert, you will still see the footprints that his huge horses left among the rocks.

1. What do you think is true about Pecos Bill?

   _____

   _____

   _____

2. Underline phrases or statements that you think might be exaggerated.

3. What other great feats or tricks would you like to see Pecos Bill do?

   _____

   _____

   _____

   _____

   _____

   _____

Name _____

WORDS THAT CONFUSE

Freddie is terribly confused about the spelling of these words. Maybe it's because these are some words that are spelled wrong very often. Help him out by deciding which spelling in each word group is correct. Circle the right one.

1. busness
   buziness
   business
   busyness

2. twelth
   twelvth
   twelfth
   twelveth

3. suprise
   suprize
   surprice
   surprise

4. cafateria
   cafetaria
   cafeteria
   cafeterria

5. calandar
   calendar
   calender
   calander

6. balloon
   baloon
   ballon
   baloone

7. embarrass
   embarass
   embbaras
   emmbarass

8. lisense
   lisence
   license
   licence

9. memary
   memory
   memry
   memmory

10. bannana
    bananna
    bannanna
    banana

11. memarise
    memorize
    memorise
    memmorize

12. nesessary
    nessessary
    necessary
    nessecary

13. Flordia
    Florida
    Floirda
    Floirida

14. restrant
    resturant
    restaurant
    restaurent

15. marshmellow
    marshmalow
    marshmallow
    marshmelow

16. reconize
    reconise
    recognize
    recognise

17. receive
    recieve
    resieve
    reseive

18. advertisement
    advertizment
    advertisment
    advertizement

19. trubble
    troubble
    troble
    trouble

20. vegtable
    vejetable
    veggetable
    vegetable

Name _____

WHO'S RIGHT?

Frannie and Frankie both studied for their spelling test. Who studied the hardest?
Look at both tests. Circle the numbers of the correctly spelled words.

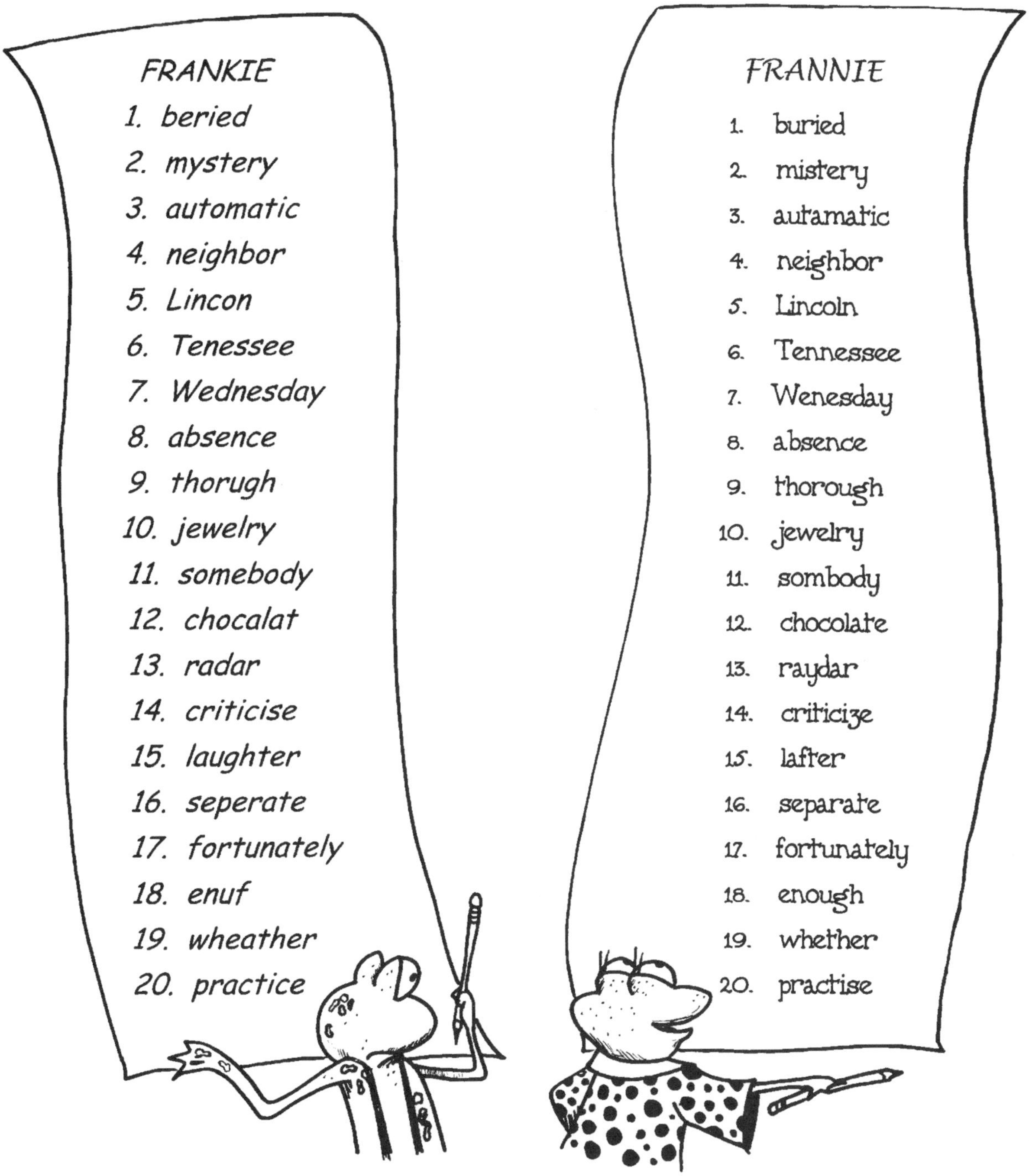

FRANKIE
1. beried
2. mystery
3. automatic
4. neighbor
5. Lincon
6. Tenessee
7. Wednesday
8. absence
9. thorugh
10. jewelry
11. somebody
12. chocalat
13. radar
14. criticise
15. laughter
16. seperate
17. fortunately
18. enuf
19. wheather
20. practice

FRANNIE
1. buried
2. mistery
3. autamatic
4. neighbor
5. Lincoln
6. Tennessee
7. Wenesday
8. absence
9. thorough
10. jewelry
11. sombody
12. chocolate
13. raydar
14. criticize
15. lafter
16. separate
17. fortunately
18. enough
19. whether
20. practise

A. Which speller did the best job on the test? _____ Frankie _____

B. Which words were spelled correctly by both spellers? (List numbers.) ____ 4 _____

Name _____

THE OUTSTANDING, OUTRAGEOUS O

O's show up lots of places in words: in the beginning, in the middle, or at the end! Ophelia Phrog, the famous opera singer, warms up her voice by singing a lot of Ooooooooooooo's.

Find the words with mistakes. Write each one correctly next to the misspelled word.

1. trio _____
2. carret _____carrot_____
3. studio _____
4. pilat _____pilot_____
5. molacule _____molecule_____

6. volcono _____v_____
7. people _____
8. docter _____
9. oppisite _____
10. memary _____

11. gerilla _____
12. octapus _____
13. Octobor _____
14. kazoo _____
15. scorpian _____

16. cacoon _____
17. shampoo _____
18. masquito _____
19. abdamen _____
20. dinasaur _____

21. lasso _____
22. ooze _____
23. oder _____
24. foolish _____
25. goon _____

Name _____

QUARTETS, QUICKSAND, & QUEENS

Find a **Q** word to match each clue. (The word will have a *q* in it!)
Write the word.
Spell it correctly!

QUIXOTIC

Uh oh

A quartet of quirky queens in the quicksand.

1. unusual   u __ __ qu __

2. ask   i __ qu __ __ __

3. take over   c __ __ qu __ __

4. smash   __ qu __ sh

5. feast   b __ __ qu __ __

6. line around
Earth's middle   __ qu __ __ __ r

7. in a hurry   qu __ __ __ ly

8. not noisy   qu __ __ __

9. follow-up
story   s __ qu __ l

10. heavy
blanket   qu __ __ __

11. four singers   qu __ __ t __ __

12. tests   qu __ z __ __ __

13. fish tank   __ qu __ __ __ __ m

14. argue   qu __ __ __ __ l

15. often   __ __ __ qu __ __ __ ly

16. to ask   qu __ __ t __ __ __

17. tools   __ qu __ __ __ ent

Name

WILY WORDS

The word *wily* means *tricky* or *slippery*! Many words with *y* are tricky to spell. Sometimes it's tough to figure out where the *y* belongs in the word!

Use the clues to help you unscramble these words. Make sure you spell them right!

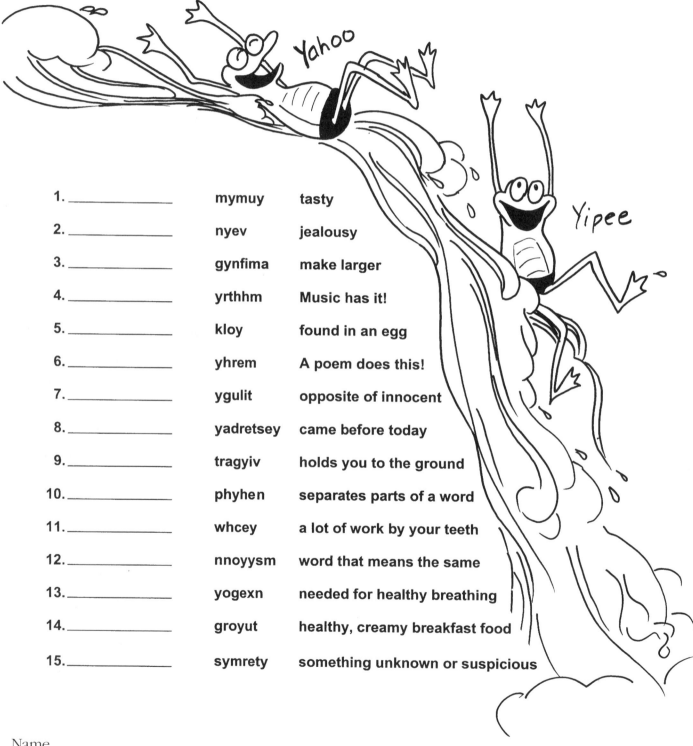

1. _____   **mymuy**   **tasty**

2. _____   **nyev**   **jealousy**

3. _____   **gynfima**   **make larger**

4. _____   **yrthhm**   **Music has it!**

5. _____   **kloy**   **found in an egg**

6. _____   **yhrem**   **A poem does this!**

7. _____   **ygulit**   **opposite of innocent**

8. _____   **yadretsey**   **came before today**

9. _____   **tragyiv**   **holds you to the ground**

10. _____   **phyhen**   **separates parts of a word**

11. _____   **whcey**   **a lot of work by your teeth**

12. _____   **nnoyysm**   **word that means the same**

13. _____   **yogexn**   **needed for healthy breathing**

14. _____   **groyut**   **healthy, creamy breakfast food**

15. _____   **symrety**   **something unknown or suspicious**

Name _____

EXTRAORDINARY WORDS

When Casey Frog comes to bat, the fans have high expectations! They cheer and shout out a lot of words that contain *x* !

This word puzzle contains at least 25 words that contain *x*.
Use the clues to help you find the words (horizontal or vertical).
Circle the words.

```
E X P E C T R E X P E L L M O X I E
G O X E U S A X O P H O N E L I T T
E X T I N C T P R E F L E X B L A X
M E E X C E L L E N T E X I S T X P
H M X G G N R O N P E E X C L A I M
H A A J X E W D E E K F F O X E S I
E X M C C X Y E X C I T I N G P P X
X I I C C T M N E X T I N C T O O T
A M N O D S L Q R E X T R E M E K U
G U E X P R E S S W A Y E E E T L R
O M J Y W E Z Z K F L E X I B L E E
N R W G E X C U S E K K A B O X E S
E O M E P I F F E X E R C I S E H H
M D S N O T X L K E E X T E R I O R
```

Excellent!

Exceptional!

Extraordinary!

1. throw out of school
2. musical instrument
3. species no longer alive
4. country south of USA
5. tighten a muscle
6. absolutely great
7. look at closely
8. to be
9. a six-sided figure
10. the greatest amount
11. shout
12. thrilling
13. what comes after this
14. animals with bushy tails
15. severe
16. gas needed for life
17. reason for something
18. moving the body
19. the outside
20. bendable
21. stuff stirred together
22. go out
23. know something will happen
24. burst or blow up
25. freeway

Name

LOOK-ALIKE WORDS

Is Freddy, the hot-air balloonist, checking out his attitude or his altitude?
He needs to know the difference between the two words in order to be sure!

Be careful with the spelling of words that look a lot like each other.
Color the puzzle parts that contain words used (and spelled) correctly.

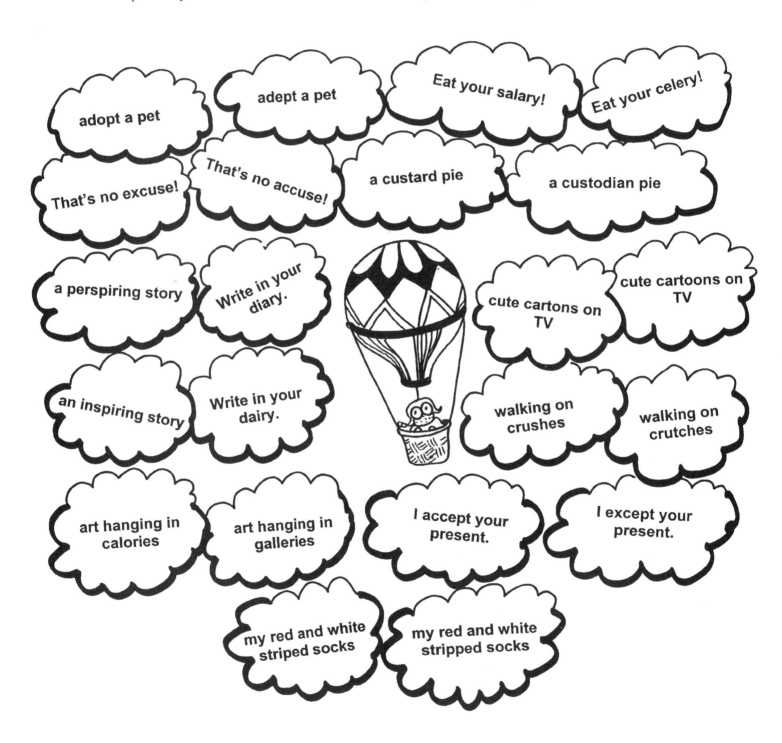

adopt a pet

adept a pet

Eat your salary!

Eat your celery!

That's no excuse!

That's no accuse!

a custard pie

a custodian pie

a perspiring story

Write in your diary.

cute cartons on TV

cute cartoons on TV

an inspiring story

Write in your dairy.

walking on crushes

walking on crutches

art hanging in calories

art hanging in galleries

I accept your present.

I except your present.

my red and white striped socks

my red and white stripped socks

Name

WORDS WITH PIZZAZ

Dazzling!

The letter *z* puts pizzaz into words. (That means sparkle and excitement!) Use correctly spelled words with *z* to finish the puzzle below!

ACROSS

1. trophy
3. closes up your jacket
5. flies do this in your ear
7. say you're sorry
9. place to keep ice cream
11. amount equal to nothing
13. severe snowstorm
16. to slowly burn out
17. a kind of music
18. comfortable and warm

DOWN

2. get things in order
4. hug
6. dangerous situation
8. twelve of something
10. figure something out
12. not working hard
14. wobbly from spinning
15. full of bubbles

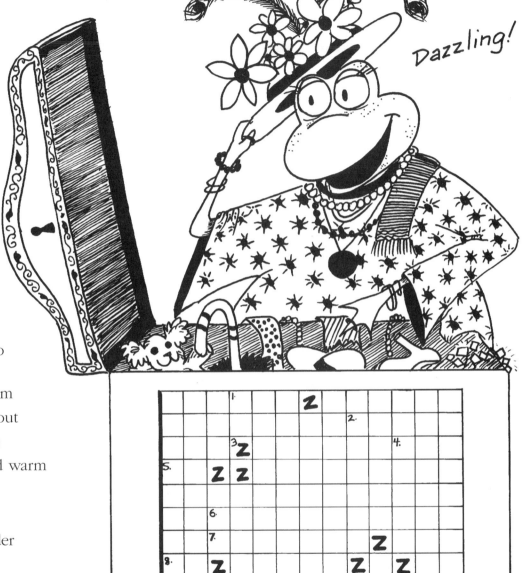

Name

ADDITIONS TO THE BEGINNING

Thousands of words have little word parts added to their beginnings. If you know how to spell these prefixes, you'll have a good start on correct spelling of the whole word!

These frogmen make a lot of use of a prefix that means "under."
Use your knowledge of prefixes to spell these words right.
Write a word to match each clue.

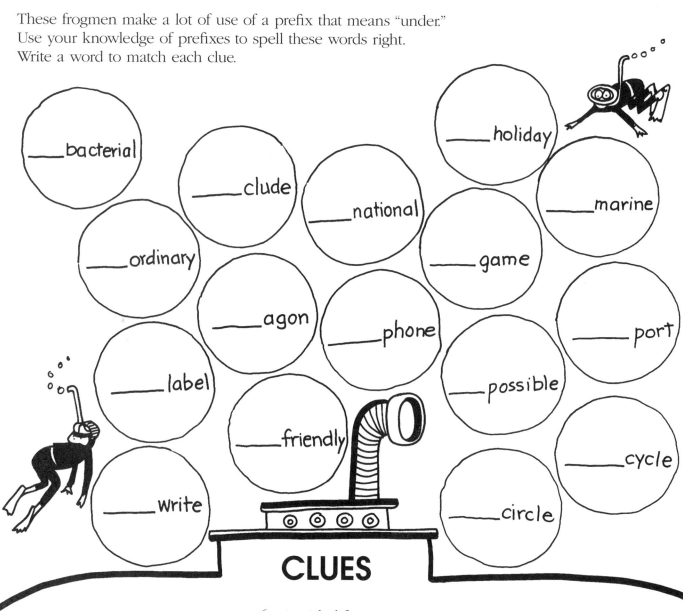

_____bacterial

_____clude

_____holiday

_____national

_____marine

_____ordinary

_____game

_____agon

_____phone

_____port

_____label

_____possible

_____friendly

_____cycle

_____write

_____circle

CLUES

1. under the ocean
2. a tiny phone
3. beyond the ordinary
4. to write again
5. a cycle with one wheel
6. six-sided figure
7. not possible
8. between nations
9. label something wrong
10. carry something across
11. to leave out
12. before the game
13. after the holidays
14. against bacteria
15. half of a circle
16. not friendly

Name _____

ADDITIONS TO THE END

Phoebe's hope (see picture) is made possible by some of those little word parts called suffixes. If you know how to spell suffixes, you'll have a better chance at ending up with the correct spelling of the whole word!

Color the parachutes that have words spelled correctly. Pay special attention to those suffixes.

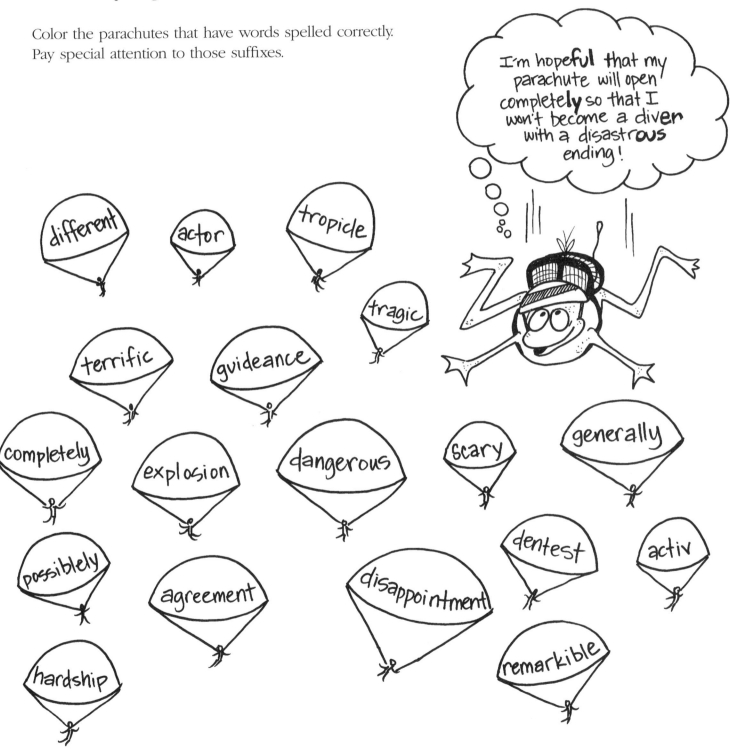

I'm hopeful that my parachute will open completely so that I won't become a diver with a disastrous ending!

different
actor
tropicle
tragic
terrific
guideance
completely
explosion
dangerous
scary
generally
possiblely
agreement
disappointment
dentest
activ
remarkible
hardship

Name _____

BON VOYAGE!

"Bon voyage!" is what people say when you leave on a ship. It means "Good trip on the water!" "Trip on the water" is only the **denotation** (dictionary definition) of the word *voyage*. This word might also make you think of wild waves, rough seas, adventure, mystery, fog, whales, sharks, pirates, or big parties. All of these things are the **connotations** (suggested meanings) of the word!

Read each of the definitions below. Write **D** next to each denotation. Write **C** next to each connotation. Then figure out what the word is, and write it in the box!

1. [   ]

_____ a large body of salt water

_____ cold, waves, surfing, deep, monsters, fish, swimming, drowning, hurricanes, sailing, diving, fun, danger, beaches

2. [   ]

_____ cold, penguins, danger to ships, shipwrecks, tall, mysterious, white

_____ a large, floating mass of ice detached from a glacier

3. [   ]

_____ splash, dive, float, wet, cold, wave jumping, beaches, summer, pools, fun, danger

_____ to propel oneself through the water by natural means

4. [   ]

_____ a mollusk with eight muscular arms lined with suckers

_____ ugly, creepy, squeezing, big eyes, grabbing, wrapping, danger, scary, hiding beneath the water

5. [   ]

_____ a small, strong, buoyant boat carried by a ship

_____ emergency, danger, rescue, oars, stormy seas, sinking ship, sharks, screaming people

6. [   ]

_____ fun and excitement, adventure, sunshine, skiing, swimming, relaxing, travel, trip, family, money

_____ time spent away from home for a rest, change, or break from something

7. [   ]

_____ something of value accepted as an exchange for buying goods; usually coins and/or paper

_____ wealth, savings, banks, toys, buying, spending

Name _____

WORDS WITH A PAST

Did you know that the word fudge was supposedly named after Captain Fudge, a seaman who had a reputation for not telling the truth? Today, when you fudge on the truth, it means that you're not telling the whole story! Many words have interesting histories. A good dictionary will give you the history, or **etymology,** of many words. Often it is in brackets at the end of the definition.

fret (fret) v. 1. to cause to be uneasy; distress, vex 2. to gnaw or wear away
(Middle English freten, to devour or eat away)

Use your dictionary to find out something about the history of some of these words. Learn about at least 10 of them. Find out what or who the word was named after, or discover something about its meaning.

1. Ferris wheel _____

2. Frisbee® _____

3. March _____

4. Monday _____

5. angel _____

6. guppy _____

7. cologne _____

8. magnolia _____

9. teddy bear _____

10. pedigree _____

11. leotard _____

12. comet _____

13. paper _____

14. sardine _____

15. Chihuahua _____

16. America _____

Name _____

LITTLE SHOP OF OPPOSITES

> **Antonyms** are words
> that mean
> the opposite of
> each other.

When customers come to the beach
shop, they seem to say the opposite of
what they mean!

Write the antonym for each word in
parentheses to make the sentences
correct.

1. "This shop has the (worst) stuff on the beach!" _____

2. "Let's get some (bad) quality diving supplies." _____

3. "Everything in this shop is too (cheap) for me to afford." _____

4. "I'll loan you some money," said my (Uncle) Martha. _____

5. "My swim mask and snorkel are always (straight)." _____

6. "I need to (sell) a(n) (ugly) (old) swimsuit." _____

   _____ _____

7. "The wet suit is so (light)—it must weigh a ton!" _____

8. "This is on sale because it has a (temporary) stain." _____

9. "Look at what a (stingy) size this raft is!" _____

10. "These beach towels are made of a really (flimsy) fabric." _____

11. "What an (ordinary) color this shirt is!" _____

12. "Won't you need two (weak) people to carry this boat?" _____

Name _____

WILD SURF

Synonyms are words that have the same or similar meanings.

Sal is working at staying on top of the wave. The words in the surf didn't do so well. They've been tossed around and totally scrambled! Each word in the list below has a synonym lost in the waves. First, find the matching wave-tossed synonym for each word. Then unscramble the synonym and write it on the line.

1. thrilling _____

2. amateur _____

3. feat _____

4. incredible _____

5. danger _____

6. astonish _____

7. massive _____

8. respond _____

9. slobber _____

10. genuine _____

11. gesture _____

12. horde _____

13. horror _____

14. journal _____

15. penalize _____

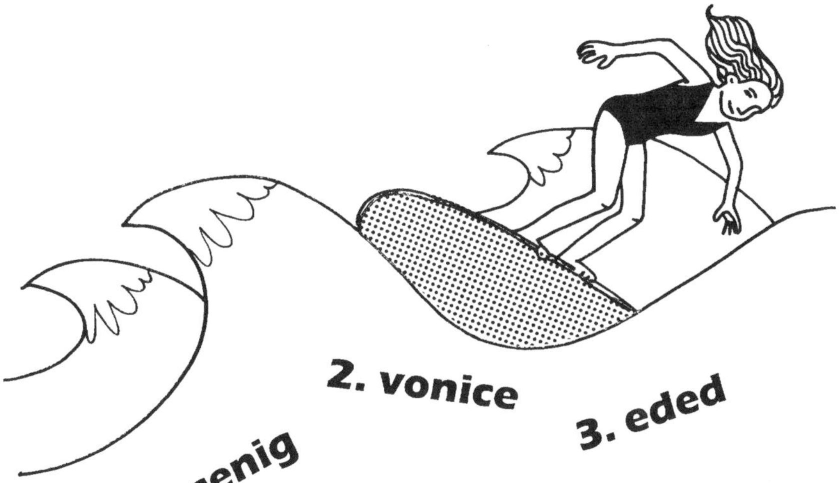

1. tixcenig

2. vonice

3. eded

4. baiblevunlee

5. ripel

6. zamae

7. eugh

8. warnes

9. lorod

10. laer

11. tovemenm

12. omb

13. rerrot

14. raidy

15. shinup

Name _____

UNFORGETTABLE!

When you come face-to-face with a weird sea creature, it is a truly unforgettable experience! The word *unforgettable* is built from the root word *forget*. Then other word parts (a prefix and a suffix) are added to the word. If you know your roots, you can create and figure out all kinds of words!

Choose the right root from the box to form each of the words described.

Root Meaning

act	(act, do)
aqua	(water)
carn	(flesh)
dorm	(sleep)
dynam	(energy)
flam	(burn)
fug	(flee)
labor	(work)
mon	(warn)
phobia	(fear)
port	(carry)
scend	(climb)
tele	(far)
vis	(see)

1. _____ivore   eater of flesh

2. zoo _____   fear of animals

3. _____itive   one who flees

4. ad_____ition   warning

5. _____ible   able to be seen

6. _____tic   pertaining to water

7. _____ion   the act of doing

8. _____mable   easily burned

9. de _____   climb down

10. _____ic   full of energy

11. _____itory   place to sleep

12. _____scope   instrument for seeing far

13. trans _____   carry across

14. _____atory   place to work

15. arachna _____   fear of spiders

16. _____able   able to be carried

17. phobo_____   fear of fear

18. a _____   to climb up

uh oh!

Name _____

54

STARS ON THE BEACH

Gloria thought she was the star of the beach! Now she has to share the spotlight with another star. What are these two meanings of the word *star*?

1. _____

2. _____

The other words around this page also have more than one meaning. Choose any three of them. For each word you choose, illustrate two or more meanings of the word in one of the circles.

Everybody wants to be a star!

Gloria Glamorous

out

set

arms

pupil

trunk

coast

saw

pick

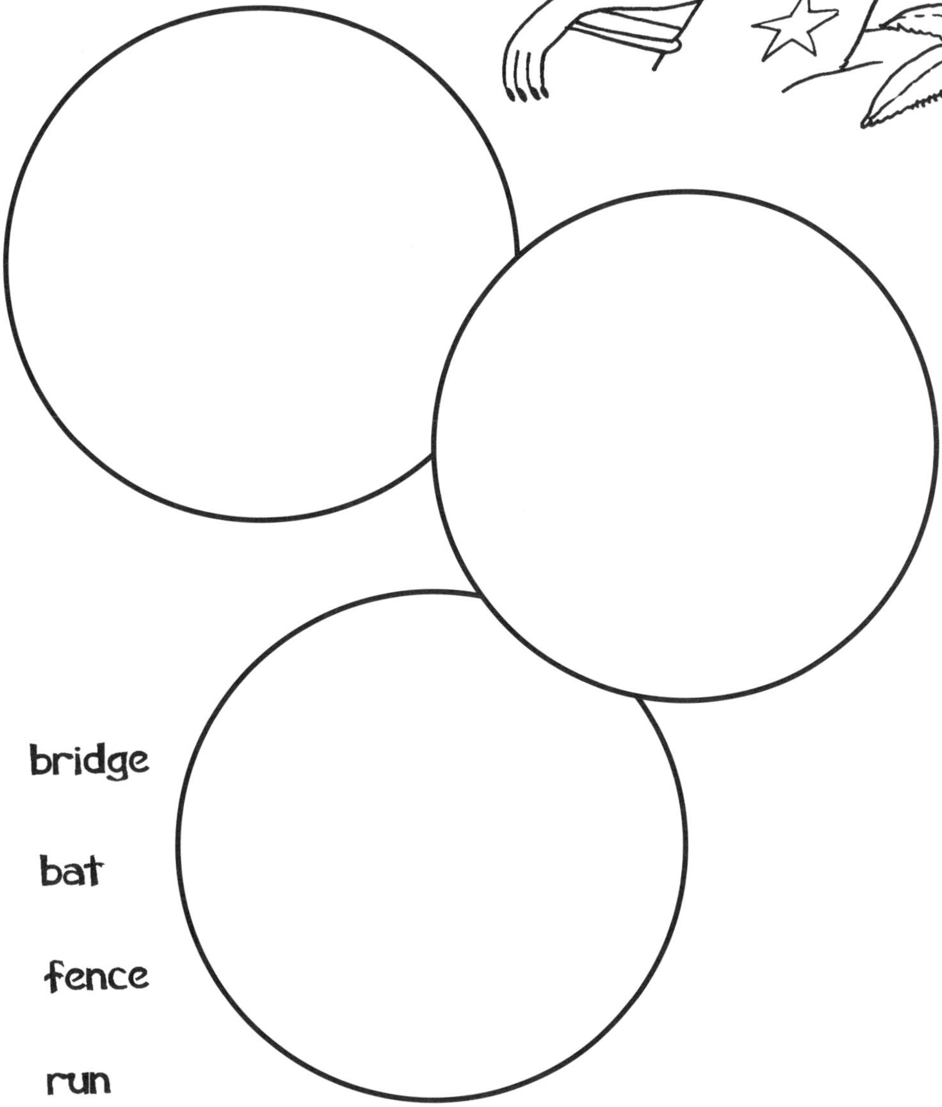

bridge

bat

fence

run

ride

quarter

back

down

time

line

count

light

Name _____

AFTER DARK

There's nothing quite like the beach at night! Everything looks, sounds, and feels so much different after the sun goes down and the shadows take over.

Look at the words at the bottom of the page. Find the meaning of each word and write it on the line. Then search the picture for something to match each word. Color that part of the picture with the color written next to the word. (*Ex: Find something to match the word **vessel** and color it blue.*)

vessel		(blue)
lunar		(yellow)
luminous		(orange)
biped		(red)
savory		(white)
merriment		(green)
pentapod		(pink)
gritty		(beige)
murky		(gray)
kindling		(brown)

Name

Samantha's letter to her friend Bo is full of figurative language.

Circle all the examples of figurative language you can find in her letter. Try to find out what each one means, if you don't already know!

How many examples of figurative language did you find?

_____

HO, HUM!

Dear Bo,

Ho, hum! What a dull, dull day! Here I sit in this new bathing suit that cost me an arm and a leg, with the sun beating on me, the waves pounding like drums, and the seagulls squawking as loud as a choir. I love the beach—just like my dad. I'm a chip off the old block! The water and sky are as pretty as a picture.

I do love the beach, but nothing is happening! Yes, the crabs are racing around faster than greased lightning, but there's no real action! My day is as dry as dust and as dull as a doorknob.

If only something outrageous would happen, this could turn out to be a red-letter day. I wish a giant waterspout would go bananas across the ocean. Or I wish a lifeguard would blow her top and go off her rocker right in front of everyone. Or wouldn't it take the cake if a dreadful sea monster appeared in the water, breaking up ships like toothpicks? Just think of how people would go running down the beach, scared stiff and screaming bloody murder! And wouldn't it be the last straw if all this happened, and I missed it because I was sleeping?

Well some say, "Out of sight, out of mind," but I say that absence makes the heart grow fonder. I miss you. I wish I could just snap my fingers and you'd be here, quick as a wink! Make no bones about it, today is a wipe out! If only you were here, then this day would not be deader than a doornail!

Love,
Samantha

Help!

Help!

Help!

WRITING WITH A SPARK

Investigative reporters Charlie Scoop and Murphy Green work for a new magazine, SPARK. They investigate all kinds of stories and write enticing pieces for the top-selling magazine. Today, Charlie and Murphy are polishing sentences by replacing dull words with better ones.

Look at each word that has been crossed out. Find another word that says the same thing, but is much more colorful, sparkling, interesting, or unusual.

Just after the bank robbery, the police came ~~walking~~ into the bank.

People had ~~scared~~ looks on their faces. They were ~~shaking~~.

The fingernails ~~tapping~~ against the window glass ~~hurt~~ my ears.

It was a ~~dark~~ afternoon and the wind was ~~blowing~~.

How could this ~~funny~~ worm get inside my ~~perfect~~ apple?

Three ~~strange~~ characters came ~~slipping~~ down the stairs to the subway.

Pass me some of that ~~tasty~~ hot fudge!

The comet ~~moved~~ across the night sky with amazing speed.

A ~~big~~ avalanche surprised and ~~worried~~ the skiers.

MURPHY GREEN

Use with page 59.

Name

WRITING WITH A SPARK, CONT.

Look at each word that has been crossed out. Replace it with another word with a similar meaning that is much more specific, colorful, interesting, or unusual.

The family had to run for their lives as the ~~awful~~ storm approached.

Have you ever watched ~~busy~~ snowboarders do their tricks?

You'll never believe the ~~awful~~ color of the dress she was wearing!

I have never seen waves as ~~big~~ as the ones I rode today!

Have you ever heard the ~~interesting~~ sound of a tornado coming?

Sirens ~~sounded~~ as the fire engines ~~went~~ toward the burning school.

How would you describe the ~~bad~~ taste of this ~~old~~ sandwich?

This wasn't the first time that the ~~little~~ chimp had been in trouble.

Catch the act! See the ~~funny~~ gorilla juggle ~~big~~ chairs at the zoo today.

It must have been ~~scary~~ to come face-to-face with Bigfoot.

The escaped elephant, ~~happy~~ to be free, ~~went~~ across the freeway.

~~Huge~~ waves ~~moved~~ closer to the house.

Three ~~big~~ walruses came ~~crawling~~ across the beach.

~~Good~~ syrup slowly ~~moved~~ over my pancakes.

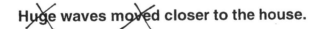

CHARLIE SCOOP

Use with page 58.

Name

FEATURE YOURSELF

Charlie is going to be the featured reporter in next month's issue of SPARK magazine. This is a monthly column where readers can get to know some personal information about one of the reporters. You can be the feature of this page, too. Finish the same sentences Charlie will finish. Make sure that the words you write make each sentence clear and interesting.

My greatest fear is a big hairy spider. I'd like to be emperor of my own island someday ...and,...

ABOUT MYSELF

1. Once, I _____

_____, but I probably will never do that again.

2. It wasn't too long ago that I _____ .

3. The greatest thing about me is _____ .

4. I wish I could _____ .

5. Wild horses could not drag me to _____ .

6. Last year, I _____ .

7. Yesterday, I _____ .

8. _____ is my greatest fear.

9. Nothing makes me madder than _____ !

10. If I could change something in the world, it would be _____

_____ .

11. I think _____ .

12. In 10 years, I expect to be _____ .

13. I would really like to try _____ .

14. Something else fascinating about me is _____ .

Name _____

WEATHERED WORDS

When Charlie goes out on an assignment to cover wild weather, his words become turbulent, too. They start taking the shape of lightning and tornadoes!

Choose one of the weather topics and make a painted writing piece about it in the space below. Make the shape of the words match the topic.

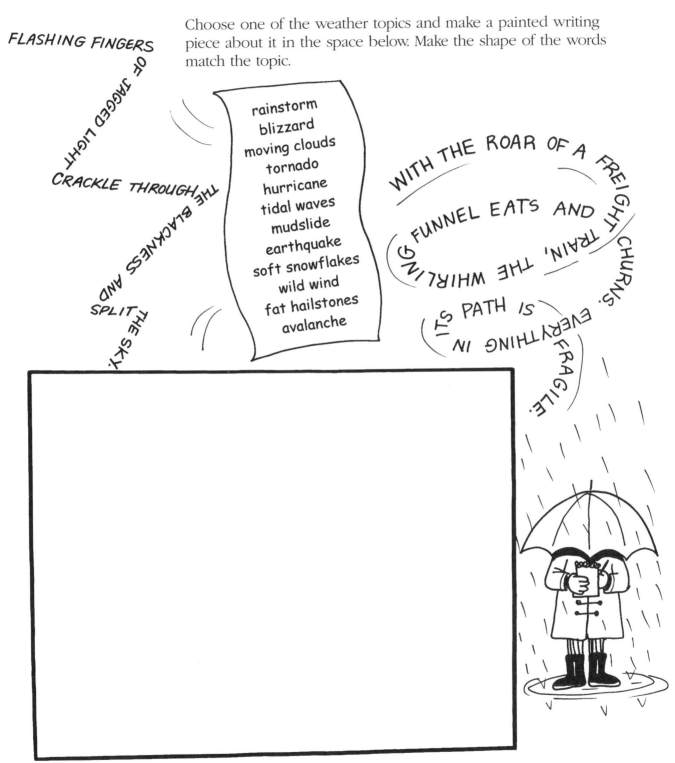

FLASHING FINGERS OF JAGGED LIGHT CRACKLE THROUGH THE BLACKNESS AND SPLIT THE SKY.

rainstorm
blizzard
moving clouds
tornado
hurricane
tidal waves
mudslide
earthquake
soft snowflakes
wild wind
fat hailstones
avalanche

WITH THE ROAR OF A FREIGHT TRAIN, THE WHIRLING FUNNEL EATS AND CHURNS. EVERYTHING IN ITS PATH IS FRAGILE.

Name _____

BETTER BEGINNINGS

Reporters know that a beginning needs to grab the reader. Whether it is a story, an essay, an article, or a report—the beginning is important. If a beginning is dull, the reader may give up right there. So Charlie is trying some different beginnings for his report on last night's school board meeting, where middle school students staged a protest. Which beginning do you think is best?

GREASY GRUB IS GROSS!

BETTER CHOW NOW!

Some Ash Middle School students protested at the school board meeting.

Students demanded that the school board discuss the poor lunches.

No one could remember a school board meeting like this one.

There were fireworks at the school board meeting last night.

Who dared to deliver rotting meat loaf and slimy Jell-o® to a school board meeting?

"Down with bad lunches!" was the cry heard at the school board meeting.

Rewrite each of these beginnings to make them more attention grabbing.

1. The food in the school cafeteria is pretty awful. _____

   _____

2. It was an average day in July. _____

   _____

3. Andrea left for school at 8 o'clock. _____

   _____

4. In the summer of 1969, American astronauts walked on the moon. _____

   _____

5. My mom got a new hairstyle, and she asked my opinion of it. _____

   _____

6. One day after school, Dan and his friends sat around with nothing to do. _____

   _____

7. School starts at 8:30 A.M. _____

   _____

8. There are many earthquakes every day. _____

   _____

9. Jamie asked me to take care of her pet skunk. _____

   _____

Name _____

GOOD QUESTIONS

Charley is getting ready to interview several different people for a magazine article he is writing. Charley is thinking about the questions he wants to ask. Write clear, complete questions that ask exactly what Charley will need to know!

1. *a rock star* _____

_____

_____

_____

2. *a 100-year-old person* _____

_____

_____

_____

3. *a witness to a robbery* _____

_____

_____

_____

4. *someone who's been struck by lightning* _____

_____

_____

_____

Name _____

WHAT CHARACTERS!

SPARK magazine held a contest for the Believe It or Not column. The magazine wanted to feature stories about people who had done unusual and unbelievable things. They printed an ad inviting people with special talents or accomplishments to come to the magazine office for interviews. To write about these interesting characters, the reporters need to collect some good words for describing people. The words on pages 64 and 65 are examples of good words for writing about characters.

For each character on these two pages, write a list of interesting words that you might use to describe her or him.

peppy
suspicious
athletic
outrageous
adventurous
quirky
elderly
eccentric
limber
offensive
arrogant
courageous
sleazy
droopy
cheerful
rotund
musical
insomniac
fearless
annoying
dependable
hilarious
clever
serious
stubborn
mature
precocious
massive
patient

1. owner of the world's smallest pony

2. person who's gone the longest time without sleep

3. holds the world paddleball-bounce record

4. the oldest skydiver in the country

Use with page 65.

Name

comical
lazy
mean
humble
delightful
unpredictable
forgetful
wicked
energetic
miserable
watchful
talented
creative
old-fashioned
persistent
foolish
rebellious
reasonable
unreasonable
attractive
joyous
sparkling
gloomy
mischievous
mysterious
lonely
reclusive
jolly

Create a name for each of the characters on pages 64 and 65.

1. _____   5. _____

2. _____   6. _____

3. _____   7. _____

4. _____   8. _____

Write a list of interesting words that you might use to describe each character. Then choose one of the eight characters and write at least one paragraph describing that character. Use another sheet of paper.

5. owns a potato shaped like Abraham Lincoln.

6. inventor of a machine that translates animal language

7. claims to be Elvis Presley

8. person who walks only on his hands

Use with page 64.

Name

CLIFF-HANGERS

Everybody loves a cliff-hanger! It's a tale that leads you to an exciting, breathtaking, mysterious, or dangerous point—and leaves you hanging! You don't know what happens next. Charlie loves cliff-hangers. He loves to write them, and he loves to finish them. Finish Charlie's cliff-hanger and give it a title. Use a separate sheet of paper.

> Joe knew it was not a good idea to be in the school at night. He would never have gone there, if it weren't for that math test tomorrow. He just had to have the math book he had left in his locker. Otherwise, he would fail the test. He had hoped to find a janitor working at the school, but there was no one there. Surprisingly, the door from the parking lot was unlocked. "I'll just run in, grab my book, and race right back out!" he told his mom. He flipped on the hall light and hurried to his locker. His hands shook as he tried the combination. He had to do it twice. Just as he got the math book and slammed his locker shut, the light went out. He heard no sounds. Everything was black! Quickly, he headed back down the hall to the door and pushed against it. To his shock, the door was locked. He could not get out! "It's a good thing Mom is waiting just outside the door in the car!" he said to himself. "She'll see me and get help." When he looked out the window, the parking lot was empty!

Next, write the beginning to your own cliff-hanger. Include something surprising, mysterious, or unusual to catch the interest of your reader. (See the Idea List.) Then, trade cliff-hangers with your friends. Finish each other's tales to tell what happened next!

Idea List

an accident
an unexpected visitor
a secret
a dream that isn't a dream
a missing friend
a strange shadow
caught on the train track
the trunk in the attic
the forbidden cave
a flash flood
a mysterious building
an unusual code
the scary computer

Name _____

CONVINCE ME!

Murphy's jingle has been a great success! Since it was first placed in the magazine three months ago, the sales of MBG (Mystery Bubble Gum) have tripled! Now, many companies want her to convince people to buy their products. Give her some help. Write a jingle (the text), a catchy slogan, an ad, or a short argument that will convince buyers to try these products.

MBG is the bubblegum for me
I don't care if it's got broccoli!

Carrots, peas, and berries
Onions, beans, and cherries
It's got fruits galore
And veggies twenty-four.

We buy packs by the dozen.
I share them with my cousin.
I love to chew and pop it.
No vitamin can stop it.

I don't care if it's got broccoli
'Cause MBG is the bubblegum for me!

Write a paragraph, poem, advertisement, or song that could convince someone to **do** one of these things. (Or you may choose something else!)

... try eating chocolate-covered ants
... learn to use the Internet
... take a trip to the Bermuda Triangle
... buy organic food
... learn to ride a wild bull
... never get a tattoo
... search for Bigfoot in a deep forest
... ride an upside-down roller coaster
... go to summer school

tuna-artichoke ice cream

a parrot hat

try eating chocolate-covered ants

Name

STRANGE DISAPPEARANCES

Science cannot explain the shocking weekend news from southern Florida. Murphy made this scientific mystery the subject of her Science Curiosities column in last week's edition of SPARK magazine.

MISSING IN THE ATLANTIC
by Murphy Green

Four strange disappearances were reported to the Coast Guard in Miami last weekend. On Friday at noon, the Quick family headed east into the Atlantic Ocean for an afternoon sailing trip on their new 20-foot catamaran. They did not return.

Several hours later, SunAir Flight 23 from Puerto Rico disappeared into the clouds over Miami and never came out.

On Saturday, two fishing boats in the same area did not come back to the harbor at the end of the day.

A fourth disappearance was reported on Sunday. A Miami woman and her husband were parasailing off the coast of Bermuda. Relatives watched them disappear into a wall of mist. They have not been seen since.

Searchers have been covering the area for days. So far, they have found no trace of any of the missing boats, persons, or aircraft. Scientists are not able to explain the cause of many strange disappearances that have been reported in this area known as "The Bermuda Triangle."

Mrs. Chalk, a second-grade teacher, thought this news report would be great for her students, but Murphy's article was too hard for them to read. Rewrite Murphy's news report, simplifying it enough for Mrs. Chalk's second graders to read and enjoy.

_____
(title)

_____
_____
_____
_____
_____
_____

Name

68

COMING ALIVE!

This week's Literature Page features examples of a tool used often in literature by writers who want their writing to be interesting. This tool or "literary technique" is called **personification.** When writers use personification, they give characteristics of living things to objects that are **not** alive.

My toaster is a sizzling, hungry monster.
It swallows my toast into its fiery jaws,
And hands it back to me, all crumbly and black.
Jennifer G., Gr. 4

I am a pot with a black handle,
People pour water in and out.
"Stop! Stop! My belly is on fire!" I yell.
"My belly my belly, it's on fire!"
"Help me!"
Elizabeth P., Gr. 4

The river sings a lazy bubbling tune to me.
The notes are low and soft, and her voice is like a lullaby.
Angela D., Gr. 5

In the desert
A massive bridge of rock
Rises against the sky
Gazing up at snow-capped
Mountains.
Nelson K., Gr. 5

The wind licks at my chapped face.
The wind plays games with my umbrella.
She tickles my eyelashes,
and whispers silly sayings into my ears.
Jordan J., Gr. 5

Write a line or a short poem about 4 of these objects. Use personification to give characteristics of a person or other living thing to each of the objects.

numbers on a math test	a mirror	my mailbox	spaghetti	my cereal
snow, hail, or rain	the sun	a blender	a lemon drop	the fog
an ocean wave	candles	the shower	my gym shoes	my pillow
an ice cream sundae	my umbrella	a headache	the sidewalk	a skateboard

Name _____

QUITE BY ACCIDENT

Murphy was in such a hurry to get this accident report written that she got it all mixed up. Can you straighten it out before it goes to press?

When I arrived, I found Farmer McCully's pigs looking shocked. No one was hurt, not even the pigs. Farmer McCully called 911 at noon to report a loud roaring sound that was shaking the earth near his farm. Just then, I heard terrible screaming in addition to the loud roaring sound. Unbelievably, a bathtub was whirling through the air. I was in the area, so I raced to the farm. I looked up in the sky toward the terrible noise. Fortunately, the tub landed safely in the pig pen. A young man in the tub was screaming for his life.

Write the sentences in a better sequence, so that the report makes sense and is interesting to the readers.

_____

_____

_____

_____

_____

_____

_____

_____

_____

_____

Name

UNSOLVED MYSTERIES

SPARK magazine has received some entries for "The Mystery Corner." Every one of them has sentence trouble! The sentences are all short and choppy. Writing is more interesting if the length and structure of the sentences vary.

Rewrite each of these mysteries. Combine or rearrange the sentences so that they form a smooth-flowing paragraph with a variety of sentence lengths. Use a separate piece of paper to rewrite the mysteries.

The Case of the Missing Pizzas

At noon it was discovered.
Thirteen pizzas were missing from Papa Gino's.
Size 10 footprints were found at the scene.
Three suspects were caught.
Bart had pizza sauce on his shirt.
Burt had cheese shreds in his hair.
Brett had a guilty smirk on his face.
Burt wears size 12 shoes.
Bart slept until noon.
Brett wears size 8 shoes.
Police solved the mystery.
They arrested one of the suspects.
Who stole the pizzas?

The Great Escape

The room has one door.
The door is locked.
It cannot be unlocked from inside.
The room has no windows.
The room has a cracked skylight.
There is a ladder in the room.
The man in the room has no tools.
At midnight it was raining.
By 2:00 P.M., the temperature was below freezing.
The cat slept on the outside step.
The cat has not been disturbed.
The man is not in the room.
How did he escape?

A Crash in the Night

The night is dark.
Long shadows lurk in every corner.
The streets are empty.
Only a lone streetlight lights a corner.
Heavy mist hangs in the air.
There is not a sound.
Nothing is moving.
Suddenly, a crash splits the silence.
Shattered glass sprinkles to the ground.
Then it is quiet again.
What caused the crash?

Name

71

COURTROOM IMPOSTORS

What confusion there was in the Miller County Court! Five people, all claiming to be Pat Pagoo, showed up to claim a large sum of money left by a wealthy relative. How will the judge ever figure out who the four impostors are?

Read the court reports below. Each report on these two pages (72 and 73) has one or more details that are not related to the report. These details have slipped into the writing, but do not belong. Track down any details that are not helpful to the article's purpose, and cross out these "impostors"!

Thursday, February 19

CASE #1

Five people showed up in Judge Law's courtroom today. All of them claimed to be Pat Pagoo, heir to a twenty-million-dollar fortune. Judge Law had just had a turkey club sandwich for lunch when the case began. All five Pat Pagoos brought birth certificates to prove their identity. Judge Law coughed from a bad cold. Then Judge Law postponed the case until authorities could investigate the background of the people and determine which ones were impostors.

Will the real Pat Pagoo please stand up?

CASE #2

Daphne Hart brought a complaint against Anthony Pilfer. Anthony was wearing a suit and tie in court today. Daphne claimed that Anthony left her candy shop on Valentine's Day without paying for some chocolates. Miss Hart told the judge that Mr. Pilfer had a 20-pound box of chocolates under his raincoat when he slipped out the back door of the shop. Mr. Pilfer pled "not guilty" and reported that he is allergic to chocolate.

Mr. Pilfer pled "not guilty."

CASE #3

Mrs. Grundy lives in a pink house on Blossom Street. She told the judge that her grandchildren visit her every Saturday. She is suing her next door neighbors, the Jeffersons. She wants them to pay $400 for the tulip bulbs and daffodil bulbs that their dog dug up from her garden. The Jeffersons claimed that they do not have a dog. Mrs. Grundy has a cat. The judge found that a dog named Tulip is registered under this family's name. He ordered the Jeffersons to pay Mrs. Grundy $400.

Mrs. Grundy swore to tell the truth.

Use with page 73.

Name

Cross out the details that are not helpful to the purpose of the writing.

Cream puff fakery?

CASE #4

The Cream Puff Heaven Bakery was brought into court today and charged with false advertising. Mr. Charles E. Claire buys four cream puffs every day from the bakery. He also buys a dozen sticky buns and two pumpkin pies. According to Mr. Claire, the bakery is using artificial whipped cream in its puffs. He brought in the bakery's newspaper ad, which claims that genuine whipped cream is used in all their pastries. The judge ordered the bakery owner to bring him a dozen cream puffs to sample, so that he can decide if the cream is fake.

CASE #5

Judge Law heard the case of Arthur Rush next. Arthur Rush makes his living designing socks for the Shoes & Socks Emporium. Mr. Rush received four speeding tickets in one week. Mr. Rush drives a Mustang and Judge Law drives a Volkswagen. The judge ordered Mr. Rush to pay all fines and to attend Speeder's School for eight weeks.

"Pay the fine," ordered the judge.

CASE #6

A problem tree.

Agatha Abernathy is suing the city of Millerstown. The city has ordered Mrs. Abernathy to cut down a diseased tree in front of her house. The city has a population of 21,000. Her house has three stories. The city claims the tree will cause a hazard when it dies. She claims the tree belongs to the city because its roots are under the street, which is city property. The judge agreed with Mrs. Abernathy and ordered the city to remove the tree.

Write a court report for the last case of the day. Include one or more details that do not belong. Ask a friend or classmate to search your report for the "impostors." Draw a picture to go along with your report.

CASE #7

There are 20 kids. They break a window Playing ball. The

Use with page 72.

Name

LOST HEADLINES

These news stories Murphy has prepared for the magazine have lost their headlines. Read each one. Then add a good, short headline. Remember that a headline must give readers a good idea about what will be in the story or report.

Spark Magazine   Page 1

An unusual rash of spider bites has been reported in the county this month. Officials are puzzled by the statistics. In the past four weeks, 127 bites by scorpions and other spiders have been reported. Most of the bites have occurred in the homes of the victims. Local scientists are trying to determine if there is an increase in the number of spiders in the area.

Spark Magazine   Page 2

Schools throughout the city were closed at noon yesterday. School officials would give no reason for the closure, except to insist that it was necessary. Students and parents have been guessing about the reasons. Some believe that the water supply at one of the schools was contaminated.

Spark Magazine   Page 3

People in cities and towns along the coast are suffering from attacks by killer bees. Thousands of animals and people have been stung by the bees. The stings produce strong flu-like symptoms. Hundreds of people have become critically ill, and 45 animals have died.

Spark Magazine   Page 4

A local librarian is enjoying her good luck today because she is $132,000 richer than she was yesterday. Mrs. Leslie Anne Ruddenbacher, assistant librarian at the Ames County Library, found a $100 bill stuck in every page of a recently returned book. The person who last borrowed the book said that the money did not belong to her.

Spark Magazine   Page 5

The Lynwood–Crater football game was a thriller down to the final seconds. Lynwood controlled the ball and led by 1 point with 15 seconds left. Then the Crater defense got to the quarterback and brought him down behind the goal line, giving Crater 2 points for a safety. This is the seventeenth win in a row for the Crater Comets. Their win broke a seven-game winning streak for the Lynwood Lions.

Spark Magazine   Page 6

Citizens of Millerstown are staying indoors this week. An eight-year-old lion escaped from a circus train as the train passed through the town last Monday. The train was making a brief stop for supplies when a conductor noticed the gate on the lion's cage was broken. Searchers are combing the area. Anyone catching sight of the lion should not approach the animal, but should call the Miller County Police.

Use with page 75.

Name

Add a good, short headline for each news story.

Spark Magazine

Page 7

Six high school skiers won medals at the state ski meet this weekend. Jonathan Mogul, a freshman, took first place in the slalom. Tom Turner, also a freshman, finished second. Tina Vann set a new state record with a win in the downhill. Her teammates Anna Georges and Teresa Gomez took second and third. Jana Jensen won gold in the freestyle event.

Spark Magazine

Page 8

A strange robbery took place Saturday night at the local sandwich shop—or did it? Juan Mirana, owner of Subs to Go, found twenty long loaves of wheat bread, a box of onions, and two large jars of pickles missing from his shop on Sunday morning. There was no sign of a break-in, however, and the doors were still locked when he arrived.

Spark Magazine

Page 9

Police reported a sharp increase in traffic tickets in Millerstown this year. Parking tickets inside city limits increased by fifty percent. The number of speeding tickets jumped from 25 last year to 380 this year. Tickets for reckless driving have doubled in the last year. It is not clear whether these increases are caused by more careless drivers or by better police work.

Spark Magazine

Page 10

Five hundred people attended a unique wedding last Saturday at the Jeston Chapel. Three couples were married in a triple ceremony. The three brides are triplets Molly, Polly, and Lolly Bridges. Each bride had a maid of honor, a flower girl, and three bridesmaids. There were three ministers in charge of the ceremony, Rev. Starks, Rev. Sparks, and Rev. Marks. The couples had a triple reception following the ceremony.

Spark Magazine

Page 11

A busload of tourists claims to have seen Bigfoot on Sunday. The tour bus was headed south on I-5 near Salem, Oregon, when a large creature appeared out of the woods. All 43 passengers on the bus testified to seeing the creature.

Spark Magazine

Page 12

A record-setting pumpkin was grown in Dade County this fall. Farmer Butch Appleby's prize pumpkin weighed 980 pounds. After officials decided it was the heaviest pumpkin grown in the county, Farmer Butch got out his chainsaw and turned the pumpkin into a fantastic Jack-O-Lantern.

Use with page 74.

Name

WRAPPING IT UP

At last, Bartholomew Gerkins had been found. After a mysterious five-year disappearance, he was returned to his family. Everything was finally back to normal. Only his little daughter still wondered. As she watched him write in his journal, she said to herself, "I was so sure my dad was left-handed like me!"

The End

Do you like mysterious endings like this one, where you are not really sure how things turned out? Imaginative endings are great fun to write. It's important to have strong endings. After all, that's the last thing the reader sees!

With a good ending you can . . .

. . . totally surprise the reader

. . . give an unexpected solution

. . . tie up all the loose ends

. . . ask a question or answer a question

. . . finish an explanation

. . . solve a problem

. . . make the reader laugh

. . . teach a lesson

. . . leave the reader looking forward to your next story

. . . leave the reader with a mystery

These are some of my best endings, if I do say so myself!

MURPHY GREEN

And that was the end of that...or was it?

The magician whispered to himself, "I'll never try that trick again."

Of course, the second act was yet to come.

I wonder what will happen on next year's field trip!

At least that's the story we told our parents.

She was lucky to escape with her life!

Eat it with whipped cream or chocolate sauce, but never with gravy!

The next day, we had a new substitute.

Would you ever shop at that store?

You can imagine what our report cards looked like!

Practice writing good endings of your own. Use the spaces on the next page (page 77) to write a sample ending for each piece of writing described.

Use with page 77.

Name _____

WRAPPING IT UP, CONT.

Write a strong ending that might be used for each of the writing examples below. Then cut the strips apart and pass them to classmates or friends. Ask each one to write a beginning that leads to the ending on the strip.

a poem about an escaped wild animal

a letter to an editor expressing a complaint about something

a surprising or funny event that happened at school

a news report about an accident or fire

an explanation of how to get your homework done on time

a warning about an unhealthy or dangerous activity

a report of a mysterious disappearance

a lesson on making a good milkshake

Use with page 76.

Name

GREAT CHOICES

"Looking for a great place to visit on your next vacation?" Murphy has a good start on her travel column for next week's magazine, but her article needs details added to tell about each place. Choose three strong supporting details to support her main statement for each paragraph. Use the ideas in the box below, or write your own.

Catch a glimpse of a mirage.

Enjoy cool drinks in a green oasis.

The sun will shine until midnight!

Enjoy some unusually fine fishing.

Get some close-up photos of big crocodiles.

Climb on glaciers and photograph icebergs.

Find out what it's really like to ride on a camel.

Spend a whole day watching playful penguins.

See for yourself the most mammoth ice shelf in the world.

See some of the most beautiful tropical birds in the world.

You might catch a glimpse of a cheetah or an anaconda.

Find plants and animals that survive on very little water.

Watch the wind create dunes and patterns in the sand.

Experience a lush tropical rain forest first hand.

Do you have a vacation coming up? Would you like to visit an exciting, unusual spot? Call your travel agent today, and make your next trip one you won't forget!

Stock up on sunscreen and head for the Great Sahara Desert.

Grab your mosquito netting and your camera for an adventure on the great, wide Amazon River.

If you don't mind getting a bit cold, try the adventure of a lifetime in frosty Antarctica!

Use with page 79.

Name

TERRIBLE CHOICES

Butterfly hunting in Quick-Sand Swamp is probably a "no-no."

Maybe Murphy should expand her travel column and warn readers about places not to visit! Get her started on this feature for the next SPARK edition.

Complete the outline to get started on your column. For each main section of the outline, write a topic sentence describing a place to avoid. Then write three or more supporting sentences giving details about why everyone should stay away from that place.

TERRIBLE CHOICES FOR YOUR VACATION

I strongly recommend that you stay far away from these places on your next vacation. Believe me, I know about these spots. I barely survived them myself!

I. _____

   A. _____

   B. _____

   C. _____

II. _____

   A. _____

   B. _____

   C. _____

III. _____

   A. _____

   B. _____

   C. _____

IV. _____

   A. _____

   B. _____

   C. _____

Use with page 78.

Name _____

WHERE IS CAMP LOOKOUT?

All over the country, people are talking about wild and wacky Camp Lookout. Read the sentences below. Punctuate each sentence correctly and then label it according to the box below. Use the clues in the sentences to help you unscramble the name of the state in which the camp is located.

> **Kinds of sentences:**
> **Interrogative sentences** (I) ask a question and end with a question mark.
> **Exclamatory sentences** (E) express strong feelings and end with an exclamation point.
> **Imperative sentences** (IM) give an order and end with a period.
> **Declarative sentences** tell (D) something and end with a period.

_____ 1. How do we get to Camp Lookout

_____ 2. Find the atlas

_____ 3. There have been Bigfoot sightings in that region of the United States

_____ 4. Many mountains, rivers, and lakes are found there

_____ 5. Don't get too close to the waterfalls when you're rafting

_____ 6. Get your fishing pole ready

_____ 7. Your tent is falling down

_____ 8. Which ghost story was too scary

_____ 9. Is that plant poison oak

_____ 10. Stay away from the bears

_____ 11. The camp is in a state that borders the Pacific Ocean

_____ 12. Oh, no, there's a skunk in our tent

_____ 13. You'll never forget Camp Lookout

The scrambled name of the state is NHGONWISAT.

Unscrambled, it is _____.

Now write your own example of each kind of sentence.

Interrogative _____

Exclamatory _____

Imperative _____

Declarative _____

Name _____

STEP BY STEP

Campers must be careful when climbing the rickety ladder to the tree house at Camp Lookout. If you can catch the subject and predicate in the sentence for each rung of the ladder, they will get to the top before it collapses. Start with Rung #10. Circle the simple subject for each sentence. Underline the simple predicate for each sentence.

> The **subject** tells who or what is doing something.
> The **predicate** tells what the subject is doing.
> *Example: Sometimes the mother bear growls at her cubs.*
> The **simple subject** is **bear**.
> The **simple predicate** is **growls**.

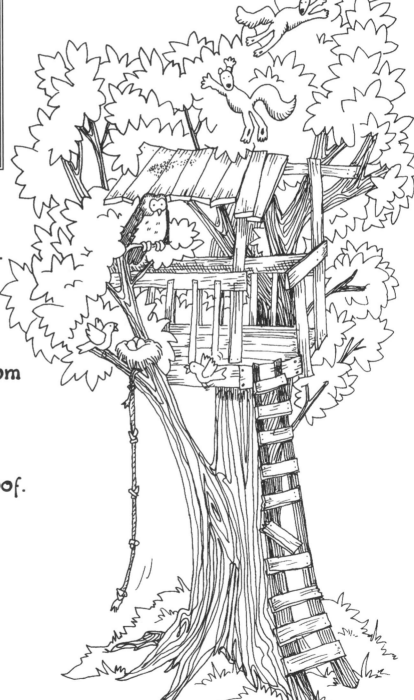

10. The tree house is reached at last!

9. Sometimes a coyote howls.

8. Sometimes an owl hoots.

7. Squirrels jump from limb to limb.

6. A swinging rope hangs from one of the branches.

5. Birds have built a nest in the tree.

4. Moss is growing on the roof.

3. Some of the boards are falling off.

2. The tree house looks old.

1. The ladder shakes with each step.

Name

CAMPER CARL'S COMPOUND PROBLEM

A **simple sentence** is a group of words that expresses a complete thought.

A **compound sentence** combines two, related simple sentences with the conjunctions *and, or,* or *but.*

Examples:
  Simple sentence: Four campers went horseback riding.
  Compound sentence: Four campers went horseback riding, and two of them
                were riding bareback.

Counselor I. M. Wacky is at it again! He has asked Carl to solve a strange problem. Please help Carl with this problem.

  1. Read each sentence below carefully. Write **S** for simple or **C** for compound in the blank before each sentence.

  2. Try to find a way for Carl to get to the other side of the lake with the instructions Counselor Wacky gave him.

_____ Carl was a camper at Camp Lookout. _____ He was a kind, considerate camper, and he always did what he was told. _____ He was asked by a counselor to run an errand. _____ Counselor I. M. Wacky told him that the job might be hard, or it might be easy. _____ Carl was asked to get an owl, a chipmunk, and a ten-pound bag of marshmallows across the lake. _____ The counselor told Carl it's not something he should try at home, but Carl wouldn't anyway because he doesn't live by a lake.

_____ The biggest problem was that Carl had room in his kayak only for himself and either the owl, the chipmunk, or the marshmallows. _____ He didn't want to leave the chipmunk alone with the marshmallows. _____ The chipmunk might eat them. _____ He didn't want to leave the owl alone with the chipmunk. _____ The owl might eat the chipmunk.

Using another sheet of paper or the back of this sheet, tell what Carl needs to do to get all three to the other side of the lake.

Name _____

RUNNING OUT OF CONTROL

Boulders are running out of control! Rewrite the run-on sentences and fragments correctly, before the boulders go crashing into Camp Lookout!

> A **run-on sentence** contains two or more sentences that have not been separated by the proper punctuation or connecting words.
> A **fragment** is part of a sentence that does not express a complete thought.

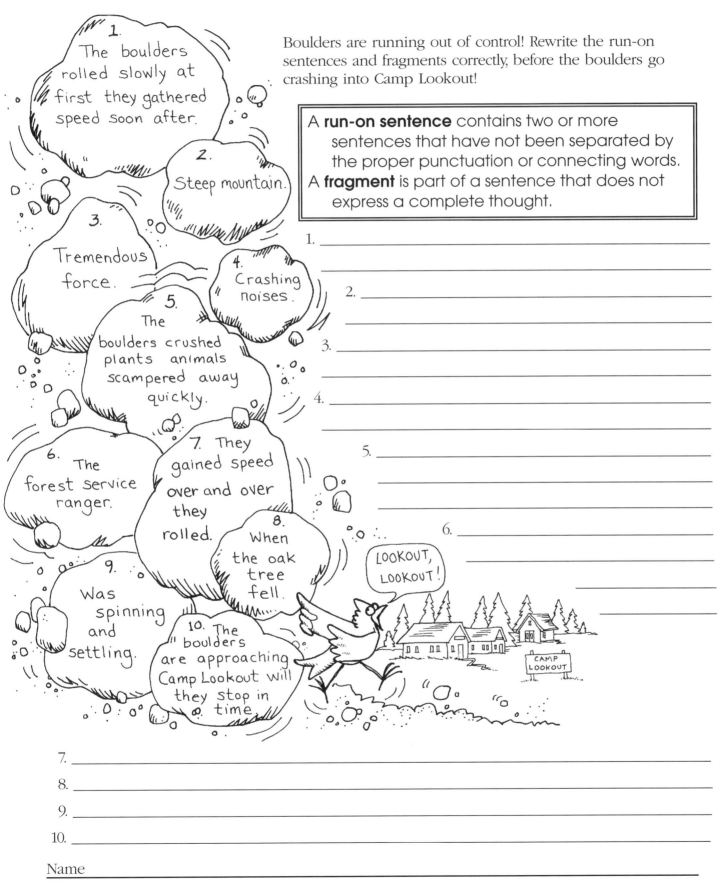

1. The boulders rolled slowly at first they gathered speed soon after.

2. Steep mountain.

3. Tremendous force.

4. Crashing noises.

5. The boulders crushed plants animals scampered away quickly.

6. The forest service ranger.

7. They gained speed over and over they rolled.

8. When the oak tree fell.

9. Was spinning and settling.

10. The boulders are approaching Camp Lookout will they stop in time

LOOKOUT, LOOKOUT!

CAMP LOOKOUT

1. _____

2. _____

3. _____

4. _____

5. _____

6. _____

7. _____

8. _____

9. _____

10. _____

Name _____

THE GREENHORNS CAMP OUT

Justin and Isaac decided to go camping on their own, away from Camp Lookout. It was their first camping experience. Read to see how these greenhorns managed. (Find out what greenhorn means!)

In the sentences below, make the noun in parentheses plural.

> **Singular** is one.
> **Plural** is more than one.
> To form plurals:
>   **Add s** to most singular nouns.
>   **Add es** to nouns ending in **x, s, ch,** or **sh.**
>   **Add s** to nouns ending in a **vowel and y.**
> When the letter before an ending **y** is a consonant, change the **y** to **i** and add **es.**

1. Justin and Isaac decided to take their tent to an area near several _____. (marsh)

2. They were from big _____ and hadn't had any camping experience. (city)

3. They brought _____ to help them with directions. (compass)

4. They talked about school and some of their favorite _____ . (holiday)

5. They sang some of their favorite camp _____ . (song)

6. Two _____ could be seen in the distance. (fox)

7. Deer watched from the _____ as they tried to set up their tent. (bush)

8. The _____ kept falling down after each one was hammered in. (pole)

9. There were _____ of poison oak nearby. (bunch)

10. After building a campfire, Justin cut one of the _____ from a poison oak bush without realizing what it was. (branch)

11. He removed the leaves and took out a package of _____ . (marshmallow)

12. The _____ moaned that evening when, as they curled up in their sleeping _____ , the tent collapsed again. (camper, bag)

Name _____

A GRAND MESS IN THE MESS HALL

Stay clear of the camp dining area, the mess hall. There are some strange things going on! The sentences tell about them. As you read them, write the plural form of the singular noun in the blank provided.

> To make these singular nouns **plural:**
>   If it ends in **f** or **fe,** change the **f** to **v** and add **es** or **s.**
>   If it ends with a **vowel and o,** add **s.**
>   If it ends with a **consonant and o,** add **es** to some and **s** to others.
>   Some plural nouns have **different spellings** (foot—feet; child—children).
>   Some nouns are the **same** in singular and plural forms (sheep; deer).

1. No one could understand how _____ ended up in the mess hall. (sheep)

2. Food began flying when several _____ ran across the floor. (mouse)

3. _____ of the campers' voices rang through the hall. (echo)

4. Three _____ were hit in the face with pizza. (child)

5. Carl had cheese dripping from his chin, while Lisa was hit with mashed _____. (potato)

6. Manuel lost two _____ trying to eat a slice of bread. (tooth)

7. The _____ of bread were so hard, the _____ could barely cut through them. (loaf, knife)

8. Several campers didn't like the _____ that were served. (trout)

9. One camper threw his trout across the room, and it landed on a tray of sliced _____. (tomato)

10. Someone turned up the volume on all the _____ so no one could hear anything except squealing and music. (radio)

11. Then some of the campers began stomping their _____. (foot)

12. The Camp Lookout counselors' _____ would never be the same. (life)

13. The place looked as if it had entertained a stampeding herd of _____. (moose)

Name _____

PICTURE THE OWNER

Lots of things get lost at Camp Lookout.
Campers and counselors are always
trying to find out who owns what!
You can show ownership (possession) by changing words. Add 's to the words in Column A so
they will show possession. Then match the words in Column A with the words in Column B, and
write them above or below each picture. The first one is done for you.

> To make a **singular noun** show **ownership** add **'s**.

A

1. tent
2. skunk
3. camper
4. tree house
5. rabbit
6. counselor
7. Bigfoot
8. wolf

B

ears	footprints
compass	door
T-shirt	poles
teeth	babies

6. _____

5. _____

3. _____

7. _____

4. _____

2. _____

1. tent's poles

8. _____

Now write three sentences using the singular possessive forms of any of the nouns above.

1. _____

2. _____

3. _____

Name _____

LOST & FOUND

More stuff is missing at Camp Lookout! There are some strange things in the Lost & Found. Use the rule about plural possessives to add either *'s* or an *'* by itself to the words in Column A so they will show possession. Then match the words in Column A with the words in Column B, and write them above or below each picture. The first one is done for you.

> To make a **plural noun** show **ownership** add **'s.**
> If the word already ends in **s,** add an **'** only.

A

1. flowers
2. children
3. cooks
4. mice
5. campers
6. deer
7. boats
8. counselors

B

tails
treasure map
petals
sleeping bags
caps
aprons
sails
food

5. _____

8. _____

3. _____

2. _____

¹ flowers' petals

6. _____

7. _____

4. _____

Write three sentences using the plural possessive forms of any of the nouns above.

1. _____

2. _____

3. _____

Name _____

87

PACK RATS

Maria and Heidi are getting ready for their two-week visit to Camp Lookout. They're having a hard time fitting everything into the trunk! Read the sentences that tell about their packing. Look for **subject pronouns.** Circle any that you find. Notice that not every sentence has one!

> A **pronoun** is used to replace a noun. **Subject pronouns** replace the subject.
> *Examples:* **I, we, they, he, she, it,** *and* **you.**
> *She lost the key. (**She** is the subject pronoun.)*

1. The two girls studied the map of Camp Lookout.

2. "It looks so exciting!"

3. Maria and Heidi were packing for their trip.

4. They checked each other's list.

5. Maria had forgotten to include a flashlight.

6. She also forgot to pack a camera.

7. Heidi had packed too much.

8. She couldn't close her suitcase.

9. "I could take less."

10. Maria couldn't decide where to put her fishing gear.

11. The last piece of luggage would not fit in the trunk of Maria's father's car.

12. "You have too much stuff."

Rewrite the sentences that did not have subject pronouns. Make sure your new sentences each have a subject pronoun. See the first example.

They studied the map of Camp Lookout.

_____

_____

_____

_____

_____

Name

GETTING THERE

The pack rats have finished packing. Now Maria and Heidi are finally on their way to Camp Lookout! Circle the object pronouns in the sentences below, and learn about their ride to camp.

> A **pronoun** is used to replace a noun.
>
> **Object pronouns** replace nouns used after action verbs.
>
> *Examples:* **them, us, it, her, him, me,** *and* **you.**
>
> *Campers bring them to their cabins. (***Them** *is the object pronoun.)*

1. In the car, Maria's father told us about his childhood.

2. Heidi asked him how long he lived in Mexico.

3. He told her twenty years.

4. At noon her father showed them his favorite restaurant.

5. The waitress gave us seats with a view of the pond.

6. Although the food was good, Heidi couldn't eat it all.

7. Maria's father showed us many different kinds of wildlife along the way.

8. He described them in detail.

9. Maria helped me roll down the window to get a better look at the animals.

10. We wanted them to come with us to camp.

11. We didn't ask him to stop.

12. At last we arrived. Maria's father drove us straight to the Camp Lookout Office.

Use some of the object pronouns listed above to create your own sentences. Remember that the object pronoun follows an action verb. It receives the action of the verb.

1. _____

_____

_____

2. _____

_____

_____

Name _____

BEAR CREEK

Bear Creek is well named. Many bears have been spotted in the area. Campers are warned to be careful. Find out what will be happening soon at Bear Creek by filling in the blanks with the future tense of the verbs. The first one is done for you.

A **future tense** verb tells what is going to happen.

To form the future tense, add the helping verb **will** to the main verb. **Shall** can also be used as a helping verb when the subject is **I** or **we.** But **shall** is not used very often in American English.

*Example: Sam **will fall** in the creek today.*

---

1. Isaac and his cabin roommates _____***will go***_____ to Bear Creek. (go)

2. They _____ the creek environment. (study)

3. Manuel _____ nets for scooping up larvae and eggs. (bring)

4. Billy _____ to find a frog for the frog jumping contest. (try)

5. Carl _____ his binoculars for bird watching. (take)

6. Some of the birds _____ nesting. (be)

7. They _____ food during the day. (find)

8. The baby birds _____ only at night. (fly)

9. The counselor _____ for bear tracks. (look)

10. The bear _____ berries near the creek. (eat)

11. They _____ for their cubs who are searching for berries also. (care)

12. We _____ the cubs and their mothers do not come too close. (hope)

Write a short story telling about something that might happen at Bear Creek in the future. Use future tense verbs in the sentences to tell what **will happen.**

_____

_____

_____

_____

Name _____

IRREGULAR BEINGS

There are some strange, out-of-this-world happenings at Camp Lookout. Read the sentences and fill in the blanks with the correct form of the irregular verbs to discover what is happening. The first one is done for you.

> **Regular past tense verbs** are formed by adding **ed** or **d. Irregular past tense verbs** show what has happened in the past by using a special form.
> *Example: Present tense —go, write.*
> *Past tense—went, wrote.*

1. Carl ___*thought*___ the sky had suddenly become an eerie pink color. (think)

2. As Manuel looked straight ahead he _____ something land in a meadow. (see)

3. Carl and Manuel _____ behind some trees and peeked around to see an unusual spacecraft in the distance. (hide)

4. The light around the spacecraft _____ brighter. (grow)

5. A tiny being, four inches tall, _____ out. It's antennas seemed to be sending signals. (come)

6. It was green and _____ something that looked like polka-dotted pajamas. (wear)

7. It picked and _____ some grass in the meadow. (eat)

8. It _____ very close to where Carl and Manuel were hiding. (go)

9. It _____ when it saw them. (run)

10. Almost as quickly as it had appeared, the spacecraft _____ out of sight. (fly)

11. Manuel and Carl quickly headed for Camp Lookout where they _____ everyone their exciting news. (tell)

12. They also _____ home to tell their parents. (write)

Write a sentence or two about a strange happening. Use some irregular past tense verbs in your sentences.

_____

_____

_____

Name

GHOST STORY

There was lots of action last night in one of the girls' cabins. A full moon was the backdrop for the ghost story Heidi decided to tell her cabin mates. Circle the action verbs in the story.

> **Scream, leap, swallow,** and **gobbled** are **action verbs** because they show action.
> **Was, were,** and **am** are not action verbs. They are **passive.**

Heidi's story began . . .

It was midnight. The only sounds were the ticking clock and the blowing window shutters. Suddenly, from her bed, the old woman noticed a hand that appeared outside on the window ledge. The fingers scratched at the window. They wiggled up and down as if they were playing a piano. Then she heard a voice whisper, "Where are my creepy fingers?" The dog crawled under her bed. The old woman sat up. She tried to figure out where the voice was coming from. This time the voice was louder, "Where are my creepy fingers?"

The old woman noticed that the hand didn't seem attached to anything. She listened. The window creaked and opened. The hand moved inside. The old woman hid under the covers. The voice got louder. "Give me my creepy fingers." The woman hid deeper under the covers and pillows. She heard an even louder voice. "Give me my creepy fingers!"

At this point Heidi grabbed Lisa, who jumped out of bed screaming.

Write a few sentences telling what would have happened next in this story.
Use lots of action verbs.

Name _____

SURVIVAL TRAINING

Carl is lost in the woods. Find the helping verb and the item in each sentence that will help Carl survive and get back to Camp Lookout. Circle each helping verb. When you find the item in the sentence, look for it in the maze. Be sure to find the items step by step, in order. This will show the correct path for Carl to follow to get back.

Helping verbs are sometimes used with main action verbs.

Common helping verbs: has, had, have, should, shall, will, were, are, was, am, is.

---

1. He is wearing the pants without a whistle in the pocket.
2. The matches were sitting on the mess hall table.
3. He will try to understand how to use the compass.
4. He is going to find materials to make a shelter.
5. Carl has seen water near the alien sighting.
6. He had taken the knife to the arts and crafts center for soap carving.
7. He has left a blanket under the bed.
8. I am afraid the flashlight was left near the boat dock.
9. He remembers he should gather wood to build a fire.
10. Then he will look for berries.
11. Near the food, he should see the entrance to the camp.
12. His friends are hoping he will find his way back to camp.

Name

WET, WETTER, WETTEST

Campers will be testing their skills at the Camp Lookout Water Competition. Write the correct form of the adjective in these sentences about the competition. The first one is done for you.

> **Er** is added to most adjectives to compare two things. The new word with the **er** ending is called the *comparative form.*
>
> **Est** is added to most adjectives to compare more than two things. The new word with the **est** ending is called the *superlative form.*

1. Carl had the _____*tiniest*_____ balloon in the water balloon toss. (tiny)

2. Manuel's balloon was _____ than his friend Nick's. (large)

3. Unfortunately, Isaac had the _____ balloon, which broke on Carl's head. (big)

4. Carl became the _____ camper at Camp Lookout. (wet)

5. Ann was the last one to arrive for the frog jumping contest. She was the _____ . (late)

6. She found her frog, which was the _____ , in a nearby swamp. (slimy)

7. Maria's frog was the _____ in the competition. (small)

8. After much debate, it was decided that her frog jumped the _____ . (far)

9. Nick's frog was the _____ . (fat)

10. It surprised everyone when his frog jumped the _____ . (high)

11. The kayaking competition took the _____ time. (long)

12. Carl was _____ than Isaac. (fast)

13. Eventually Isaac and Manuel fell out of their kayaks, so they were the _____ . (slow)

14. Although Ann paddled the _____ of all the campers, Maria won the race. (fast)

At the end of these activities and other Water Competition events, there were five top winners. Can you figure out what place ribbon each of the following campers received? Write their names on the ribbons. **Nick placed after Maria and before Isaac. Ann placed after Isaac and before Carl.**

Name _____

CAMP FIELD DAY

Field Day was planned for the week following the Water Competition. Field Day is always one of the most fun days at camp! This year, it was full of fun and surprises. Help the sentences below make sense by filling in the correct adjective form (more, most, worse, worst, better, best). The first one is done for you.

> To compare adjectives:
>
> If an adjective has two or more syllables use **more** or **most** instead of **er** or **est**.
>
> **Good** and **bad** have special forms for comparison.
> **One** person, place, or thing: **good** or **bad**
> **Two**: better or worse
> **Three** or more: **best** or **worst**

1. The _____**most**_____ unusual event was the egg-on-a-spoon race.
2. During the race Justin was _____ careful than Manuel.
3. However, the _____ thing happened to Justin.
4. As Justin approached the finish line first, in the _____ position, the raw egg dropped from his spoon and splattered on his shoe.
5. The wheelbarrow race was the _____ awkward event of the day.
6. Billy and Isaac were the _____ nervous.
7. Consequently, they got the _____ start.
8. Ann and Maria were the _____ skillful in their ability to maneuver.
9. Passing an orange from neck to neck was the _____ difficult event.
10. Carl was _____ careful than most campers when he passed the orange.
11. However, because it was the _____ slippery, it dropped and became a juicy, gooey mess.
12. Lisa had the _____ time trying to pass that messy orange to Isaac.

Write four sentences in which you use more, most, worse, worst, better, or best.

1. _____
2. _____
3. _____
4. _____

Name _____

MEET BILLY B. GOOD

Have you met camper Billy B. Good? He is famous here at Camp Lookout. He is just the kind of camper you do not want to have around. Find out why by reading about Billy. Fill in the correct adverbs in the following sentences. The first one is done for you.

> When using adverbs to **compare two actions,** add **er** to most short adverbs.
>
> To **compare three actions,** add **est** to most short adverbs.
>
> If an adverb has two or more syllables, add **more** or **most**.

1. Billy B. Good is the son of camp counselor, Mr. O. B. Good. Almost everyone thinks the father should handle his son ___**_more firmly_**___. (firmly)

2. Billy is known to many as the camp prankster. He awakens the _____ each morning. (early)

3. When he awakens, he sneaks around the mess hall _____ than anyone can imagine. (cleverly)

4. He moves the _____ in the kitchen. (fast)

5. There he exchanges sugar for salt in all the shakers, _____ than a fox. (skillfully)

6. _____ than not he is the first one to arrive for breakfast. (often)

7. He waits _____ than the rest of the campers for everyone to arrive. (eagerly)

8. In the mess hall, his laugh fills the room. It can be heard _____ than all the other campers' voices put together. (loudly)

9. In the afternoon, when campers are busy with activities, Billy is working _____ than ever. (busily)

10. He sneaks in each cabin and works _____ than a mouse. (quietly)

11. He works _____ than most campers would ever consider. His work consists of putting frogs and ants in sleeping bags, exchanging items in campers' suitcases, and switching the boys' and girls' restroom signs. (long)

12. Even though he is treated _____ than other campers by the counselors, his pranks still continue. (harshly)

Name _____

GETTING NOWHERE

Ten adventuresome campers are going on a trail ride. Discover what happens on their ride!
As you read, choose the correct word to fill in the blank.

> Words that mean **no** are called **negatives.**
>
> *Examples: not, never, nowhere, nothing, nobody, no one, aren't, doesn't, haven't, wouldn't.*
>
> Two negatives **should not be used** in the same sentence.

1. Not one of them _____ have missed going on the trail ride, except maybe Manuel. (would, wouldn't)

2. Manuel hadn't _____ been on a horse before. (never, ever)

3. He was assigned Pokey. Nobody else would have _____ to do with that horse on a trail ride. (nothing, anything)

4. Manuel could hear the other riders' voices far away in the distance. "Doesn't _____ want to ride with me?" he complained. (nobody, anybody)

5. Pokey smelled the flowers and chewed grass. There wasn't _____ he didn't enjoy seeing or eating. (nothing, anything)

6. It was for sure that Manuel and Pokey were getting _____ fast. (nowhere, anywhere)

7. The other riders had brought lunches, but hungry Manuel had not brought _____ . (anything, nothing)

8. He had hoped to get a horse fast enough to bring him back by lunchtime, but Pokey would have _____ to do with his schedule. (anything, nothing)

9. Suddenly, in the middle of the trail, Pokey stopped and wouldn't move for what seemed like hours. Manuel could get _____ to help. They were all too far ahead. (no one, anyone)

10. He tried pushing and pulling him, but there wasn't _____ he could do to make him move. (anything, nothing)

11. Manuel and Pokey had barely ridden beyond the stables. In the distance, they could hear voices. "We haven't gone _____ !" said Manuel bitterly. (nowhere, anywhere)

12. "Where have you been?" asked the riders. It wasn't _____ Manuel wanted to talk about. (anything, nothing)

Name _____

GO FISH

It's time to do some fishing. Circle the direct object in each sentence. Then fish around in the word search pond. If the object you have circled is correct, you will be able to find it in the pond. There is only one direct object in each sentence. Good luck!

> The **direct object** is a noun or pronoun that receives the action of the verb.
> *Example: The squirrel ate acorns in the tree.*
> **Squirrel,** *a noun, is the subject.* **Ate** *is the verb.* **Acorns** *is a noun and the direct object.*

1. Manuel and Justin dug worms.
2. Maria packed several lunches for the trip.
3. Heidi searched the cabins for fishing gear.
4. The campers searched the creek for their favorite fishing spot.
5. They noticed deer nearby.
6. They located a good fishing hole.
7. Manuel cast his line into the water.
8. The line caught Justin's cap on the way.
9. Justin's cap splashed the water as it hit.
10. Heidi climbed a rock and knelt over the water trying to retrieve the cap.
11. Maria pulled a huge fish out of the water after her first cast.
12. Maria fed her friends the fish for dinner.

```
A Z M R L P R X Y D B J T
H C G N O I K O A C E D U
F R E F H C N J C K W E V
I E L M F L K E N A O P R
S E G W O R M S Q R P U B
X K I A C S I V D O L W E
F W A T E R F E G H O C S
R O C E D H R I N J K F L
I L U N C H E S Z D M I D
E Y W P R U H T L A S S V
C H O L E P Q F G C T H R
E B X D H W C A B I N S Z
```

Name _____

TAKEN BY STORM

Swimming in the Camp Lookout pool is one of the most popular activities. Below is a description of a day in the pool. Fill in the blanks with one of the homophones listed below so the description will make sense.

> **Homophones** are words that sound the same but are spelled differently.

they're   there   their   to   two   too   for   four

>   your   you're   by   bye   buy

1. Many campers were walking from _____ cabins _____ the swimming pool.

2. Some ran, hoping _____ be the first ones _____ .

3. Campers jumped in the water _____ and _____ at a time.

4. They left _____ towels _____ the grassy area.

5. "_____ running _____ fast along the edge of the pool!" yelled a counselor _____ the lifeguard.

6. The lifeguard, Ima Float, was _____ busy _____ notice what the children were doing.

7. "_____ being a nuisance," Ima called. "Mind _____ own business," she said as she continued putting on makeup and combing her hair.

8. Campers could _____ refreshments at a stand _____ the pool entrance.

9. _____ was lots of time for campers to eat and do _____ swimming tricks.

10. Maria and Heidi began doing _____ tricks in the water.

11. They did a handstand and _____ somersaults.

12. _____ hoping to get into water ballet classes some day.

13. Billy did a cannonball near _____ heads.

14. "Watch out, you big, bully billy goat!" yelled Maria. "_____ jumping too close to us."

15. All of a sudden, _____ was lightning and thunder. It began _____ pour.

16. "Grab _____ towels and run," yelled Ima, as the makeup dripped down her face.

17. Campers grabbed _____ towels, dressed quickly, and headed _____ _____ cabins. Snug and safe inside, they listened _____ the storm and played games.

"GRAB YOUR TOWELS AND RUN!!"

Name _____

GETTING THE PICTURE

Isaac has made a drawing of Camp Lookout. Look on the next page (page 101) to see it. Notice that he made quite a few spelling mistakes when he labeled it. Cross out the errors and write the correct words. Five of them are already labeled correctly. After you finish, choose fifteen sets of the homophones below and write a sentence that uses all the words in the set. See the first example.

> **Homophones** are words that sound the same but are spelled differently.

tow toe   sent cent scent   braid brayed   pair pare pear

for four   bare bear   night knight   dear deer

hair hare   flea flee   sale sail   whole hole   eye I

meat meet   pale pail   peace piece   bee be   wood would

plane plain   flour flower   horse hoarse   son sun

*The bear is at **peace** while eating the **piece** of meat.*

1. _____

2. _____

3. _____

4. _____

5. _____

6. _____

7. _____

8. _____

9. _____

10. _____

11. _____

12. _____

13. _____

14. _____

15. _____

Use with page 101.

Name

Use with page 100.

CAMPSIDE CAPERS

Somebody's having a great old time in the camp garbage tonight. One camper has been sneaking around quietly to listen in on their conversation. This camper has written down everything Freddy Raccoon and Moe Mouse have said, but something is missing!

Insert quotation marks before and after the exact words that are being said. Write the conversations into the talk balloons for the animals. These words in the balloons will not need any quotation marks or explanations about who is talking!

Raiders of the Camp Cans

Tonight we'll raid the garbage cans outside the mess hall. Are you ready? asked Freddy.

You bet! exclaimed Moe.

There's a gold mine in this can! There's even a book. Have you ever read Monster Madness? asked Moe.

No! Why are you messing with books? I hear a noise. Grab your stuff and run, said Freddy.

I got corn cobs, potato peels, apple cores, bread crusts, and some mozzarella cheese. Yummm. What did you get? questioned Freddy.

Moe answered cheerfully, It looks like I got everything but the kitchen sink.

Name _____

A COUNSELOR'S MIDNIGHT HIKE

The camp counselor, Mr. O. B. Good, wrote a journal entry about his experience on a midnight hike. He forgot to include punctuation. See if you can add all the missing marks.

CAMP LOOKOUT

July 24

Dear Diary

Last night I took the boys in our cabin on a midnight hike It was a disaster I'm young (forty) and think of myself as having a lot of patience but last night tested my limits These boys behave worse than any kids in the whole camp They're always arguing never minding me and playing jokes on each other Nick had the nerve to bring a water balloon on the hike He hit Carl in the back I almost returned them to our cabin I should have

I asked the kids to stay on the trails and they claimed they couldn't see them This was not true since there was a full moon and they had flashlights They used their flashlights as weapons to zap each other This was a constant thorn in my side However the worst experience of the hike was when we saw a skunk Manuel warned everyone by yelling We're going to get sprayed Complete chaos broke loose for everyone except Justin He has to be the slowest moving snail on the planet so of course he got sprayed The smell was horrible The kids went wild It was all I could do to get us safely back to camp

After getting the kids to their bunks I had the job of filling a tub with tomato juice I brought Justin to the tub and told him to get in He acted like I'd lost my mind And I had

Painfully yours

O B

HELLO MOTHER, HELLO FATHER

Some of the campers are writing home. Their postcards, on this page and the next, need some punctuation and capitalization so the parents will be able to read them. Edit each one, and rewrite it on the lines below.

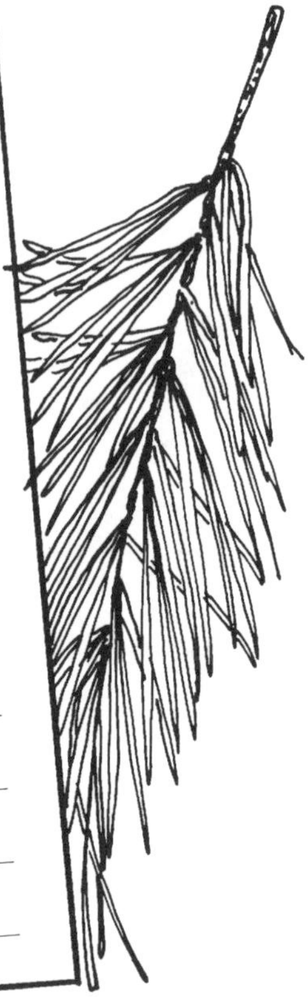

hello mother hello father
    here i am at camp lookout camp is very entertaining i went rafting and almost went down a waterfall i went fishing and caught justins hat i went horseback riding on the slowest horse in the world, pokey i had frog legs for dinner and oh yes i saw an alien can i stay longer
    xoxoxo, manuel

_____

_____

_____

_____

_____

_____

dear mom and dad
camp is fun i got lost for a day and a tornado hit our camp the counselor asks me to do fun stuff like take an owl raccoon and bag of marshmallows across the lake in a kayak the food is great
                                    your loving son carl 

_____

_____

_____

_____

_____

Use with page 105.

Name _____

Edit and rewrite the postcards on this page.

hi mom
    remember the ghost story you told me ive been telling give me my creepy fingers to everyone the girls get really scared and our counselor asked me not to tell it anymore nothing else is new except i did see bigfoot

                                                hugs and kisses heidi

dear mom and dad
    heidi and i found a treasure map were planning which toys wed like to buy with the money well get from selling the treasure also i caught a huge fish saw bigfoot and my frog jumped the farthest in the frog jumping contest
                        your loving daughter maria

MY FISH ↑

HAVE A NICE DAY !   hi mom
        you wouldnt believe how good ive been everything is going great i get along very well with all the counselors and kids i have lots of work to do but I dont even mind my favorite part of camp is breakfast how much longer can i stay   your obedient son billy

Use with page 104.

Name

TREASURE HUNT

The map below was found by Heidi and Maria. They hope to discover buried treasure somewhere close to Camp Lookout. Unfortunately, there are many errors in the directions, and the map is hard for them to read. Help by rewriting the directions with correct punctuation, capitalization, and spelling. You will need to use a separate piece of paper for this task. Then follow the directions, and put an **X** on the spot where you think the treasure is hidden.

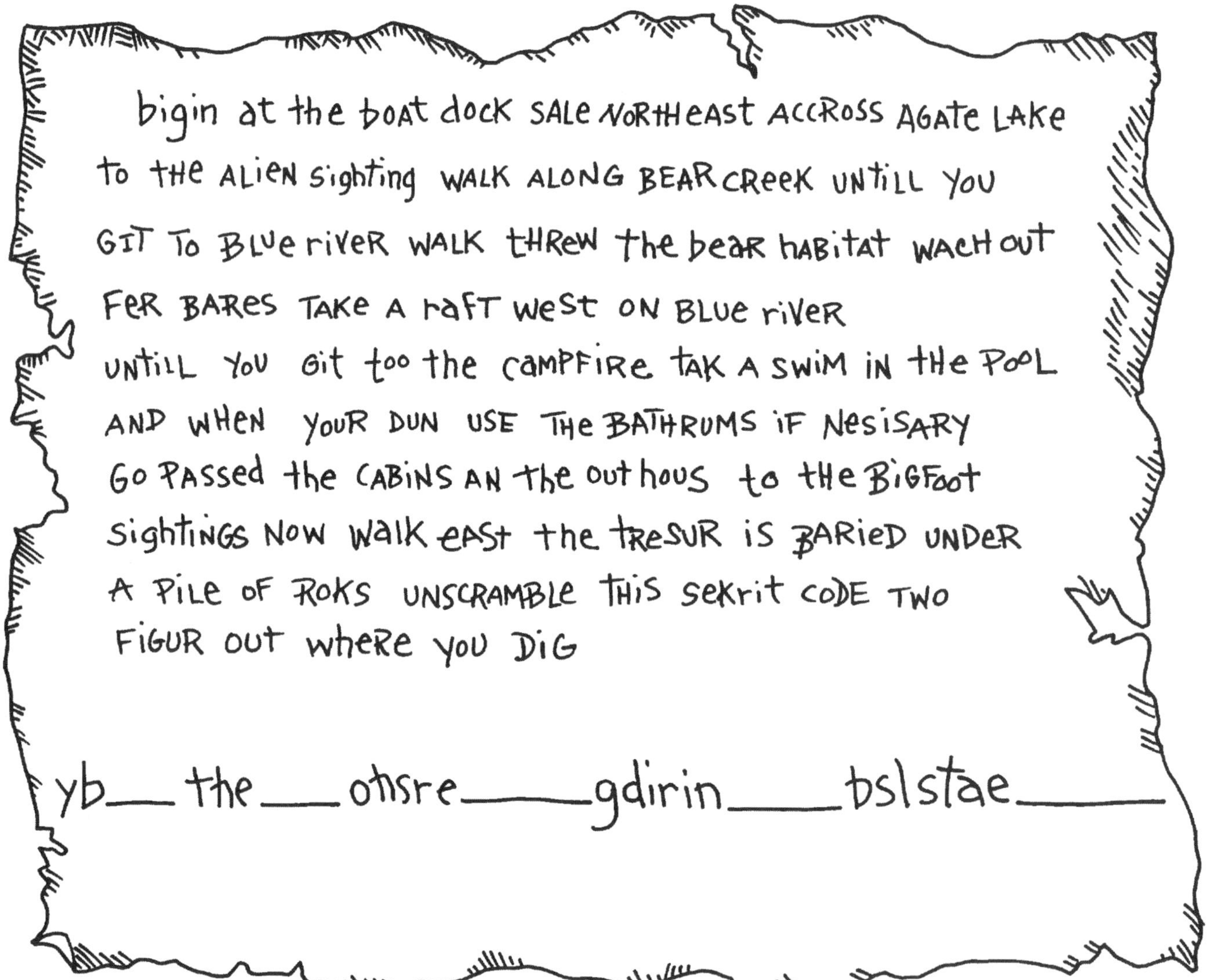

bigin at the boat dock sale northeast accross agate lake
to the alien sighting walk along bear creek untill you
git to blue river walk threw the bear habitat wach out
fer bares take a raft west on blue river
untill you git too the campfire tak a swim in the pool
and when your dun use the bathrums if nesisary
go passed the cabins an the outhous to the bigfoot
sightings now walk east the tresur is baried under
a pile of roks unscramble this sekrit code two
figur out where you dig

yb___ the___ ohsre_____ gdirin_____ bslstae_____ _____

Use with page 107.

Name

CAMPFIRE

NORTH

BEAR HABITAT

BLUE RIVER

SWIMMING POOL

BEAR CREEK

ALIEN SIGHTING

AGATE LAKE

BOYS GIRLS
BATHROOMS

BOAT DOCK

MESS HALL

BUNK HOUSES   CABINS

BIG FOOT SIGHTINGS

HORSE RIDING STABLES

Use with page 106.

Name

SOCIAL STUDIES

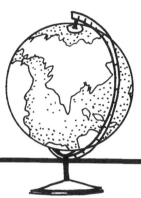

Skills Exercises
Grade Five

SKILLS CHECKLIST
U.S. HISTORY, GOVERNMENT, & CITIZENSHIP

✔	SKILL	PAGE(S)
	Identify dates and places of major events in U.S. history	112, 113, 127, 140, 146
	Identify and describe a variety of major events in U.S. history	112, 115, 140, 144
	Identify features and locations of some Native American cultures	114, 115
	Use maps to find locations of events in U.S. history	114, 115, 130, 144
	Identify and describe features of the early development of America	114–117, 127
	Identify some of the early explorations of the North American continent	116
	Identify some key persons in U.S. history	116, 131, 132, 136, 149
	Identify some key events and places of the colonial period	117
	Examine some of the contents and ideas of the Declaration of Independence	118
	Describe important U.S. traditions, symbols, and documents	118, 120–125, 128, 148
	Recognize and sequence some events of the Revolutionary War period	119
	Describe some rights and responsibilities of American citizens	120, 121, 128, 148
	Identify rights and key concepts in the U.S. Constitution	120–126, 128, 129
	Identify the persons and duties of the legislative branch of the U.S. government	122, 123, 126
	Identify the persons and duties of the executive branch of the U.S. government	122, 124
	Identify the persons and duties of the judicial branch of the U.S. government	122, 125
	Describe the structure of the U.S. federal government and features of each branch	122–126
	Identify offices and officials in local, state, and federal governments	122–126, 148
	Examine the process by which Congress makes laws	126
	Identify the first states to join the union	127
	Examine and interpret the Bill of Rights	128, 129
	Identify some facts and features of the Louisiana Purchase	130
	Identify some key persons and events in the westward expansion of the U.S.	131, 135, 137
	Identify some key events and persons related to the argument over slavery	132
	Identify events and persons related to the Civil War and Reconstruction periods	133, 134
	Identify some key persons in the U.S. Industrial Revolution	136
	Identify some important inventions and technological advances in U.S. history	136
	Examine patterns of European immigration to the U.S.	138, 139
	Find information on graphs	138, 139
	Describe some key issues and events of recent U.S. history (20th century)	140
	Identify some key persons and events related to the Cold War and the Space Race	141
	Identify government establishments and other locations in Washington, D.C.	142, 143
	Identify and locate key places in U.S. history	144, 145
	Make and read timelines of major events in U.S. history	146, 147
	Identify current local, state, and national officials	148
	Identify U.S. presidents and other key persons in U.S. history	149

SKILLS CHECKLIST
MAP SKILLS & GEOGRAPHY

✔	SKILL	PAGE(S)
	Identify different map tools and resources	150–153
	Place labels and titles correctly on maps	152
	Identify many different kinds of maps	152, 153
	Use a road map	152, 153
	Make and use map keys	152–153
	Identify and find directions on a map	152–153, 155, 156, 165, 166
	Use maps and globes to find and compare locations	152–153, 155, 156, 165, 166
	Identify parts of a map: key, title, symbols, compass, scale	152–154
	Identify, draw, and use map symbols	152–154
	Use a variety of maps to find information	152–153, 154–155, 156, 159–165, 166
	Use a variety of maps to answer questions	152–153, 154–155, 156, 159–165, 166
	Use scales to determine distances on maps	154
	Identify four hemispheres on maps and globes	155
	Recognize continents and bodies of water on world and U.S. maps	155–156
	Identify names, locations, and shapes of all states in the U.S.	156, 166
	Recognize and use a variety of geographic terms	158
	Locate places on a grid map	159
	Locate and place objects on grids	159–163
	Locate and identify major lines of latitude	160
	Become familiar with lines of latitude and longitude	160–163
	Find locations using lines of latitude and longitude	160–163
	Identify many countries on world or continent maps	160–163
	Use a floor plan to locate places	164
	Find information on a weather map	165
	Use a time zone map; recognize U.S. time zones	166
	Make maps as a representation of actual or fictitious places	168
	Make maps from information given	168

SKATING INTO THE PAST

Sam has always been interested in the past. Maybe this has something to do with the influence of his Great-Great-Great-Uncle Sam! Whatever the reason, he likes digging around in news from the past. Now he's got a wonderful idea:

> "Why not ride my time-traveling skateboard into the past and see some of the stuff that's happened in the United States?" he says.

While Sam is getting ready for some time travel, take a look at these news headlines from the past. In the space below each headline, write the name of the event that is the subject of the news story.

1. Nation's News 1914
Ship Passes from Atlantic to Pacific

2. Promontory Gazette 1869
LAST SPIKE HAMMERED

3. The Tribune 1917
WAR DECLARED

4. Daily Tribune 1927
LINDBERGH SUCCEEDS

5. Sun Times 1920
Women Celebrate!

6. Weekly News 1946
WAR BEGINS WITHOUT GUNS

7. New York Times 1929
It's A Thundering Crash

8. Gazette 1939
POLAND INVADED

9. Washington Tribune 1956
Ike Does It Again

10. The Tribune 1959
USA Welcomes 49 & 50

Use with page 113.

Name _____

11. Early Times 1962
CRISIS in the CARIBBEAN

12. Missouri Gazette 1843
WAGONS HEAD WEST

13. Gazette 1776
WE DECLARE!

14. Washington News 1974
SCANDAL ROCKS NATION

15. Tribune 1865
IT'S OVER AT LAST!

16. Boston Times 1770
TROOPS FIRE ON PROTESTERS

17. Daily News 1773
TEA DUMPED IN HARBOR

18. Gazette 1849
The Rush Is On!

19. The Times 1803
$15 Million Land Deal

20. Morning News July 1969
BIG STEP IS CHEERED

21. Virginia Gazette 1607
English Folks Settle In

22. The Gazette 1804
EXPLORERS REACH PACIFIC

23. New York News 1789
INAUGURATION DAY!

24. The Post 1971
GOOD NEWS FOR 18-YEAR OLDS

Sam is off, skating into the past. Have a good trip, Sam!

Use with page 112.

Name _____

THEY WERE HERE FIRST!

The United States is over 200 years old, but its history actually began thousands of years ago when the first immigrants came to North America. These earliest Americans crossed the Bering Land Bridge from Asia to the North American continent. They were probably hunting for woolly mammoths and bison. The descendants of these early Americans formed many large groups called **nations**, which were then divided into smaller groups called **bands**.

Use colored pencils and the map on page 115 to help Sam get a good idea of where these Native American nations lived. You may need help from a U.S. map, too!

I. Use a blue pencil to label the following rivers and bodies of water.

Atlantic Ocean	Puget Sound	Lake Erie	Río Grande
Pacific Ocean	Lake Huron	Lake Superior	St. Lawrence River
Gulf of Mexico	Lake Ontario	Lake Champlain	Colorado River
Chesapeake Bay	Lake Michigan	Mississippi River	Columbia River

II. In 1650, eight major Native American nations were found in what are now the lower 48 states. Find each nation's territory and color it as directed.

1. ORANGE: The Navajo Shepherds lived in this smallest area.
2. YELLOW: South of the Navajo Shepherds, in an area that extends along the Río Grande River, were the Desert Dwellers.
3. RED: A group of Seed Gatherers lived in the small area to the north of the central section of the Desert Dwellers.
4. RED: Another group of Seed Gatherers lived in the large area that is west of the Navajo Shepherds and goes all the way to the coast.
5. BROWN: The Pueblo Farmers lived in the remaining small southwestern area.
6. BLUE: The Northern Fisherman lived along the northwestern coast.
7. PURPLE: The large central area was the land of the Hunters of the Plains.
8. GREEN: The remaining area was home to the Woodsmen of the Eastern Woodlands.

III. Choose one area and research it to find the names of some of the nations and tribes of this area.

Use with page 115.

Name

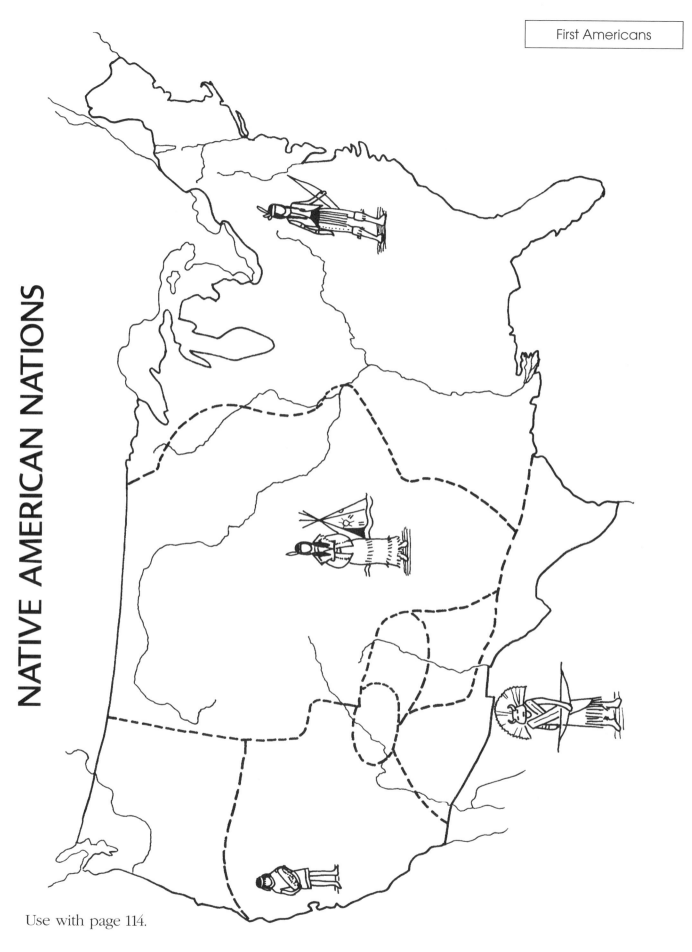

NATIVE AMERICAN NATIONS

Use with page 114.

Name

THE GREAT EXPLORERS

When Sam dropped in on some of the earliest explorers of North America, he was shocked to find that none of them were English! Because most Americans speak English, he expected that England would have been the first country to explore the New World.

Who were these early explorers, and what did they find as they explored the new continent? For each explorer, write the area of America that he explored and the European country from which he came. (You may need some help from your history book or encyclopedia!)

1 *In 1524, I explored the_____. I am Giovanni da Verrazzano from_____.*

2 *My name is Juan Ponce de Leon. I'm the famous explorer who looked for the Fountain of Youth in the area of _____ around 1513. I'm from_____.*

3 *I'm Samuel de Champlain from _____. From 1603–1609, I explored _____.*

4 *In 1528, I explored _____. My name is Panfilo de Narvaez, and I'm from the country of_____.*

5 *I'm Henry Hudson from _____. In 1610, I discovered and named the _____.*

6 *I'm Jacques Cartier from _____. In 1535, I discovered the_____.*

7 *I am a Franciscan Father named Marcos, from _____. In 1539, I explored the area of _____.*

8 *From 1539–1542, I looked for gold in the new continent. My name is Hernando de Soto. In 1541, I discovered the _____. I'm from _____.*

9 *I searched for gold in the area of _____ from 1540–1542. I'm Francisco de Coronado from _____.*

Name _____

SETTLING DOWN

Colonists are people who move from their country to a new land. A settlement in a new land is called a colony.

Once the New World was discovered, people began coming from other countries far away. They came for all kinds of reasons and settled in colonies. French, Spanish, English, and Dutch citizens were among the European settlers in what is now the United States. The period from 1565 up to the Revolutionary War is known as the **American Colonial Period.** Solve the puzzle below using the names of people, settlements, and events of this period.

ACROSS

2. island colony purchased by the Dutch for $24
4. the last of the 13 colonies
5. William Penn's second colony
8. colony on the Hudson River claimed by the Dutch
10. Quaker founder of Pennsylvania
11. a person from the first colony
12. religious group settled in Pennsylvania

DOWN

1. Quaker "City of Brotherly Love"
2. colony owned by George Calvert
3. colony settled by the Swedish
5. colonists came to Georgia to be free from _____
6. the number of original colonies
7. Pilgrims' ship that landed at Plymouth
9. many settlers came to America in search of _____ freedom

Name _____

AN IMPORTANT PIECE OF PAPER

It's one of the most important pieces of paper in U.S. history!
It's the **Declaration of Independence,** and this is how it begins:

When, in the Course of human events, it becomes necessary for one people to dissolve the political bands which have connected them with another, and to assume, among the powers of the earth, the separate and equal station which the Laws of Nature and of Nature's God entitle them, a decent respect to the opinions of mankind requires that they should declare the causes which impel them to the separation.

We hold these truths to be self-evident, that all men are created equal, that they are endowed by their Creator with certain unalienable Rights, that among these are Life, Liberty, and the pursuit of Happiness.

That, to secure these rights, Governments are instituted among Men, deriving their just powers from the consent of the governed,

That, whenever any Form of Government becomes destructive of these ends, it is the Right of the People to alter or to abolish it, and to institute new Government, laying its foundation on such principles, and organizing its powers in such form, as to them shall seem most likely to effect their Safety and Happiness.

Thomas Jefferson, along with several others, wrote the Declaration of Independence as a statement of human rights as well as of complaints against the British king. This formal announcement of the colonists' independence was made on July 4, 1776. Although the words were written over 200 years ago, they are still the basis of American democracy. Some of the wording may seem strange to you, because people in Jefferson's time spoke differently. Write what you think the following phrases mean.

1. In the first paragraph, who were the "people"?

_____

2. To whom were the colonists politically bound?

_____

3. "That all men are created equal . . ." means _____ .

4. What does "unalienable" mean? _____ .

5. "That they are endowed by their Creator with certain unalienable Rights . . ." means

_____

6. Name the "unalienable Rights." _____

_____

Name _____

"THE BRITISH ARE COMING!"

Sam is trying to get his facts about the American Revolution straight. He has some of the important events written down in a travel log, but he has not kept track of what happened when. After you've learned about the Revolutionary period, put these events in the right order.

_____ Paul Revere rides through the night warning, "The British are coming!"

_____ British General Charles Cornwallis surrenders at Yorktown, Virginia.

_____ British General Howe arrives from Britain with 32,000 troops.

_____ Washington's army winters at Valley Forge, Pennsylvania.

_____ Battle of Kings Mountain is fought in North and South Carolina.

_____ The Declaration of Independence is completed.

_____ The British Parliament passes the Stamp Act.

_____ The Battle of Bunker Hill is fought.

_____ The British Parliament passes the Townshend Acts.

_____ The British Parliament passes the Sugar Act.

_____ America signs a treaty for help from France.

_____ The final peace treaty is signed in Paris, France.

_____ The U.S. Constitution is written.

_____ The Boston Tea Party takes place.

_____ The Boston Massacre occurs.

Name _____

POWERFUL WORDS

"Whatever is a preamble?" wonders Sam! His trip back to 1787 when the Constitution was written should answer this question. A preamble is something that comes at the beginning. This is the Preamble to the U.S. Constitution:

We the people of the United States, in order to form a more perfect Union, establish justice, insure domestic tranquillity, provide for the common defense, promote the general welfare, and secure the blessings of liberty to ourselves and our posterity, do ordain and establish this Constitution for the United States of America.

The ideas in this preamble were not new. The Iroquois League of Indians and other groups throughout history formed governments based on similar beliefs. Like the Declaration of Independence, the Constitution has unusual language. It may seem strange now, but it was normal more than 200 years ago!

Reread the Preamble. Then rewrite it in common, everyday language.

The Preamble Rewritten

We ARE the people.....

Name _____

THE MAIN DOCUMENT

What luck to stumble across the 1787 Constitutional Convention in Philadelphia, Pennsylvania, and sneak into the secret meetings! These meetings were held in an upstairs room of the State House, with guards placed at every door. The pavement in front of the building was covered with dirt and sawdust so that the noise of the traffic would not disturb the delegates as they wrote the document that formed the U.S. government! Use the clues to solve this puzzle about the U.S. Constitution.

Across

2. number of senators from each state
8. the highest law of the U.S.
9. Congress makes the _____
12. to change the Constitution
13. serves a 6-year term

Down

1. made up of the Senate plus the House of Representatives
3. only colony that did not take part in the Constitutional Convention
4. branch of government that has courts
5. Chief Executive Officer of the U.S.
6. the U.S. government is a system of checks and _____
7. number of representatives from each state depends on the state's _____
10. number of branches of U.S. government
11. president's refusal to approve a law

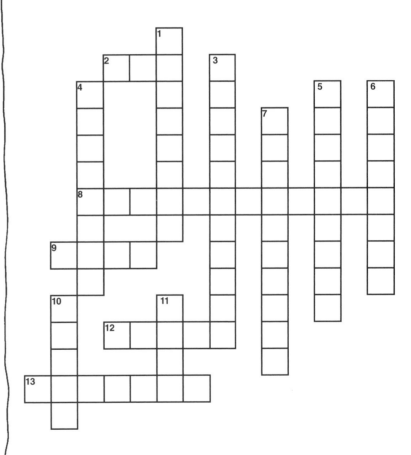

Name _____

CHECKS AND BALANCES

Balance is very important right now for Sam, who has just landed on the top of the U.S. Capitol Building. Balance is important in government, too. The U.S. Constitution formed a government with three branches, or parts.

Each branch is equally important, and each branch has some control over the other two branches. In this way, no one person or branch can become too powerful. The branches serve as a system of **checks** and **balances** for each other.

In the diagram below, label each branch of the U.S. government. In the space below, write WHO is part of that branch and WHAT the duties and responsibilities are for that branch. Find out how each branch has some control over the other two.

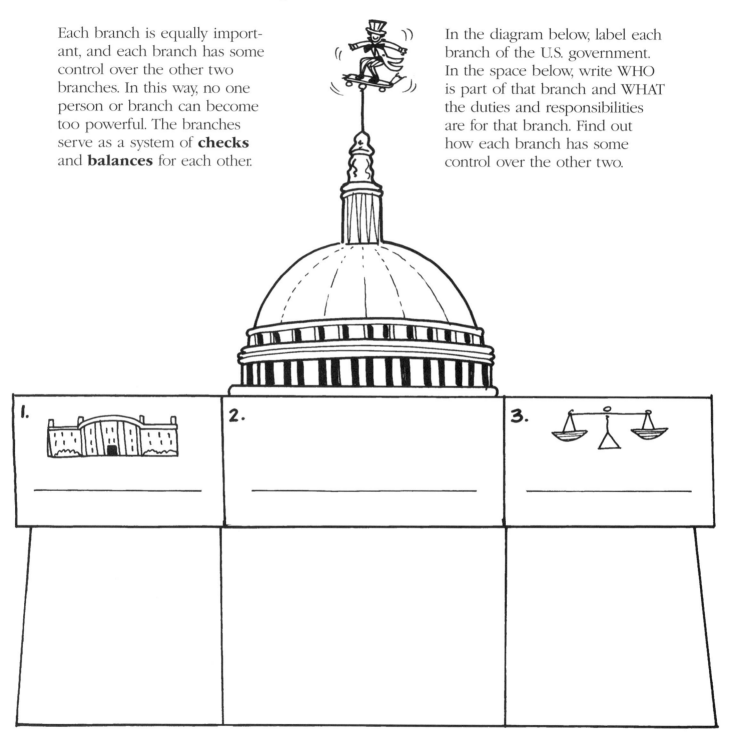

1. _____

2. _____

3. _____

Name _____

A CONGRESSIONAL MAZE

Sam has come to a screeching halt in front of the Capitol Building. Inside, the representatives and senators of Congress are doing the business of the U.S. government. Visitors are allowed, so he finds his way inside. The Constitution set guidelines for Congress. Find Sam's way through the maze of hallways by coloring a path to connect the true statements about Congress. Do not travel through sections with false statements.

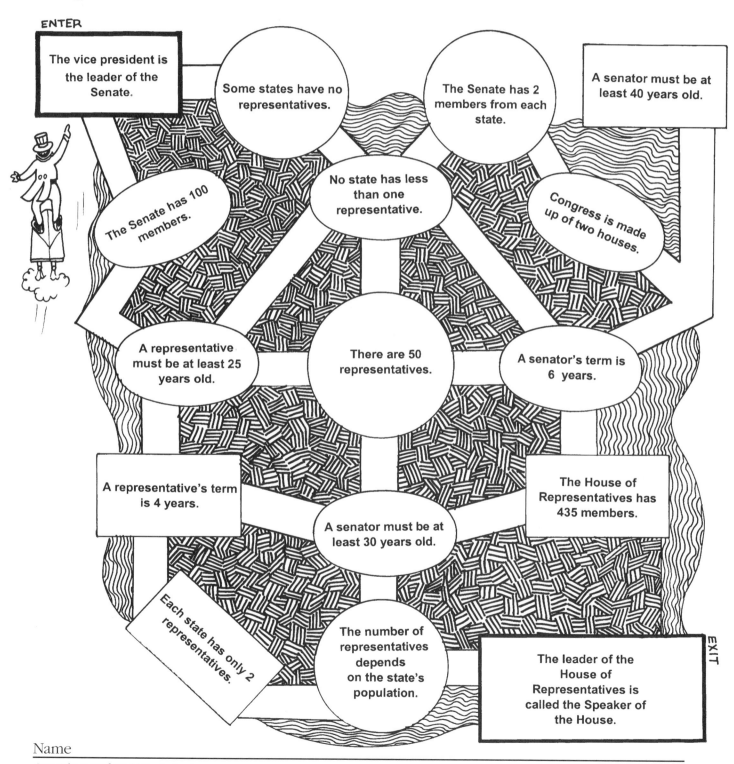

ENTER

The vice president is the leader of the Senate.

Some states have no representatives.

The Senate has 2 members from each state.

A senator must be at least 40 years old.

The Senate has 100 members.

No state has less than one representative.

Congress is made up of two houses.

A representative must be at least 25 years old.

There are 50 representatives.

A senator's term is 6 years.

A representative's term is 4 years.

A senator must be at least 30 years old.

The House of Representatives has 435 members.

Each state has only 2 representatives.

The number of representatives depends on the state's population.

The leader of the House of Representatives is called the Speaker of the House.

EXIT

Name

"I DO SOLEMNLY SWEAR"

It is the big day—Inauguration Day, 2009! Sam watches as Barack Obama takes the oath to be president of the United States and Joe Biden takes the oath as vice president. What duties do they promise to carry out? Show what you've learned about the role of the executive branch by filling in the missing information. You may need some help from your textbook, encyclopedia, or other reference materials.

1. Persons in the executive branch

2. Qualifications for the president and vice president
- Age
- Citizenship
- Residency

3. Length of term

Number of terms

4. Duties of the president

5. Reasons a president can be removed

6. Name some Cabinet members

7. Some titles for the president

8. The order of succession if a president dies
A.   B.

C.   D.

9. What the Cabinet does

Name _____

ORDER IN THE COURT!

Every courtroom is supposed to have order. You can be pretty sure you'll find order in the highest court of the United States. Can you figure out which of the statements Sam is reading about the judicial branch are really true? Mark each one **T** or **F**.

Chief Justice

Out of order!

1. The highest court in the United States is the Circuit Court. T　　F	**5.** The Supreme Court is located in its own building in New York City. T　　F	**9.** A Supreme Court justice cannot be removed from office. T　　F
2. It is the duty of the courts to pass laws. T　　F	**6.** Another name for a Supreme Court judge is *justice.* T　　F	**10.** The length of a Supreme Court justice's term is 10 years. T　　F
3. The executive branch is responsible for enforcing the laws. T　　F	**7.** The duties of the Supreme Court are written in the Constitution. T　　F	**11.** In addition to the Supreme Court, the judicial branch has several other court systems. T　　F
4. It is the courts' job to interpret or explain the laws. T　　F	**8.** Women cannot be on the Supreme Court. T　　F	**12.** Supreme Court justices are appointed by the Senate and approved by the president. T　　F

Name _____

THE ROAD FROM BILLS TO LAWS

How does a bill become a law? Place the letters on the path in the right order to show the steps that a bill follows to become a law.

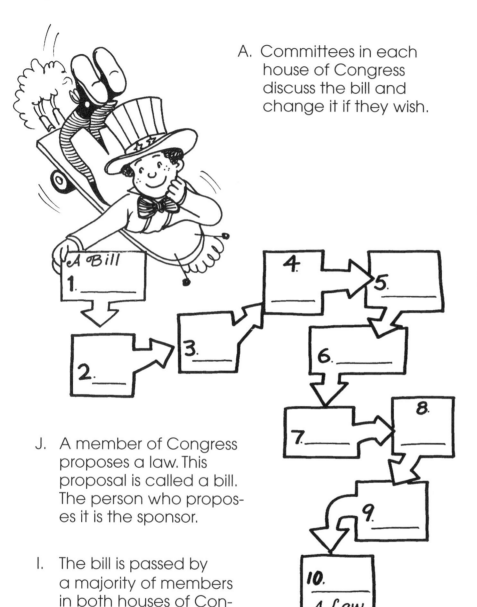

A. Committees in each house of Congress discuss the bill and change it if they wish.

B. If the House and Senate pass different versions of the same bill, members of the two houses meet to try to agree on one version.

C. The president signs the bill into law.

D. The bill, with final changes, goes back to the houses for a vote.

E. If the president does not sign the bill, this is a veto. The veto may be overridden by a two-thirds vote in both houses of Congress. It then becomes law without the president's signature.

F. The bill is introduced in both houses of Congress.

G. The committee votes on the bill.

H. If the committee has approved a bill, it goes to the full House of Representatives or Senate to be debated and voted on.

I. The bill is passed by a majority of members in both houses of Congress.

J. A member of Congress proposes a law. This proposal is called a bill. The person who proposes it is the sponsor.

Name _____

13 ORIGINALS

Did you know that all of the original 13 colonies did not enter the United States at the same time? Each colony became a state only after it ratified the new Constitution. (**Ratify** means to approve.) The clues below show the date each colony joined the United States and one reason that the colony was originally formed. Write the name of the correct state next to the appropriate clue. Some letters are provided for you.

1. December 7, 1787
Trade
_ _ L _ _ _ _ _ _

2. December 12, 1787
Religious & Political Freedom
_ _ _ _ _ Y _ _ _ _ _

3. December 18, 1787
Religious & Political Freedom
_ _ _ J _ _ _ _

4. January 2, 1788
Haven for Debtors
_ _ _ _ _ _ A

5. January 9, 1788
Religious & Political Freedom
_ _ N N _ _ _ _ _ _

6. February 6, 1788
Religious Freedom
_ _ _ _ _ _ _ _ _ _ _ T S

7. April 28, 1788
Religious & Political Freedom
M _ _ _ _ _ _ _

8. May 23, 1788
Trade
_ O _ _ _ _ _ _ _ _ _ A

9. June 21, 1788
Trade
_ _ W _ _ P _ _ _ _

10. June 25, 1788
Trade & Agriculture
_ _ _ _ I _ _

11. July 26, 1788
Trade
_ _ W _ _ _ K

12. November 21, 1789
Trade & Agriculture
_ _ _ _ _ H _ _ _ O _ _ _ _

13. May 29, 1790
Religious Freedom
_ _ _ _ D _ I _ _ _ _ _

Name

10 BOLD STATEMENTS

The **Bill of Rights** is made up of the first 10 amendments to the U.S. Constitution. They were written because the citizens of the United States insisted on it! After the Constitution was written and the states began to give their approval, citizens demanded that statements be added to protect their rights. As a result, these amendments (or changes) were added.

Sam has come across some interesting situations in his travels through time. Use the Bill of Rights to help him find answers to his questions. You can find a copy of the Bill of Rights in your history book or encyclopedia.

— Amendment 1 —

Freedom of Religion, Speech, Press, Assembly, and Petition

Sam hears a bus driver criticizing the mayor of the city. The bus driver is very loud and angry about the mayor's decisions. Can he be arrested for badmouthing a city official?

— Amendment 2 —

Right to Keep and Bear Arms

A family that Sam visits in Philadelphia has a collection of 37 antique rifles, 5 shotguns, and 2 handguns. Their next-door neighbor is afraid of guns and has reported them to the police several times. Is it legal for this family to have guns?

— Amendment 3 —

Right to Refuse Quartering of Soldiers

Another family Sam meets lives down the road from an Army base. There is a fire in one of the barracks on the base. An Army captain bangs on their door and tells Mrs. Marshall to give him and his soldiers supper and a place to sleep. Does she have to do this?

— Amendment 4 —

Unreasonable Searches and Seizures

A police officer stops Sam for riding his skateboard in a "No Boards" zone. As the officer is writing a warning, he notices Sam's backpack and begins searching through it. During the search, the officer discovers Sam's box of allergy pills and arrests Sam on suspicion of illegal drug possession. Is this legal?

Use with page 129.

Name

— Amendment 5 —

Rights of Accused Persons

Sam is having bad luck in this town. In a local shop, a shopkeeper sees that Sam is wearing a great watch—the kind he sells in his store for $100. He calls the police, who take the watch from Sam and send him to jail. They say he must stay there for three months. Have his rights been violated?

_____

— Amendment 6 —

Right to a Fair, Speedy, and Public Trial

The shopkeeper insists that Sam stole the watch! Sam doesn't have much money with him on his Time Travel Trip. He is told he will have to wait one year for a trial and that he must get a lawyer for himself. Will Sam be forced to wait this long for a trial? Will he have to appear in court without a lawyer if he can't afford one?

_____

— Amendment 7 —

Trial by Jury in Civil Cases

If Sam's case goes to trial, can he insist on a jury trial?

_____

— Amendment 8 —

Limits of Bails, Fines, and Punishments

Sam has finally convinced everyone that the watch belonged to him. On his next stop, however, he sees two boys stealing doughnuts from a bakery. As they are running away, two police officers catch them. At their hearing, the judge states, "I'm going to teach you boys a lesson, even though this is your first offense!" He sets their bail at $500,000 each.

Can the judge do this? _____

— Amendment 9 —

Rights of the People

At another stop, Sam meets a family who has just moved onto a large piece of property. They have started to raise goats and chickens. The children play loud music all day and night. They have bright outdoor lights that they burn all night while they work on their noisy motorcycles. Can the neighbors do anything about this?

_____

— Amendment 10 —

Powers of the States and People

In a fast-growing city, a group of parents in a neighborhood have written to Washington, D.C., asking the federal government to build a school for their neighborhood. Education is not mentioned in the Constitution. Is it the job of the federal government to build the school?

_____

Use with page 128.

Name

SUCH A BARGAIN!

What a great buy! Land for only 3¢ an acre! The Louisiana Territory was the biggest piece of land ever added to the United States at one time. And the price was unbelievably low! The United States purchased the Louisiana Territory from the French Emperor Napoleon in 1803. Its boundaries stretched from New Orleans, up the Mississippi River, and west to the Rocky Mountains—approximately 828,000 square miles.

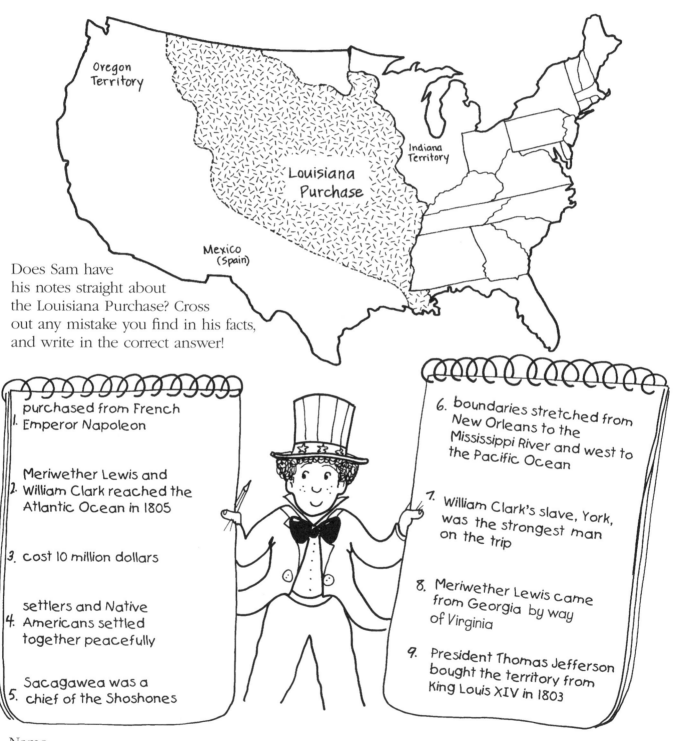

Oregon Territory

Louisiana Purchase

Indiana Territory

Mexico (Spain)

Does Sam have his notes straight about the Louisiana Purchase? Cross out any mistake you find in his facts, and write in the correct answer!

1. purchased from French Emperor Napoleon

2. Meriwether Lewis and William Clark reached the Atlantic Ocean in 1805

3. cost 10 million dollars

4. settlers and Native Americans settled together peacefully

5. Sacagawea was a chief of the Shoshones

6. boundaries stretched from New Orleans to the Mississippi River and west to the Pacific Ocean

7. William Clark's slave, York, was the strongest man on the trip

8. Meriwether Lewis came from Georgia by way of Virginia

9. President Thomas Jefferson bought the territory from King Louis XIV in 1803

Name _____

SECRETS OF THE WEST

Many secrets of the western United States were discovered by **explorers** who took trips sponsored by the government. Another group of explorers called **frontiersmen** also did plenty of discovering of their own. **Mountain men**—a group of adventurous fur trappers—were responsible for uncovering some of the best secrets. They blazed many of the trails that opened up the west for the settlers who followed.

Match the name of each mountain man, frontiersman, and explorer with his description.

_____ 1. Opened the route that went from Independence, Missouri to Oregon.

_____ 2. Blazed a trail from Independence, Missouri to Santa Fe, New Mexico through the Cimarron Desert.

_____ 3. Created the Gila Trail from Santa Fe, New Mexico to San Diego, California.

_____ 4. Failed in his attempt to climb the Colorado Peak that now bears his name.

_____ 5. Drew a map of the plains he crossed and labeled them the Great American Desert.

_____ 6. Explored the Louisiana Territory.

A. Zebulon Pike
B. Jim Bridger
C. William Becknell
D. John Jacob Astor
E. Meriwether Lewis & William Clark
F. William Ashley
G. Robert Stuart
H. Daniel Boone
I. Antonio Armijo
J. Jed Smith
K. Hugh Glass
L. Stephen Long

_____ 7. Formed the American Fur Company.

_____ 8. Nearly killed by a grizzly bear and crawled 150 miles before he was rescued.

_____ 9. Organized the yearly rendezvous (gathering) where men traded furs for supplies.

_____ 10. Much admired mountain man who always carried his Bible and did not swear, drink, or smoke.

_____ 11. Old Gabe, famous for his yarns and tall tales, took a small boat down the Bear River and discovered the Great Salt Lake.

_____ 12. Found the Cumberland Gap through the Appalachian Mountains to Kentucky.

Name _____

THE BIG ARGUMENT

FREEDOM!

Sam's travels back in time have landed him in the middle of a major argument in U.S. history. While America was gaining new territories in the early 1800s, a disagreement over slavery divided the nation. Anti-slavery groups wanted to keep slavery from spreading, especially into the new territories. Some wanted to end slavery altogether. Find an important name or term related to this argument, using the clues to help you. At the end of each line, write the underlined letter from the answer. If you solve the clues correctly, the letters will spell out the name for anti-slavery supporters.

a. Harriet Tubman

d. John Brown

f. Phillis Wheatley

c. ABOLISH

g. Underground Railroad

b. Harpers Ferry

e. Uncle Tom's Cabin

_____ 1. arsenal in Virginia that was attacked by an anti-slavery group _____

_____ 2. man from Kansas who planned to start a slave revolt _____

_____ 3. female slave who was freed in New York in the 1820's _____

_____ 4. means "to get rid of" _____

_____ 5. slave who became a conductor on the Underground Railroad _____

_____ 6. famous novel that criticized slavery _____

_____ 7. organizer of the American Anti-Slavery Society _____

_____ 8. a Supreme Court case that tried to settle the slavery question _____

_____ 9. system of helping slaves escape to the Northern States or Canada _____

_____ 10. founder of *The North Star,* an anti-slavery newspaper _____

_____ 11. educated slave who was a poet _____

_____ 12. black preacher who led a slave revolution in Virginia _____

_____ 13. Henry Clay was called the Great _____ _____

h. William Lloyd Garrison

k. Sojourner Truth

l. Compromiser

i. Dred Scott

j. Nat Turner

m. Frederick Douglass

The ___ ___ ___ ___ ___ ___ ___ ___ ___ ___ ___ ___ ___ spoke out against slavery.

Name _____

A NATION DIVIDED

"How could this happen?" Sam wonders. "How could citizens fight against each other?"

Yes, Sam's skateboard has found its way into the middle of the American Civil War. A **civil war** is one that is fought within a country. Each fact below is about an event or person during the Civil War. Set a time limit and try to write a QUESTION for each answer. How many points can you get?

1. 5 Points-**Withdrawal of a state from the Union**

2. 10 Points-**Capital of the Confederacy**

3. 5 Points-**President of the United States during the Civil War**

6. 5 Points-**Confederate President**

5. 5 Points-**Major military leader of the Southern forces**

4. 10 Points-**Site of Southern surrender, ending the Civil War**

7. 10 Points-**The place where Lincoln was assassinated**

8. 10 Points-**Executive order that freed the slaves of the Confederacy**

9. 15 Points-**Amendment to Constitution that freed the slaves**

12. 10 Points-**Fast ships that dodged Union warships**

11. 20 Points-**During the Civil War, these were called the Border States**

10. 10 Points-**Northern ironclad that fought the *Merrimac***

13. 15 Points-**Army that General Lee commanded**

14. 15 Points-**Site of the first major battle of the Civil War**

15. 15 Points-**Northern general who defeated Lee**

POSSIBLE SCORE
160
YOUR SCORE: _____

Name _____

CARPETBAGGERS & SCALAWAGS

Until Sam visited the actual time and place, he could never have imagined what the country was like after the Civil War. Things were a mess! The period from 1865 to 1877 was called **Reconstruction**. During this time, the whole structure of society in the American South went through many changes. In addition, there was a great deal of bitterness on both sides. Many people had been wounded or killed, and large areas of the country were destroyed. During the Reconstruction period, the country tried to rebuild itself.

Match the important terms about this period (found in the carpetbags) with the definitions.

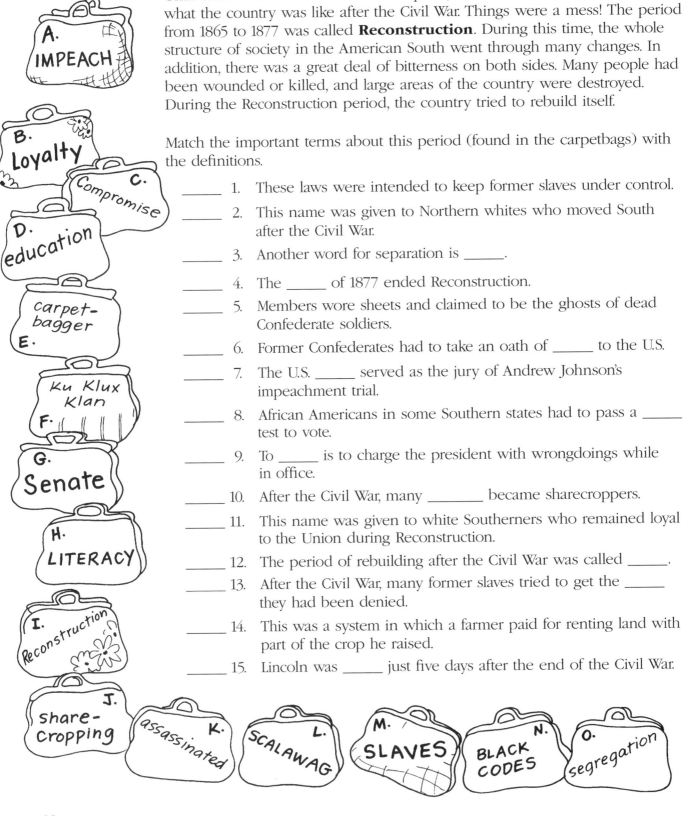

A. IMPEACH

B. Loyalty

C. Compromise

D. education

E. carpet-bagger

F. Ku Klux Klan

G. Senate

H. LITERACY

I. Reconstruction

J. share-cropping

K. assassinated

L. SCALAWAG

M. SLAVES

N. BLACK CODES

O. segregation

_____ 1.   These laws were intended to keep former slaves under control.

_____ 2.   This name was given to Northern whites who moved South after the Civil War.

_____ 3.   Another word for separation is _____.

_____ 4.   The _____ of 1877 ended Reconstruction.

_____ 5.   Members wore sheets and claimed to be the ghosts of dead Confederate soldiers.

_____ 6.   Former Confederates had to take an oath of _____ to the U.S.

_____ 7.   The U.S. _____ served as the jury of Andrew Johnson's impeachment trial.

_____ 8.   African Americans in some Southern states had to pass a _____ test to vote.

_____ 9.   To _____ is to charge the president with wrongdoings while in office.

_____ 10. After the Civil War, many _____ became sharecroppers.

_____ 11. This name was given to white Southerners who remained loyal to the Union during Reconstruction.

_____ 12. The period of rebuilding after the Civil War was called _____.

_____ 13. After the Civil War, many former slaves tried to get the _____ they had been denied.

_____ 14. This was a system in which a farmer paid for renting land with part of the crop he raised.

_____ 15. Lincoln was _____ just five days after the end of the Civil War.

Name _____

THE GOLDEN SPIKE

Sam is just in time for the hammering of the Golden Spike! The east and west coasts were finally linked by the Transcontinental Railroad. Before the railroad, people traveled by wagon or stagecoach. The train made the long trip across the country faster, cheaper, and safer. The railroad took years to finish. The final Golden Spike was driven into place with a silver hammer at Promontory Point, Utah, on May 10, 1869.

The answer to each of the questions below is included in the word search. Fill in each blank, and circle the words in the puzzle, which may appear vertically, horizontally, or backward.

```
P  S  I  E  R  R  A  N  E  V  A  D  A  S  C
U  R  E  A  S  T  W  A  R  D  L  L  I  P  O
N  N  O  T  B  T  I  E  S  Q  R  F  E  I  B
I  G  A  N  G  S  T  E  R  P  O  I  N  K  R
O  N  I  A  R  T  K  R  O  W  A  S  S  E  E
N  M  A  R  T  H  A  S  S  E  R  W  T  S  O
P  R  O  M  O  N  T  O  R  Y  P  O  I  N  T
A  J  E  V  U  O  J  K  D  G  P  J  I  Y  E
C  E  N  T  R  A  L  P  A  C  I  F  I  C  Y
I  C  O  N  G  R  E  S  S  I  T  O  N  D  D
F  E  S  E  N  I  H  C  N  N  V  T  A  X  P
I  N  D  O  P  D  E  B  D  A  O  R  X  P  P
C  R  O  C  K  Y  M  O  U  N  T  A  I  N  S
```

WORD SEARCH CLUES

1. In 1862 _____ passed the Pacific Railroad Act.

2. The _____ Railroad began laying tracks westward.

3. The Central Pacific Railroad began laying tracks _____.

4. The Union Pacific workers lived on a _____ that followed them across the plains.

5. First, workers made a smooth _____.

6. Squared-off logs laid across a roadbed are called _____.

7. Iron rails were set on the ties and held in place with large nails called _____.

8. Grenville Dodge's Union Pacific crew laid tracks across the _____.

9. Charles Crocker, a Sacramento merchant, was in charge of the _____ Railroad.

10. When crews reached the _____ foothills, most of them took off to dig for gold.

11. _____ workers built most of the eastbound tracks.

12. The two crews met at _____, Utah.

Name _____

MACHINES REPLACE MUSCLES

By the time the United States was 100 years old, the country was in the middle of the Industrial Revolution. The U.S. had become the world's leading industrial nation. Factories were mass-producing products that had once been made by hand. The free enterprise system allowed almost anyone to start a business. If the business failed, they lost their money. If it succeeded, they kept the profits. This system encouraged people to invest in new ideas and inventions. Some of the most notable characters during the Industrial Revolution are named below. Connect them to the event, organization, or invention that made them famous.

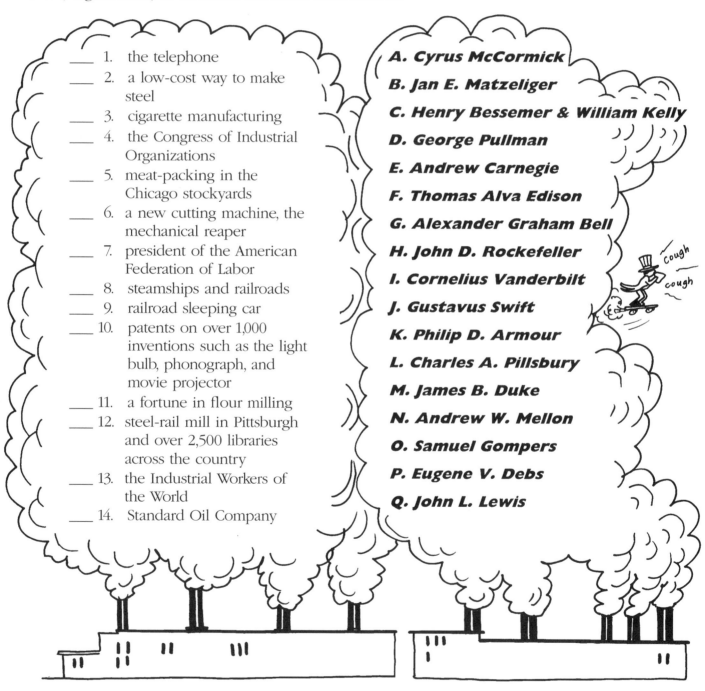

_____ 1. the telephone

_____ 2. a low-cost way to make steel

_____ 3. cigarette manufacturing

_____ 4. the Congress of Industrial Organizations

_____ 5. meat-packing in the Chicago stockyards

_____ 6. a new cutting machine, the mechanical reaper

_____ 7. president of the American Federation of Labor

_____ 8. steamships and railroads

_____ 9. railroad sleeping car

_____ 10. patents on over 1,000 inventions such as the light bulb, phonograph, and movie projector

_____ 11. a fortune in flour milling

_____ 12. steel-rail mill in Pittsburgh and over 2,500 libraries across the country

_____ 13. the Industrial Workers of the World

_____ 14. Standard Oil Company

A. Cyrus McCormick

B. Jan E. Matzeliger

C. Henry Bessemer & William Kelly

D. George Pullman

E. Andrew Carnegie

F. Thomas Alva Edison

G. Alexander Graham Bell

H. John D. Rockefeller

I. Cornelius Vanderbilt

J. Gustavus Swift

K. Philip D. Armour

L. Charles A. Pillsbury

M. James B. Duke

N. Andrew W. Mellon

O. Samuel Gompers

P. Eugene V. Debs

Q. John L. Lewis

cough cough

Name

THE OLD WEST

It is exciting to be in the Old West, but Sam is wondering just exactly where he is! Who are these people called "cowboys"? Why in the world did they go west? Was there anyone there to greet them when they arrived?

You've probably heard about cowboys, railroads, the Gold Rush, and the cruel *displacement* (removal) of Native Americans. Do you know enough about the Old West to finish these sentences? Use the words in the lasso to complete the statements about the Old West.

> homesteaders   transcontinental   Central Pacific
> reservation   Little Bighorn   Promontory   spike
> Chisholm   Pikes Peak   bison   gold   Chinese
> Golden   Nez Perce   lasso   saddle   Sioux

1. Many people headed west to California in search of _____.

2. A large nail, or _____, is used in building railroad tracks.

3. _____ were the folks who were given free land to farm.

4. Sitting Bull and Crazy Horse led the _____ people at the Battle of Little Bighorn.

5. The last spike of the transcontinental railroad, the _____ Spike, was driven in at _____, Utah.

6. Herds of longhorn cattle were driven from Texas to Kansas along the _____ Trail.

7. The transportation system that joined the East to the West was called the _____ railroad.

8. Two important pieces of cowboy equipment are the _____ and _____.

9. An area set aside for Native Americans to live on is called a _____.

10. _____ _____ is the place in Colorado where gold was discovered in 1859.

11. The large animals that roamed the Great Plains were called _____.

12. Chief Joseph marched a group of his people, the _____ _____, toward Canada.

13. The Union Pacific and the _____ _____ were the two railroad companies that built the transcontinental railroad.

14. _____ _____ was a famous battle in the 1876 Indian wars.

15. Asian immigrants who helped build the transcontinental railroad were the _____.

Name _____

COMING TO AMERICA

The Statue of Liberty welcomes people to America. From 1820 to 1930, more than 37 million people came to the United States. Over half of them entered through Ellis Island in the years between 1899 and 1931. Those people who came to America were looking for adventure, religious freedom, a better life, or escape from governments that offered little freedom. Over the years, the patterns of immigration from Europe changed. Use the graphs on the next page (page 139) to answer questions about these patterns.

1. There are five separate time periods on the graphs. During which of these time periods did the greatest number of immigrants come to the United States? _____

2. In the time period from 1881 to 1890, which area of Europe sent the most people? _____

3. Overall, which area of Europe sent the fewest immigrants? _____

4. From 1881 to 1890, _____ Europe sent about 2 million immigrants to the U.S.

5. Southern Europe sent the most immigrants from _____ to _____.

6. In the period from 1881 to 1900, approximately _____ million people came to the U.S. from Europe.

7. During what years did the most immigrants come from Central Europe? _____

8. How many immigrants came from Central Europe between 1901 and 1920? _____

9. During what years did the fewest number of immigrants come from Southern Europe? _____

10. What two sections of Europe had almost the same number of immigrants between 1891 and 1890? _____

Find out where the Statue of Liberty is located. _____

Find out where the Statue of Liberty came from. _____

Use with page 139.

Name _____

PATTERNS OF EUROPEAN IMMIGRATION TO AMERICA
1871–1920

FROM **NORTHWESTERN EUROPE**
Britain, Ireland, Netherlands, Belgium,
Switzerland, France, Luxembourg, Scandinavia

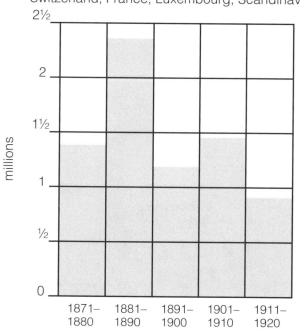

FROM **CENTRAL EUROPE**
Germany, Poland, Hungary, Austria

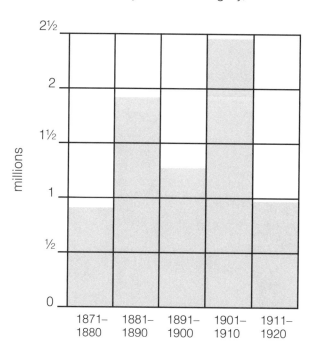

FROM **EASTERN EUROPE**
Russia, Turkey, Romania, Bulgaria

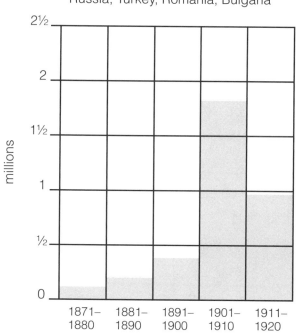

FROM **SOUTHERN EUROPE**
Spain, Italy, Greece, Portugal

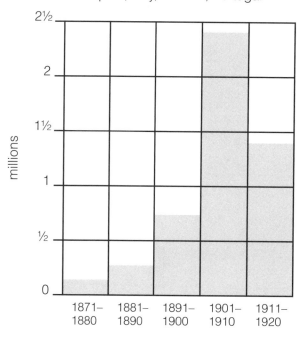

Use with page 138.

INTO THE RECENT PAST

Sam lives in the early years of the 21st century. Now, he wants to research the events that happened in the 100 years before he was born.

See if you can find the dates of each of the 20th-century events below. Write the date by each event. Then number them in the order in which they happened. Circle those events that could NOT have been broadcast on the radio. Try to figure out why they weren't on the radio.

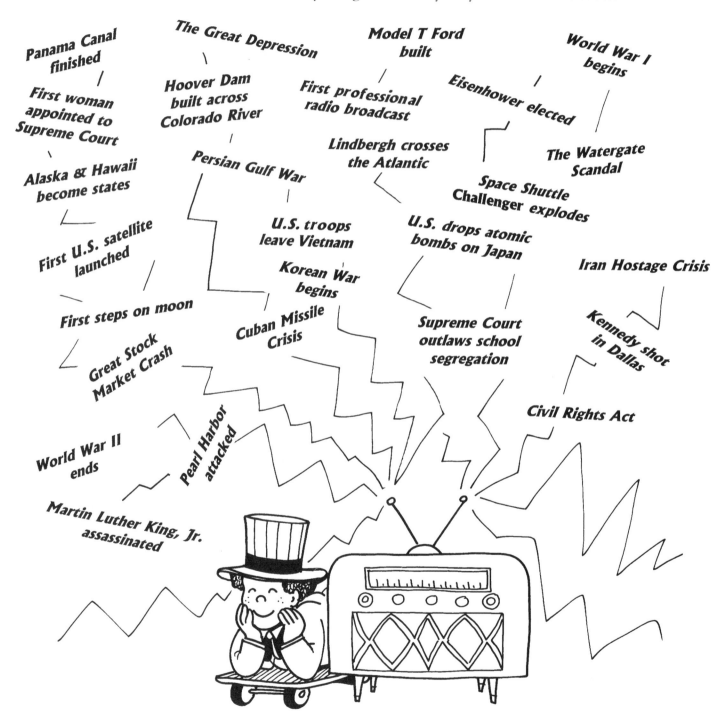

Panama Canal finished

The Great Depression

Model T Ford built

World War I begins

First woman appointed to Supreme Court

Hoover Dam built across Colorado River

First professional radio broadcast

Eisenhower elected

Alaska & Hawaii become states

Persian Gulf War

Lindbergh crosses the Atlantic

The Watergate Scandal

Space Shuttle Challenger explodes

First U.S. satellite launched

U.S. troops leave Vietnam

U.S. drops atomic bombs on Japan

Iran Hostage Crisis

First steps on moon

Korean War begins

Supreme Court outlaws school segregation

Kennedy shot in Dallas

Great Stock Market Crash

Cuban Missile Crisis

Civil Rights Act

World War II ends

Pearl Harbor attacked

Martin Luther King, Jr. assassinated

Name _____

THE BIG CHILL

It was called the Cold War because there was no heat in the form of bombs, guns, or fiery explosions. Instead of outright war, there was a high level of tension—mostly between the United States and the Soviet Union. The tension was complicated by the fact that both super-powers had a dangerous weapon that could be used at any time. The Cold War began after World War II when the Allies, who had fought together to win the war, divided up responsibility for many of the European countries that Hitler had controlled.

The puzzle below is about the Cold War. Unlike most puzzles, the answers are here but the clues are missing! Write the clues for each word in this puzzle about the Big Chill!

Across

3. _____

6. _____

8. _____

10. _____

11. _____

Down

1. _____

2. _____

4. _____

5. _____

7. _____

9. _____

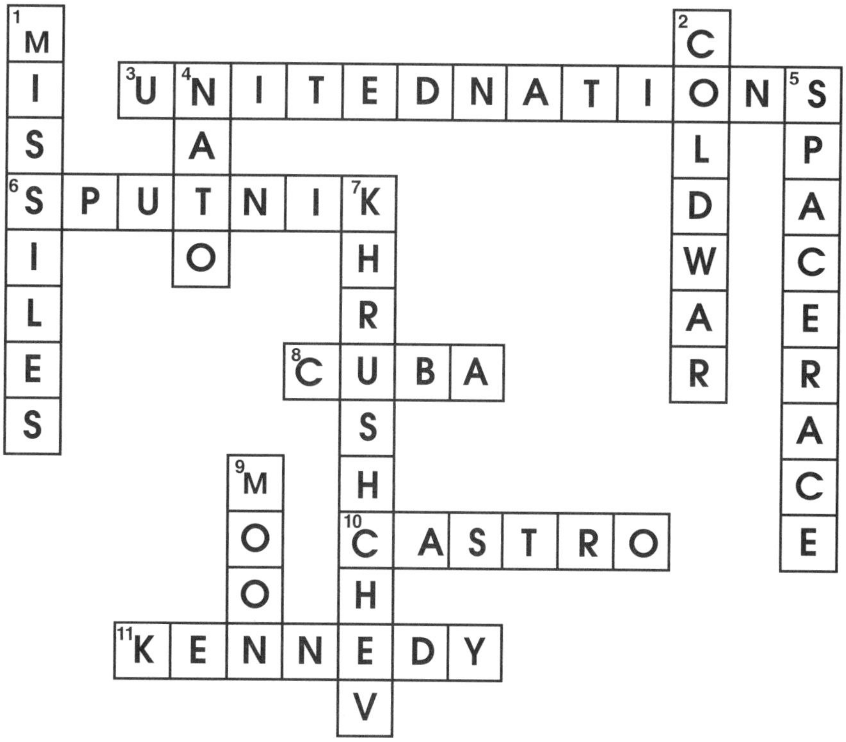

Crossword grid answers:
1 Down: MISSILES
2 Down: COLDWAR
3 Across: UNITEDNATIONS
4 Down: NATO
5 Down: SPACERACE
6 Across: SPUTNIK
7 Down: KHRUSHCHEV
8 Across: CUBA
9 Down: MOO
10 Across: CASTRO
11 Across: KENNEDY

CRUISING THE CAPITAL

Sam never realized how many interesting places and spaces there are to see in the District of Columbia. This is his first visit to the nation's capital, and he's going to see it all. As he buzzes around the streets of Washington, here are some of his stops. Use the map on page 143 to find each place described below. Write the name, and then color it on the map.
(G = green, Y = yellow, O = orange, P = purple, R = red, B = blue, BR = brown, S = silver)

1. _____ (Y)
place that makes the U.S.'s paper money

2. _____ (O)
home of the highest crime-fighting agency in the U.S.

3. _____ (S)
tall, white, marble pillar dedicated to the first U.S. president

4. _____ (S)
white sandstone residence of the president

5. _____ (G)
serves as the national library, with 80 million items in 470 languages

6. _____ (P)
collection of 14 museums

7. _____ (R)
huge building with a statue of a seated president inside

8. _____ (P)
home of the highest court in the U.S.

9. _____ (B)
offices of the judicial system

10. _____ (Y)
home of important documents, such as the Constitution, Declaration of Independence, and Bill of Rights

11. _____ (R)
black granite, V-shaped wall with the names of the 58,000 soldiers who died in the war

12. _____ (BR)
home of the U.S. Congress

Use with page 143.

13. _____ (P)
home of the Treasury offices

14. _____ (G)
place where President Lincoln was assassinated

15. _____ (BR)
long, narrow parklike area that stretches from the Capitol to the Washington Monument

16. _____ (B)
headquarters of U.S. mail system

17. _____ (O)
traces the history of flight; holds planes used by the Wright brothers and Charles Lindbergh

18. _____ (Y)
place that prints government documents

Name _____

WASHINGTON, DISTRICT OF COLUMBIA

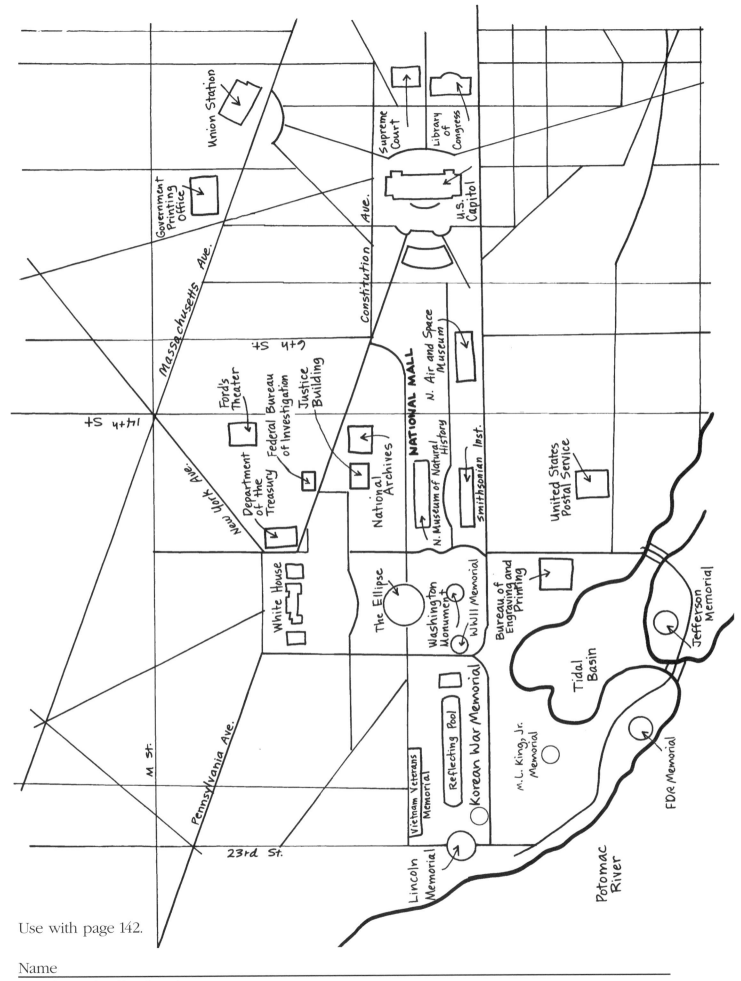

Use with page 142.

Name

WHERE DID IT HAPPEN?

The fascinating, exciting, spectacular, and tragic events of history took place all over the
continent. See if you can remember where! If Sam is visiting the sites of the events listed on
the next page (page 145), where will he go? Write the number of each event
next to the spot on the map where it happened. Then
label each state with its abbreviation.

Use with page 145.

Name

A. Write the number of each event below in RED on the spot where it happened.

1. battle at the Alamo
2. landing of Pilgrims at Plymouth Rock
3. Daniel Boone explored this state
4. Confederacy establishes first capital
5. Battle of Little Bighorn
6. Lincoln's log cabin moved from Kentucky

7. birth of Martin Luther King, Jr.
8. eruption of Mt. St. Helens in 1980
9. founding of Las Vegas

10. driving of the Golden Spike in 1869
11. assassination of John F. Kennedy in 1963
12. birth of film industry in America
13. arrival of the Statue of Liberty
14. Japanese bombing of Pearl Harbor in 1941
15. discovery of Pikes Peak in 1806
16. beginning of the Oregon Trail
17. end of the Oregon Trail
18. birth of the P.T. Barnum Circus
19. presidents' faces carved on Mt. Rushmore

20. Battle of Gettysburg
21. 1849 Gold Rush
22. first skyscraper built
23. Yellowstone becomes a national park
24. state purchased from Russia for $7.2 million
25. first airplane flight in Kittyhawk
26. invention of light bulb
27. Cowboy Hall of Fame established
28. JFK buried in 1963
29. Space shuttle *Challenger* launched
30. Battle of New Orleans

B. Color yellow the states that were the first 13 to enter the U.S.

C. Color green the last two states to enter the U.S.

Use with page 144.

Name _____

WHEN DID IT HAPPEN?

The history of the United States spans over 200 years. If Sam makes these stops on his travels back through time, what years will he visit?

Match each event written on page 147 to the year it occurred by writing each one on the timeline. For each event that is already written on the timeline, fill in the missing year.

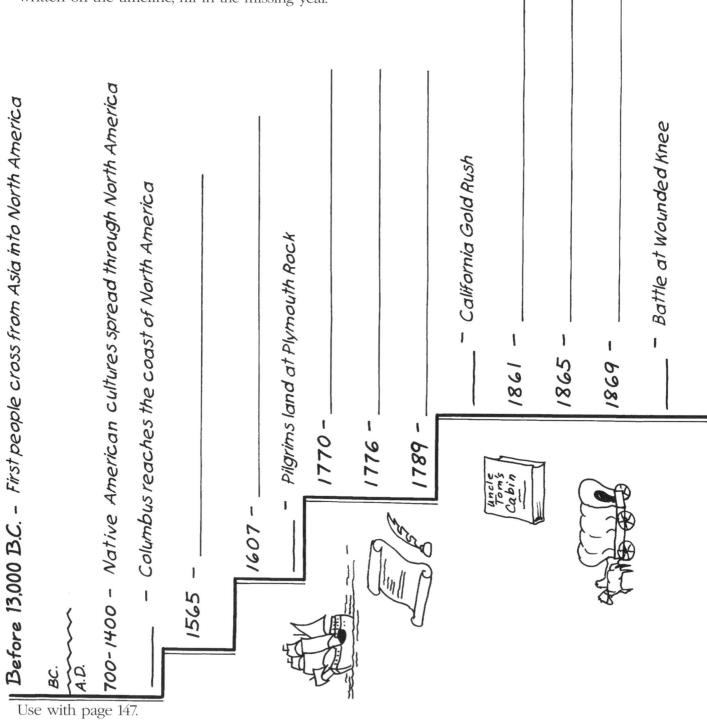

Before 13,000 B.C. – First people cross from Asia into North America

B.C.

A.D.

700–1400 – Native American cultures spread through North America

– Columbus reaches the coast of North America

1565 –

1607 –

– Pilgrims land at Plymouth Rock

1770 –

1776 –

1789 –

– California Gold Rush

1861 –

1865 –

1869 –

– Battle at Wounded Knee

Use with page 147.

Name _____

146

Events on timeline (top)

1908 –
— Panama Canal completed
1927 –
— Stock market crash & Great Depression
1933 –
— Japanese bomb Pearl Harbor
1945 –
1950 –
— J. F. Kennedy elected president
1964 –
— Assassination of Martin Luther King, Jr.
— First walk on moon
1973 –
1979 –
— Space shuttle Challenger explodes
1989 –
— Terrorist attacks on the World Trade Center and Pentagon buildings
2008 –

Events to place (bottom)

Civil War ends

Model T invented

Civil Rights Act

Korean War begins

Roosevelt's New Deal

Civil War begins

Loma Prieta earthquake in San Francisco

Barack Obama elected president

U.S. troops leave Vietnam

George Washington inaugurated

U.S. drops atomic bombs on Japan

First English settlement, Jamestown

Lindbergh flies across the Atlantic

St. Augustine, Florida, oldest city settled

Use with page 146.

Name

BACK TO THE PRESENT

What a trip! Sam has been flying and sailing through hundreds of years of United States history! It's good to be back home in the present. He's learned a lot about his country's history. How much does he know about its present? How much do you know? Fill in these facts about your country.

1. What is your state's nickname (and how did it develop)? _____

   _____

2. Who is your state's governor? _____

3. Who is your representative to Congress?

   _____

4. How many representatives does your state have? _____

5. Who are your two state senators? _____

   & _____

6. Who is your town's mayor? _____

7. Name one representative to
   your city or town council. _____

8. Who are your representative and senator to your state
   government? _____

   _____

9. What is the legal age for voting? _____

10. When did your state become a state? _____

11. Who is the current U.S. president? _____

12. Who is the current U.S. vice president? _____

13. Name two members of the president's Cabinet. _____

    & _____

14. What is the U.S. motto? _____

Draw the U.S. flag here.

Draw the U.S. Great Seal here.

Name _____

MYSTERY VIPS

Which **V**ery **I**mportant **P**erson in America's history is which? Match each quote with the person who would have said it by putting the number of the quote next to the correct name.

1.
My warriors defeated General Custer at the Battle of Little Big Horn.

2.
I invented the telephone and started the American Bell Telephone Company.

3.
I became president after John F. Kennedy was shot.

4.
I was the U.S. president during the Great Depression and World War II.

5.
I was the first person to walk on the surface of the moon.

6.
I was the U.S. president during World War I.

7.
I am an African American political leader who campaigned to become a candidate for president in 1984 and 1988.

8.
I was the first woman appointed to serve on the Supreme Court.

9.
I refused to give up my seat on a public bus in Montgomery, Alabama. This started a bus boycott in the Civil Rights movement in 1955.

10.
I was a nurse who helped wounded soldiers in the Civil War and started the American Red Cross.

11.
I was a Boston silversmith who rode a horse in 1775 to warn the people of Concord that the British were coming.

12.
I was a slave who escaped to the North and helped other slaves reach freedom on the Underground Railroad.

WOODROW WILSON

FRANKLIN D. ROOSEVELT

Clara Barton

Neil Armstrong

Alexander Graham Bell

Paul Revere

Harriet Tubman

Crazy Horse

Rosa Parks

Sandra Day O'Connor

Jesse Jackson

Lyndon B. Johnson

Name

WE DELIVER!

Oliver D. World and his partner, Ivanna Gough, are the busy owners of Excellent Delivery Service (EDS). They promise to deliver anything, anywhere in the world, anytime! In their business, they would be lost without these tools:

A **globe** is a model of the Earth. Like the Earth, it is a sphere. It shows land and water formations. Find the globe. Color the land green and the water blue.

A **map** is a flat picture of a place. There are many different kinds of maps. Draw a red border around the map.

A **scale** is a tool that tells distances on a map. A scale shows how the measurements on a map compare to the measurements of the real place. Circle the scale in yellow.

A **compass rose** is a tool that tells directions on a map or globe. Find the compass rose and trace it in orange. Add the four missing directions: NE, NW, SE, and SW.

An **atlas** is a collection of different maps put together in a book. There are many kinds of atlases. Some contain different kinds of maps of the same location (such as political maps, climate maps, product maps, population maps, topographic maps, and so on). Color the cover of the atlas purple.

Use with page 151.

Name

ANYTHING! ANYWHERE!

Help Ivanna and Oliver choose the right tools for their deliveries. On the line provided, write the tools they will need to complete each delivery or to solve each problem they have. Choose from map, globe, atlas, scale, or compass rose. Use the descriptions on page 150 to help you.

_____ 1. A pizza has been ordered for delivery to 123 Cheesy Street.

_____ 2. Ivanna and Oliver must get a crocodile from Florida to a zoo in China. They are trying to decide if they should go by land or by sea.

_____ 3. The U.S. government wants to send a new flag to the U.S. embassy in every South American country. Oliver needs to find out how many flags to pack.

_____ 4. They are going to be picking up 4,000 crates of bananas in Costa Rica to deliver to a pudding factory in New Mexico. They need to find out if their cargo might get rained on in Costa Rica.

_____ 5. They need to deliver hot dogs to Tibet. They know how high their delivery plane can fly, but they need to know if it will fly high enough to get over the Himalayan Mountains.

_____ 6. Someone has requested that a shipment of microwave ovens be delivered to the Arctic and to Antarctica. Oliver is trying to see how many different ways he can get to these places.

_____ 7. They've been hired to deliver three dozen squealing pigs to Indonesia. They need to find out exactly where Indonesia is!

_____ 8. Ivanna is trying to figure out how far her plane will need to travel and in what direction she must fly to take sunflower seeds from Sacramento, California to Houston, Texas.

_____ 9. Oliver is searching for a route to deliver souvenirs from the Cowboy Hall of Fame in Oklahoma City to some cowboy fans in Norway.

_____ 10. An employee is leaving the office in Kanopolis, Kansas, with a load of whipped cream to deliver across the city. The delivery girl is waiting for Oliver to give her directions.

Use with page 150.

Name _____

MUDDY MAP DISASTER

Today the Excellent Delivery Service has been hired to deliver baskets of sour grapes to Irate County. OOPS! The delivery man dropped his only copy of the map into the murky waters of Lake Grumpy. Some of the writing washed off. Luckily, he can still read the key.

1. Read the list of deliveries he needs to make. The list tells where each person lives.

2. Use the map key to find the right place for each delivery.

3. Write the name of each place on the map at the correct spot. (Each spot has an X.)

4. Write a good title for the map.

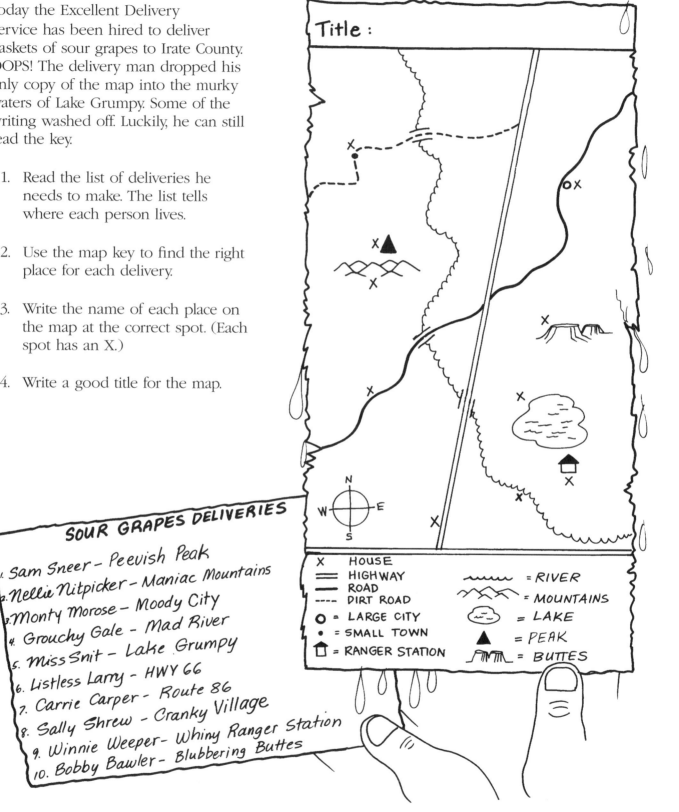

Title :

SOUR GRAPES DELIVERIES

1. Sam Sneer - Peevish Peak
2. Nellie Nitpicker - Maniac Mountains
3. Monty Morose - Moody City
4. Grouchy Gale - Mad River
5. Miss Snit - Lake Grumpy
6. Listless Larry - HWY 66
7. Carrie Carper - Route 86
8. Sally Shrew - Cranky Village
9. Winnie Weeper - Whiny Ranger Station
10. Bobby Bawler - Blubbering Buttes

X   HOUSE
≡≡≡   HIGHWAY
——   ROAD
----   DIRT ROAD   ∿∿∿∿ = RIVER
O = LARGE CITY   ⌒⌒⌒ = MOUNTAINS
• = SMALL TOWN   ☁ = LAKE
⌂ = RANGER STATION   ▲ = PEAK
                                        ᴍᴍᴍ = BUTTES

Name

WATCH OUT FOR GHOSTS!

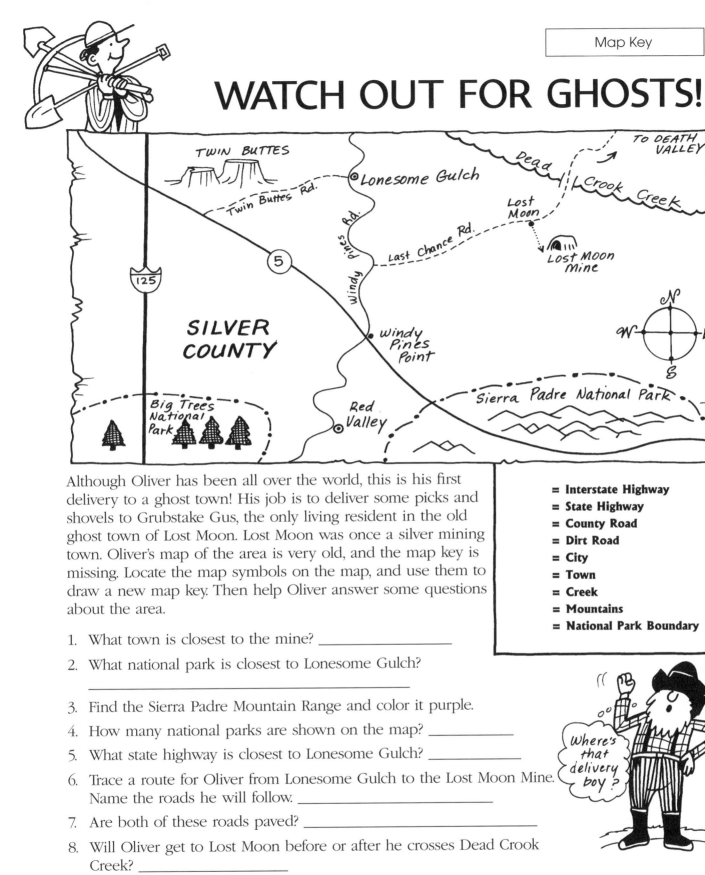

SILVER COUNTY

Although Oliver has been all over the world, this is his first delivery to a ghost town! His job is to deliver some picks and shovels to Grubstake Gus, the only living resident in the old ghost town of Lost Moon. Lost Moon was once a silver mining town. Oliver's map of the area is very old, and the map key is missing. Locate the map symbols on the map, and use them to draw a new map key. Then help Oliver answer some questions about the area.

```
___ = Interstate Highway
___ = State Highway
___ = County Road
___ = Dirt Road
___ = City
___ = Town
___ = Creek
___ = Mountains
___ = National Park Boundary
```

1. What town is closest to the mine? _____

2. What national park is closest to Lonesome Gulch?
   _____

3. Find the Sierra Padre Mountain Range and color it purple.

4. How many national parks are shown on the map? _____

5. What state highway is closest to Lonesome Gulch? _____

6. Trace a route for Oliver from Lonesome Gulch to the Lost Moon Mine. Name the roads he will follow. _____

7. Are both of these roads paved? _____

8. Will Oliver get to Lost Moon before or after he crosses Dead Crook Creek? _____

9. If he continues on the road past Dead Crook Creek, what will he see? _____

10. What roads would he take to get from Big Trees National Park to Lost Moon Mine?
    _____

Name _____

A SUNDAE DELIVERY

Ivanna has to get into her helicopter for this delivery! She's been hired to deliver a giant cherry to the top of the world's tallest ice cream sundae. Find out how big this sundae really is by answering these questions. Pay attention to the scale! *(Hint: To measure along the way, use a piece of string and a ruler.)*

1 cm = 2 meters

Give answers to the nearest meter.

1. How high is the sundae? _____

2. How wide is the dish? _____

3. How long is the licorice trail up to the top? _____

4. How tall is the ladder? _____

5. How long is the big candy cane? _____

6. How tall is the cherry (including the stem)? _____

7. How far is it from Raisin Face Curve to Candycane Crossing? _____

8. How far is it from Candycane Crossing to Candy Heart Ridge? _____

9. How far is it from Marshmallow Cliffs to Cherry Top Peak? _____

Name _____

BUSINESS IS BOOMING

The Excellent Delivery Service has a busy week. They have instructions to pick up "orders" from every hemisphere and deliver these things to a small town in Kansas. For each order, write the hemispheres they will visit for the pick-up.
*(Write **N** for Northern, **S** for Southern, **E** for Eastern, and **W** for Western.)*

Pick-up # 1
one kangaroo and one platypus
from Australia   S,E

Pick-up # 2
decorations for
Chinese New Year celebrations
from China

Pick-up # 3
27 grass skirts from Hawaii

Pick-up # 4
camel hair from Egypt

Pick-up # 5
three penguins
from Antarctica

Pick-up # 6
safari posters from Kenya

Pick-up # 7
Eiffel Tower T-shirts
from France

Pick-up # 8
4 geese from Canada

Pick-up # 9
50 pounds of Turkish taffy
from Turkey

Pick-up # 10
coffee from Colombia

Pick-up # 11
wool from Argentina

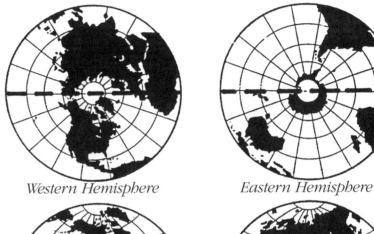

Northern Hemisphere   *Southern Hemisphere*

Western Hemisphere   *Eastern Hemisphere*

Name _____

DENTIST'S NIGHTMARE

The Excellent Delivery Service is getting ready for a big sale at the "We Don't Care About Cavities Candy Company." They will have deliveries in every state! The candy company is making several special new candies. The name of each new candy starts with the same letter as the name of a state.

1. Angelic Apple-bites
2. Chewy Coco Chunks
3. Delicious Devils
4. Fruities
5. Gooey Gut Grabbers
6. Heavenly Hoh-hohs
7. Icy Igloos
8. Krazy Krunchies
9. Licorice Laces
10. Monster Muffins
11. Nutty Nougat
12. Orange Owls
13. Peppermint Pops
14. Red-Hot Rockets
15. Super Sour Strips
16. Tons o' Taffy
17. Utterly-Butterlies
18. Vanilla Vines
19. Way-Good Wafers

Appleyard

Sweet Home

Citrus Heights

Strawberry Point

Orange Cove

Pumpkin Center

Pearblossom

Cherry Knolls

Fruitvale

Use with page 157.

Name

Ivanna is making a map to show which kind of candy will go to each state. Help her out by labeling each state with its name. Then draw the symbol on each state for the candy that will be delivered there! (HINT: Each kind of candy will be delivered only to the states that begin with the same letter as the candy!)

Sugar Creek

Hershey

Cheesequake

Sweet Springs

Limecrest

Sassafras

Sugar Grove

Berryville

Cherry Grove

Cherryville

Berry

Honey Grove

Sweetwater

Which state has the most towns with "sweet" names?

_____

Sugarland

Coconut

Citrus Springs

Cocoa

Use with page 156.

Name

HELP WANTED!

HELP! The Excellent Delivery Service is so successful that they must hire some new helpers. Jack is about to take a test to see if he knows enough for this job. To get the job, he must get at least 17 correct answers. Circle the answers that Jack got right. Fix each wrong answer. Will Jack get the job? _____

I'll "ace" this test with your help!

JOB APPLICATION
Excellent Delivery Service

Name:

Other Work Experience:

Define these Geographical and Map Terms.

1. hemisphere– *half of the Earth*
2. equator– *imaginary line dividing Earth in half, north and south*
3. continent– *large body of land*
4. scale– *something to weigh people*
5. globe– *a model of the Earth*
6. key– *something to unlock doors*
7. North Pole– *Santa Claus's home*
8. compass rose– *a flower with points*
9. atlas– *a book of maps*
10. plateau– *a high mountain in the desert*
11. Tropic of Cancer– *line of latitude at 23°30' south of the equator*
12. Arctic Circle– *line of latitude at 66°30' north of the equator*
13. prime meridian– *0° line of latitude*
14. time zone– *a machine that lets you travel through time*
15. grid– *a system of crossing lines to help locate things*
16. South Pole– *bottom of the Earth—90° south latitude*
17. latitude– *distance east or west of the prime meridian*
18. longitude– *distance north or south of the equator*
19. Tropic of Capricorn– *line of latitude at 66°30' south of the equator*
20. Antarctic Circle– *top of the Earth—90° north latitude*

SCORE_____

Passed ☐   Failed ☐

Name _____

OFF TO SADDLESORE ACRES

All the cowpokes and their ponies are waiting for the hay delivery in Cheyenne County. The Excellent Delivery Service has provided a grid and a street guide for the driver of the 2-ton hay truck. Help the driver locate the places where he needs to make deliveries.

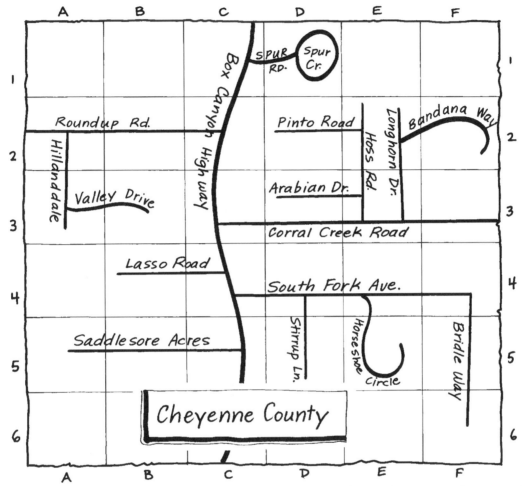

Write the grid location for each of these places. (For example: Spur Circle is in D 1. Corral Creek Road is in C 3, D 3, E 3, and F 3.)

1. Arabian Dr. _____

2. Bandana Way _____

3. Box Canyon Hwy. _____

4. Hillanddale _____

5. Horseshoe Circle _____

6. Lasso Rd. _____

7. Longhorn Dr. _____

8. Pinto Rd. _____

9. Roundup Rd. _____

10. Saddlesore Acres _____

11. Stirrup Ln. _____

12. Valley Dr. _____

13. Bridle Way _____

14. South Fork Ave. _____

15. Hoss Rd. _____

16. Spur Rd. _____

Name

UPS & DOWNS

Cousin Nirvanna has gotten the big delivery assignment that all the EDS employees call the "North Pole, South Pole, and Just about Everything in Between" trip! She's reviewing her notes about the lines that will help her find her way up, down, and around North and South America. Use the map and your knowledge of latitude to help Nirvanna find the right countries and places for her deliveries.

Lines of latitude help locate points north or south of the equator.

90°N
NORTH POLE

GREENLAND

Fort Yukon

66°30'N
ARCTIC CIRCLE

Nuuk

CANADA

Boston

Reno   U.S.A.

Houston

30°N

MEXICO

23°30'N
TROPIC OF CANCER

0°
EQUATOR

Quito

SOUTH
AMERICA

23°30'S
TROPIC OF
CAPRICORN

Porto
ALEGRE

30°S

66°30'S
ANTARCTIC CIRCLE

ANTARCTICA

1. When Nirvanna gets to 90° S with her delivery of wool socks, she'll be at _____.

2. Folks in Houston are waiting for cowboy hats. What latitude is Houston? _____

3. When she delivers armadillo cages at the Tropic of Cancer, she's in the country of _____.

4. Kids in two towns on (or near) the Arctic Circle can't wait to get their new video game, *Slime 4*. What are the towns? _____ and _____

5. Nirvanna needs to find the city of _____, right on the equator, to drop off the llama treats.

6. Nirvanna is in a panic. She has to get some air conditioners to Porto Alegre. She can't remember if it is north or south of the Tropic of Capricorn. Which is it? _____

7. She has lobster traps to deliver to a city north of the Tropic of Cancer on the Atlantic Ocean. That city is probably _____.

8. The last stop is a delivery of raincoats to folks on the very tip of South America. About what latitude is this? _____

SOUTH POLE — 90°S

Name

WHERE'S THE TEA?

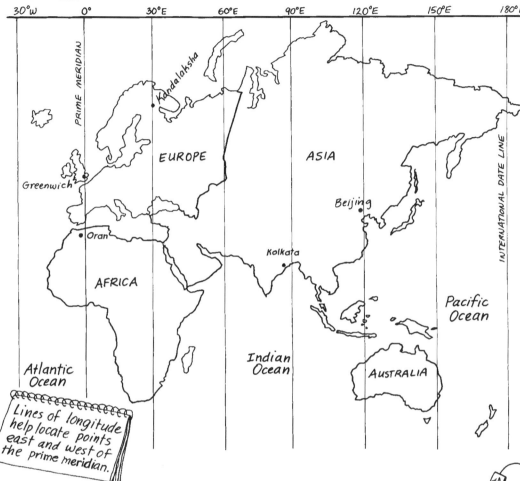

It is tea time in Greenwich, England, and the Queen is impatiently waiting for the Excellent Delivery Service to bring the tea she has ordered. Brush up your knowledge about longitude and follow these directions. *(Remember, Greenwich is at 0° longitude, which is called the **prime meridian!**)*

The Queen isn't the only one waiting for her tea. Deliveries of tea go to VIP tea drinkers all over the world. Draw a tea bag on the map to show the location for each delivery below. Write the corresponding number on the tea bag. You may need to use a world map to help you find the locations.

1. The Queen of England at the prime meridian
2. The Raja in an Indian city at 88° E
3. King Kualapu on the International Date Line (180° E)
4. Captain Klinger on his ship at 60° E in the Indian Ocean
5. Princess Frederika on her royal yacht at 30° W
6. Sheik Fahan in a north African city close to the prime meridian
7. A champion snake catcher somewhere between 120° and 150° E in Australia
8. A candle maker in a northern Russian city at 30° E
9. A prize-winning scientist on an island east of Africa at approximately 50° E
10. An expert climber in the Swiss Alps at about 8° E

Name

WORLDWIDE PIZZA PARTY

Pietro is celebrating the grand opening of his newest pizza parlor. He has hired the Excellent Delivery Service to deliver his pizzas all over the world. Help Oliver deliver the pizzas on time to the locations written on the list. (Remember, latitude is given first, then longitude). Put a fat, red dot and the name of each of the cities on the world map. (See page 163.) You may need some help from an atlas or a world map.

Work quickly, so the pizzas will get there while they are still hot!

PIETRO'S PIZZA DELIVERIES

artichokes & olives	Cairo, Egypt	30°N, 31°E
onions and peppers	Caracas, Venezuela	10°N, 66°W
gorgonzola & anchovies	Oslo, Norway	60°N, 10°E
spiced chicken & olives	Cape Town, South Africa	33°S, 18°E
pork & sausage	Pontianak, Borneo	0°, 109°E
sauerkraut & beef	Belgrade, Yugoslavia	44°N, 20°E
veggie without onions	Carson City, NV, USA	39°N, 119°W
hot chilies & mushrooms	Barrow, AK, USA	72°N, 158°W
pepperoni & hot mustard	Rio de Janeiro, Brazil	22°S, 43°W
beef, olives, & mushrooms	Accra, Ghana	6°N, 0°
double cheese	Winnipeg, Canada	49°N, 97°W
red peppers & ham	Wellington, New Zealand	41°S, 176°E
pineapple & mushrooms	Honolulu, HI, USA	21°N, 157°W
ants, pecans, & olives	Canberra, Australia	35°S, 149°E

Oi, such a lot of pizzas!

Hurry— the plane's waiting.

1. Oliver picks up the pizzas from Pietro in his hometown of Kanopolis, Kansas. Write the location of Kanopolis.

_____

2. Where should Oliver deliver your pizza? (Give the latitude and longitude.)

_____

What kind of pizza do you want?

_____

Use with page 163.

Name _____

THE WORLD

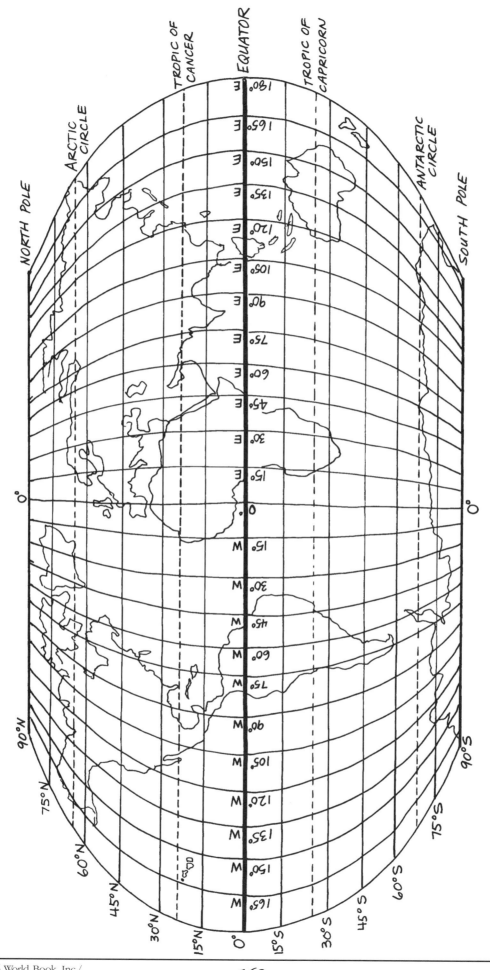

Name

FOR ANIMALS ONLY

Today, Ivanna has several deliveries for a mall, but this is a very unusual mall! Its customers are animals! Help her read the mall directory to find the shops for her deliveries.

1. Where will Ivanna deliver the scissors for trimming cat whiskers? Shop # _____

2. On which level should she deliver the box of books? _____

3. Where should she deliver the case of neon dog collars? Shop # _____

4. Where should she deliver the CDs of *You Ain't Nothing but a Hound Dog?* Shop # _____

5. Ivanna has hair bows and flea powder for the Shaggy Dog Salon. Color it pink.

6. Find the shop where she should deliver the frog fly treats. Color it green.

7. Where should she deliver the two cases of worms? Shop # _____

8. Where should she deliver the XXXXXXX-large sweatsuits? Shop # _____

9. On what level should she deliver a load of rawhide pretzels? _____

10. She has a case of iguana shampoo. Where does this go? Shop # _____

11. Where should she deliver a box of 40 lion-sized combs? Shop # _____

12. Which store is right for a delivery of zebra-striped nail polish? Shop # _____

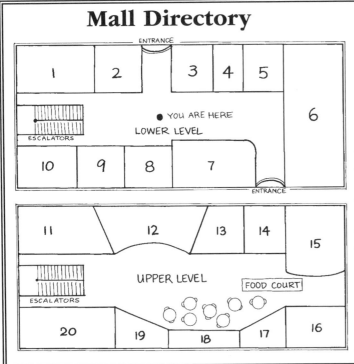

Mall Directory

1. Crazy Collars Shop
2. Ellie's Elephant Apparel
3. Savanna Manicures
4. The Shaggy Dog Salon
5. The Bookworm
6. Reba's Reptile Grooming
7. Big Foot Shoes
8. The Fancy Feline
9. Howling Wolf Music
10. The Mane Event
11. Underground Furnishings
12. Baa Baa Baby Supplies
13. Mouse Houses, Inc.
14. Toys for Tiny Tigers
15. Rats R Us
16. Porcupine Boutique
17. Froggie Fries & Flies
18. Fins & Feathers Eatery
19. Hot Rawhide Pretzels
20. The Big Cheese Café

Name _____

HAZARDS OF THE JOB

The most exciting and frightening "occupational hazards" of a delivery person's job are the natural hazards that can appear quite suddenly. Erupting volcanoes, earthquakes, tsunamis (tidal waves), and icebergs can cause major catastrophes! Even the everyday stuff, such as crossing a very hot, dry desert, can be an adventure! The map below shows the natural hazards in and near Australia. Use it to complete these activities.

NATURAL DISASTERS
- ⌒ —TSUNAMI
- ⌂ — ICEBERG
- ⩘ —EARTHQUAKE
- ▲ —VOLCANO
- ◀--- STORM ROUTE
- ▭ - DESERT

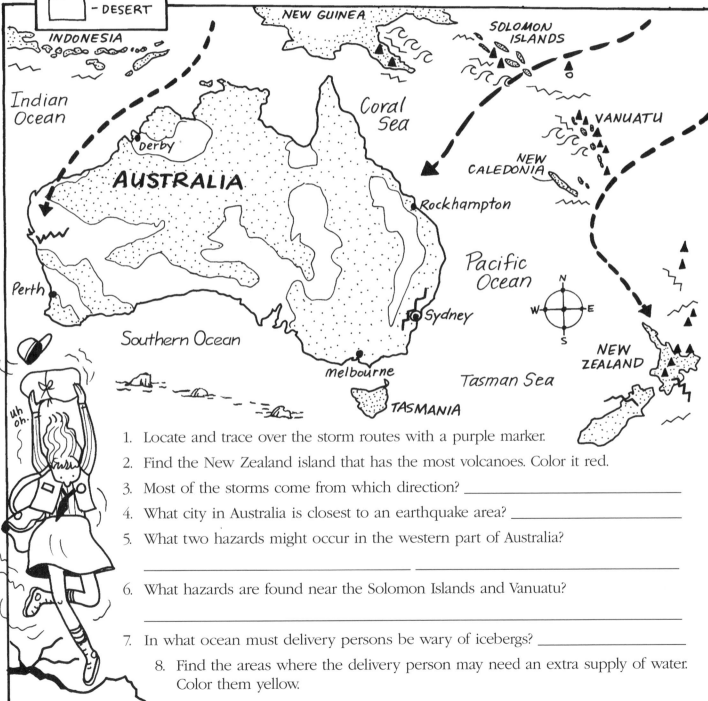

1. Locate and trace over the storm routes with a purple marker.

2. Find the New Zealand island that has the most volcanoes. Color it red.

3. Most of the storms come from which direction? _____

4. What city in Australia is closest to an earthquake area? _____

5. What two hazards might occur in the western part of Australia?

   _____   _____

6. What hazards are found near the Solomon Islands and Vanuatu?

   _____

7. In what ocean must delivery persons be wary of icebergs? _____

8. Find the areas where the delivery person may need an extra supply of water. Color them yellow.

Name _____

165

IT'S ABOUT TIME!

Whoops! Some people need to get their time zones straight! They are waking Oliver and Ivanna up in the middle of the night! Each of these calls, e-mails, faxes, and letters has a time question. The map on page 167 shows the time zones of the United States. Use it to figure out the answers to these questions. (Remember, Ivanna and Oliver are in Kanopolis, Kansas, which is in the Central Time Zone.)

1. This is Dolly, calling from Hollywood, California, darling! I simply have to have my hair stylist in New York City send me some mousse! It's 2 A.M. here. What time is it in New York?

_____

2. I'm calling to complain about your terribly tardy delivery service! I said I wanted my dear, rich great-uncle's birthday present delivered to him exactly at noon in Hawaii. It's 10 past noon here in Chicago now—and he does not have his present yet! (Why not?)

_____

3. I live in Montana. My flowers from Hawaii were supposed to be delivered at noon, Hawaii time. It's noon here. When will my flowers be delivered?

_____

4. Why do you sound so groggy, Oliver? It's 8 A.M. here in Miami. I need to order slippers for my dog to chew. What time is it there, anyway?

_____

5. Your delivery plane leaves Chicago at 5 P.M. and lands in Portland, Oregon at 7 P.M. Does this mean that you can get my ice cream all the way across the country in two hours? _____

6. Pierre's hair salon in New York opens at 10 A.M. Eastern Time. If you call when they open, what time will it be on your time, Oliver?

_____

7. Please deliver a singing birthday message—in person—to my senator in Washington, D.C. right now! She works every night until midnight! (If it's 11 P. M. in Kansas, can Oliver deliver this message on time?)

_____

8. Please get my wig shipped out right away. It's only 9:30 P.M. here in Alaska. Why aren't you open? What time is it there?

_____

Use with page 167.

Name

TIME ZONES OF THE UNITED STATES

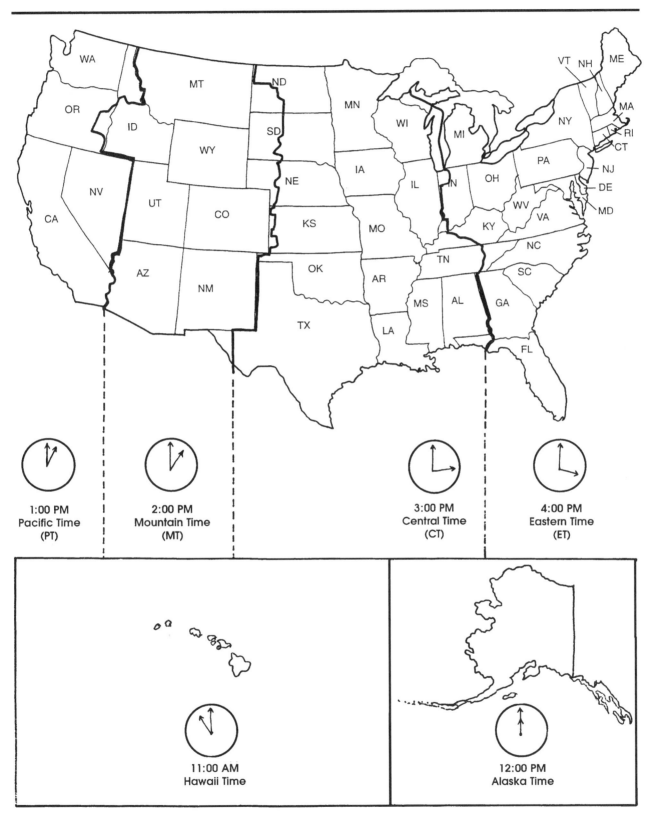

1:00 PM
**Pacific Time
(PT)**

2:00 PM
**Mountain Time
(MT)**

3:00 PM
**Central Time
(CT)**

4:00 PM
**Eastern Time
(ET)**

11:00 AM
Hawaii Time

12:00 PM
Alaska Time

Use with page 166.

THE WEIRDEST DELIVERY

Oliver has made some pretty weird deliveries, but never one as strange as the stone sarcophagus he's delivering to Count Dracula's Transylvania Theme Park. Oliver has a map of the park (see page 169), but when he gets there he discovers that the park is not yet finished. It is *your* job to design the park! Include some of the things listed below. You can also add your own ideas to the map! Draw symbols to show the location of each place, then make a key for your map. Also add a scale and a compass rose.

Features for the Transylvania Theme Park . . .

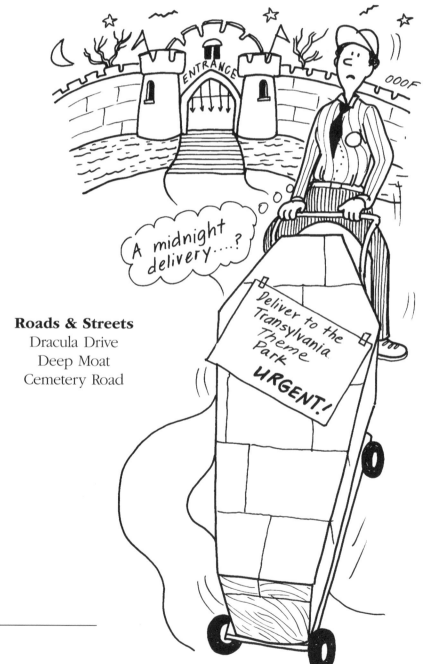

Rides
The All-Night Twister
The Flying Bat Coaster
The Fang-Mobile
The Countdown Cruise
Float the Moat
The Dungeon Drop
Werewolf Water World
Spider Web Climb
Nighttime Skydive

Village Shops & Businesses
Moat Boat Rentals
The Cape Shoppe
All-Night Movies
The Blood Bank
Anti-Garlic Factory
Bats and Other Toys
Night School
Sunstroke Emergency Room
Night Court
Dental School

Roads & Streets
Dracula Drive
Deep Moat
Cemetery Road

Restaurants
Full Moon Café
Midnight Soup Stop
Juicy Stake Cafeteria
Frozen Ghost Toasties
Ghoulash Parlor

What is a sarcophagus? _____

Use with page 169.

Name

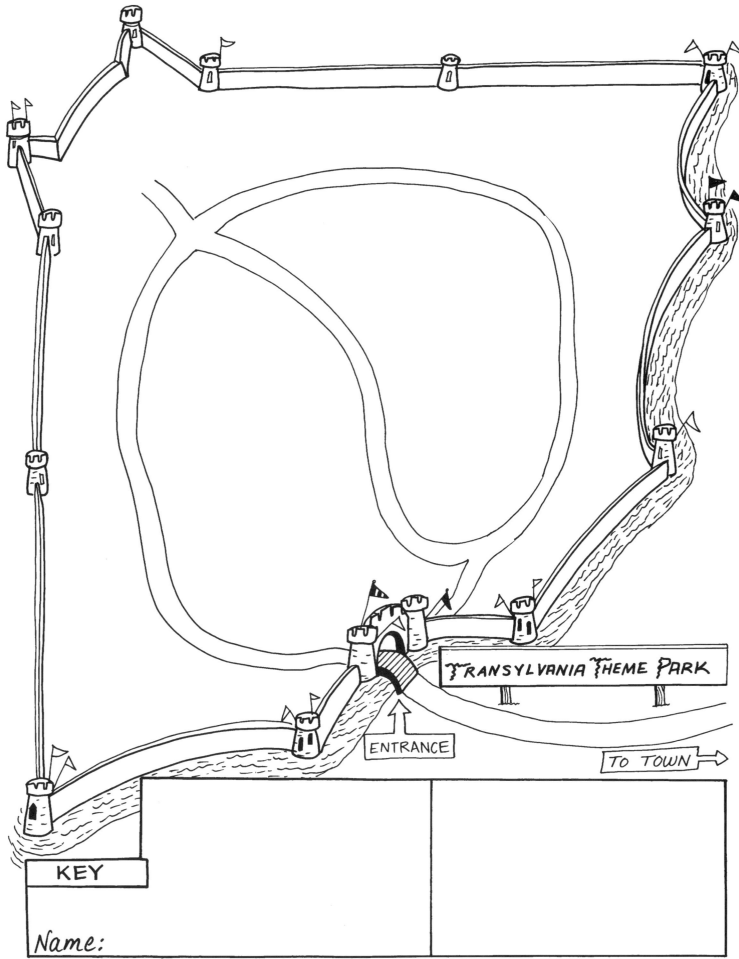

TRANSYLVANIA THEME PARK

ENTRANCE

TO TOWN →

KEY

Name:

Use with page 168.

SCIENCE

Skills Exercises
Grade Five

astronomy

chemistry

biology

geology

anatomy

earth science

SKILLS CHECKLIST
SCIENCE

✔	SKILL	PAGE(S)
	Describe components and benefits of health and physical fitness	173
	Define vocabulary terms related to the human body and health	173, 174
	Describe some ways the body defends against disease	173, 174
	Identify organs and functions related to human body systems	174
	Describe compounds; read and write chemical formulas	176
	Identify the components of matter: atoms and molecules	176, 179
	Distinguish between physical and chemical changes in matter	178
	3 states of matter	179
	Define and describe concepts and terms related to heat	180
	Define terms and explore concepts of electricity and current	181
	Identify and describe properties and behaviors of light	182
	Define and give examples of forces	183
	Identify and describe concepts and laws related to energy	183
	Identify and describe concepts and laws related to motion	183
	Draw a model of solar system; show Earth's relationship to other bodies	184
	Identify and compare characteristics of each planet	184
	Define and describe characteristics of other objects in the solar system	186
	Define, describe, and differentiate among movements of objects in space	186
	Identify and describe features of Earth's surface	188–192, 197
	Describe earthquakes, volcanoes, and other internal Earth processes	188, 197
	Identify characteristics of rocks	189
	Define and describe properties of air and Earth's atmosphere	190
	Identify weather patterns and forms of precipitation	190
	Describe and define different features of the ocean	192
	Define terms related to earth, space, physical, and life sciences	193–196
	Review facts related to earth, space, physical, and life sciences	193–196
	Science Terms	200

FITNESS SEARCH

Every body has defenses against disease, but Dr. de Plant knows that keeping fit and healthy makes the body's defense job easier. The puzzle hides 17 words that have to do with health and fitness. The clues at the bottom give hints about the words. Find and circle all 17 words. They may be written up, down, forward, backward, or diagonally.

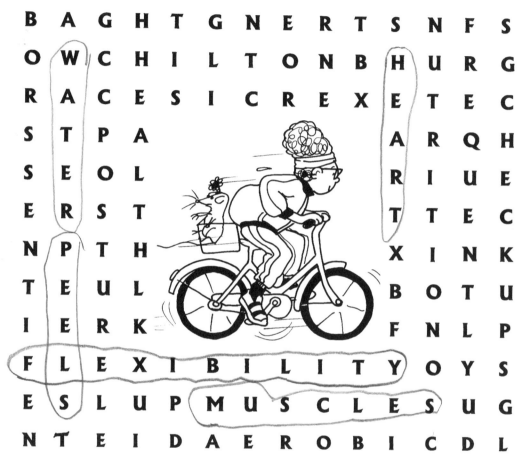

```
B A G H T G N E R T S N F S
O W C H I L T O N B H U R G
R A C E S I C R E X E T E C
S T P A         A R Q H
S E O L         R I U E
E R S T         T T E C
N P T H         X I N K
T E U L         B O T U
I E R K         F N L P
F L E X I B I L I T Y O Y S
E S L U P M U S C L E S U G
N T E I D A E R O B I C D L
```

1. Get plenty of _____, mostly at night.
2. Drink plenty of _____ every day.
3. Kind of exercise that swimming provides: _____
4. Lifting weights increases _____.
5. Say _____ to drugs and other harmful stuff.
6. Aerobic exercise is good for your _____.
7. Gently stretching muscles increases _____.
8. Take your _____ to see how fast your heart is beating.
9. Eat a healthy _____.
10. Warm up your _____ before exercising so you don't pull them!
11. How often you should exercise? _____
12. Opposite of sickness: _____
13. Stand up straight for good _____.
14. Dr. de Plant has a _____ plan.
15. Get _____ regularly from your doctor.
16. Skiing is a form of _____.
17. _____ is the study of food and the body's use of it.

Name _____

ATTACK OF THE "GERM"-INATORS

Today Dr. de Plant has invited some students to her laboratory for a funny film about the body's defense system. In the film, some germs are closing in for an attack. If a statement about the body's defense system is true, color the matching spaceship green. If the statement is false, cross out the matching ship.

We're on our way to attack an earthling. Are these statements about its defense system true?

1. A germ is a bacteria or a virus.

2. Acid in the stomach can kill many germs.

3. Mucus in the nose and throat helps keep germs out.

4. The body system that helps protect against germs is the limp system.

5. Vaccinations put dead or weak viruses or bacteria into the body.

6. Dried, clotted blood that forms on the skin is called rabies.

7. Antibiotic drugs can destroy viruses.

8. The body can kill some germs that get inside it.

9. All germs can be passed from person to person.

10. Immunity is the ability of the body to defend itself against a disease.

11. The body has natural defenses against germs and disease.

12. Antibodies can destroy the poison in germs.

Pay attention. Quiz tomorrow!

Use with page 175.

Name _____

Help me survive the attack of the germs! If a statement is true, color **all** the sections with that number red. If the statement is false, color **all** the sections with that number black.

1. The top layer of protective skin is the epiglottis.
2. A scab is made from dry, clotted blood.
3. Tears or sweat can kill germs.
4. It is not easy for germs to enter the body through the mouth.
5. Germs cannot get through healthy skin.
6. Germs love cool, bright places.
7. It is easy for germs to enter the body through the hair and nails.
8. Saliva helps defend against germs.
9. All diseases are caused by viruses.
10. Ear wax and nose hairs can catch germs.
11. Some white blood cells surround and swallow whole germs.
12. Sun, fresh air, and healthy food are good weapons against disease.
13. The body can make antibodies to protect against disease.
14. The body is only attacked by germs once in a while.
15. Diseases can be carried to the body by insects.
16. Harmful bacteria cannot live in water.
17. An antibiotic can never stop the growth of bacteria.
18. Soapy water cannot protect against germs.

Use with page 174.

Name

HANGING TOGETHER

The microscope seemed like a good tool for Robo Rat to find out more about matter. He overheard Dr. Sparks talking about how matter is made up of small particles called **atoms,** which combine together to make different substances called **compounds.** When Robo looked in the microscope, he saw some atoms hanging around together in groups (called **molecules**). For any compound, a formula can be written to show what atoms combine to make the molecules of the compound.

Read the compound names below. Then try to write the formula for each molecule that Robo saw. Number 3 is done for you as an example!

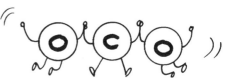

1. HYDROGEN CHLORIDE

2. CARBON DIOXIDE

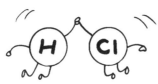

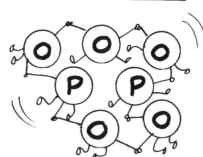

3. PHOSPHORUS PENTOXIDE

$P_2 O_5$

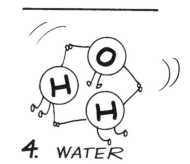

4. WATER

6. SILICON DIOXIDE

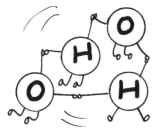

5. HYDROGEN PEROXIDE

Symbols

Bromine	Br
Calcium	Ca
Carbon	C
Chlorine	Cl
Fluorine	F
Hydrogen	H
Lead	Pb
Nitrogen	N
Oxygen	O
Phosphorus	P
Silicon	Si
Silver	Ag
Sodium	Na

Color the molecules. Use the same color for an element every time you use it.

Grab your partners and 'do-se-do'!

Use with page 177.

Name

7. CARBON MONOXIDE

_____

8. SODIUM CHLORIDE (SALT)

_____

9. LEAD MONOXIDE

_____

11. SILVER NITRATE

_____

10. HYDROGEN BROMIDE

_____

12. SODIUM PEROXIDE

_____

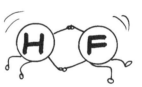

13. HYDROGEN FLUORIDE

_____

14. SILVER CHLORIDE

_____

Look at the formula for
chalk. Draw the molecule.

15. NITROGEN DIOXIDE

_____

16. CALCIUM CARBONATE (CHALK)
$Ca\ C\ O_3$

Use with page 176.

Name

A CHANGEABLE DAY

What a day Dr. Sparks has had! There have been so many changes! Some of them have been physical changes, and some have been chemical changes. Write **P** for physical or **C** for chemical before each change that happened today.

(Remember: No new substance is formed in a physical change. In a chemical change, one or more new substances are formed.)

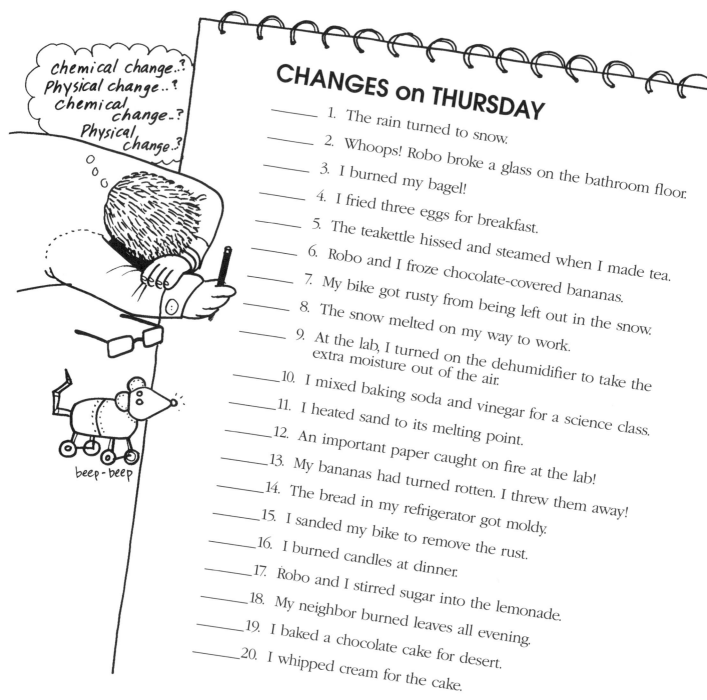

CHANGES on THURSDAY

_____ 1. The rain turned to snow.

_____ 2. Whoops! Robo broke a glass on the bathroom floor.

_____ 3. I burned my bagel!

_____ 4. I fried three eggs for breakfast.

_____ 5. The teakettle hissed and steamed when I made tea.

_____ 6. Robo and I froze chocolate-covered bananas.

_____ 7. My bike got rusty from being left out in the snow.

_____ 8. The snow melted on my way to work.

_____ 9. At the lab, I turned on the dehumidifier to take the extra moisture out of the air.

_____ 10. I mixed baking soda and vinegar for a science class.

_____ 11. I heated sand to its melting point.

_____ 12. An important paper caught on fire at the lab!

_____ 13. My bananas had turned rotten. I threw them away!

_____ 14. The bread in my refrigerator got moldy.

_____ 15. I sanded my bike to remove the rust.

_____ 16. I burned candles at dinner.

_____ 17. Robo and I stirred sugar into the lemonade.

_____ 18. My neighbor burned leaves all evening.

_____ 19. I baked a chocolate cake for desert.

_____ 20. I whipped cream for the cake.

Name _____

A-MAZING MATTER

While physicist Dr. Thermo Sparks is describing the three states of matter, his pet rat is worrying about his next meal. Here's how you can help him. Color the squares about liquids red, the squares about gases green, and the squares about solids yellow. Then draw a line on the yellow path for Robo Rat to get to the cheese.

LIQUID	**SOLID**	has a definite size but no definite shape			Water takes this form above 100° C.
has a definite size & shape	**GAS**	has no definite size or shape		can be poured	
		Water takes this form below 0° C.	takes the shape and size of any container		Things take this form when they freeze.
takes the shape of the container but not the size		Water takes this state between 0° and 100° C.	Water changes to this state above 100°C.		
	Solids take this state when they melt.				Liquids take this state when they evaporate.

A HOT JOKE

Dr. Sparks is in a joking mood today. He has a joke about heat. Robo thinks he can get the answer, but actually he needs a little help! Fill in the missing words to make the "hot" facts correct. Then write the letters that match the numbers on the lines below. You'll spell the answer to Dr. Sparks' joke.

1. Heat is a form of thermal __ __ __ __ __ __.
    ₁₀   ₄

2. A __ __ __ __ __ __ is the unit used to measure heat.
    ₂₀

3. __ __ __ air rises and __ __ __ __ air sinks.
       ₁₆   ₅ ₁₃

4. The transfer of radiant energy in waves is __ __ __ __ __ __ __ __ __.
                                              ₁₂   ₉

5. __ __ __ __ __ __ __ __ __ __ is the transfer of heat by movement of
    ₁₄   heated liquids or gases.

6. A __ __ __ __ __ __ __ __ __ measures heat.
       ₁   ₁₉

7. Wood is a poor __ __ __ __ __ __ __ __ __ of heat.
                    ₇

8. Radiation can __ __ __ __ __ __ __ __ heat through empty space.
                    ₈

9. A temperature of 100 °C or 212 °F is the __ __ __ __ __ __ __ point of water.
                                              ₂

10. Upward and downward movement of air is a convection __ __ __ __ __ __ __.
                                                        ₁₇   ₃

11. Material that slows heat transfer is called __ __ __ __ __ __ __ __ __ __.
                                                  ₁₁   ₁₅

12. __ __ __ __ __ __ __ __ __ is the transfer of heat from particle to
    ₁₈   ₆   particle of matter.

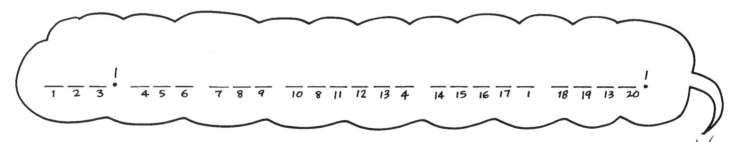

1 2 3 ! 4 5 6   7 8 9   10 8 11 12 13 4   14 15 16 17 1   18 19 13 20 !

AN ELECTRIFYING TOPIC

Experimenting with electricity can be a hair-raising experience! It looks as if Dr. Sparks did not have his thinking cap on when he matched these terms about electricity with their definitions. Look at the answers he has given. If an answer is not correct, cross it out and write the letter of the answer he should have given.

_D_ 1. electric charge
_B_ 2. static electricity
_C_ 3. electric current
_L_ 4. circuit
_G_ 5. insulator

_F_ 6. electrons
_I_ 7. conductor
_E_ 8. switch
_K_ 9. battery
_O_ 10. static discharge

_H_ 11. DC
_N_ 12. power
_J_ 13. ampere
_M_ 14. volt
_A_ 15. AC

A. alternating current
B. material electrons can move through
C. movement of electrons along a path
D. a path through which current flows
E. a device used to open or close a circuit
F. atom particles with a negative electrical charge
G. a poor conductor of electricity
H. electric charge built up in one place
I. charge with an unequal number of protons and electrons
J. temporary source of electric current
K. amount of work done per unit of time
L. direct current
M. unit that measures rate of electron flow in a circuit
N. unit that measures electric potential
O. movement of electrons from one object to another

I think Dr. Sparks got his wires crossed!

Name

A LIGHT STUDY

Only a scientist would go on vacation at the Arctic Circle to study light! Dr. Sparks is relaxing under the Arctic sky as he watches the Northern Lights. The puzzle is filled with words that describe some of the properties of light. You will notice that the puzzle is already finished for you, but something is missing—the clues! You need to write a clue for each word in the puzzle.

1. _____

2. _____

3. _____

4. _____

5. _____

6. _____

7. _____

8. _____

9. _____

10. _____

11. _____

12. _____

13. _____

14. _____

15. _____

Name _____

SNOW PROBLEMS

It takes energy, motion, and force to get in a snowball fight! Some force has to put energy into the motion that makes the snowball soar through the air! What force causes the motion of most flying snowballs?

Match these explanations to the terms on the snowballs. Write the correct number on each snowball.

1. the changing from one position to another

2. measure of how far an object moves in a period of time

3. any change in speed or direction of a moving object

4. the push or pull of one object against another

5. the force of attraction between objects

6. the amount of force applied to a particular area

7. measure of the force gravity pulls on an object

8. amount of matter that is in an object

9. can't be seen, but can be stored and then set free to work

10. result of a force moving an object through a distance

11. tendency for an object to resist any change in its speed or direction

12. a force that slows down and stops moving objects when they move across each other

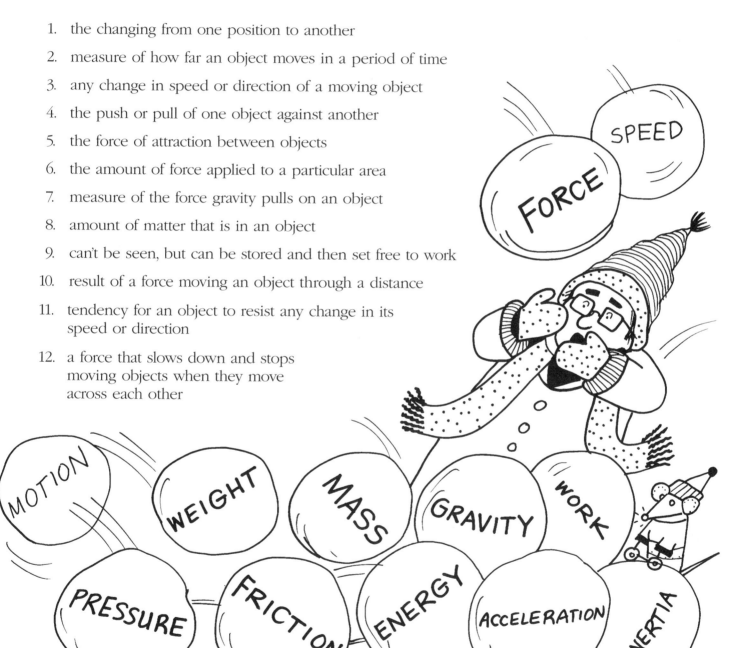

IT'S OUT OF THIS WORLD

Dr. Cosmo Quake and his faithful pet rat, Asteroid, are fortunate to be able to enjoy space travel. They have studied the solar system for years. Use the facts you know to finish the charts on these two pages (pages 184 and 185). Then draw the planets of the solar system in the proper orbits. (This is just a diagram of the solar system, so the sizes of the planets will not be exactly in proportion and the distances will not be correct. Give the general idea of the location, size, color, and look of the planets!)

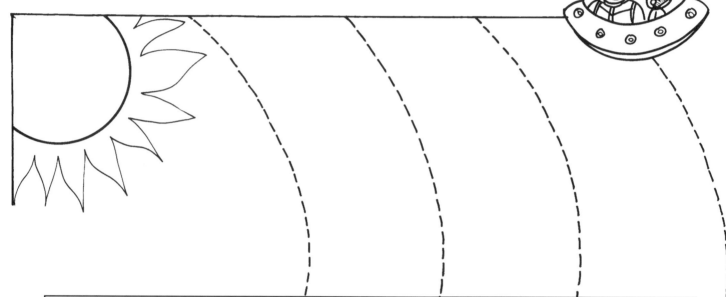

The Inner Planets

Number in Order from the Sun	PLANET	Number of Known Satellites	Colors, Features, Special Characteristics

Use with page 185.

Name

IT'S OUT OF THIS WORLD, cont.

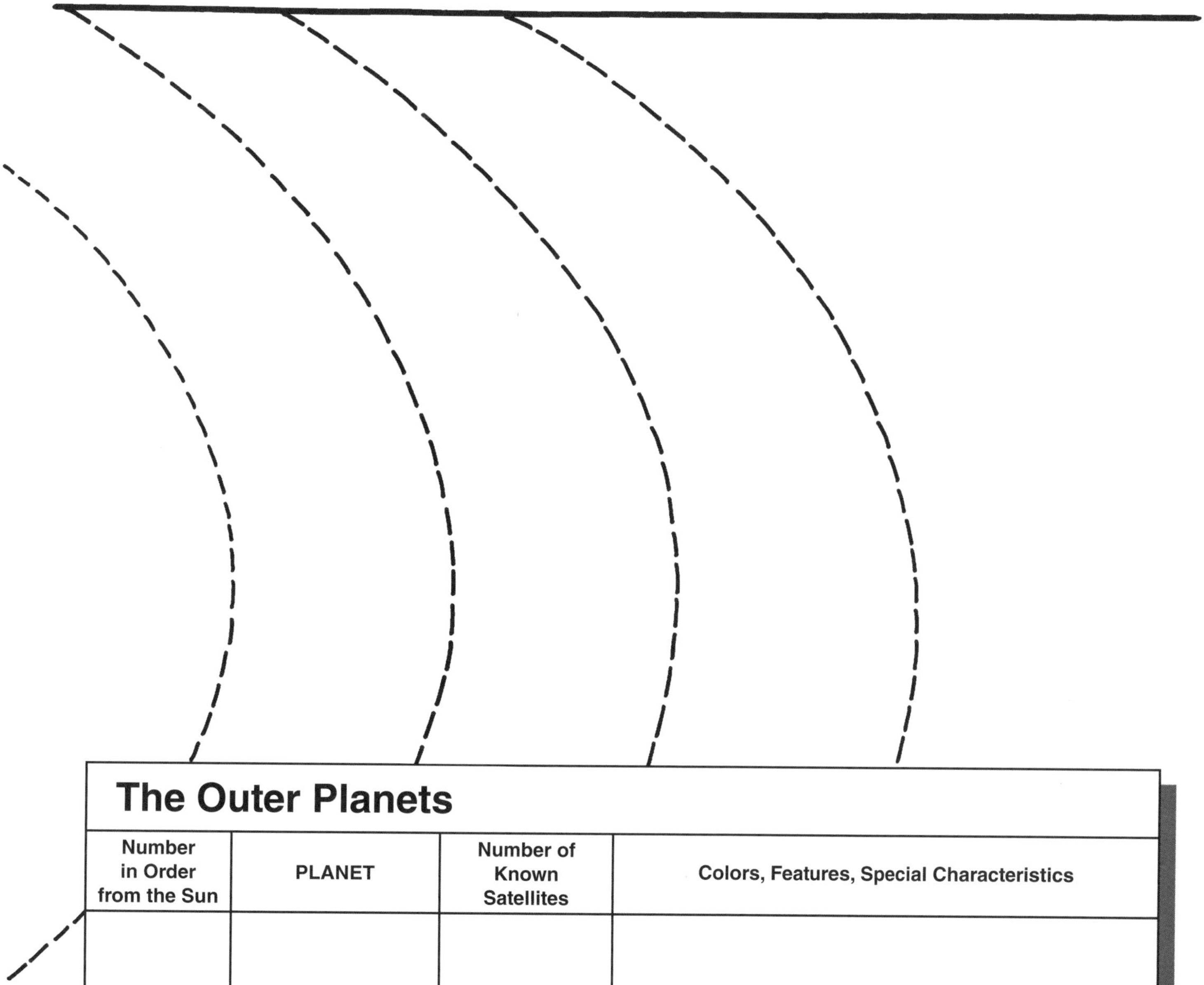

The Outer Planets

Number in Order from the Sun	PLANET	Number of Known Satellites	Colors, Features, Special Characteristics

Use with page 184.

Name

STRANGE ENCOUNTERS

There's a lot more out there to see than just planets! It looks as if Asteroid and Cosmo are finding space to be pretty full. Read the description of each space item. Write the number of the picture that matches the description. You will see that some of them are jokes or just silly—but all their names are words of things you could really find in space. Write the correct name in the blank to the right of each description.

_____ A. a collapsed star (gravity is so strong that no light can escape) _____

_____ B. exploding star _____

_____ C. largest ball of hot gas in the solar system _____

_____ D. frozen masses of dust and ice that orbit the sun _____

_____ E. the biggest and brightest stars _____

_____ F. a tight group of stars _____

_____ G. burst of gas from the sun's surface _____

_____ H. large numbers of asteroids between Jupiter and Mars _____

_____ I. two stars that orbit each other _____

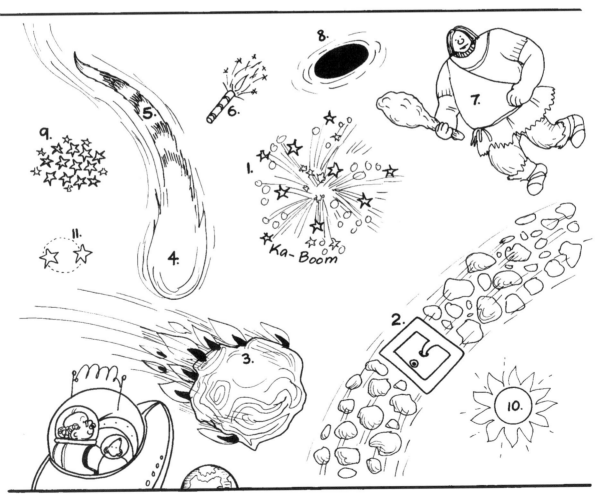

Use with page 187. Color the space stuff as you find it.

Name _____

_____ J.   long tail of dust that follows the comet _____

_____ K.   rock-like objects that move through space (burn upon entering Earth's atmosphere) _____

_____ L.   absence of atmosphere or air in space _____

_____ M.   path an object follows when orbiting another object _____

_____ N.   space traveler _____

_____ O.   vehicle for traveling in space _____

_____ P.   extremely dense, dying star _____

_____ Q.   a theoretical opening in space that may pass to another dimension _____

_____ R.   an object that orbits another body _____

_____ S.   large body of rock, liquid, and gases that orbits the sun _____

_____ T.   natural satellites that orbit the Earth and other planets _____

_____ U.   huge group of stars that form a spreading spiral _____

_____ V.   large rock chunks broken from a planet that orbits the sun _____

_____ W. smaller rock substances that orbit the sun in groups _____

Use with page 186. Color the space stuff as you find it.

Name _____

Copyright © 2016 World Book, Inc./
Incentive Publications, Chicago, IL

A VACATION PARADISE?

Dr. Quake thought for sure he would have a nice relaxing vacation if he headed west. You decide how relaxing it was! On his trip, he saw some sights and had some experiences caused by changes deep within Earth. He wrote about these in his trip notes. For each note, write a word that tells what feature, place, event, or tool he might be describing.

1. I feel very warm next to an opening in Earth's surface. Oh, my! Is that lava I see coming out?

2. As I drove along, the road disappeared into a funnel-shaped opening in the Earth caused by dissolving limestone beneath the surface.

3. The hotel bed began to slide across the room. The floor was shaking violently because of sudden rock movements within Earth.

4. An hour after the violent shaking of my bed, just when I thought everything had quieted down, the bed began to shake all over again.

5. Yesterday, I visited the spot on Earth directly above the focus of last month's earthquake.

6. I left the beach resort early today. I heard that a huge wave, formed by the force of an earthquake, was headed this way!

7. I took pictures of a huge hole filled with a beautiful lake. The hole was formed when a volcano blew its top.

8. Tomorrow I will visit an earthquake study center and look at the instruments that measure the strength of quakes.

9. What a beautiful sight Old Faithful was! Hot water and steam were shooting in the air, forced out of a small hole in Earth's surface by pressure underground.

10. I almost rode my little rented moped right into an opening in the road along a crack where fractured rocks had moved apart.

Name

A ROCKY BUSINESS

These rock hounds (or rock rats!) know about the different kinds of rocks. They are putting each kind of rock into a separate pile. The three kinds of rocks are classified according to how the rocks were formed. Show what you know about rock classification. Label each description below to show what kind of rock is connected to each word, name, or phrase. Use **M** (for metamorphic), **I** (for igneous), or **S** (for sedimentary).

_____ 1. formed from hardened lava

_____ 2. formed from sediment deposits

_____ 3. gravel and pebbles for conglomerate

_____ 4. limestone formed from minerals and sea shells

_____ 5. obsidian and basalt

_____ 6. heat and pressure form these from other rocks

_____ 7. dissolved minerals cement sediments together

_____ 8. slate, marble, and gneiss

_____ 9. can be extrusive or intrusive

_____ 10. banded and nonbanded

_____ 11. sandstone

_____ 12. any rocks can become these

_____ 13. used to make floors and tabletops

_____ 14. formed from melted rock

_____ 15. some form chemically

_____ 16. shale is the most common of this kind

_____ 17. layers cemented together

_____ 18. granite

_____ 19. coal is this kind of rock

_____ 20. can be formed from all three kinds

Name

EVERYBODY TALKS ABOUT IT!

It seems that everybody is always talking about the weather! That's because weather affects life every day. Cosmo and his scientist cousins are talking about it over their picnic lunch. So are their helpful rats! Read each comment about the weather. Then choose the word that tells what weather they are describing. Write the weather word on the line.

1. Last Tuesday, we were notified that a tornado had been spotted in our area.

_____

2. Yesterday, the air was moving at very fast speeds. My sun umbrella blew all the way across town!

_____

3. The ground got so cold that water vapor in the air condensed into little drops that collected all over the grass.

_____

4. The freezing rain left the whole town covered with ice.

_____

5. Last summer, this county went for months without any kind of precipitation.

_____

6. There's bad weather forming where two large masses of air with different temperatures have bumped into each other!

_____

7. Oh, oh! I think tiny water droplets have joined in the clouds and are falling to the ground! They will ruin our picnic!

_____

8. This morning water droplets in clouds were hovering close to the ground. I could hardly see to drive to work!

_____

9. I just love a picnic on days when the temperature is warm and there is not a cloud in the sky!

_____

windy   dew   front   fog   sunshine   drought   rain   ice storm   tornado warning

Use with page 191.

Name

10. Have you ever been around during one of those big storms where there is heavy snow blown around by high winds?

_____

11. When I lived in Kansas, I watched a whirling funnel of air that formed between the bottom of a storm cloud and the ground. It was moving very fast, and it sounded like a speeding train!

_____

12. I remember a storm where rain was falling through a layer of air colder than –3° C and the rain turned to freezing, icy, sloppy drops.

_____

13. We had better not be out here when electricity gets released from thunderclouds.

_____

14. Just look at the interesting shapes made by those tiny water droplets that have collected together and are suspended in the air!

_____

15. When the ground cools and makes the air around it cool just as freezing temperatures arrive, dew that is on the ground will freeze to make everything look white!

_____

16. Stay away from the beach when terrible storms with very high winds form over warm tropical ocean water!

_____

17. Oh! I just hate it when the air expands at great speeds and causes those horrible booming sounds. It scares me to death!

_____

18. Do you remember the summer of '95? The temperatures were above 110° F for weeks. It was so hot, I couldn't even eat cheese!

_____

19. Once I got lost in huge piles of tiny crystals formed when water froze on ice pellets in the clouds.

_____

20. One time, I was caught outside when water froze in layers around small balls of ice. These kept blowing up and down during a terrible thunderstorm. They built up more and more ice until they were as big as golf balls. It is so very dangerous for a rat to be out in a storm when that is happening. I thought I would never survive!

_____

hail
heat wave
frost
blizzard
thunder
snow
sleet
lightning
tornado
hurricane
clouds

Use with page 190.

Name

OCEAN SNOOPING

What will Dr. Quake and his helper find while they're snooping around in the ocean? What will they learn? For each thing they discover or "bump into," write the word (or words) that tells what they have learned or found! Choose from the words beneath the water!

1. They feel a movement where the water is rising and falling.

2. Their boat gets pushed up on the very top of a wave.

3. Their boat dips down to the lowest point of the wave.

4. Their boat gets caught in the movement of more dense sea water toward an area of less dense sea water.

5. Asteroid gets a mouthful of ocean water and finds that it is not fresh to taste. He wonders where this taste comes from!

6. Slowly, their boat washes toward shore with the shallow water waves caused by the pull of gravity.

7. Dr. Quake tells Asteroid that these waves happen twice a day in most oceans because of the gravitational pull that some space bodies exert on each other.

8. Dr. Quake also teaches Asteroid that cold water brings high amounts of something to the surface for ocean animals to feed on.

9. They don't get a good look at the steeply dropping outer edge of the continental shelf, which dips down to the deep ocean basin.

10. Dr. Quake explains about the system of cracks in Earth's crust deep under the Atlantic Ocean where melted rock comes through.

11. The ocean is too murky today to see any of the animals that live along the bottom of the ocean.

12. They do see plenty of tiny plants and animals that drift along the ocean surface.

BENTHOS   CONTINENTAL SHELF   TROUGH
WAVES   PLANKTON   CONTINENTAL SLOPE
PLAIN   CREST   EARTH
TIDES   SUN   MOON
EVAPORATES   COOLER   CURRENT
NUTRIENTS   RIFT ZONES
DISSOLVED SALTS   WARMER

Name _____

WHERE WOULD YOU FIND IT?

Would you find a **supergiant** in your bathtub? Is a **cirrus** likely to be found at a circus?
Where would be a good place to search for a **newton**? Dr. Quake knows these answers, do you?
For each science feature below choose the answer that tells where to find it.

1. **a supergiant?**
   a. under a microscope
   b. in your bathtub
   c. through a telescope

2. **some benthos?**
   a. in a volcano
   b. at the ocean bottom
   c. in the ocean surf

3. **an aurora?**
   a. in the Earth's core
   b. on a reptile
   c. in the sky

4. **a crest?**
   a. on a wave
   b. in a test tube
   c. in a crystal

5. **a fault?**
   a. in the earth's crust
   b. on the sun's surface
   c. in a cloud

6. **a corona?**
   a. in a cell's nucleus
   b. around the sun
   c. inside a mineral

7. **a continental slope?**
   a. on a ski hill
   b. in a science lab
   c. beneath the ocean surf

8. **a mantle?**
   a. in a machine
   b. inside Earth
   c. on a magnet

9. **a plankton?**
   a. in an ocean current
   b. in the desert
   c. in an electrical current

10. **a stratus?**
    a. in a prism
    b. in the sky
    c. in a fossil

11. **a moraine?**
    a. orbiting Earth
    b. at the edge of a glacier
    c. in a mixture

12. **a comet?**
    a. orbiting the sun
    b. orbiting Earth
    c. orbiting the moon

13. **some magma?**
    a. inside a volcano
    b. in the jet stream
    c. in a geyser

14. **a trench?**
    a. in the atmosphere
    b. on the ocean floor
    c. in a tornado

15. **an asteroid?**
    a. between Earth & Mars
    b. between Mars & Jupiter
    c. between Earth's layers

16. **geyser?**
    a. in a soda shop
    b. on a glacier
    c. shooting into the air

17. **a newton?**
    a. measuring water
    b. measuring force
    c. measuring plants

18. **an anemometer?**
    a. measuring heat
    b. measuring wind force
    c. measuring air pressure

Name _____

SCIENCE CHALLENGE

The three scientist cousins have decided to settle their dispute about who is the smartest, once and for all. They're taking the science challenge. You take the challenge, too! See if you can get all the right answers! Write the answer for each challenge question. Then use the answer key to add up your score. Each correct answer receives the points shown. For each wrong answer, subtract the amount shown from your total. Correct answers on BONUS squares receive twice the points shown. (Incorrect answers lose twice as much!)

When you finish this challenge, try the Super Science Challenge! (See page 195.)

LIFE SCIENCE	**EARTH & SPACE SCIENCE**	**PHYSICAL SCIENCE**
1. an animal phylum of soft bodies with hard shell coverings **100 pts** (–50)	**1.** causes Earth's day and night **100 pts** (–50)	**1.** measure of the amount of matter in an object **100 pts** (–50)
2. animals no longer living on Earth **200 pts** (–100)	**2.** planet closest to sun **200 pts** (–100)	**2.** change from a liquid to a gas **200 pts** (–100)
BONUS **3.** animal protection in which body color blends in with surroundings **300 pts** (–150)	**3.** number of days for 1 revolution of Earth around the sun **300 pts** (–150)	**BONUS** **3.** change from gas to liquid **300 pts** (–150)
4. kind of biome where cactus is found **400 pts** (–200)	**BONUS** **4.** three kinds of rocks **400 pts** (–200)	**4.** change of position of an object **400 pts** (–200)
5. plant process that produces oxygen **500 pts** (–250)	**5.** major agent of change on Earth's surface **500 pts** (–250)	**5.** ability to do work **500 pts** (–250)

TOTAL _____   TOTAL _____   TOTAL _____

GRAND TOTAL _____

Dr. Iris de Plant

Dr. Thermo Sparks

Dr. Cosmo Quake

Name _____

SUPER SCIENCE CHALLENGE

Write the answer for each challenge question. Then use the answer key to add up your score. Each correct answer receives the points shown. For each wrong answer, subtract the amount shown from your total. Correct answers on BONUS squares receive twice the points shown. (Incorrect answers lose twice as much!) Add up your total score from both pages (pages 194 and 195).

LIFE SCIENCE	EARTH & SPACE SCIENCE	PHYSICAL SCIENCE
1. term for animals that keep constant body temperature **200 pts** (–100)	**1.** layer beneath Earth's crust **200 pts** (–100)	**1.** measure of the force of gravity on an object **200 pts** (–100)
2. pollution caused by water droplets combined with sulfur dioxide in air **400 pts** (–200)	**BONUS** **2.** when a meteor changes to a meteorite **400 pts** (–200)	**2.** happens when force moves an object over a distance **400 pts** (–200)
BONUS **3.** class of arthropods with 8 legs **600 pts** (–300)	**3.** these are broken in the process of weathering **600 pts** (–300)	**BONUS** **3.** two substances combine to form a new substanc **600 pts** (–300)
4. chemicals that cause change in the body **800 pts** (–400)	**4.** two known planets farthest from sun **800 pts** (–400)	**4.** the amount of space occupied by an object of matter **800 pts** (–400)
5. largest sense organ in the body **1,000 pts** (–500)	**5.** what stalactites and stalagmites are formed from **1,000 pts** (–500)	**5.** the unit used to measure force **1,000 pts** (–500)

TOTAL _____   TOTAL _____   TOTAL _____

TOTAL THIS PAGE _____

TOTAL BOTH PAGES _____

Name _____

DEFINITELY NOT TRIVIAL

Trivia actually means that something is rather unimportant. These bits of science information may look short, but they are not at all trivial! If you can answer the questions, you'll show that you know some important science facts about Earth and space. (If Asteroid knew a little more about stalactites, he might have worn a different outfit today!) Be ready to explain your answers to anyone who might ask!

1. Which is not wet: a tsunami, a geyser, or a drought? _____

2. How is an orchestra leader like a carrier of electricity? _____

3. Would you put your family pictures on Earth's mantle? _____

4. If you are revolving around Earth, are you on a planet? _____

5. In 1957, where would you have found something called *Sputnik*? _____

6. What did a falling apple help Isaac Newton understand? _____

7. Is an ozone layer part of a cake? _____

8. Where would you find a crest and a trough?

   _____

9. Where would you find a stalactite?

   _____

10. Where would you find a stalagmite?

    _____

11. What was named after Edmond Halley?

    _____

12. Would you keep your books on a continental shelf? _____

13. Could you weigh your pet monkey on a Richter Scale? _____

14. What did Yuri Gagarin do that only dogs had done before? _____

15. Does Betelgeuse have anything to do with beetles or juice? _____

16. How are Earth's faults different from your faults? _____

17. If you visit the solar system's largest planet, will you be on Jupiter? _____

18. What would a baron (or anyone else) do with a barometer? _____

Really, Asteroid! You don't need a space suit to hunt for stalactites!

Name _____

SUCH ODD STUFF!

There are some strange, mysterious features on and just below Earth's surface. Find out what these mysteries are. (See the list below.) Which mysterious sight would you be near in each of these examples?

A. HOT SPRINGS

B. FUMORALE

C. GEYSER

D. LACCOLITH

E. VOLCANIC NECK

F. SINKHOLE

G. CALDERA

H. MUDSPOTS

I. SOLFATARAS

J. BATHOLITH

K. DIKE

SPLURP

_____ 1. You take a swim in a lake-filled crater formed when a volcano blew its top and the volcano's cone collapsed into the vent.

_____ 2. You are filming a natural hot spring that is shooting hot water high up into the air through a small opening in Earth's surface.

_____ 3. Your cousin is videotaping you as you relax in a steaming hot pool of underground water which was heated by magma in a thermal region before it rose through cracks into the pool.

_____ 4. You're recording the strange popping noises as you watch the plopping, spurting patterns made by hot water squirting up through mud.

_____ 5. You hold your nose because this spot smells like rotten eggs. It's an outlet in Earth's surface where steam, chlorides, sulfurs, and other gases are given off by cooling magma. The rocks around the edges are yellow from the sulfur, and wow! Does it smell!

_____ 6. More rotten eggs! This dying volcano gives off sulfur vapors all the time.

_____ 7. You have to envision this one, because it's beneath the surface. A large mass of intrusive igneous rock forms the core of a mountain you're admiring. This solid mass extends far down into Earth.

_____ 8. You saw it with your own eyes! A road disappeared, and a truck with it—into a funnel-shaped depression in the earth caused by dissolving limestone beneath the surface.

_____ 9. Another underground marvel—a mushroom-shaped body of igneous rock, formed as lava hardens in this strange shape.

_____ 10. The earth has eroded away to leave a tall skinny mass of rock that was formed underground when magma entered a vertical crack and hardened.

_____ 11. An inactive volcano had magma solidified in its pipe. As the softer, outer rock wore away, this remained resistant to erosion.

Name _____

SCIENCE TERMS

adaptation—ability of a living thing to survive in its environment

asteroids—rocky or metallic objects smaller than planets that orbit a star

astronomy—study of objects in space

atmosphere—layer of gases that surrounds Earth

atom—the smallest unit of an element that has all the properties of that element

bacteria—simple living thing that causes decomposition or disease

barometer—instrument used to measure air pressure

bedrock—the solid rock layer under the soil

biome—region with distinct climate, plants, and animals

botany—the study of plants

cell—basic unit of structure and function in living things

chemical change—change in which a substance becomes another substance

chemical formula—a group of symbols that tells the atoms in a compound

chlorophyll—substance that makes a plant green and traps light energy to make food

circuit—a closed-loop path for electricity to follow

climate—the average of all weather conditions over an area

comet—mass of frozen gases, dust, and small rocks that orbits the sun

community—all the organisms that live together in a certain area

compound—a substance containing atoms of two or more elements chemically combined

conduction—energy transferred through matter from particle to particle

conductor—material that electrons can flow through

consumer—organism that lives from eating others

convection—transfer of heat energy by the movement of warmed liquids and gases

continental shelf—the flat part of the continent that is covered by sea water

continental slope—the steeply sloping surface between the continental shelf and the ocean basin

core—the innermost layer of Earth

craters—depressions on the surfaces of some planets and their moons

crest—highest point of a wave

crust—the outermost layer of Earth

current—areas where water is moving from places of high density to lower density; the flow of electrons in a conductor

decomposer—organism that causes decay of dead organisms

delta—fan-shaped deposit that develops where moving water slows down as it enters a larger body of water

drought—a period of time with little precipitation

earthquakes—vibrations caused by sudden movement in Earth's rocky outer shell

eclipse—one object passes into the shadow of another

ecology—study of interactions between organisms and the environment

ecosystem—system in which living organisms interact with each other and with their nonliving environment

electron—a negatively charged particle that orbits the nucleus of an atom

element—substance made of one kind of atom

endangered—a species that only has a few members living

environment—everything that is outside of a living thing

epicenter—the point on Earth's surface that is directly above the focus of an earthquake

erosion—process by which Earth materials are carried away and deposited elsewhere

evaporation—process by which a liquid becomes a gas

extinction—total disappearance of a species

faults—fractures in rock

food chain—pathway of food and energy through an ecosystem

food web—complex series of food chains

force—a push or pull one body exerts on another

friction—force that slows or stops motion when two things rub against each other

front—area where two air masses of different temperatures meet

galaxy—large system of stars, gases, and dust in space

gas—state of matter that has no definite size or shape

germination—early growth of a plant from a seed

geology—study of all processes affecting Earth

geysers—hot springs that erupt in water and steam

glaciers—thick masses of slowly moving ice

gravity—the attraction between two objects because of their mass

igneous rock—rock formed from melted Earth material

inertia—property of a body that resists change in speed

insulation—material that slows the flow of electricity

invertebrates—animals without a backbone

joule—unit for measuring work or energy

lava—melted rock (magma) that is released from Earth

during volcanic eruptions

light—the only visible part of the magnetic spectrum

liquid—state of matter that has definite volume but no shape

magma—molten material found beneath Earth's surface

magnet—any object that has a magnetic field and exerts force on other magnets

magnetic field—area of magnetic lines of force

magnetic poles—locations of strongest force on a magnet

mantle—the middle layer of Earth

mass—amount of matter in an object

metamorphic rocks—rocks that form from other rocks due to heat and pressure

meteorites—meteors that strike Earth

meteoroids—small fragments of matter moving through space

meteorology—the study of weather patterns and climates

meteors—meteoroids that burn up in Earth's atmosphere

mineral—naturally occurring inorganic solid

mixture—two or more elements blended together without combining chemically

motion—change in position

nimbus—dark gray cloud usually producing rain or snow

nucleus—central part of the atom; contains neutrons and protons

opaque—material that absorbs light

orbit—the path followed by a planet

organism—a complete living thing

ovary—the female plant part

parasite—organism that gets its food from another organism (host) but harms the host

photosynthesis—process in which plants use energy from light to make food and oxygen

physical change—change in size, shape, color, or state without a change in chemical composition

physical science—study of matter and energy

pistil—female organ of a plant

pitch—quality of a sound determined by its frequency

pollination—transfer of pollen grains to ovules in flowers

power—amount of work done per unit of time

predator—animal that captures another for food

prey—animal eaten by a predator

producer—organism that makes its own food from photosynthesis

radiation—transfer of energy that does not require matter; travels in waves

reflection—bouncing back of a wave or light ray

refraction—bending of a wave or light ray

respiration—process by which cells release energy from food molecules for their activities

revolution—the movement of a body around another

Richter Scale—scale for measuring intensity of earthquakes

rift zone—system of cracks in Earth's surface

rocks—Earth materials made of one or more minerals

rotation—turning motion of an object on an axis

sedimentary rocks—rocks formed as the result of weathering and repositioning of Earth materials

sediment—loose Earth materials resulting from weathering

simple machine—one of six devices that make work easier

skeleton—frame of bones or cartilage that shapes, supports, and protects an organism

solar eclipse—eclipse occurring when Earth is in the shadow of the moon

sound wave—a wave caused by vibrations

stars—bright, hot spheres of gas

stratosphere—layer of the atmosphere that contains the ozone layer

thermosphere—uppermost layer of the atmosphere

tides—shallow water waves caused by the gravitational attraction among Earth, the moon, and the sun

tissue—a group of cells with similar shape and function that perform a job together

tornado—funnel-shaped wind that moves over land in a narrow path

translucent—material that transmits light but cannot be seen through

transpiration—loss of water vapor through *stomata* (small holes) of a leaf

transparent—having the property of allowing light to pass through

troposphere—layer of the atmosphere nearest Earth

trough—lowest point of a wave

tsunami—powerful tidal wave caused by an earthquake

velocity—speed and direction of a moving object

vertebrate—animal with a backbone

vibration—rapid back-and-forth movement

volcano—mountain formed by material forced out of Earth's interior

volt—unit to measure electric potential

volume—loudness of a sound

watt—unit to measure power

wave—rhythmic movement transferring energy from one place to another

MATH

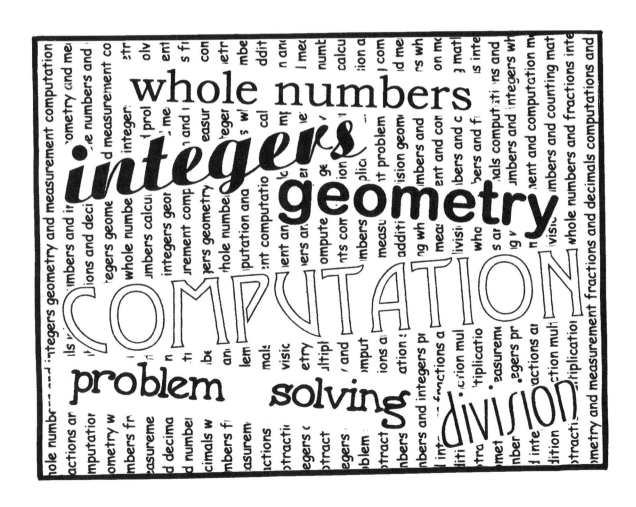

Skills Exercises
Grade Five

SKILLS CHECKLIST
PROBLEM SOLVING

✔	SKILL	PAGE(S)
	Identify information that may be missing from a problem	206
	Identify information needed for solving a problem	206, 207
	Solve a variety of word problems	206–209, 211, 215–217, 220–236
	Eliminate excess information	207
	Choose correct equations to solve problems	208
	Find solutions to equations	208, 209
	Translate problems into equations	208, 209
	Solve problems using statistical data	210, 211, 223, 230
	Solve problems using information from charts, graphs, and tables	210, 211, 230
	Solve problems involving U.S. customary measurements	212
	Solve problems using information from diagrams and illustrations	212, 218, 228, 225, 228, 229
	Solve problems involving metric measurements	213
	Solve problems using fractions	214
	Solve problems using decimals	215, 216
	Solve multistep problems	216, 217, 219, 222, 223, 228–230
	Solve problems using money	216, 223
	Select appropriate operation(s) for solving problems	217
	Use formulas to find perimeter, area, and volume of geometric figures	218, 219
	Solve problems involving ratios	220
	Solve problems involving percent	220, 221, 223
	Solve problems involving time	222
	Solve consumer problems involving taxes and discounts	223
	Use estimation to solve problems	224, 232, 233
	Create diagrams, models, or charts to help solve problems	225
	Use mental math to solve problems	226, 227, 232–234
	Use logic to solve problems	228, 229
	Find more than one solution to a problem	230, 231
	Choose an appropriate strategy to solve a given problem	232, 233
	Write explanations of how problems were solved	234, 235
	Check the accuracy of problem solutions	236

SKILLS CHECKLIST
COMPUTATION & NUMBERS

✔	SKILL	PAGE(S)
	Read and write whole numbers	237, 238,
	Solve word problems with whole numbers	237, 238, 240, 244, 246
	Add and subtract whole numbers	239, 240
	Multiply whole numbers	240–243, 245
	Choose among a variety of whole number operations	240
	Select the proper operation for a given computation	240, 246
	Identify common factors and greatest common factors	241, 242
	Solve equations with whole numbers	243–246
	Divide whole numbers	244, 245
	Solve multistep problems with whole numbers	245
	Identify and use properties of operations	247
	Name fractional parts of a whole or set	248
	Read and write fractional numbers and mixed numerals	248–255
	Solve word problems with fractional and decimal numerals	248, 251, 257, 258, 260
	Compare and order fractions	249, 250
	Identify equivalent fractions	251
	Write mixed numerals as fractions and fractions as mixed numerals	252, 253
	Write and solve equations with fractions and decimals	254
	Add and subtract fractions and mixed numerals	254
	Multiply and divide fractions and mixed numerals	255
	Read and write decimals and mixed numerals	256–260
	Round decimals	256
	Add and subtract decimals	257
	Solve problems with decimal numerals	257–260
	Multiply and divide decimals	258
	Change fractions to decimals and decimals to fractions	259, 260
	Understand, read, and write percents	260
	Write decimals as percents and percents as decimals	260
	Write fractions as percents and percents as fractions	260
	Read, write, compare, and order integers	261
	Add and subtract integers	261

SKILLS CHECKLIST
GEOMETRY & MEASUREMENT

✔	SKILL	PAGE(S)
	Identify kinds of lines: perpendicular, parallel, and intersecting lines	262
	Identify and describe points, lines, line segments, rays, and planes	262
	Identify plane figures	263
	Identify and define kinds of triangles: (scalene, equilateral, isosceles, right)	263
	Use formulas to find perimeter, area, and volume	264
	Determine time measurements	265
	Identify and define different kinds of polygons	266
	Identify, define, and distinguish among different kinds of quadrilaterals	267
	Identify symmetrical figures and lines of symmetry	268
	Identify transformations in plane figures	269
	Compare and convert among U.S. customary measurements	270
	Use metric units for measuring length	271
	Find the circumference of circles	272
	Find the area of plane figures	273, 274
	Find the area of circles	274
	Use metric units to find the volume of cubes and rectangular prisms	275
	Use U.S. customary units to find the volume of cubes and rectangular prisms	276

SKILLS CHECKLIST
GRAPHING, STATISTICS, & PROBABILITY

✔	SKILL	PAGE(S)
	Read & interpret tables of statistics	279–281
	Read & interpret frequency graphs	278
	Construct a frequency table from statistical data	279
	Analyze data to find range, median, and mode	280
	Use tables of statistics to solve problems	281
	Solve problems from statistics shown on a graph	282
	Find locations on a coordinate grid	283
	Find probability of an event	284–286
	Find the odds of an event	287
	Describe all the possible outcomes of two events	288
	Find probability of two events	289
	Identify possible combinations of sets within a larger set	290
	Use random sampling to make probability predictions	291
	Use probability concepts and calculations to solve problems	292

SOMETHING'S MISSING!

When Suzie heads down the slalom slopes, it's hard to get her to stop—even though she is missing something important for her race! Something is also missing in each of these problems. For each problem, tell what other facts are needed to find the answer.

Something's missing...

1. The wind at the top of Suzie's run is 26 mph. She skis down the mountain at 38 mph. How much faster is the wind blowing at the top of the run than at the bottom?
   _____

2. There are 4,866 skiers on the slopes at Holiday Hollow today. Some are intermediate and expert skiers, and $\frac{1}{5}$ of them are beginners. How many are expert skiers?
   _____

3. New skier, Abigail, fell 17 times during the first hour of her lesson. She fell twice that many times during the second hour. How many times did she fall all together during her 3-hour lesson? _____

4. Last week, 1,700 ski passes were sold. In previous weeks, 7,100 were sold. How many more were sold this season than last? _____

5. Suzie spent $139 for her new ski jacket and $520 for her new skis. How much more did the skis cost than the boots? _____

6. Suzie brought $28 for lunches during her ski trip. How much would she be able to spend each day? _____

7. The ski patrol rescues many skiers in trouble each day. Of those, 15% have broken bones. How many broken bones are there a day? _____

8. Anthony has won 7 major slalom races this year. Scott has won 4. Thomas has won twice as many as Will. How many have the four boys won all together? _____

9. Last night 15 inches of new snow fell on the ski hill. How much snow does the ski hill have now? _____

10. There were half as many collisions on the ski hill today as there were on Tuesday, and twice as many as on Monday. How many collisions were there today?
    _____

Name _____

MORE THAN ENOUGH

Wild Will has given a lot more information about his favorite snowboard tricks than is really need-ed to solve these problems. Cross out the information in each problem that is not needed for the solution. Then, solve the problems.

1. What a great day I had today! This is the 14th competition I've won this year. I won 13 last year with my new $700 snowboard. Today is my 14th birthday, too! How many competitions have I won in the past two years? _____

2. I impressed the crowd with my tricks today. My first run included 4 Tail Grabs and twice as many Tail Rolls. I did 17 tricks in all, including 3 Flips. How many of the tricks were not Tail Grabs or Tail Rolls? _____

3. My last run down the hill took 3 minutes 20.21 seconds. This was 0.33 seconds faster than my first run. I did 3 Backscratchers, 2 Iguana Back Flips, and 5 Nose Rolls. How fast was my first run? _____

4. This season, I've done 200 Ollies and 400 Fakies in practice. I've practiced my McTwist 12 times more than my Fakies. How many McTwists have I done in practice? _____

5. I have practiced my tricks a total of 246 hours so far this season. I've been at the snowboarding park 82 times. It takes 45 minutes to get to the park from my home. My season pass cost $350. About how many hours did I snowboard each time I went to the park? _____

6. This year, 1,200 snowboarders each bought a pass for $350. Anyone under 12 got a 10% discount. There were 180 boarders under 12. There were 70 boarders over 16 who bought passes. How much did the passes cost for kids under 12? _____

7. Julia said she'd take me to a movie if I could do more Slob Airs than she did (without falling). The movie tickets cost $6.50 each. She did 17 Slob Airs without falling. I did 3 times as many as that, but I fell 39 times. Did she have to take me to the movie? _____

8. I fall about 4 times for every 200 feet I snowboard. I have 37 bruises on my body, 6 cuts on my face, and 1 broken finger. If I cover 13,000 feet a week on my snowboard, about how many times will I fall? _____

9. I ate 6 tacos, 2 hot dogs, and 4 energy bars today. I've eaten 9 dozen energy bars this season. How many energy bars did I eat before today? _____

Name _____

WILD WHITEWATER WHIRL

Kayakers will have a much better chance of getting down wild rivers safely if they choose the best path. You'll have a better chance of solving math problems correctly if you can find the equation that best fits the problem. Circle the correct equation and solve each problem. If you get them right, you'll help Will find the right path down the river.

1. Will puts his kayak in at the dam. The first set of rapids is 3 miles downstream, the next is 4 miles farther, and the next is $2\frac{1}{2}$ miles farther. He gets out 2 miles after the third set. How many miles has he paddled? _____
    a. $3 + 4 = n$
    b. $n = 3 + 4 + 2\frac{1}{2}$
    c. $3 + 4 + 2\frac{1}{2} + 2 = n$
    d. $3 \times 2 \times 2 \times 2\frac{1}{2} = n$

2. It takes 6 hours to drive to Raging River without stopping. If Wanda and Will stop twice for $\frac{1}{2}$ hour each time and once for a 1-hour lunch, how long will their trip take? _____
    a. $n = 6 + \frac{1}{2} + \frac{1}{2}$
    b. $n = 6 + \frac{1}{2} - \frac{1}{2} + 1$
    c. $6 + \frac{1}{2} + \frac{1}{2} + 1 = n$
    d. $6 - \frac{1}{2} - \frac{1}{2} - 1 = n$

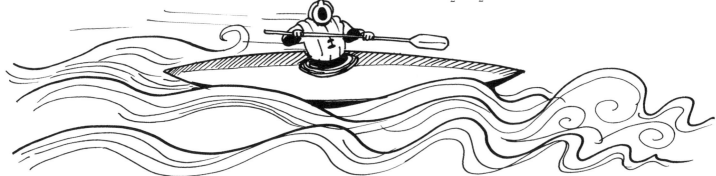

3. Will and his 12 teammates each have a helmet, paddle, wetsuit, and splashskirt to carry in their kayaks. How many items of gear do they have in all? _____
    a. $12 \times 4 = n$
    b. $n = 4 \times 13$
    c. $12 + 4 = n$
    d. $1 + 1 + 1 + 1 + 12 = n$

4. This summer Will entered 17 whitewater rodeos. This was 9 more than last year. How many rodeos did he enter last year?
    _____
    a. $17 + 9 = n$
    b. $n = 17 \times 9$
    c. $n = 17 - 9$
    d. $17 \div 9 = n$

5. The Whitewater club has 24 members with kayaks. If each car-top rack holds 4 kayaks, how many cars will they need to travel? _____
    a. $n = 24 \div 4$
    b. $n = 24 \times 4$
    c. $24 + 4 = n$
    d. $24 - 4 = n$

6. Will got dunked 5 times. Wanda got dunked 3 times. Wayne got dunked twice the number of times that Will and Wanda did. How many times did Wayne go in? _____
    a. $n = 2(5 + 3)$
    b. $n = 2 + 8 + 3$
    c. $2 \times 5 + 3 = n$
    d. $5 + 3 + 2 \times 5 = n$

Name _____

SINK THAT BASKET

The Panthers and the Warriors are big rivals. This game is the big one! The championship is at stake. To solve these problems about the teams and the game, change each problem into an equation. Read the problem, write an equation, and then solve the equation to find the answer.

1. The Warriors scored 42 two-point baskets and 7 three-pointers. What was their final score?

    _____

2. In this game and the last two games, the Panthers scored the exact same number of points. The total of all these was 216. What was their score for each game?

    _____

3. To get to the game, the Panthers traveled 195 miles less than the Warriors, who traveled 400 miles. How far did the Panthers travel to the game?

    _____

4. The Warriors bought 96 pairs of court shoes at the beginning of the season. They had to buy 28 more a month later to replace the ones that had worn out. How many did they **not** have to replace?

    _____

5. A typical player breathes seven quarts of air a minute while sitting on the bench and 20 times that much per minute while playing a strenuous game. How many quarts per minute would that be?

    _____

6. There were 155 more Panther fans than Warrior fans at the game. There were 2,224 Warrior fans. Among all of the fans, 350 had to stand. How many fans had seats?

    _____

7. The concession stand took in $4,500 at the game. Of that, $1,850 was for food, and $570 was for souvenirs. The rest was for drinks. How much was spent on drinks?

    _____

8. Player Sarah Peters dribbled the basketball a total distance of 4,788.5 feet. Her sister Denise dribbled it half that far. How far did Denise dribble the ball?

    _____

Name _____

A SLIPPERY SLOPE

The climbing team is having some trouble this week. On an expedition to the top of Mount Slick, the climbers are finding the slopes to be very slippery. Each day they make progress upward, but on many steps they slide backward. Look at the record of each climber's progress over 3 days. For each one, tell how far they've moved up the mountain by the end of day 3.

| Climber | DAY 1 | | DAY 2 | | DAY 3 | | Total |
	Feet Up	Feet Slipped Back	Feet Up	Feet Slipped Back	Feet Up	Feet Slipped Back	Feet Gained
Jose	1,295	416	1,001	227	1,720	173	
Abby	1,510	307	1,421	196	1,666	214	
Dylan	2,103	519	1,933	225	1,166	197	
Jessica	1,111	87	1,609	210	2,100	414	
Ryan	1,794	360	1,510	314	1,987	121	
Brad	1,600	765	1,799	201	2,206	316	
Lauren	2,166	409	1,995	179	1,611	209	
Andy	1,618	399	1,816	533	1,159	166	
Alexa	1,999	255	2,030	485	2,000	289	
Denise	1,277	310	1,909	79	1,683	110	

1. Which climber has gotten the farthest? _____

2. If the total climb is 5,000 feet, has any climber reached the top? _____

Name _____

GOAL OR NOT?

Some of the attempts the Bay City Blues soccer players make to score a goal end up being only attempts. Other attempts end up with a goal! Read the graph to find out how many of the attempts are successful. Use the information on the graph to answer the questions.

1. Tess scored goals on what percent of her attempts? _____% How many goals did she make? _____

2. Who scored the most goals for the season? _____ Who was next? _____

3. What was the difference between the number of Patti's attempts and the number of her goals? _____

4. What was the total number of goals the Blues scored for the season? _____

5. Who made the least goals for the season? _____ How many goals did she make? _____

6. What was the total number of attempts for the season? _____

7. Write a fraction that shows the total goals compared to the total attempts for the team. _____

8. Who scored on $\frac{9}{10}$ of her attempts? _____

9. What fraction shows the ratio of Carla's goals to her attempts? _____

10. Who made $\frac{2}{19}$ of the total goals? _____

11. Which players made over 50% of the goals they attempted?

    _____

    _____

12. Which two players together made exactly 50% of the total goals for the season?

    _____

    _____

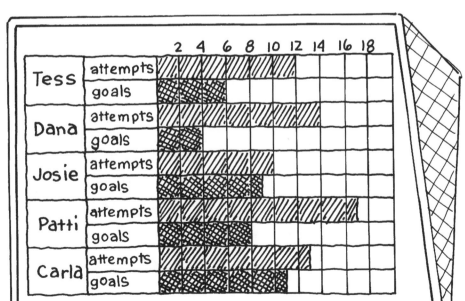

JUST IN CASE

Just in case anyone has wondered about Mochaville Middle School's athletic abilities, the proof of their excellence can be found in the school trophy case. Just step into the lobby of the gym and take a look. Look closely at these trophies! Each one holds a measurement. Several pairs of trophies have measurements that stand for the same amount. Choose 10 different colors of markers or crayons. Color the pairs of matching measurements with the same color.

1. 5,280 feet
2. 20 qt
3. 54 in.
4. 108 in.
5. 3 yd
6. 4 cups
7. 3½ lb
8. 1½ tons
9. 56 oz
10. 3,000 lb
11. 1½ yd
12. 2 pints
13. 8 cups
14. 80 pints
15. 1 mile
16. 2 quarts
17. 5 gal
18. 4 yards
19. 12 feet
20. 10 gal

Name

AMAZING FEET

Athletes do amazing things with their feet, and they wear all kinds of interesting footwear while they do these feats. Find the length (in centimeters) of each of these feet (in the shoes or other coverings they wear for their sport). Measure carefully, and pay attention to this scale: 1 centimeter in the picture = 6 centimeters on the real footwear.

Write your answer next to each picture.

$\overline{1 \text{ cm}} = 6 \text{ cm}$

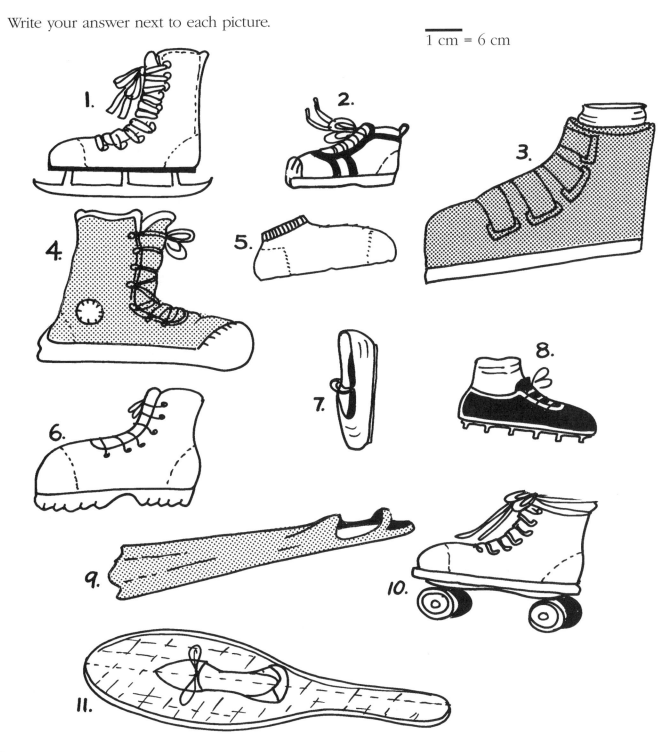

Name _____

BRUNO'S BURLY BREW

Big Bruno makes energy shakes for all his weight-lifting pals. One batch makes enough for 4 big weight lifters. Follow the directions to change the recipe for different groups of his friends. (You'll have to multiply some fractions and mixed numerals to do this.)

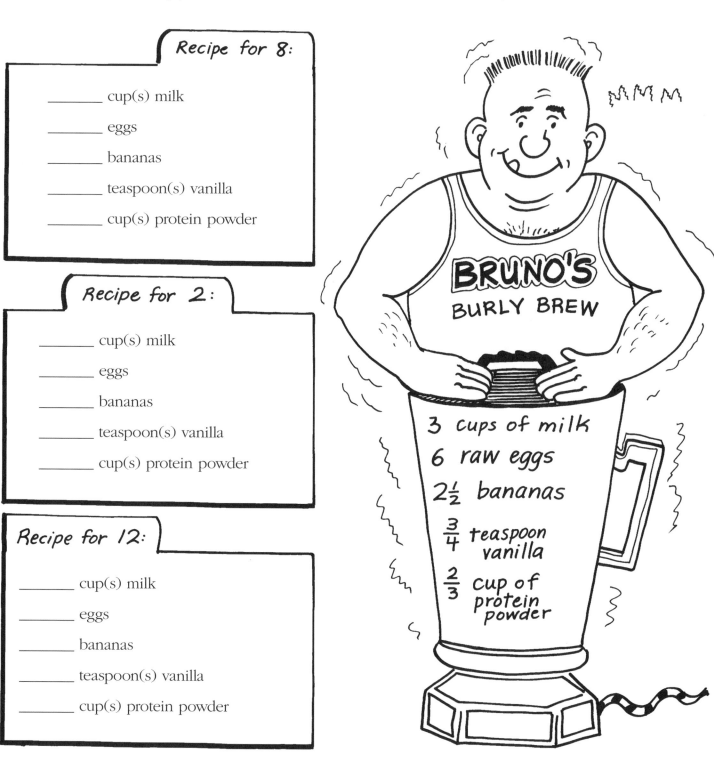

Recipe for 8:

_____ cup(s) milk

_____ eggs

_____ bananas

_____ teaspoon(s) vanilla

_____ cup(s) protein powder

Recipe for 2:

_____ cup(s) milk

_____ eggs

_____ bananas

_____ teaspoon(s) vanilla

_____ cup(s) protein powder

Recipe for 12:

_____ cup(s) milk

_____ eggs

_____ bananas

_____ teaspoon(s) vanilla

_____ cup(s) protein powder

3 cups of milk

6 raw eggs

$2\frac{1}{2}$ bananas

$\frac{3}{4}$ teaspoon vanilla

$\frac{2}{3}$ cup of protein powder

Name _____

"FIGURING" OUT DECIMALS

Tamara is working on perfecting her figures for a skating competition. They must be precise for the judges. Numbers with decimals can be tricky, too. You can practice decimals by finding the decimal number in Jenny's figure 8 that matches the problem. Circle each one with the correct color.

_____ 1. one-tenth more than 7 RED

_____ 2. five-hundredths more than 6.3 BLUE

_____ 3. the difference between 10.8 and 10.2 PINK

_____ 4. one hundred plus twelve-hundredths BLACK

_____ 5. 3 tenths more than 6 hundredths YELLOW

_____ 6. 0.05 plus 0.04 PURPLE

_____ 7. 9 tenths less than ten TAN

_____ 8. two-tenths more than 14 ORANGE

_____ 9. 5 hundredths more than 2 BROWN

_____ 10. one-tenth less than one TAN

_____ 11. two-tenths plus four-hundredths SILVER

_____ 12. 9 tenths plus 9 hundredths GREEN

_____ 13. ten plus twelve-hundredths RED

_____ 14. eight-hundredths more than eight BLUE

_____ 15. one-tenth less than ten GREEN

_____ 16. two-tenths less than nine PINK

_____ 17. ten less than 12.4 PURPLE

_____ 18. 0.004 more than 0.005 RED

_____ 19. ten less than 10.22 ORANGE

_____ 20. 0.6 more than three YELLOW

_____ 21. two-tenths more than 0.3 BLUE

_____ 22. 5 tenths less than fifty-one GREEN

_____ 23. five-tenths less than 21 SILVER

_____ 24. one hundred plus two-tenths PURPLE

Name _____

WHERE'S THE FOOD?

After the volleyball tournament, the team is hungry. The girls have all ordered the food they want, but they're wondering what's taking so long! Meanwhile, the coach is wondering just how much this is all going to cost. Find the total cost for each player.

EAT AT THE

MENU TREE

Tacos .... 80¢
Burritos .... 99¢
Hot Dogs $1.50
Hamburgers ... $1.75
Pizza Slice $1.25
Sandwiches ... $1.90
Rice Bowl $1.00
Fries .... 95¢
Salad $1.10
Chips .... 50¢
Shakes $1.50
Drinks .... 99¢
Ice Cream ...... 95¢
Candy .... 45¢

Annie Ace
salad
burrito
choc. shake
2 tacos
TOTAL

Movin' Marika
fries
hamburger
3 candy bars
van. shake
TOTAL

Daring Donna
fries
salad
sandwich
choc. shake
TOTAL

Suzie Spiker
2 pizzas
drink
chips
ice cream
TOTAL

Jumpin' Julie
2 fries
3 hot dogs
choc. shake
pizza
TOTAL

Colleen Cool
salad
rice bowl
pizza
drink
TOTAL

Towering Tara
pizza
salad
hamburger
drink
ice cream
TOTAL

No-Foul Fran
hot dog
3 burritos
fries
van. shake
3 candy bars
TOTAL

Sally Smasher
salad
2 fries
van. shake
candy
TOTAL

Nellie Net
2 chips
rice bowl
taco
sandwich
TOTAL

Sara Server
3 hot dogs
pizza
choc. shake
taco
TOTAL

Power Pam
2 chips
2 tacos
3 candy bars
choc. shake
TOTAL

Name _____

BUMPS, BRUISES, & BREAKS

The Blue Berg Hockey Team never makes it through a game without some injuries. It looks as if Bruiser is out of the game for a while! Help the team solve some of their injury problems by deciding what operation is needed for each one. (Some may need more than one.) Write **A** (add), **S** (subtract), **M** (multiply), or **D** (divide) next to each problem. Then use a separate piece of paper to find the answers.

_____ 1. The cost of hospital trips for the Blue Bergs averages $125,000 a season. If the season is five months long, what is the average monthly hospital cost for the season? _____

_____ 2. The Blue Bergs had a total of 396 teeth intact when they started the season. They lost 45 of them. How many teeth did the team have left at the end of the season? _____

_____ 3. Pierre, the goalie, lost an average of 27 minutes per game because of bloody noses. How many games did he play in if he lost 135 minutes total for his nosebleeds? _____

_____ 4. Each defensive player bumped his shins and bruised his nose a total of 26 times in each game period. There are 3 game periods and 2 defensive players. At this rate, how many bumps and bruises will they get in the entire game? _____

_____ 5. In one season, 12 of the 130 total injuries were broken bones and torn ligaments, 53 were broken or lost teeth, and 30 were black eyes. The rest were bumps and bruises. How many were bumps and bruises? _____

_____ 6. Two team members got food poisoning the morning of the big game. Twice that many had colds and couldn't play. Three more were on crutches. If there are 18 players on the team, how many were left to play the game? _____

_____ 7. During one game, a referee called minor penalties on Big Bruno and Biffo for roughing. Five more players got minor penalties for tripping and 3 more for high sticking. If a minor penalty is 2 minutes in the penalty box, how many total minutes did the team spend in the penalty box during the game? _____

_____ 8. In one game alone, there were these injuries: one player had a hockey stick broken over his head, two guys got in a bloody fist fight, and five more got cut by skates to the cheek. All of them had to take time out from the game. How many players got called off the ice for injuries? _____

Name _____

BEACH BAG JUMBLE

When Megan returned from her swimming workout in the ocean, she dumped her beach bag on the blanket and settled down for a snack. Find the perimeter (**P**), area (**A**), or volume (**V**) for each of the items that were in her bag. Choose the right formula to find each answer.

Perimeter = sum of all sides

Area of triangle = $\frac{1}{2}$ b x h

Area of circle = π x r^2

Volume of cylinder = π x r^{2}x h

Circumference of circle = π x d

Area of rectangle = l x w

Volume of cube = s x s x s

Volume of rectangular prism = l x w x h

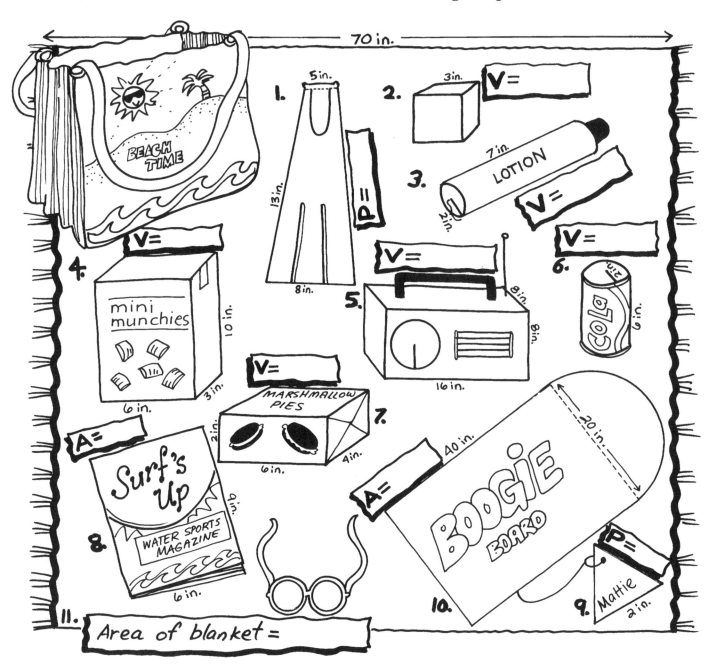

Name

DIAMONDS, RINGS, & COURTS

Athletes do plenty of running around, swimming, shooting across, or working with big surfaces. What area is covered by their sport? Choose the right formula from the center to find the area of each sports surface shown in the pictures. Write each answer in square units on the line.

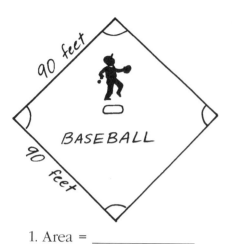

90 feet

90 feet

BASEBALL

1. Area = _____

TENNIS

36 feet

78 feet

2. Area = _____

BOXING

16 feet

16 feet

3. Area = _____

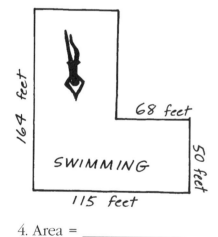

164 feet

68 feet

50 feet

SWIMMING

115 feet

4. Area = _____

FORMULAS FOR AREA

square $A = s \times s$

rectangle $A = l \times w$

circle $A = \pi \times r^2$

triangle $A = \frac{1}{2} b \times h$

trapezoid $A = h \times \frac{a+b}{2}$

ARCHERY

75 feet

15 feet

5. Area = ___ _____

WRESTLING

12 feet

6. Area = _____

TRACK

200 feet

600 feet

7. Area = _____

18 feet

3 feet

12 feet

SAILING

8 feet

8. Area = _____

Name _____

HANG TEN PERCENT

The surf's up at Shark Beach! One hundred surfers showed up on Saturday to "hang ten" for the awesome waves. If a surfer is "hanging ten percent"—what would that mean? See if you can figure it out!

Choose the correct percentage from the waves below to match the fraction in each problem. Write the answer on the line. Some answers may be used more than once.

Remember: To write a fraction as a percent, you have to write an equivalent fraction with a denominator of 100. For example: $\frac{1}{5} = \frac{20}{100} = 20\%$!

____% 1. $\frac{3}{4}$ of the surfers fell off their boards.

____% 2. $\frac{1}{10}$ can hang ten.

____% 3. $\frac{1}{5}$ forgot their sunscreen.

____% 4. $\frac{9}{10}$ are afraid of sharks.

____% 5. $\frac{1}{4}$ wear sunglasses at all times.

____% 6. $\frac{8}{10}$ wax their own boards.

____% 7. $\frac{1}{2}$ have been stung by jellyfish.

____% 8. $\frac{4}{10}$ have sand in their swimsuits.

____% 9. $\frac{1}{20}$ have never seen a shark.

____% 10. $\frac{6}{20}$ saw a shark today.

____% 11. $\frac{55}{100}$ have had surfing injuries.

____% 12. $\frac{3}{20}$ are very sunburned.

____% 13. $\frac{27}{30}$ learned to surf very young.

____% 14. $\frac{9}{12}$ forgot to eat breakfast.

____% 15. $\frac{10}{100}$ are over 50 years old.

____% 16. $\frac{4}{16}$ did not fall today.

____% 17. $\frac{3}{10}$ never had a surfing lesson.

____% 18. $\frac{2}{5}$ got smashed by the last wave.

____% 19. $\frac{4}{5}$ are high school students.

____% 20. $\frac{11}{22}$ have on wet suits today.

90% **75%** **50%** **25%** **5%** **150%** **80%** **10%** **30%** **20%** **55%** **40%**

Name _____

"BUT COACH, CAN WE REST NOW?"

What are the coaches cooking up now? They are probably trying to figure out ways to keep their players working, improving, and winning. Here are some of the statistics the coaches must consider. Help them use percentages to find the numbers they need.

To find 30% of 80, move the decimal 2 places to the left and multiply: 0.30 x 80 = 24.0 or 24.

Find the number that represents each percentage.

_____ 1. Of the 20 players on Coach Jammin's team, 40% can dunk.

_____ 2. Rob swam 60% of the 120 laps that Coach Samantha Swimm asked for him to do.

_____ 3. Coach Strikeout ordered 20 new ball caps for his team. Only 5% arrived on time.

_____ 4. There were 360 runners at Coach Swift's home meet, but only 15% ran the hurdles.

_____ 5. Coach Wrencher's wrestlers won 75% of their 24 matches.

_____ 6. Only 10% of the 30 wrestlers want Coach Wrencher's bulldog Daisy to be the team mascot.

_____ 7. Coach P. J. Puck's hockey team traveled 1,200 miles last year, and 80% of the travel was on the team bus.

_____ 8. Coach Vicki Volley was not happy when 80% of the 30 players threw their towels on the locker room floor.

_____ 9. When Coach George T. Down invited his 80 football players to dinner, 90% of them ate the pizza he served.

_____ 10. By the end of the season, 15% of Coach Marcy Mogul's 60 skiers were injured.

Name _____

TIME OUT

The Cramville basketball team is crammed into their bus for the big game. It is a long ride to Eagleton, and the Cramville Comets are having some unexpected stops along the way. Solve these problems about their trip.

_____ 1. The team left Cramville at 8:00 A.M. They stopped for gas at 9:05 A.M. How long were they on the road before stopping?

_____ 2. They got stuck in the mud at the gas station, so their gas stop ended up being 45 minutes. What time did they get underway again?

_____ 3. Oops! A flat tire at 10:50 A.M. took them 20 minutes to change. What time was it when they got back on the road?

_____ 4. Just 90 minutes later, they hit a terrible snowstorm that stopped them for another hour. What time did they start moving again?

_____ 5. The van stopped for a snack and restroom break at 2:55 P.M. They headed toward Eagleton again at 3:15 P.M. How long was their stop?

_____ 6. An accident backed up traffic for miles. They stopped at 4:10 P.M. and didn't move again for 55 minutes. What time was it when they got moving again?

_____ 7. At 5:50 P.M., they were held up again! This time a fierce windstorm had knocked trees down across the road. The road was cleared at 6:20 P.M. How long did they wait?

_____ 8. Everyone was starved for dinner. Their hour-long dinner stop ended at 8:35 P.M. When did they stop for dinner?

_____ 9. Two hours and twenty minutes after their dinner stop ended, the Comets finally arrived at their motel in Eagleton. What time did they arrive?

_____ 10. The trip was expected to take 6 hours. How much longer than that did it take?

Name

RACK UP THE SAVINGS

When athletes shop for sports clothing, they need to have some good math skills to figure out their costs. Taxes add to the cost of the clothing. Discounts lower the prices. Solve these problems for the shoppers. (Round prices to the nearest penny.)

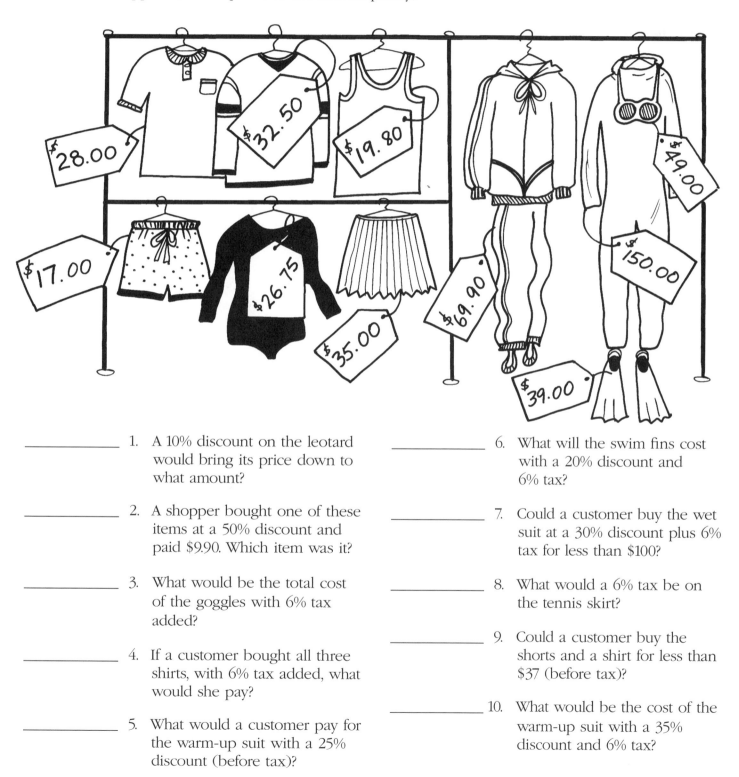

_____ 1. A 10% discount on the leotard would bring its price down to what amount?

_____ 2. A shopper bought one of these items at a 50% discount and paid $9.90. Which item was it?

_____ 3. What would be the total cost of the goggles with 6% tax added?

_____ 4. If a customer bought all three shirts, with 6% tax added, what would she pay?

_____ 5. What would a customer pay for the warm-up suit with a 25% discount (before tax)?

_____ 6. What will the swim fins cost with a 20% discount and 6% tax?

_____ 7. Could a customer buy the wet suit at a 30% discount plus 6% tax for less than $100?

_____ 8. What would a 6% tax be on the tennis skirt?

_____ 9. Could a customer buy the shorts and a shirt for less than $37 (before tax)?

_____ 10. What would be the cost of the warm-up suit with a 35% discount and 6% tax?

Name _____

CHILL OUT

Athletes drink lots of refreshing drinks, use plenty of towels, and get many uniforms dirty. You won't need to know an exact answer for these problems about their drinks, towels, and uniforms. Sometimes a close answer is just fine! Practice your estimation skills by circling the closest answer.

1. Each kid on the track team drinks about $2\frac{1}{2}$ gallons of water at each meet. There are 12 on the team. How much water do they drink each meet?

    10 gal   50 gal   30 gal   24 gal

2. There are eight tug-of-war teams with 10 or 11 on each team. They each use 2 towels apiece. About how many towels will they use?

    11   110   160   800

3. Each drinking cup at the snack shack gets filled with about $\frac{1}{4}$ cup of ice. On Sunday, 20 cups of ice were used. How many drinking cups were used?

    4   80   120   40

4. After the game, half of the football team uses 2 sticks of deodorant each. The other half uses 1 stick each. There are usually about 25 team members at a game. How much deodorant do they need?

    40 sticks   400 sticks
    4,000 sticks   100 sticks

5. A 5-gallon jug of SLAM Sports Drink serves about 30 thirsty kids. If 88 kids show up at Field Day, how many jugs will be needed?

    30   50   3   300

6. Three kids on the relay team made T-shirts to replace the worn-out shirts for their team. They bought the shirts for $3 and sold them for $5.95. If they bought 30 shirts and sold them all, about how much money did they make?

    $900 $190 $90 $180

7. The coach found 3 lockers full of smelly socks at the end of the season. He counted 23 pairs in one locker. If the others had about the same, how many pairs would he need to wash?

    75 pairs   50 pairs
    90 pairs   150 pairs

8. If seven runners each wear out about four pairs of $90 shoes a year, how much will they spend on shoes (total of all 4)?

    $2,800 $560 $360 $800

9. Mothers of the soccer players wash the uniforms 3 times a week. How many washings will take place for 22 players over a 10-week season?

    220   66   660   6,600

Name

FANTASTIC FINISHES

Who finished first? Pictures, diagrams, or models can help you figure out which runner is the winner in problem #1. For problems 2–5, draw a picture or diagram to help you figure out who finished first in each of these races.

1. Toby crossed the finish line ahead of Tony but behind Timothy. Terence and Tiny finished ahead of Timothy. Tiny was 3 places ahead of Toby. Label the runners in the picture.

2. In a softball throwing competition, the Frequent Fliers threw farther than the Airborne Aces, but not as far as the Iron Arms. The Speed Demons threw farther than the Airborne Aces, but not as far as the Frequent Fliers. Who won first place?

3. In the volleyball tournament, the Pacers won more games than the Panthers but fewer than the Grizzlies. The Panthers won more games than the Giants. Who came in first?

4. Skateboarder Sam finished his race ahead of Sara who finished behind Suzie and Stuart. Serena finished 4 places ahead of Sara. Who finished first?

5. Runner Thomas finished ahead of James and behind Ramon. Andrew finished behind James. Michael came in ahead of Andrew but behind James. Who came in first?

Name

CRISS-CROSS BIKE RACE

In this bicycle race, each cyclist will follow a different path. The four paths will cross each other many times. Start with biker #1. Using mental math, do the operation on the first flag. (Add 7 and 1.) Draw a path to the circle that has that answer. Then take that answer and do the operation shown on its flag. Draw the path to the next circle. Keep drawing the path until the cyclist arrives at a trophy.

Go back and draw the paths for the other three cyclists the same way. Use a different color to draw each path. Always pay attention to what the flags tell you to do with the numbers!

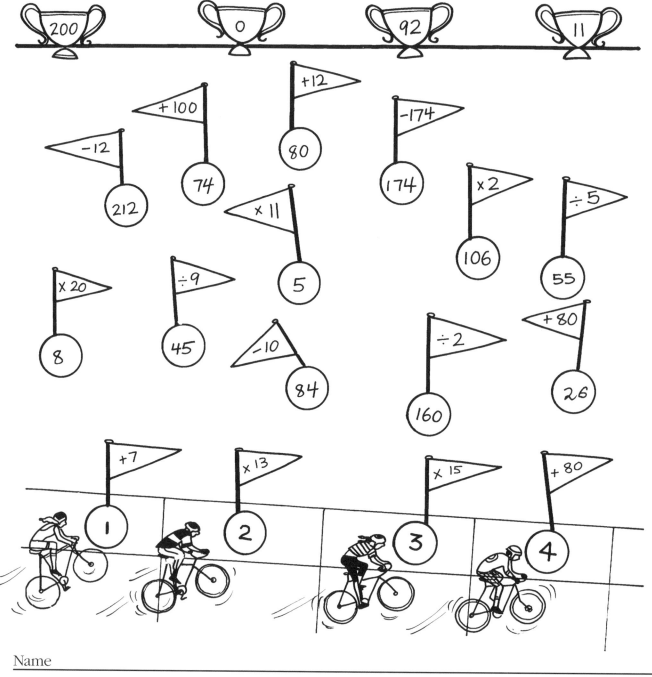

Name _____

HITTING THE BRICKS

If you're going to learn to break bricks with your hand, you will have to practice a few times (or more) before you get it right! Sometimes you might not get it quite right. **Trial and Error** is one strategy for problem solving. Here's how it works: You choose an answer you think might work and try it out. If it doesn't fit, keep trying until you find one that works!

Lee is getting ready for a karate demonstration at his dojo next week. Each day he breaks a different number of bricks to get ready. By thinking about the clues, find the number he breaks each day.

SUNDAY

An even 2-digit number
Larger than 6 but smaller than 12

_____

MONDAY

Multiple of 40
Greater than 100
Less than 600
No digits of 1, 2, 3, 6, or 8
Only one 0

_____

TUESDAY

A 2-digit multiple of 7
Less than 50
Greater than 20
An even number
No digits over 5

_____

WEDNESDAY

An even 2-digit number
Multiple of 3
Digits add up to 6
Over 16
Less than 30

THURSDAY

An odd number less than 99
Two digits
Divisible by 25

FRIDAY

Even number between 50 and 150

Digits total 1

_____

SATURDAY

An even number between 50 and 70
Digits total 11

Digits are in order (small to large)

_____

Name _____

LOCKER ROOM LOGIC

Coach Crunch has been looking all day for the tennis player who left a Gorgonzola cheese in her locker. It's leaking out and getting pretty stinky. Whose locker is this? The players whose lockers are in this area are Chrissy, Cathy, Carla, Camille, and Cass. Use the clues and logical thinking to figure out who is the owner of the stinky locker.

1. Cass's locker is next to Camille's.

2. Camille's locker is #20.

3. The cheese is not in Cathy's locker.

4. Carla's locker number is 10 less than Chrissy's.

5. Cathy's locker is next to Chrissy's.

The cheese is in _____'s locker.

Just after the Coach Crunch settled the cheese problem, he found out that someone could not open their locker. The coach needs your help again to find the owner of Locker #46. The locker list shows these names: Randy, Reed, R.J., Rick, and Ray.

1. Ray's and Randy's lockers are not together.

2. Randy's locker is on one end.

3. Reed's locker has the highest number.

4. Rich's locker is next to Reed's.

_____ could not open his locker.

Name _____

LOGICAL LINEUP

Finally, the Bigtown Bears are in the playoffs. The ticket line has been growing since early morning. Solve the problems about the lineup by looking at the pictures and using logical thinking.

Problem 1: Jamie forgot the money, but hasn't discovered it yet. Figure out which one is Jamie. Circle Jamie.

1. Jamie is in front of a person with curly hair.

2. Jess is in front of Jamie, but behind Moe.

3. Moe is first in line.

4. Lee is last in line.

5. There are two people between Jamie and Moe.

Problem 2: Two of these fans will get seats in the front row. Put a box around each of them.

1. Neither of them is first in line.

2. Neither wears glasses.

3. One of them is in the last half of the line.

4. Neither of them is a Bear's fan.

Name

GRIDIRON SOLUTIONS

A gridiron is another name for a football field. The aim of a football game is to score more points than the other team by crossing the opponent's goal line with the ball. Points are scored in many ways. The chart under the goalpost below shows the ways to score points. Notice that extra points with kicks, runs, or passes can only occur after a touchdown!

If the Grizzlies scored 30 points in a game, they might have collected these points in a few different ways. Here are a few:

5 TD = 30 points	4 TD + 3 XK + 1 FG = 30 points
10 FG = 30 points	3 FG + 3 TD + 1 XRP + 1 XK = 30 points
3 TD + 3 XK + 3 FG = 30 points	1 S + 3 TD + 2 XRP + 2 FG = 30 points

TD = touchdown = 6 points

XK = (kick) extra point after touchdown = 1 point

XRP = (run or pass) extra point after touchdown = 2 points

FG = field goal = 3 points

S = safety = 2 points

OOOF

Write 3 or more equations to show how the Grizzlies might have scored their points in each game described.

1. The first game of the season ended with a 16 to 16 tie.

   _____

   _____

   _____

2. The Grizzlies won the second game 49 to 18.

   _____

   _____

   _____

Use with page 231.

Name _____

GRIDIRON SOLUTIONS, cont.

Write 3 or more different equations to show how the Grizzlies might have scored their points in each game described.

3. In the game against the Cougars, the toughest game of the season, the Grizzlies scored 37 points.

    _____

    _____

    _____

4. Oh, oh! The only loss of the season came to the Vikings. The Grizzlies lost in a close one: 21 to 20.

    _____

    _____

    _____

5. The homecoming game was a great victory. The Grizzlies won 56 to 18.

    _____

    _____

    _____

6. The final game of the season ended in another tie. The score was 29 to 29.

    _____

    _____

    _____

Use with page 230.

Name

JUST HANGING AROUND

STRATEGIES
- Trial and Error
- Write an Equation
- Draw a Diagram
- Make a Chart
- Make a Graph
- Use Mental Math
- Use a Formula
- Estimate

Gymnasts hang around the gym a lot. They practice for hours and plan strategies for winning at their sport. For every one of these problems about gymnasts, choose the strategy that you think would best help you find the answer. Then use that strategy to solve the problem.

1. The rings are suspended 98 in. from the floor. Is this about 8 ft? _____
    a. draw a diagram
    b. use mental math
    c. write an equation

2. The gymnasts are lined up at the drinking fountain. Fred is 2 people behind Ned. Ned is 3 people in front of Ted. Ed is just behind Ned. Who is last in line?

    _____

    a. write an equation
    b. draw a diagram
    c. trial and error

3. There are 6 events in men's gymnastics. If the judges each score only 1 event, and each event has 5 judges, how many judges will there be? _____
    a. use mental math
    b. write an equation
    c. make a graph

4. The bleachers in the gym are 22 ft long. How many people can sit in a row if each person takes up about 2 ft of space?

    _____

    a. make a chart
    b. estimate
    c. use a formula

5. The coach added up the number of gymnasts he has coached in each of the last 6 years. The numbers were 13, 10, 20, 7, 8, and 8. What is the total number he has coached? _____
    a. use mental math
    b. make a chart
    c. make a graph

6. The mat on which Scott will do his floor routine is 12 meters by 12 meters. What is the area of the mat? _____
    a. trial and error
    b. use a formula
    c. write an equation

Name _____

PRACTICE MAKES PERFECT

Gymnasts practice for hours. These hours add up to weeks, months, and even years! Practice your problem-solving skills by choosing strategies to solve these problems about the gymnasts and their sport. Choose the strategy you think is best for each problem and find the answer if possible.

STRATEGIES
- Trial and Error
- Write an Equation
- Draw a Diagram
- Make a Chart
- Make a Graph
- Use Mental Math
- Use a Formula
- Estimate

1. Terry's balance beam routine includes a walkover into a somersault. The walkover takes about 5 feet to execute, and the somersault takes about twice that. Can she do both on the 16.5-foot beam?

   _____

2. The floor exercise area is a 40-foot square. If Terry's routine takes her across and back 6 complete times, how many feet will she travel?

   _____

3. At the State meet, the Flips earned 123 points. The Stars earned 63 less, while the Swoop won with three times what the Stars earned. What was the Swoop's score?

   _____

4. The High School meet started at 2:30 P.M. The 4 events each took $\frac{1}{2}$ hour with a ten-minute break after each and a $\frac{1}{2}$-hour awards ceremony at the end. What time was the meet over?

   _____

5. Lucy fell off the beam fewer times than Jana. Jana fell less than Terri but more than Pasha. Terri fell more than Raina, and Raina fell more than Jana. Pasha fell more than Lucy. Who fell the least of all?

   _____

6. Three gymnasts are each 6 years apart in ages. The total of their ages is 33. What are their ages?

   _____

Name _____

SUBMERGED SOLUTIONS

Often when you solve a problem, all that shows on paper is the answer. The way that you solved the problem is not shown. It is submerged in your mind, but no one else can see it. Sometimes, you don't even stop to think about what you **did** to solve the problem.

When you solve these underwater problems (on pages 234 and 235), pay attention to how you go about getting the answer. Solve each problem, write your answer, and then explain how you found the solution. You may draw diagrams or pictures as a part of your explanation.

1. A school of barracudas swam past Samantha. She saw twice as many lobsters as barracudas, and three more angelfish than lobsters. She saw 25 angelfish. How many barracudas did she see?

   _____

   How did you solve this problem?

   _____

   _____

   _____

   _____

2. Scuba diver Samantha got to the sunken ship before Seth, but not before Tabitha and Josiah. Dara got to the ship before Josiah, but after Tabitha. Who got to the ship last?

   _____

   How did you solve this problem?

   _____

   _____

   _____

   _____

Use with page 235.

Name _____

3. Josiah spent $280 on new scuba gear. Then he bought a new underwater camera for $112 and an underwater watch for $56. Since he made some money from the sale of his old gear, he only had to come up with $362 for the new gear. How much did he get from the sale of the old gear?

_____

How did you solve this problem?

_____

_____

4. The divers fed the fish half of the food in a cube-shaped container. Each side of the cube measured 12 inches. If the container was full to start with, what is the volume of food given to the fish?

_____

How did you solve this problem?

_____

_____

Challenge!

5. Tabitha and Dara have been diving a number of years that is half of the age of Dara. Dara is 3 years older than Tabitha. The total of their ages is 33.
How old is Tabitha? _____ How old is Dara? _____

How long have they been diving? _____

How did you solve this problem?

_____

_____

_____

_____

Use with page 234.

Name _____

HITTING THEIR STRIDE

Speed skaters need to get into a rhythm of the right stride in order to achieve their fastest possible time. See how accurate you can be in checking out the answers to these problems. If the answer to a problem is correct, color the matching section on the speed skating track.

1. Skating time of $\frac{3}{4}$ hour = 75 minutes

2. 3 races of 1500 m each = 4500 m

3. 2 feet = 0.2 of 10 feet

4. 200 m = 0.2 of 1000 m race

5. 14 hours = 140 minutes

6. $\frac{1}{2}$ of $\frac{1}{4} = \frac{1}{4}$

7. 9% of 90 = 10

8. $\frac{1}{3}$ is equivalent to $\frac{3}{9}$.

9. The formula for a perimeter of a triangle is s + s + s.

10. $\frac{5}{50}$, 10%, $\frac{1}{10}$, and 0.1 all mean the same amount.

11. 9 minutes 1 second minus 2 minutes 50 seconds is 7 minutes 51 seconds

12. The difference between −14° and +74° is 60°

13. 40% = 0.4 = $\frac{4}{10}$ = $\frac{2}{5}$

14. 0.2 seconds x 0.4 seconds = 0.008 seconds

15. Eight speed skaters ate 1.5 lb of pasta each. This totals 12 lb of pasta.

16. One hundred times one thousand is one million.

Name

ATHLETES ON PARADE

The Olympic Games begin with a parade of all the athletes who will compete in the games. In the 1996 Summer Olympic Games in Atlanta, Georgia, 10,300 athletes came from 197 countries to compete for 17 days. Hundreds of medals were given out, millions of dollars were spent, thousands of visitors attended, and billions more watched on TV. In 1998, it started all over again when 3,200 athletes from 70 nations traveled to Nagano, Japan, for the Winter Olympics.

Write the words that match the numbers for these Olympic facts.

1. There were 10,300 athletes competing in Atlanta.

   _____

2. The Atlanta Olympics cost 1,600,000,000 dollars.

   _____

3. About 2,000,000 people came to Atlanta to watch the 1996 Summer Olympics.

   _____

4. In 1896, there were about 40,000 spectators in Athens, Greece, for the first of the modern
   Olympic Games. _____

5. There were over 3,000 hours of live TV coverage of Olympic events in Atlanta.

   _____

6. The television rights for the Barcelona Summer Games in 1992 were sold for 40,100,000

   dollars. _____

7. At the Summer Olympics in Atlanta in 1996, 1,929 medals were handed out.

   _____

8. The Olympic Stadium in Atlanta held 85,000 spectators.

   _____

9. About 7,137 athletes participated in the 1988, 1992, 1994, and 1998 Winter Olympics.

   _____

10. The city of Nagano, Japan, has a population of 350,000.

   _____

Use with page 238.

Name _____

ATHLETES ON PARADE, CONT.

Write the numbers that match the words for these Olympic facts.

_____ 11. Thirty-five billion people watched the Atlanta Olympics on TV.

_____ 12. In 1992, ninety-five thousand spectators in Barcelona, Spain watched the Spanish soccer team win for the first time in the Olympics.

_____ 13. Four thousand one hundred and four athletes participated in the Summer Olympic Games in London in 1948.

_____ 14. The Reebok company spent thirty million dollars on an ad campaign to show the two Daves (Dave O'Brien and Dave Johnson) competing to win the decathlon, but Dave O'Brien failed to make the U.S. team!

_____ 15. Nine thousand three hundred fifty-six athletes participated in the Summer Olympic Games in Barcelona in 1992.

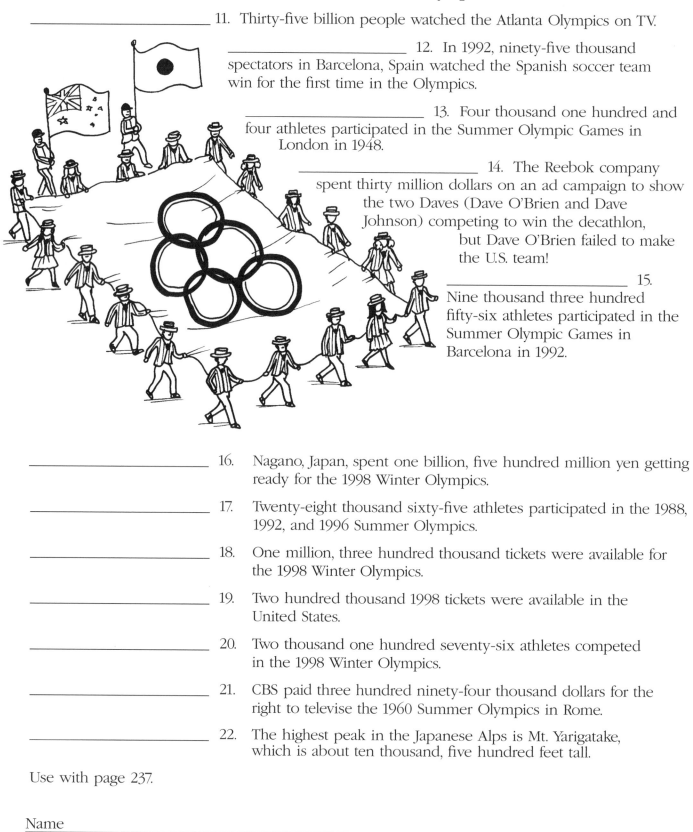

_____ 16. Nagano, Japan, spent one billion, five hundred million yen getting ready for the 1998 Winter Olympics.

_____ 17. Twenty-eight thousand sixty-five athletes participated in the 1988, 1992, and 1996 Summer Olympics.

_____ 18. One million, three hundred thousand tickets were available for the 1998 Winter Olympics.

_____ 19. Two hundred thousand 1998 tickets were available in the United States.

_____ 20. Two thousand one hundred seventy-six athletes competed in the 1998 Winter Olympics.

_____ 21. CBS paid three hundred ninety-four thousand dollars for the right to televise the 1960 Summer Olympics in Rome.

_____ 22. The highest peak in the Japanese Alps is Mt. Yarigatake, which is about ten thousand, five hundred feet tall.

Use with page 237.

Name _____

EN GUARD!

Fencing was one of the events at the first Modern Olympic Games in 1896, but it began around 4000 B.C. Fencers use various types of swords: the foil, which weighs about 500 grams; the épée, which weighs 770 grams; and the sabre, which weighs 500 grams. When the director of the bout calls "en guard," the competitors take a ready position. They begin the "bout" when the director gives the "fence" command.

Try your skill in this bout
with addition and subtraction.

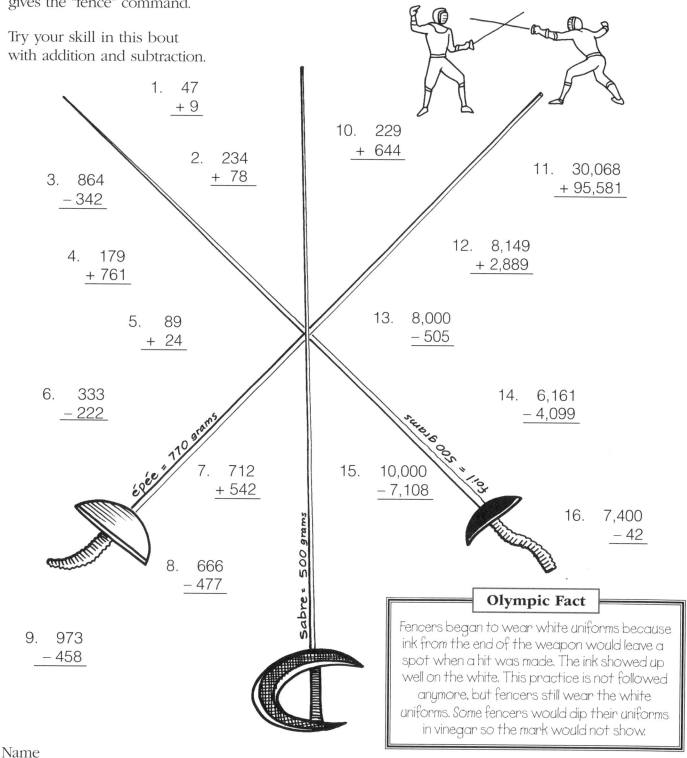

1. 47
   + 9

2. 234
   + 78

3. 864
   – 342

4. 179
   + 761

5. 89
   + 24

6. 333
   – 222

7. 712
   + 542

8. 666
   – 477

9. 973
   – 458

10. 229
    + 644

11. 30,068
    + 95,581

12. 8,149
    + 2,889

13. 8,000
    – 505

14. 6,161
    – 4,099

15. 10,000
    – 7,108

16. 7,400
    – 42

épée = 770 grams

foil = 500 grams

sabre = 500 grams

Olympic Fact

Fencers began to wear white uniforms because ink from the end of the weapon would leave a spot when a hit was made. The ink showed up well on the white. This practice is not followed anymore, but fencers still wear the white uniforms. Some fencers would dip their uniforms in vinegar so the mark would not show.

Name

BIG WINNERS

TOP 30 MEDAL WINNERS
Olympic Summer Games
1896–1996

Country	Medals
United States	2,011
Soviet Union/ Russia	1,159
Germany	1,125
Great Britain	634
France	564
Sweden	461
Italy	445
Hungary	325
Australia	293
Finland	291
Japan	280
Romania	239
Poland	227
Canada	214
The Netherlands	188
Bulgaria	177
Switzerland	170
China	164
Czechoslovakia/ Czech Republic/ Slovakia	163
Denmark	134
Belgium	132
South Korea	126
Norway	121
Greece	111
Cuba	109
Yugoslavia	87
Austria	84
New Zealand	71
Spain	69
Turkey	59

…lern Olympic Games began in 1896, 100 years before the
… Games in Atlanta. Since then, thousands of medals have
been given to hard-working athletes. The gold medal for first
place is the most prized award! A silver medal is given for second
place, and a bronze medal is given for third place. A new design
for the medals is created for each Olympic Games. Solve the
problems below with the information from the chart of top
medal-winning countries.

1. Total medals won by the top 5 countries = _____

2. Germany's medals + Canada's = _____

3. _____ won about 3 times as many as Cuba.

4. Great Britain won _____ fewer medals than the U.S.

5. This country won 211 fewer medals than Japan. _____

6. _____ won about 4 times as many as Greece.

7. The Netherlands won _____ fewer medals than France.

8. Belgium and Denmark together won _____ medals.

9. Switzerland won _____ fewer medals than Germany.

10. The top 10 winners had a total of _____ medals.

11. Before the 1996 Olympics, Spain had a total of
    46 medals. How many did Spain win in 1996? _____

12. Before the 1996 Olympics, the United States had a total of
    1,910 medals. How many did the United States win in 1996?

    _____

Olympic Fact

The gold medal is not really made
of gold. It is made mostly of silver,
but it must contain at least six
grams of pure gold.

Name _____

EXPLOSIVE SPEEDS

People began sledding over 15,000 years ago on sleds made of a strip of animal skin stretched between two pieces of wood. Today, Olympic bobsleds are high-tech machines made for speed.

Bobsledding is thrilling to watch! A crew of two or four flies down a mile-long, curvy course at speeds of up to 90 mph. An explosive start is very important for a fast racing time.

See how fast you can find factors for these bobsleds. Write four factors for the number on the sled. Write one factor on the helmet of each crew member.

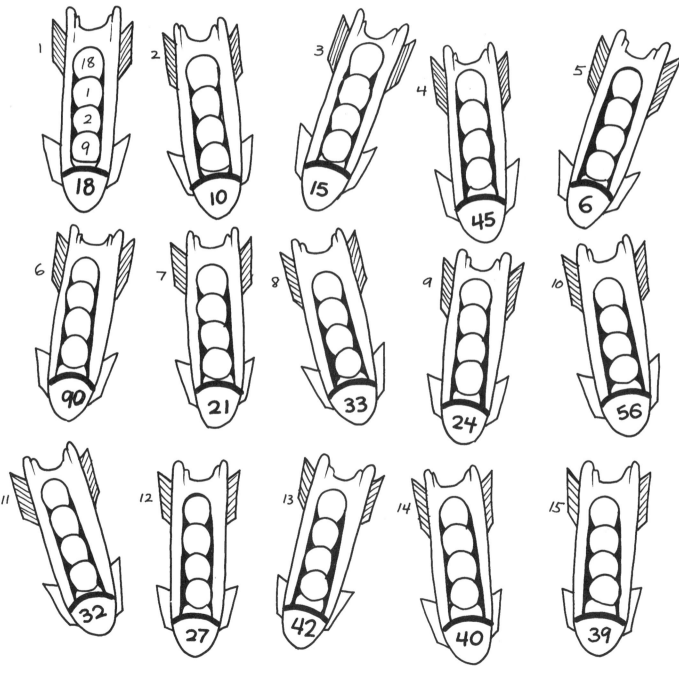

¬O BRAKES!

It is said that some of the earliest bobsleds had no brakes and were steered by a rope! The sleds were stopped in a very interesting way. Find out how by solving the puzzle below.

Write the greatest common factor for each pair of numbers. Then write the corresponding letter to your answer on the line above that answer in the puzzle at the bottom of the page. If your answers are correct, you will find out how the sleds were stopped.

1. 2 and 4 _____ R

2. 9 and 6 _____ E

3. 11 and 33 _____ T

4. 14 and 28 _____ I

5. 30 and 45 _____ V

6. 18 and 24 _____ N

7. 28 and 32 _____ D

8. 15 and 27 _____ E

9. 80 and 50 _____ A

10. 12 and 36 _____ K

11. 3 and 9 _____ E

12. 4 and 12 _____ D

13. 6 and 10 _____ R

14. 16 and 6 _____ R

15. 14 and 10 _____ R

16. 10 and 40 _____ A

17. 5 and 25 _____ G

18. 15 and 50 _____ G

19. 16 and 4 _____ D

20. 7 and 35 _____ H

21. 12 and 32 _____ D

22. 40 and 90 _____ A

23. 5 and 15 _____ G

24. 20 and 10 _____ A

25. 22 and 6 _____ R

26. 15 and 9 _____ E

27. 21 and 3 _____ E

___ ___ ___ ___ ___ ___ ___ ___ ___   ___ ___ ___ ___ ___ ___ ___
11   7   3   4   2   14 15 3   2   4   2   10 5   5   3   4

___ ___ ___ ___ ___ ___ ___   ___ ___ ___ ___   to stop the sled.
10 5   10 2   4   3   6   2   10 12 3

Name _____

MAY THE BEST SAILOR WIN

Yachting has been an Olympic sport since the 1896 games in Athens. Unfortunately, the yachting races had to be canceled at those games! The weather was just too bad. In each racing class, all the yachts must have the same design. This way, the best sailor wins the race, not the best boat!

Solve the multiplication problems in the puzzle. Use the color code to find the color for each section. If you get the answers right, the colored picture will show you one kind of yacht used in Olympic racing.

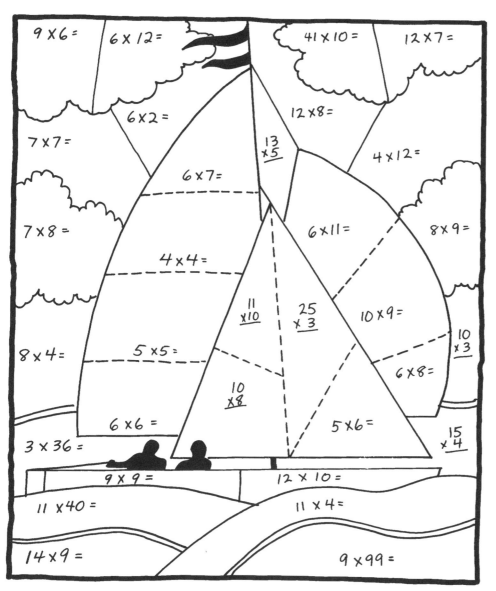

COLOR CODE

Red 66, 16	
Hot Pink 54, 56, 84, 72, 410	
Purple 42, 80	
White 25, 75	
Dark Blue 36, 440, 60, 891, 110	
Bright Green 44, 65, 90, 108, 126	

Orange 96, 49, 30	**Yellow** 12, 48, 32	**Brown** 120, 81

Olympic Fact

Competitors sail 1 race each day of the competition. The crew throws out their worst race. All the other scores are added together. The lowest score wins!

Name

 BY THE THOUSANDS

country hosts the Olympic Games, they spend many months and a lot of money getting
Most countries try to use sports arenas and areas that they already have, but many new
buildings and venues must be built for all the events and the spectators. Usually a country
builds a new Olympic Stadium. The stadium in Atlanta was built to hold 85,000 fans.

**If the 85,000 seats in Atlanta were arranged in 50 equal sections, how many seats
would there be in each section? To find the answer, you would need to divide 85,000
by 50. Use division to find the answers to these problems.**

1. Aquatic Center—swim events   14,000 seats ÷ 20 sections = _____

2. Georgia World Congress—fencing, judo   7,500 seats ÷ 25 sections = _____

3. Georgia Tech Coliseum—boxing   9,500 seats ÷ 10 sections = _____

4. Nagano's Hockey Arena—hockey   10,000 seats ÷ 50 sections = _____

5. White Ring—speed skating   7,300 seats ÷ 5 sections = _____

6. Nagano Olympic Stadium   50,000 seats ÷ 50 sections = _____

7. Atlanta Olympic Stadium   85,000 seats ÷ 50 sections = _____

8. Clark University Stadium—field hockey   5,000 seats ÷ 25 sections = _____

9. Georgia Dome—basketball   32,000 seats ÷ 8 sections = _____

10. Omni Coliseum—baseball   52,000 seats ÷ 40 sections = _____

11. $9\overline{)8,190}$ 12. $3\overline{)1,227}$ 13. $6\overline{)9,534}$ 14. $8\overline{)46,328}$

cheer   roar   hurrah   cheer

Olympic Fact

Atlanta spent $500 million on new buildings for the 1996 Olympics. The Olympic Stadium cost $209 million.

Name _____

MAKING IT OVER HURDLES

The Olympic hurdle event is a fast sprinting race with a series of barriers to jump. The hurdles are made of wood and metal, and sometimes runners knock them over as they jump. It doesn't disqualify a hurdler to knock one over, but usually it slows him or her down a little. Men and women compete in hurdle events of different lengths and with different height hurdles. (Women: 2 ft 6 in and 2 ft 9 in; Men: 3 ft and 3 ft 6 in)

Help this runner clear her hurdles by solving the problems correctly. Start with the first number, and do all the operations shown to find the final answer.

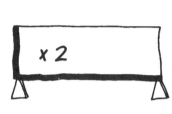

Solve these problems the same way.

1. **19** x 4 ÷ 2 + 140 – 17 = _____

2. **50** x 4 – 50 + 500 – 50 ÷ 100 = _____

3. **7,777** – 555 + 778 ÷ 4 + 2 = _____

4. **888** ÷ 4 x 3 + 111 – 222 + 333 = _____

5. **1** + 22 + 33 ÷ 2 + 2 x 30 – 900 + 1 = _____

6. **200** x 10 – 1,450 ÷ 5 + 101 – 9 = _____

7. **4,202** + 55 + 100 – 3,000 + 643 ÷ 2 = _____

8. **10,000** ÷ 10 + 1,000 x 5 – 10,000 + 1 x 10 – 10 = _____

Olympic Fact

In 1988, hurdler Gail Devers faced the biggest hurdle of her life. Due to Grave's disease, she could not walk. Doctors thought they would need to amputate her feet. Instead, she came back to win gold medals in the 100-meter sprint at the 1992 and 1996 Olympics.

Name _____

TOURIST ATTRACTIONS

Two million people attended the 1996 Olympics. They bought tickets; watched events; traveled to different venues; toured Atlanta; lived in hotels, tents, campers, and homes; and bought a lot of food and souvenirs.

Decide which operation you should use to solve each of these problems about Olympic tourists. Write the operation (add, subtract, multiply, or divide) after each problem. Then solve the problem.

Souvenirs! More souvenirs!

1. Tickets for the kayaking race cost $27. The ticket office counted $29,403 for this event. How many tickets were sold?

    Operation _____ **Answer** _____

2. If hot dogs sold for $2.00 in the Olympic Park and 986,443 hot dogs were sold, how much money was collected?

    Operation _____ **Answer** _____

3. 26,000 bus and limo drivers were hired for the Olympics. If $\frac{3}{5}$ worked every day, how many worked at one time?

    Operation _____ **Answer** _____

4. One family drove 243.33 km from their home to Atlanta for the games. They went home by a route 21.7 km longer. How long was their trip home?

    Operation _____ **Answer** _____

5. In Nagano, 10,000 people could attend a hockey game at once. Of these, $\frac{1}{5}$ had "standing room only" tickets. How many fans had to stand?

    Operation _____ **Answer** _____

6. Brielle's family bought 18 Olympic basketballs as souvenirs to take home to friends. They spent $412.20. How much did each ball cost?

    Operation _____ **Answer** _____

7. Not all sports fans can get to the Olympics, so they are televised around the world. TV rights cost $2,500,000 in 1968. In 1992, they cost 120 times that much. How much did the 1992 rights cost?

    Operation _____ **Answer** _____

8. In Nagano, tickets for good seats at the Opening Ceremony cost $350. In Atlanta, the tickets cost $636. How much did Joanna's family of 4 pay to go to both?

    Operations _____ & _____

    Answer _____

This way...

Gift Shop

Name _____

THE RIGHT PROPERTIES

Hockey players have some special properties—the equipment they need to wear on the ice. Without the right stuff, they wouldn't be able to play the game very well (or very safely)! Their equipment certainly helps them with problems on the ice.

Math operations have properties that you need to use for solving math problems. Review these properties. Then decide which ones are used in the problems below. Write the name of the property below each problem.

> Zero Property of Addition
> Zero Property of Subtraction
> Zero Property of Multiplication
> Property of One
> Opposites Property of Addition
> Commutative Property of Addition
> Commutative Property of Multiplication

1. $8 \times 4 = 32$ and $4 \times 8 = 32$

   _____

2. $8{,}633 \times 1 = 8{,}633$

   _____

3. $99 \times 0 = 0$

   _____

4. $110 \times 55 = 6{,}050$ and $55 \times 110 = 6{,}050$

   _____

5. $1 \times 99 = 99$

   _____

6. $6 \times 8 = 8 \times 6$

   _____

7. $53 + 17 = 17 + 53$

   _____

8. $666 - 0 = 666$

   _____

9. $25 + 10 = 35$ and $35 - 10 = 25$

   _____

10. $1{,}700 + 0 = 1{,}700$

    _____

11. $7{,}401 \times 15 = 15 \times 7{,}401$

    _____

12. $77 \times 0 = 0$

    _____

Name _____

WATCH THAT PUCK!

These fans are gathered for an exciting, high-speed ice hockey game. All the action in the game is focused on a little rubber disc that moves so fast that often it is hard to tell where it is and which team has it! An exciting Olympic moment for the United States was in 1980 when the U.S. team defeated Finland to win its first gold medal in 20 years.

Olympic Fact

The 1998 Winter Olympics in Japan were the first Games that permitted women to compete in ice hockey.

Pay attention to these fans to practice your fraction-hunting skills. Write a fraction to fill each blank.

1. _____ of the fans are holding balloons.

2. _____ of the fans are holding flags.

3. _____ of the flags have words on them.

4. _____ of the flags are black.

5. _____ of the flags have no words.

6. _____ of the fans are holding cups.

7. _____ of the cups have 2 straws.

8. _____ of the cups have no straws.

9. _____ of the fans are wearing boots.

10. _____ of the shoes and boots have black on them.

11. _____ of the fans are wearing earmuffs.

12. _____ of the fans are wearing hats.

13. _____ of the shoes and boots have laces.

14. _____ of the hands are wearing mittens or gloves.

15. _____ of the fans are wearing scarves.

16. _____ of the fans are hatless.

17. _____ of the hats have feathers.

18. _____ of the fans have mustaches.

19. _____ of the balloons are held by the girl with pigtails.

Name

OVER THE NET

Olympic Fact

In beach volleyball, each team has only two players. They play barefoot in the sand.

Beach volleyball began in the 1940s on the beaches of California. It was played for fun at first, but now it is a serious professional sport. It did not gain a place at the Olympic Games until 1996, when the U.S. men's teams won the gold and silver medals.

Compare each set of fractions below to see which is greater. Circle the largest fraction. If the fractions are equal, circle them both!

1. $\frac{2}{4}$ $\frac{1}{4}$

2. $\frac{5}{7}$ $\frac{3}{7}$

3. $\frac{4}{8}$ $\frac{2}{4}$

4. $\frac{2}{7}$ $\frac{1}{3}$

5. $\frac{1}{3}$ $\frac{1}{6}$

6. $\frac{5}{6}$ $\frac{1}{3}$

7. $\frac{3}{4}$ $\frac{7}{8}$

8. $\frac{2}{5}$ $\frac{4}{10}$

9. $\frac{5}{8}$ $\frac{2}{3}$

10. $\frac{7}{9}$ $\frac{11}{12}$

11. $\frac{2}{10}$ $\frac{5}{6}$

12. $\frac{1}{5}$ $\frac{2}{10}$

Rewrite the fractions in order from smallest to largest.

13. $\frac{1}{2}$ $\frac{2}{5}$ $\frac{1}{4}$

14. $\frac{3}{18}$ $\frac{5}{6}$ $\frac{2}{3}$

15. $\frac{2}{5}$ $\frac{6}{7}$ $\frac{5}{9}$

_____

_____

_____

Name _____

LOST !

Badminton may seem like a rather easy sport where you just hit the "birdie" around at a slow pace. Actually, it is the world's fastest racket sport. The "birdies" are really called shuttlecocks, and they travel as fast as 200 miles per hour. Players must be very quick, strong, and agile to compete.

Pete has gotten separated from the badminton team on the way to the competition. To help him join his teammates, compare the fractions in each box. Color the boxes that have the correct sign (<, >, or =) between the fractions. If you do this correctly, you will have colored a path for Pete.

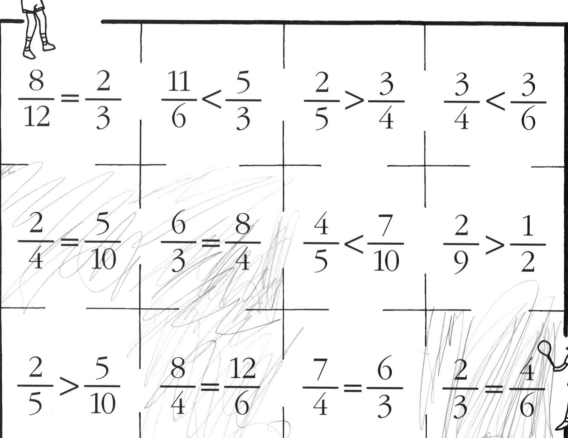

$\frac{8}{12} = \frac{2}{3}$ | $\frac{11}{6} < \frac{5}{3}$ | $\frac{2}{5} > \frac{3}{4}$ | $\frac{3}{4} < \frac{3}{6}$

$\frac{2}{4} = \frac{5}{10}$ | $\frac{6}{3} = \frac{8}{4}$ | $\frac{4}{5} < \frac{7}{10}$ | $\frac{2}{9} > \frac{1}{2}$

$\frac{2}{5} > \frac{5}{10}$ | $\frac{8}{4} = \frac{12}{6}$ | $\frac{7}{4} = \frac{6}{3}$ | $\frac{2}{3} = \frac{4}{6}$

$\frac{7}{16} = \frac{1}{4}$ | $\frac{20}{25} = \frac{4}{5}$ | $\frac{7}{12} = \frac{14}{24}$ | $\frac{0}{2} = \frac{0}{4}$

Name

WINTER OLYMPIC TRIVIA

Do you know the name of the most difficult ice-skating jump ever landed in Olympic competition? Do you know what is the oldest game played on ice? Do you know how fast downhill skiers might travel? Do you know how many people fit on a luge sled? Do you know the length of the longest cross-country ski race?

Find the answers to these and other trivia questions while you practice identifying equivalent fractions. In each problem, two of the fractions are equivalent. The fraction that is not equivalent gives the answer to the trivia question! Circle the non-equivalent fraction in each problem.

1. Luge sleds can reach speeds over

    A. $\frac{16}{18}$ 150 mph

    B. $\frac{8}{9}$ 300 mph

    C. $\frac{5}{9}$ 80 mph

2. The oldest game played on ice is

    A. $\frac{2}{3}$ curling

    B. $\frac{1}{5}$ ice hockey

    C. $\frac{6}{9}$ ice bowling

3. Downhill racers travel at speeds of up to

    A. $\frac{4}{5}$ 200 mph

    B. $\frac{7}{9}$ 80 mph

    C. $\frac{12}{15}$ 40 mph

4. The number of competitors riding each luge sled is

    A. $\frac{3}{5}$ 1 or 2

    B. $\frac{4}{7}$ 3 or 4

    C. $\frac{8}{14}$ 4 or 5

5. The first Olympics that included snowboarding was in

    A. $\frac{1}{3}$ 1992

    B. $\frac{7}{21}$ 1984

    C. $\frac{5}{8}$ 1998

6. The speedskating rink in Lillehammer in 1994 was shaped like a

    A. $\frac{7}{8}$ ice skate

    B. $\frac{9}{12}$ Viking ship

    C. $\frac{28}{32}$ snowshoe

7. People have been using skis for

    A. $\frac{1}{11}$ 9000 years

    B. $\frac{2}{12}$ 200 years

    C. $\frac{1}{6}$ 100 years

8. How far can ski jumpers fly?

    A. $\frac{3}{4}$ about 600 feet

    B. $\frac{6}{7}$ about 1 mile

    C. $\frac{18}{21}$ about 2000 feet

9. The biathlon combines

    A. $\frac{1}{2}$ skating & skiing

    B. $\frac{5}{11}$ cross-country skiing & rifle shooting

    C. $\frac{2}{4}$ luge & bobsled

10. The most difficult ice-skating jump landed in Olympic competition (as of 1997) was

    A. $\frac{1}{4}$ the quadruple lutz

    B. $\frac{2}{8}$ the triple flip

    C. $\frac{2}{6}$ the triple axle

Name

THE LONGEST JUMPS

It sounds pretty hard! An athlete runs down a short path and jumps as far as possible, landing into a pit of sand. A measurement is taken from the beginning of the jump to the impression the body leaves in the sand. If the athlete falls backward from where the feet land, the measurement will be shorter than desired!

Here are some measurements of long jumps from athletes of all ages. They are written as improper fractions. Change them into mixed numerals.

Olympic Fact

U.S. track and field athlete Jackie Joyner-Kersee won the gold medal in 1988 with a jump of 24 ft $3\frac{1}{2}$ in. U.S. jumper Carl Lewis won the gold medal in the long jump at the 1984, 1988, 1992, and 1996 Olympic Games.

1. Carl $\frac{57}{2}$ feet = _____

2. Lutz $\frac{57}{6}$ feet = _____

3. Jackie $\frac{97}{4}$ feet = _____

4. Heike $\frac{47}{2}$ feet = _____

5. Amber $\frac{32}{5}$ feet = _____

6. Yvette $\frac{85}{8}$ feet = _____

7. Arnie $\frac{88}{3}$ feet = _____

8. Ellery $\frac{83}{4}$ feet = _____

9. James $\frac{49}{4}$ feet = _____

10. Randy $\frac{109}{4}$ feet = _____

11. Tatyana $\frac{71}{3}$ feet = _____

12. Mary $\frac{63}{4}$ feet = _____

13. Bob $\frac{165}{6}$ feet = _____

14. Albert $\frac{129}{12}$ feet = _____

15. Jenny $\frac{101}{4}$ feet = _____

16. Tommy $\frac{14}{3}$ feet = _____

Name _____

GETTING TO VENUES

A venue is a place where one of the Olympic events is held. There are many venues at each Olympic Games. These Olympic athletes are trying to get to their proper venues, but their paths are blocked. Remove the obstacles along the paths by changing each improper fraction to its correct mixed numeral.

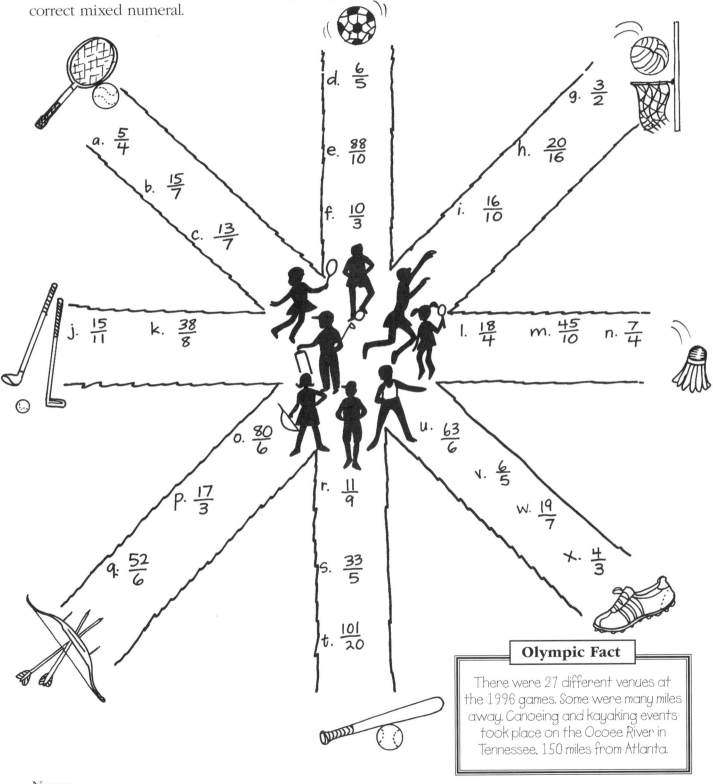

a. $\frac{5}{4}$

b. $\frac{15}{7}$

c. $\frac{13}{7}$

d. $\frac{6}{5}$

e. $\frac{88}{10}$

f. $\frac{10}{3}$

g. $\frac{3}{2}$

h. $\frac{20}{16}$

i. $\frac{16}{10}$

j. $\frac{15}{11}$

k. $\frac{38}{8}$

l. $\frac{18}{4}$

m. $\frac{45}{10}$

n. $\frac{7}{4}$

o. $\frac{80}{6}$

p. $\frac{17}{3}$

q. $\frac{52}{6}$

r. $\frac{11}{9}$

s. $\frac{33}{5}$

t. $\frac{101}{20}$

u. $\frac{63}{6}$

v. $\frac{6}{5}$

w. $\frac{19}{7}$

x. $\frac{4}{3}$

Olympic Fact

There were 27 different venues at the 1996 games. Some were many miles away. Canoeing and kayaking events took place on the Ocoee River in Tennessee, 150 miles from Atlanta.

Name

THE #1 SPORT

In ancient versions of soccer, players tossed the ball around in the air, bouncing it off their hands and heads. Today, only the goalie is allowed to touch the ball with his or her hands while it is in play on the field.

Soccer was the first team sport to be included in the Olympics. At every Olympic Games, it draws some of the biggest crowds. In Barcelona, Spain, the mainly Spanish crowd was thrilled to see the Spanish team win the gold medal!

Look on the soccer field for the answer to each problem. Circle the correct answer with the color shown next to the problem. Answers must be in lowest terms.

1. GREEN: $\frac{2}{3} + \frac{1}{6} =$ _____

2. RED: $\frac{5}{10} - \frac{1}{5} =$ _____

3. BLUE: $\frac{5}{12} - \frac{1}{3} =$ _____

4. YELLOW: $\frac{3}{4} - \frac{5}{8} =$ _____

5. PURPLE: $\frac{1}{4} + \frac{4}{16} =$ _____

6. BROWN: $\frac{10}{25} + \frac{2}{5} =$ _____

7. ORANGE: $\frac{11}{12} - \frac{3}{4} =$ _____

8. PINK: $\frac{1}{2} + \frac{2}{22} =$ _____

9. RED: $\frac{20}{30} - \frac{2}{6} =$ _____

10. BLUE: $\frac{1}{9} + \frac{2}{3} - \frac{1}{3} =$ _____

11. PURPLE: $\frac{2}{9} + \frac{8}{9} - \frac{1}{3} =$ _____

12. GREEN: $\frac{4}{7} + \frac{1}{3} =$ _____

13. ORANGE: $\frac{11}{14} - \frac{3}{7} + \frac{1}{7} =$ _____

14. BROWN: $\frac{1}{6} + \frac{3}{4} - \frac{1}{8} =$ _____

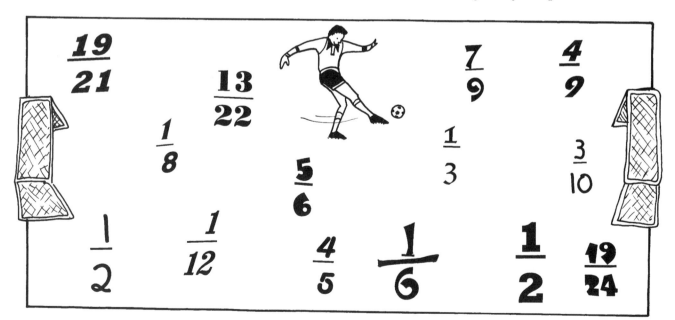

THROUGH WILD WATERS

In the Olympic kayaking events, kayakers race through wild, foaming water (called white water). They must get down the river through a series of gates safely and fast! Some of the gates require them to paddle upstream against the raging waters! Of course, sometimes the kayaks flip, but the athletes are good at turning right side up again.

To divide fractions, you need to do some flipping, too! The second number in the problem must be turned upside down. Then, you multiply the two fractions to get the answer to the division problem!

$$\frac{3}{5} \div \frac{7}{10} = \frac{3}{5} \times \frac{10}{7} = \frac{30}{35} = \frac{6}{7}$$

Flip the second fraction in all these problems to find the right answers.

1. $\frac{3}{4} \div \frac{7}{8} =$ _____

2. $\frac{4}{7} \div \frac{1}{2} =$ _____

3. $\frac{9}{11} \div \frac{2}{3} =$ _____

4. $\frac{2}{3} \div \frac{1}{5} =$ _____

5. $\frac{1}{30} \div \frac{2}{20} =$ _____

6. $\frac{2}{9} \div \frac{4}{5} =$ _____

7. $\frac{7}{8} \div \frac{5}{6} =$ _____

8. $\frac{10}{11} \div \frac{11}{10} =$ _____

9. $\frac{1}{6} \div \frac{2}{3} =$ _____

10. $\frac{4}{5} \div \frac{1}{9} =$ _____

11. $\frac{5}{12} \div \frac{1}{3} =$ _____

12. $\frac{8}{9} \div \frac{3}{4} =$ _____

13. $\frac{1}{6} \div \frac{2}{5} =$ _____

14. $\frac{3}{4} \div \frac{3}{4} =$ _____

15. $\frac{2}{5} \div \frac{5}{2} =$ _____

Name

A HUGE OBSTACLE COURSE

So many obstacles! A runner in the steeplechase race has to run 3,000 meters and jump over 28 hurdles and 7 water jumps. See if you can get past all the obstacles in this steeplechase course. At each jump, round the decimal as the directions tell you. If you get them all correct, you will have successfully completed this steeplechase course. The real Olympic course will be a lot harder than this!

Round to the nearest tenth.

1. .087
2. .86
3. 10.1420
4. .3367
5. 1.56

6. 4.888
7. 2.186
8. .0722
9. .0634
10. 4.79

Round to the nearest hundredth.

11. .18338
12. 2.8067
13. .7777
14. .0593
15. 6.0035

16. 100. 477
17. .942
18. 1.369
19. 4.601
20. 3.672

Round to the nearest thousandth.

21. .4689
22. 4.6789
23. 7.08966
24. .05555

25. 41. 5226
26. .198765
27. 5.0109
28. .02161

Round to the nearest ten thousandth.

29. .747777
30. .19991
31. .740000
32. 15.02891
33. 1.1515151
34. 4.33371
35. .59022

Olympic Fact

Michael Phelps, a swimmer from the United States, holds the record for the most medals won ever—22. He also won a record 18 gold medals.

Name

WHO WEARS THE MEDALS?

In the Olympics, the individual all-around championship is the highest achievement a gymnast can achieve. Most gymnasts dream of winning this gold medal. Gymnasts must compete in four events. Their scores from all four events are totaled to see who has the highest score.

Add up the scores for all these gymnasts. Then rank them in order from first to last.

Gymnast	Balance Beam	Floor Exercise	Uneven Bars	Horse Vault	Total Score	Place
Karin	9.932	9.912	9.955	9.680		
Sofia	9.817	9.950	9.609	9.896		
Elena	8.954	9.987	9.640	9.320		
Kim	8.999	9.690	9.800	9.975		
Kerri	9.981	9.208	9.997	9.700		
Tatiana	9.975	10.00	9.980	9.973		
Nina	9.290	9.964	9.699	9.609		
Larissa	9.956	9.866	9.057	9.666		
Svetlana	9.979	9.979	9.780	10.00		
Olga	8.974	9.401	8.899	9.789		
Kathy	10.00	9.777	9.780	9.925		
Tamara	9.966	10.00	9.224	9.099		

Who won the gold? _____ Silver? _____ Bronze? _____

Name _____

WHAT'S THE COST?

Sonja Henie was eleven years old when she entered her first Olympic Games in 1924. Even though this young figure skater finished last, she did not give up. She came back three more times and won the gold medal every time! She was known for her interesting, graceful movements and her fancy costumes. Those fancy costumes and other supplies add up to a lot of expense for a skater! You can be sure that they are all more expensive today than they were in Sonja Henie's time! Practice your decimal skills to find the costs for these skating items. Use scrap paper to solve the problems.

_____ 1. One skater paid $108.00 for 36 fancy jewels to sew on her costume. What did each jewel cost?

_____ 2. Laces for her skates were 5 pair for $13.00. What does one pair cost?

_____ 3. A pair of skate blades costs $189.00. A pair of skate boots costs 4 times that much. How much are the skates and blades all together?

_____ 4. If a skater's vitamins for one month cost $17.50, how much does one year's supply cost?

_____ 5. Every practice session at Kurt's rink costs $5.00. Kurt goes to 4 sessions a day, 6 days a week. How much does he spend each week on ice time?

_____ 6. If Jill's skating tights cost $53.60 for 8 pair, how much will 4 pair cost?

_____ 7. The coach's fees are $45.00 per hour. Jill trains with her coach 8 hours each week. How much per week does this cost Jill?

_____ 8. Last year, Scott paid $800 in entry fees for 6 competitions. If each fee was the same, about how much did each competition cost him to enter?

_____ 9. If Kristi's new skates cost $695 and she buys 3 pair each year, how much would she spend in a year on skates?

_____ 10. If Paul spent $322.00 on moleskin and cream for blisters last year, how much did it cost him per month to take care of blisters?

_____ 11. Jenni's newest costume cost twice as much as her last one. This one was $286. How much did the last one cost?

_____ 12. Todd's skating partner drinks hot chocolate twice a day at the rink. The hot chocolate costs $1.25, and they skated 290 days last year. How much did she spend on hot chocolate all year?

Name _____

OVER THE TOP

Pole vaulters sprint along a short track with a long, flexible pole. Then they plant the pole and soar upside down over another pole that might be almost 20 feet high. The goal is to make it over the top without knocking off that pole! At the 1996 Olympics, Jean Galfione from France won the gold medal with a jump over a pole that was 19 feet, 5 inches high!

If a pole vaulter makes it over the top 6 times out of 7 tries, a fraction ($\frac{6}{7}$) can show his success rate. The fraction can be changed to a decimal score. (Divide 6 by 7. The decimal is 0.86.) Find the decimal to match each fraction that shows how these pole vaulters are doing at their practice. Round to the nearest hundredth.

BOING

Athlete	Fraction	Decimal
1. Maxim	$\frac{14}{18}$	_____
2. Javier	$\frac{16}{20}$	_____
3. Sergei	$\frac{20}{27}$	_____
4. Wolfgang	$\frac{13}{18}$	_____
5. Frederick	$\frac{20}{26}$	_____
6. Quinon	$\frac{13}{16}$	_____
7. Philippe	$\frac{21}{28}$	_____
8. William	$\frac{16}{22}$	_____
9. Charles	$\frac{15}{21}$	_____
10. Grigori	$\frac{9}{12}$	_____

Name

THE DREAM TEAM

No one doubted that the United States Olympic basketball team would win gold in Barcelona in 1992. This was a team of the world's best professional players, including Magic Johnson and Michael Jordan. These players probably had pretty high percentages when it came to shooting free throws.

Each fraction shows the number of free throws that might have been made by some basketball players from the top three Olympic teams in comparison to the number of shots taken. Change each fraction into a percentage.

FREE THROW PRACTICE SHOTS

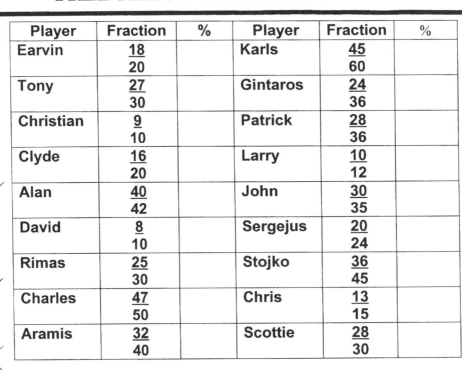

Player	Fraction	%	Player	Fraction	%
Earvin	18/20		Karls	45/60	
Tony	27/30		Gintaros	24/36	
Christian	9/10		Patrick	28/36	
Clyde	16/20		Larry	10/12	
Alan	40/42		John	30/35	
David	8/10		Sergejus	20/24	
Rimas	25/30		Stojko	36/45	
Charles	47/50		Chris	13/15	
Aramis	32/40		Scottie	28/30	

1. Which player's average was lower than Karl's?

   _____

2. Which player had the same percentage as Rimas and Larry?

   _____

3. What three players had a percentage over 90%?

   _____

4. Who had the best percentage at this practice session?

   _____

Name _____

TEMPERATURE COUNTS

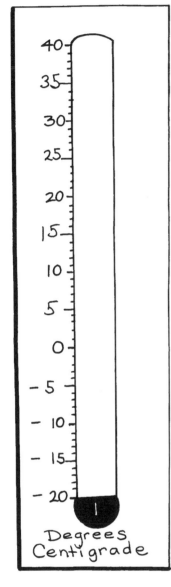

Degrees
Centigrade

The temperature really does matter for ski races. Snow conditions change with temperature changes, and this can affect the skiers' speed and control. As a result, racers, coaches, and Olympic officials pay a lot of attention to the thermometer.

Use this thermometer as a number line to help you solve these problems with integers. Remember, integers are a set of positive and negative numbers.

1. At 5 o'clock in the morning, the temperature at the top of the race course was –13°. By 10:00 A.M., it was +12°. How much had the temperature risen? _____

2. The temperature rose from +12° to + 23° by noon. How much did the temperature change? _____

3. In the afternoon, the temperature fell rapidly from +23° to -1°. How much change is this? _____

4. By 7:00 P.M., the temperature was –9°. How much had the temperature changed from 10:00 A.M.? _____

5. It continued to get colder. By midnight, the temperature was 35° colder than it had been at noon. What was the midnight temperature? _____

6. If the temperature rose 12° between midnight and 6:00 A.M. the next morning, what was the temperature at 6:00 A.M.? _____

Finish these problems.

7. 30 – 41 = _____

8. –10 + 15 = _____

9. 5 + – 7 = _____

10. – 9 + 4 = _____

11. –12 + – 4 = _____

12. 40 + –6 + –10 = _____

13. –10 + –5 + 15 = _____

14. 20 + 3 + –6 = _____

Name _____

SIGNS FROM THE CROWD

The rowdy crowd is getting ready for the opening football game of the season between the Ashland Grizzlies and the Crescent City Cougars.

Draw a line from each label to match the correct sign.

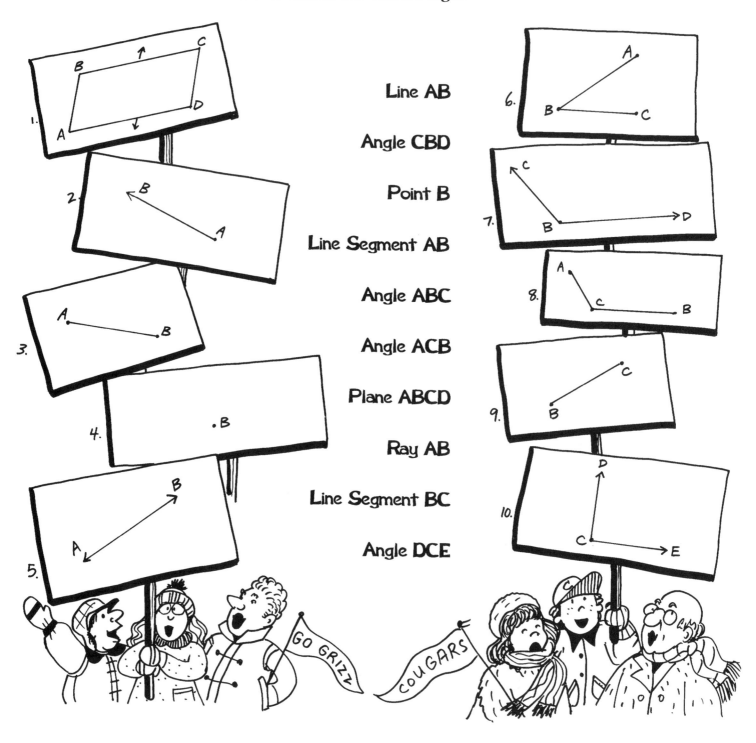

Line AB

Angle CBD

Point B

Line Segment AB

Angle ABC

Angle ACB

Plane ABCD

Ray AB

Line Segment BC

Angle DCE

Name _____

A PLANE MESS

Coach Jackson teaches math when he is not coaching volleyball. He had some great posters ready for his geometry lesson today, but, as usual, he forgot to close the window. A huge wind blew his stuff all over the floor.

Get the definition posters back together with the math terms in time for class. Draw a line from each math term to its matching poster.

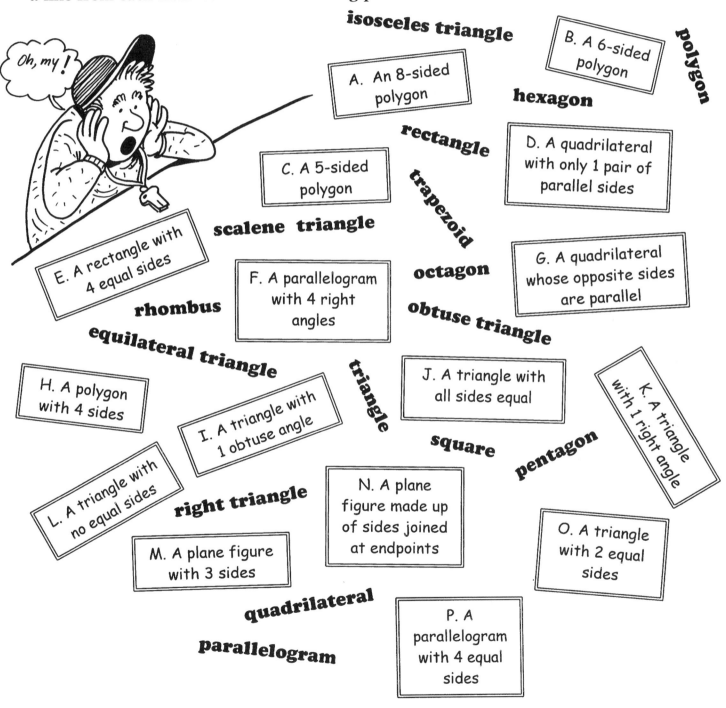

isosceles triangle

A. An 8-sided polygon

B. A 6-sided polygon

polygon

hexagon

rectangle

D. A quadrilateral with only 1 pair of parallel sides

C. A 5-sided polygon

trapezoid

scalene triangle

octagon

G. A quadrilateral whose opposite sides are parallel

E. A rectangle with 4 equal sides

F. A parallelogram with 4 right angles

obtuse triangle

rhombus

equilateral triangle

H. A polygon with 4 sides

triangle

J. A triangle with all sides equal

K. A triangle with 1 right angle

I. A triangle with 1 obtuse angle

square

pentagon

L. A triangle with no equal sides

right triangle

N. A plane figure made up of sides joined at endpoints

O. A triangle with 2 equal sides

M. A plane figure with 3 sides

quadrilateral

P. A parallelogram with 4 equal sides

parallelogram

Oh, my !

Name

DUFFEL BAG JUMBLE

Brayden just came home from tennis practice and dumped the contents of his duffel bag on the floor of his room. Everything in his bag is a geometric plane figure or space figure. Use the right formula to find the perimeter (**P**), area (**A**), circumference (**C**), or volume (**V**) of these figures. Label each answer accurately.

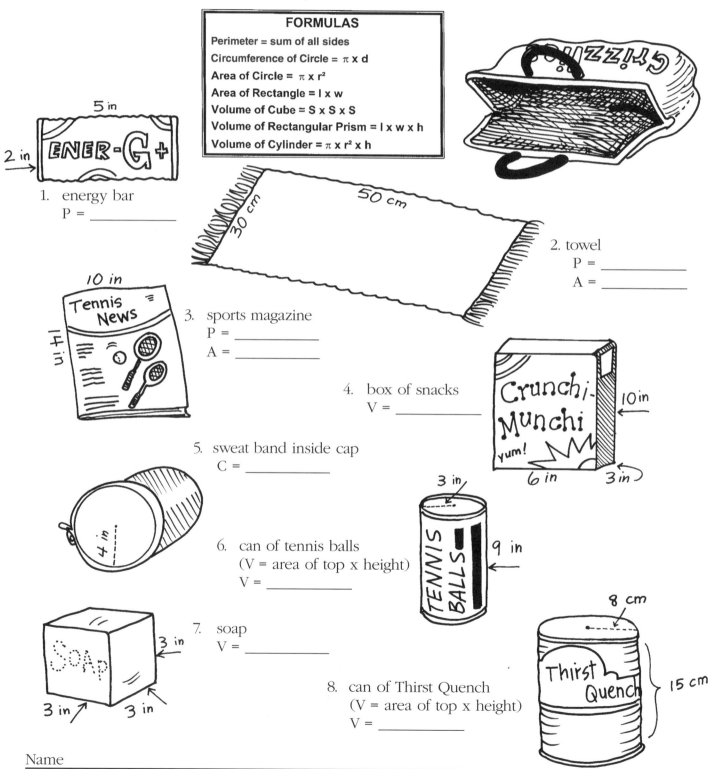

FORMULAS

Perimeter = sum of all sides

Circumference of Circle = $\pi \times d$

Area of Circle = $\pi \times r^2$

Area of Rectangle = $l \times w$

Volume of Cube = $S \times S \times S$

Volume of Rectangular Prism = $l \times w \times h$

Volume of Cylinder = $\pi \times r^2 \times h$

5 in

2 in

ENER-G+

1. energy bar
   P = _____

30 cm · 50 cm

2. towel
   P = _____
   A = _____

10 in

Tennis News

4 in

3. sports magazine
   P = _____
   A = _____

4. box of snacks
   V = _____

Crunchi-Munchi yum!

10 in

6 in · 3 in

5. sweat band inside cap
   C = _____

4 in

6. can of tennis balls
   (V = area of top x height)
   V = _____

3 in

TENNIS BALLS

9 in

SOAP

3 in

3 in · 3 in

7. soap
   V = _____

8. can of Thirst Quench
   (V = area of top x height)
   V = _____

8 cm

Thirst Quench

15 cm

Name _____

THE LONGEST PRACTICES

The Ashland Middle School Marching Band practices longer than any sports team. They work all through the year to be an award-winning band.

Use your skills with time measurement to figure out just how long and hard they work! Finish the chart to show the length of each summer practice.

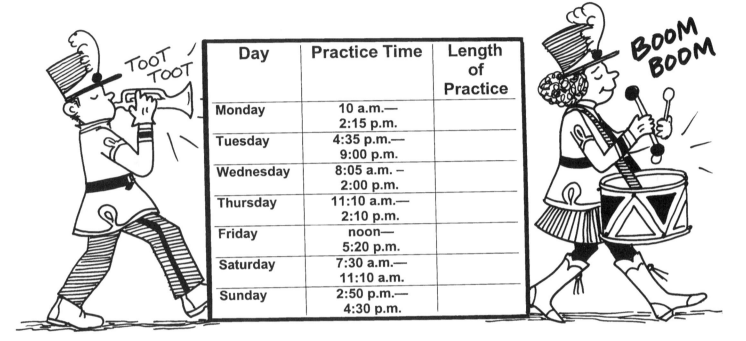

Day	Practice Time	Length of Practice
Monday	10 a.m.—2:15 p.m.	
Tuesday	4:35 p.m.—9:00 p.m.	
Wednesday	8:05 a.m. –2:00 p.m.	
Thursday	11:10 a.m.—2:10 p.m.	
Friday	noon—5:20 p.m.	
Saturday	7:30 a.m.—11:10 a.m.	
Sunday	2:50 p.m.—4:30 p.m.	

Solve these problems.

1. During February, each practice began at 3:45 p.m. and finished at 6:10 p.m. on school days. How long was each practice? _____

2. On Saturdays, the band warms up in the band room for 40 minutes. Then they practice on the field for 2 hours and 20 minutes. Then they go back to the band room for another 55 minutes. How long is the practice? _____

3. When the band traveled to the latest competition, they left school on the bus at 9:30 a.m. They arrived in Astoria and practiced until 7:15 p.m. How long did they spend traveling and practicing that day? _____

4. The trumpet section needed some extra practice. They began at 7:15 a.m. Their practice lasted 1 hour, 20 minutes. What time did it end? _____

5. The tubas practiced after school for 2 hours and 25 minutes. They ended their practice at 4:30 p.m. What time did the practice begin? _____

Name _____

THE GREAT SHAPE MATCH-UP

All the parents of the basketball players have come to watch the first home game. They're all holding up numbered cards with symbols to match the names of their kids on the team.

Search the cards to match the parents and players. Write the number of each card on the correct player.

KEEPING BUSY

Ashley never stops playing sports! As soon as one season is over, she starts a new sport. So, she has many labels: athlete, basketball player, volleyball player, tennis player, gymnast, pitcher, and swimmer.

Quadrilaterals are like that, too. They have many labels.

All quadrilaterals have four sides. But a four-sided figure can show up in many "uniforms" or different "looks."

Which figures match each description? (There may be more than one.)

1. All angles are right angles, but all sides are not equal. _____

2. Only one pair of opposite sides is parallel. _____

3. A rectangle with all sides equal

   _____

4. A figure with two pairs of opposite sides parallel _____

5. A parallelogram with all sides the same length

   _____

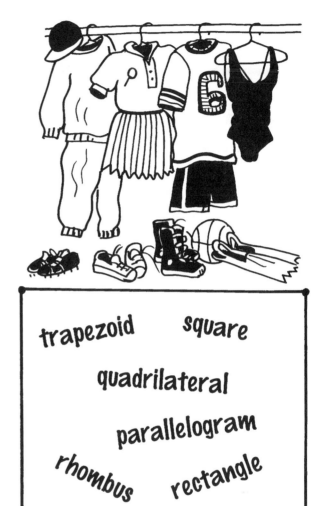

trapezoid   square

quadrilateral

parallelogram

rhombus   rectangle

6. All sides are equal, but all angles may not be equal. _____

Write (T) TRUE or (F) FALSE next to each statement.

_____ 1. All squares are rectangles.   _____ 6. All squares are rectangles.

_____ 2. All rectangles are quadrilaterals.   _____ 7. All squares are rhombuses.

_____ 3. No rhombuses are trapezoids.   _____ 8. A trapezoid is a quadrilateral.

_____ 4. Rectangles have no right angles.   _____ 9. All parallelograms are rectangles.

_____ 5. All rectangles are squares.   _____ 10. All rhombuses are squares.

Name _____

MIRROR IMAGES

Jenna often practices her dance moves in front of a mirror. She hopes the reflection shows a perfect performance.

In a symmetrical figure, each half is a perfect reflection of the other.

Look at the figures below. Color the ones that are symmetrical. Use a ruler to draw the line of symmetry in each symmetrical figure.

Complete figures I, J, and K to make them symmetrical. The line of symmetry is already given for you.

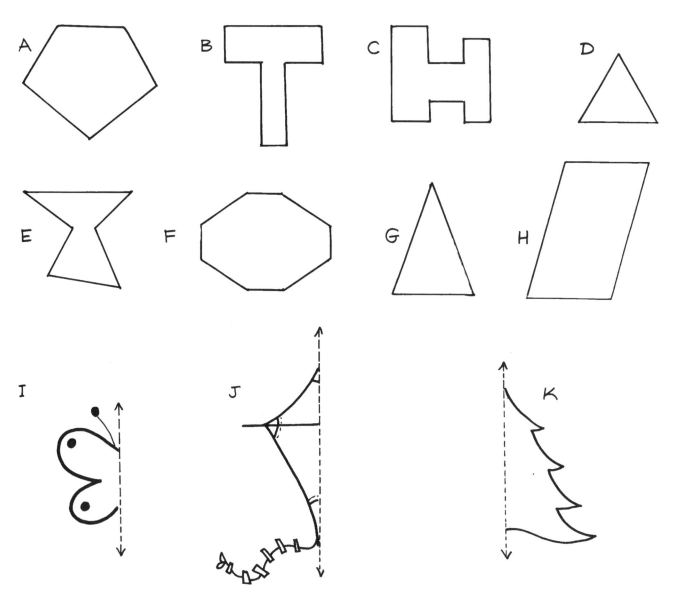

Name

OUT OF ORDER

The sports storage room is a mess. Pieces of equipment have been tossed around carelessly. Custodian George has to put things back in order.

Look at each pair of items. Tell whether the second item in each pair is a slide, flip, or turn of the first item. Write S, F, or T beside each pair. (Some pairs may have more than one label!)

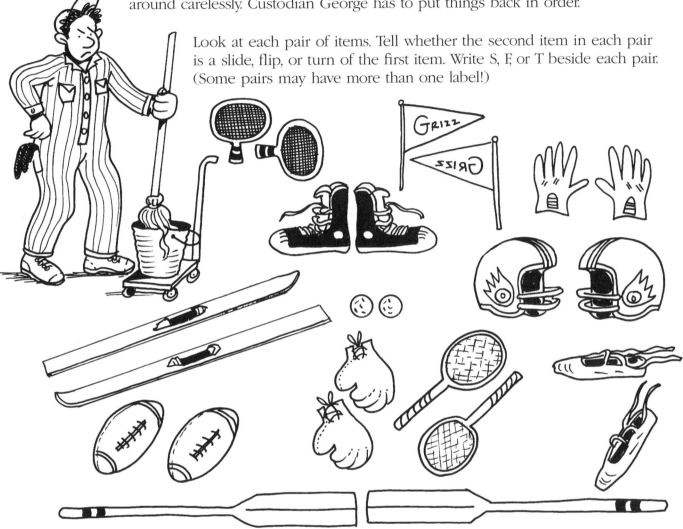

Draw a slide (translation) of this figure:

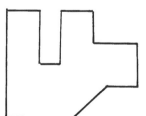

Draw a turn (rotation) of this figure:

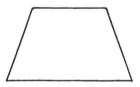

Draw a flip (reflection) of this figure:

Draw a turn (rotation) of this figure:

Name _____

MORE OR LESS?

Ooops! The weight lifters have a problem at practice today. The weights on both ends of the bars are not equal for every athlete!

Look at the measurement amounts below. They have the same problem. Compare the measures. Write > (greater than), < (less than), or = in each circle.

1.	6 pt	○	3 qt
2.	16 oz	○	1 lb
3.	9 qt	○	16 pt
4.	5 pt	○	10 c
5.	3 ft	○	36 in
6.	3 lbs	○	59 oz
7.	2 c	○	1 pt
8.	2 lbs	○	22 oz
9.	7 yds	○	21 ft
10.	2,000 lbs	○	1 T
11.	12 ft	○	3 yds
12.	6 gal	○	18 qt
13.	38 in	○	1 yds
14.	4 yds	○	100 in
15.	2 qt	○	8 gal
16.	11 in	○	1 ft
17.	4 T	○	6 tsp
18.	100 sec	○	2 mins
19.	7 hrs	○	420 mins
20.	10 gal	○	40 qt

Name

CLIMBING THE WALL

The Adventure Club uses a climbing wall at the gym to practice rock climbing skills. Draw a path up the wall for each of these climbers. The path must connect the hand-hold points.

After you draw the paths, use a centimeter ruler to measure the paths. Then find the length of the path to the nearest meter, using this scale: 1 centimeter of measure = 1 meter on the wall.

Michael

Marcy

Length of Michael's path _____

Length of Marcy's path _____

Name _____

CIRCLES EVERYWHERE YOU LOOK

Circles show up all the time in the world of sports. See below the circles of different sizes athletes find in their sports.

Use the formula for circumference ($C = \pi d$) for each circle.

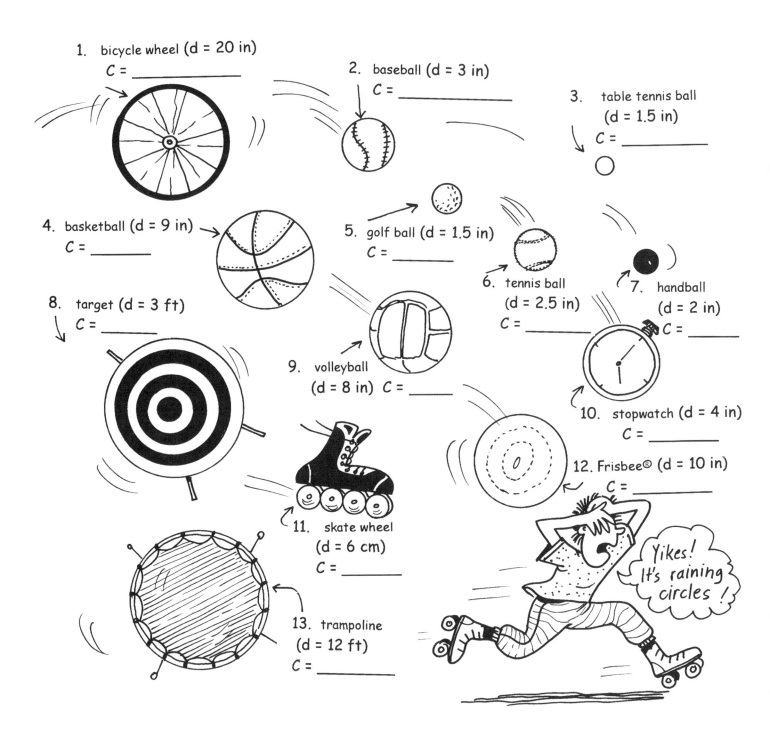

1. bicycle wheel (d = 20 in)
   C = _____

2. baseball (d = 3 in)
   C = _____

3. table tennis ball
   (d = 1.5 in)
   C = _____

4. basketball (d = 9 in)
   C = _____

5. golf ball (d = 1.5 in)
   C = _____

6. tennis ball
   (d = 2.5 in)
   C = _____

7. handball
   (d = 2 in)
   C = _____

8. target (d = 3 ft)
   C = _____

9. volleyball
   (d = 8 in) C = _____

10. stopwatch (d = 4 in)
    C = _____

11. skate wheel
    (d = 6 cm)
    C = _____

12. Frisbee® (d = 10 in)
    C = _____

13. trampoline
    (d = 12 ft)
    C = _____

Yikes!
It's raining
circles !

Name _____

SKY-HIGH MEASUREMENTS

Kites are a great way to show off your school spirit. The sky has been the limit for the Grizzly fans who got together to fly their kites before the soccer game. Find the area of each kite. Write the area on the kite or kite section.

Triangle	$A = \frac{1}{2}bh$	Rectangle	$A = l \times w$
Square	$A = s^2$	Parallelogram	$A = bh$

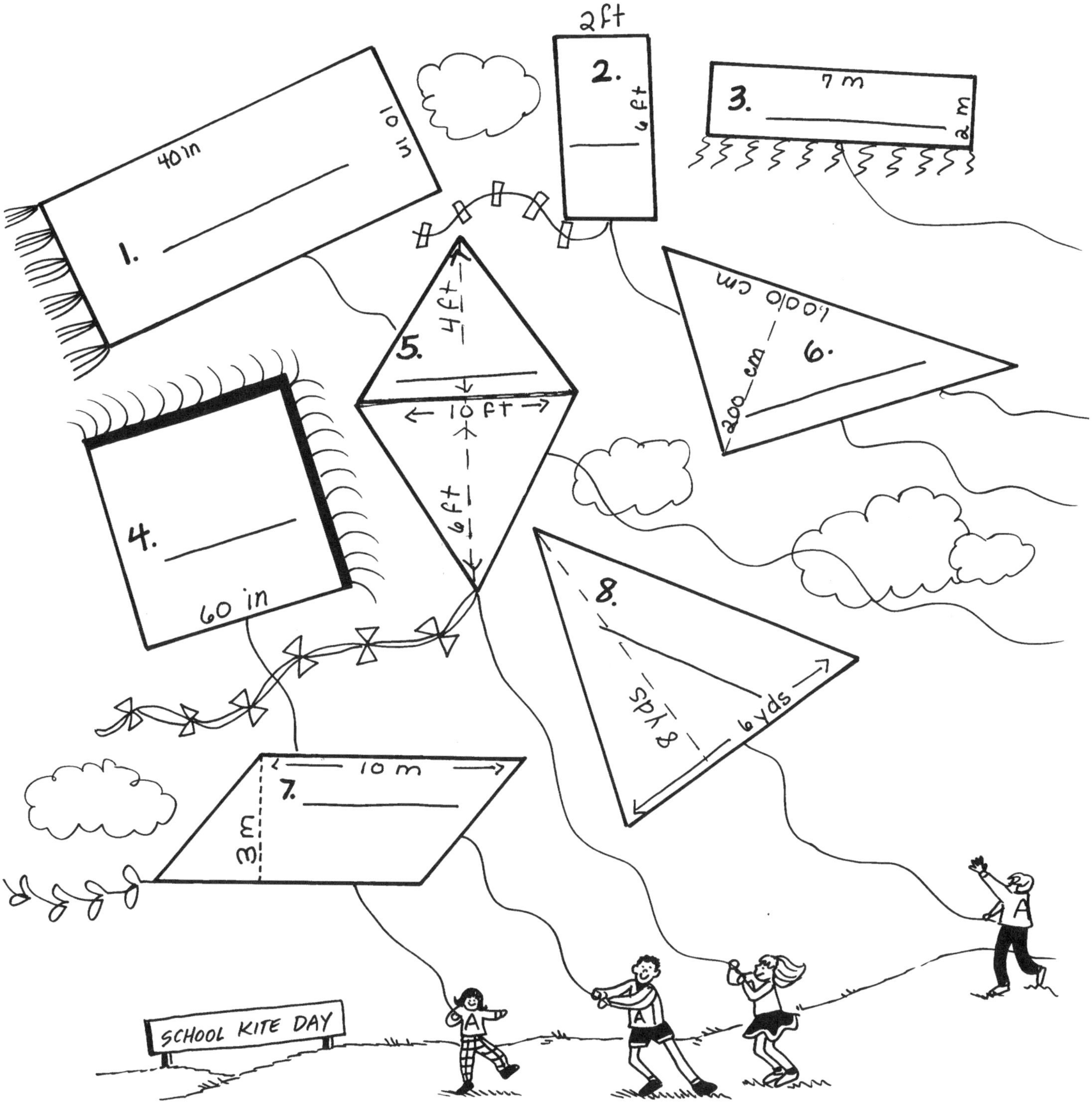

1. 40 in 10 in
2. 2 ft 6 ft
3. 7 m 2 m
4. 60 in
5. 4 ft 10 ft 6 ft
6. 1,000 cm 200 cm
7. 10 m 3 m
8. 8 yds 6 yds
SCHOOL KITE DAY
A

Name

PEP RALLY MEASUREMENTS

School ended early today so students could get ready for tomorrow's pep rally. Kids are busy making posters and decorations. How much paper did they have to buy or borrow to make these posters?

To find out the sizes of the posters, calculate the perimeter and area for each one.

1. P = _____
   A = _____

2. P = _____
   A = _____

3. P = _____
   A = _____

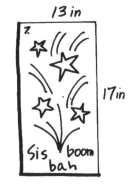

4. P = _____
   A = _____

5. P = _____
   A = _____

6. P = _____
   A = _____

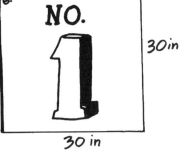

7. P = _____
   A = _____

8. Which has the largest area? _____

9. Which has the longest perimeter? _____

Name _____

HUNGRY FANS

The game has gone into overtime, and the fans are extremely hungry! They are going to need a lot of snacks before the night is over.

Find the volume of each container to discover which fan got the most to eat or drink! (Volume = length x width x height) Label your answers correctly.

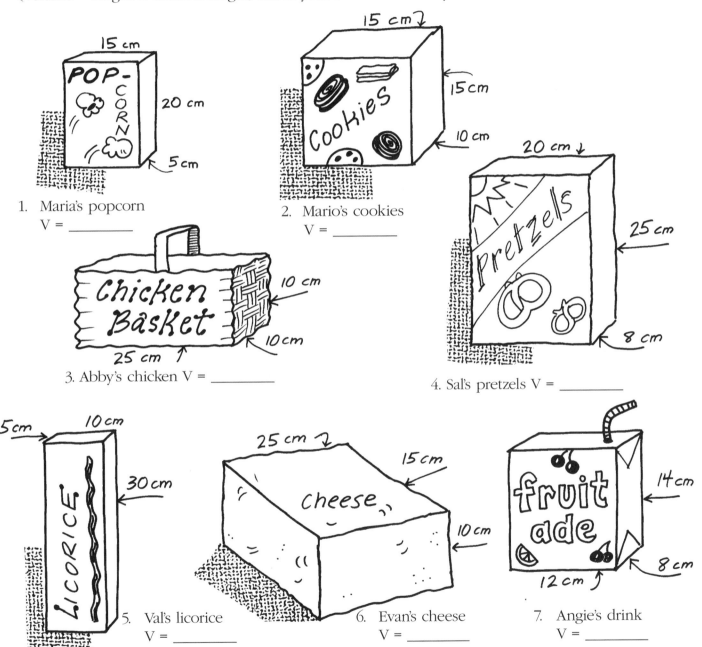

1. Maria's popcorn
   V = _____

2. Mario's cookies
   V = _____

3. Abby's chicken V = _____

4. Sal's pretzels V = _____

5. Val's licorice
   V = _____

6. Evan's cheese
   V = _____

7. Angie's drink
   V = _____

A. Which two fans ate the same volume of snacks? _____

B. Which fan ate or drank the greatest volume? _____

Name _____

UNIFORM CONFUSION

Al, the athletic director, is confused. He is passing out boxes of uniforms but doesn't know which one to give to each coach.

Identify each coach's box of uniforms from the description the coach is giving. Fill in the blank with the letter of the box.

1. My box is 1 x 1 x 2 feet. My cheerleading uniforms are in box _____ .

2. The measurements of my box are 5 x 36 x 5 inches. My swimmer's uniforms are in box ____ .

3. My football uniforms are in the box that is 15 x 33 x 11 inches. This is box _____ .

4. My box measures 30 x 4 x 15 inches. The track uniforms are in box ____ .

A. $V = 1,620$ in³

B. $V = 3,024$ in³

C. $V = 1,800$ in³

D. $V = 2$ ft³

Use with page 277.

Name _____

5.

I need the box that is 24 x 14 x 9 inches.
It holds the uniforms for my fencing team.
This is box _____.

6.

My soccer players'
uniforms are in box
_____.
This box has measurements
of 9 x 12 x 15 inches.

7.

Please give me box _____.
The volleyball uniforms are in this box
with measurements of 10 x 10 x 27 inches.

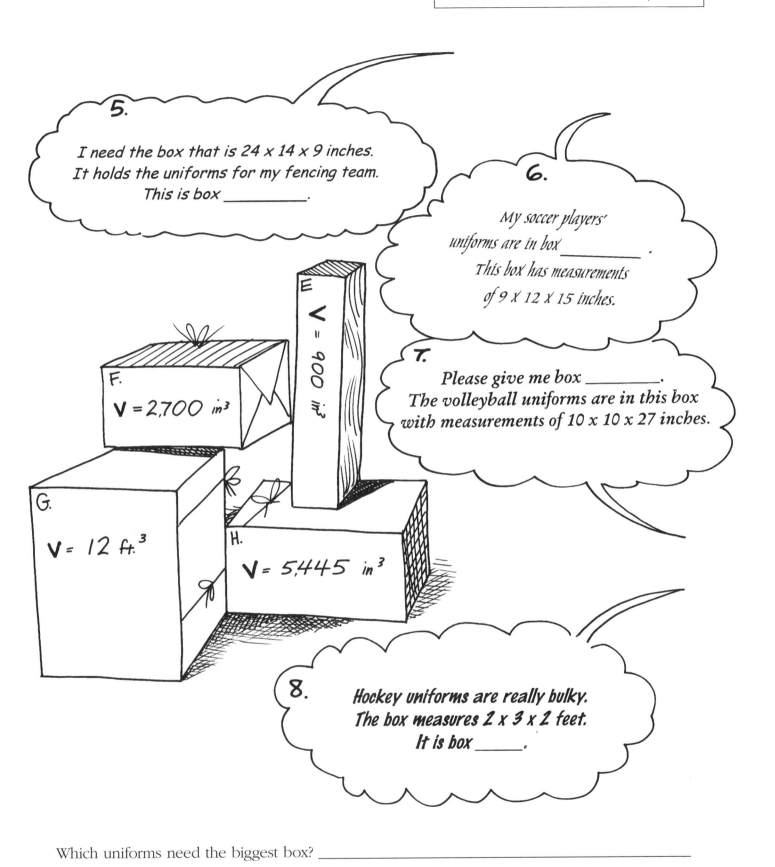

E.

V = 900 in³

F.

V = 2,700 in³

G.

V = 12 ft.³

H.

V = 5,445 in³

8.

Hockey uniforms are really bulky.
The box measures 2 x 3 x 2 feet.
It is box _____.

Which uniforms need the biggest box? _____

Use with page 276.

Name _____

SPECTACULAR BUBBLES

The biggest bubble-gum bubble ever reported was 23 inches in diameter. That's almost two feet! Susan Montgomery Williams of Fresno, California blew this bubble in 1994.
How big is your biggest bubble? Try measuring your next one. See how close you can get to 23 inches!

The graph shows the **frequency** with which different size bubbles were blown (how often) during a bubble-blowing contest. Use the information on the graph to tell whether the statements below are true or false.

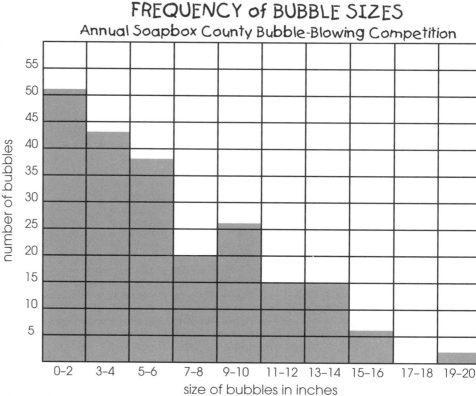

FREQUENCY of BUBBLE SIZES
Annual Soapbox County Bubble-Blowing Competition

number of bubbles

size of bubbles in inches

Write T (true) or F (false) for each statement.

_____ 1. About 300 bubbles were blown all together.

_____ 2. About 40 bubbles were over 10 inches in diameter.

_____ 3. There were about 26 bubbles 9–10 inches in diameter.

_____ 4. There were about 30 bubbles 3–4 inches in diameter.

_____ 5. There was only one bubble 19–20 inches in diameter.

_____ 6. About 150 bubbles were under 4 inches in diameter.

_____ 7. There were fewer than 5 bubbles in the 15–16 inch size.

_____ 8. There were fewer than 20 bubbles 9–10 inches in diameter.

_____ 9. The most bubbles blown were under 4 inches in diameter.

_____ 10. The fewest bubbles blown were 19–20 inches in diameter.

_____ 11. Fewer 7–8 inch bubbles were blown than 9–10 inch bubbles.

_____ 12. There were no bubbles blown larger than 18 inches in diameter.

_____ 13. The number of 11–12 inch bubbles was the same as another group.

_____ 14. In general, there were fewer bubbles blown as the sizes got larger.

Name

WONDERFUL WALLS

It may sound unbelievable, but someone has built a wall out of bubbles!
Fan-Yang of Canada built the record-setting bubble wall in 2009. It was about 166 feet long.

This **frequency table** shows the number of bubbles in 50 different walls being built for a contest. Count the number of walls that had 0-1,000 bubbles. Color a bar on the **frequency graph** to show how many walls had that many bubbles in it. Then do the same for each of the other groups shown on the graph. Color a different bar for each amount.

Frequency Table for Bubble Walls
Number of Bubbles in 50 Walls

2,410	1,190	860	3,190	2,060	5,960	2,760	3,895	3,250	2,905
3,858	4,890	2,002	4,500	2,100	3,165	4,011	4,375	1,200	4,131
4,040	2,180	3,860	2,525	4,975	1,800	2,800	3,330	4,075	2,200
2,909	2,468	1,515	4,141	2,345	3,198	5,450	2,490	1,766	4,700
1,650	3,600	5,625	2,508	4,600	2,844	3,863	3,655	3,480	2,450

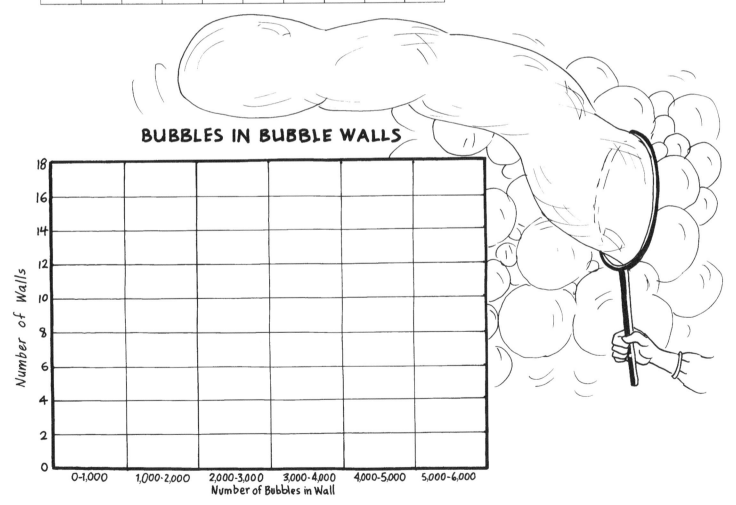

BUBBLES IN BUBBLE WALLS

Number of Walls

18
16
14
12
10
8
6
4
2
0

0-1,000   1,000-2,000   2,000-3,000   3,000-4,000   4,000-5,000   5,000-6,000
Number of Bubbles in Wall

Name _____

ENORMOUS EDIBLES

The tallest cake was created in 2008 in Indonesia. It was 108 feet tall! A lot of people probably had a wonderful time eating that cake!

Look at the data that tells about the cakes in another cake contest. The table shows the number of layers for each cake.

A. The **range** of a set of data (set of numbers) shows the smallest and largest numbers.

The range of this data is _____ to _____ .

B. The **mode** of a set of data is the number that appears most often. The mode of this data is _____ .

C. The **median** of a set of data is the number that falls in the middle if the numbers are arranged in order from smallest to largest.

The median of this data is _____ .

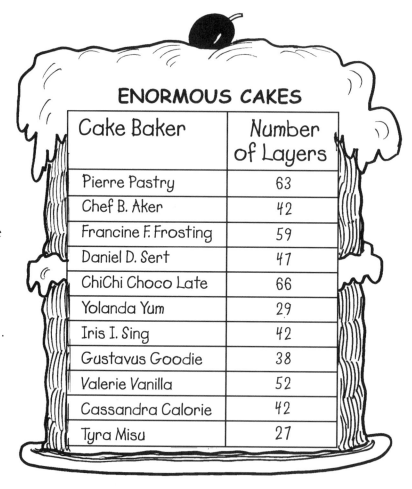

ENORMOUS CAKES

Cake Baker	Number of Layers
Pierre Pastry	63
Chef B. Aker	42
Francine F. Frosting	59
Daniel D. Sert	47
ChiChi Choco Late	66
Yolanda Yum	29
Iris I. Sing	42
Gustavus Goodie	38
Valerie Vanilla	52
Cassandra Calorie	42
Tyra Misu	27

For each set of data, find the range, mode, and median:

1. 2, 6, 1, 8, 4, 2, 9, 7, 5
   a. range = _____
   b. mode = _____
   c. median = _____

2. 90%, 84%, 72%, 92%, 72%
   a. range = _____
   b. mode = _____
   c. median = _____

3. 21, 6, 9, 23, 22, 9, 10
   a. range = _____
   b. mode = _____
   c. median = _____

4. 16%, 10%, 4%, 80%, 6%, 16%, 12%
   a. range = _____
   b. mode = _____
   c. median = _____

5. 120 mi, 119 mi, 121 mi, 221 mi, 121 mi, 200 mi
   a. range = _____
   b. mode = _____
   c. median = _____

Name _____

INCREDIBLE CREATIONS

The tallest sand castle was built by a team in Florida. The team members built the 45-foot, 10-inch-high castle in 2015.

These teams have spent a week building their castles. The table shows the hours they've worked. Use the table to solve the problems.

1. What is the mean of the hours the *Sand Wizards* worked? _____

2. What is the mean of the hours the *Builders Four* worked? _____

3. What is the mean of all the hours worked on Sunday? _____

4. What is the mean of all the hours worked on Friday? _____

5. Which team had the greatest range in number of hours? _____

6. Which team spent the most number of hours working?

    _____

7. Which team spent the least number of hours working?

    _____

8. Which range is greater: the *Sculptors'* range or the *Sand Crabs'* range?

    _____

9. Tuesday was the longest day for which two teams?

    _____

    _____

10. On which day did the workers spend less time building than they did on Friday?

    _____

SAND CASTLE CONTEST
Team Hours for Building Castles

Team	Sun	Mon	Tue	Wed	Thurs	Fri	Sat
The Sand Wizards	12	14	15	14	13	8	8
The Sand Crabs	14	16	12	8	14	10	7
The Builders Four	6	7	14	11	14	5	6
The Sculptors	10	12	17	17	6	12	8
The Castle Quartet	18	14	13	12	11	10	5

Name _____

STUDYING TO SET RECORDS

What does it take to set a record? It takes imagination, time, and a lot of work or patience. Some of the records take plenty of skill or money, too! In addition, you might need to do some research if you want to try for a record.

This is the library of a future record-setter. The graph shows the number of books she has read on each topic. Use the graph to solve the problems.

STUDYING TO SET RECORDS

Solve each equation about the number of books Agatha read.

1. Wheelbarrow Racing + Pancake Tossing = _____

2. Parking Meter Collecting – Fast Shaving = _____

3. 6 + Car Eating = _____

4. Backward Racing – _____ = Unicycle Racing

5. Egg Balancing x _____ = Pancake Tossing

6. Leapfrogging + Wheelbarrow Racing = _____

7. Car Eating – 6 = (What Event ?) _____

8. Fast Shaving + (What Event?) _____ = Pancake Tossing

I ate that book in record time!

Name _____

Copyright © 2016 World Book, Inc./ Incentive Publications, Chicago, IL

DOZENS OF DANCERS

Dancers around the world try to set records for the longest or fastest dance, or for the dance with the most people. The biggest tap dance, with 6,951 dancers, took place in New York City. The longest line dance had 18,431 dancers. The longest dancing dragon was about 3.5 miles (5.5 kilometers) long and made up of over 3,000 people.

These dancers are making their line around a coordinate grid. Write the coordinates of each dancer on the grid. Write coordinates like this: (x, y).

A. _____

B. _____

C. _____

D. _____

E. _____

F. _____

G. _____

H. _____

I. _____

J. _____

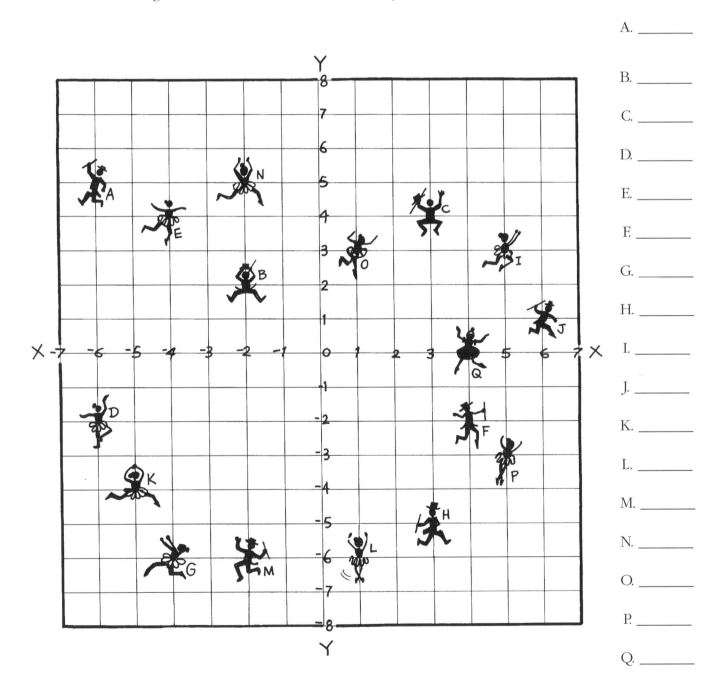

K. _____

L. _____

M. _____

N. _____

O. _____

P. _____

Q. _____

Name _____

PIGGY BANK PROBABILITIES

The world's largest piggy bank is over 26 feet (8 meters) long and over 18 feet (5.5 meters) tall.

This piggy bank has seven coins inside:

3 quarters
2 dimes
1 nickel
1 penny

A. If you shake one coin out, what is the probability (chance) that it will be a quarter?

   1. P (Q) = _____

   2. What is the chance it will be a penny?
   P (P) = _____

   3. P (D) = _____

   4. P (N) = _____

B. A piggy bank has these coins:
6 dimes, 3 quarters, 3 nickels, 2 pennies. Shake out one coin.

   1. P (D) = _____

   2. P (Q) = _____

   3. P (N) = _____

   4. P (not a dime) = _____

   5. P (not a quarter) = _____

   6. P (D or N) = _____

   7. P (Q or a P) = _____

C. A piggy bank has these coins:
7 pennies, 4 dimes, 5 nickels. Shake out one coin.

   1. P (not a dime) = _____

   2. P (N) = _____

   3. P (P) = _____

   4. P (D) = _____

   5. P (N or D) = _____

   6. P (Quarter) = _____

   7. P (D or P) = _____

Name

LOTS & LOTS OF LITTER

One day a huge number of collectors gathered to pick up litter in one place. There were 146,679 people who worked to pick up litter in Japan. This set a record for the most litter collectors.

This bag of litter contains 10 old shoes (S), 5 banana peels (BP), 5 burned out light bulbs (LB), and 10 candy wrappers (CW).

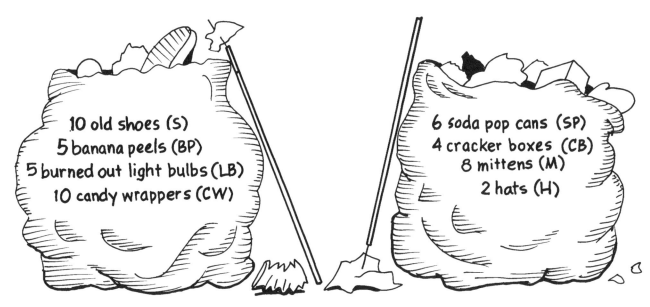

10 old shoes (S)
5 banana peels (BP)
5 burned out light bulbs (LB)
10 candy wrappers (CW)

6 soda pop cans (SP)
4 cracker boxes (CB)
8 mittens (M)
2 hats (H)

If you reach in and grab the first piece of litter you touch, what is the probability (chance) that it will be a . . . .

1. P (S) = _____

2. P (BP) = _____

3. P (LB) = _____

4. P (CW) = _____

5. P (S or CW) = _____

6. P (not a CW) = _____

7. P (not a BP) = _____

8. P (BP or LB) = _____

9. P (not a S) = _____

10. P (not a LB) = _____

Another bag of litter contains
   6 soda pop cans (SP)
   4 cracker boxes (CB)
   8 mittens (M)
   2 hats (H)

If you reach in and grab the first piece of litter you touch, what is the probability (chance) that it will be a . . .

11. P (SP) = _____

12. P (CB) = _____

13. P (M) = _____

14. P (H) = _____

15. P (M or H) = _____

16. P (not M) = _____

Name

WALKING TALL FOR NEW RECORDS

The longest walk on stilts covered over 3,000 miles. A man walked from New York to Los Angeles in 1957. The tallest stilts ever used for a walk were over 50 feet tall. A man from China walked 10 steps on these in 2006.

The spinner is a guide for kids doing a stilt race. The spinner tells them how many steps to take on each turn.

Look at the spinner to answer these probability problems.

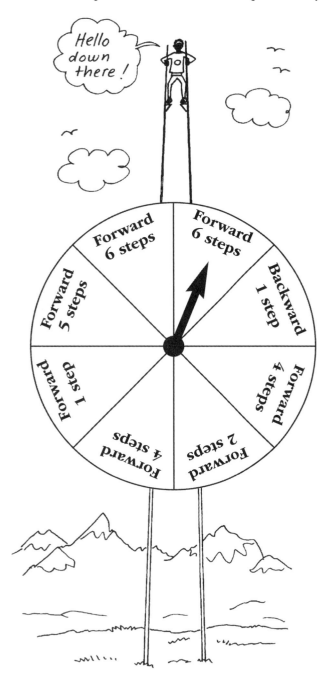

1. How many different outcomes are there for ONE spin? _____

What is the probability for each outcome below with ONE spin?

2. P (6 steps forward) = _____

3. P (5 steps forward) = _____

4. P (1 step forward) = _____

5. P (2 steps forward) = _____

6. P (4 steps forward) = _____

7. P (steps forward) = _____

8. P (steps backward) = _____

9. P (1 step in either direction) = _____

10. P (3 steps forward) = _____

11. P (less than 5 steps forward) = _____

12. P (more than 2 steps forward) = _____

13. P (more than 2 steps backward) = _____

14. P (5 or 6 steps forward) = _____

Name

WILL THERE BE LIGHT?

Six hundred thousand light bulbs would give off a lot of light. This is how many bulbs the world's greatest collector of light bulbs gathered. Is it possible that they all still work?

Out of 10 light bulbs, 4 are burned out. If you choose a bulb, what is the chance that it will be burned out? You know that the probability of choosing a burned-out bulb is $\frac{4}{10}$.

There is another way to talk about such choices. This is to describe **odds in favor of** an event and **odds against** an event.

"Odds in favor" are written like this: $\frac{\text{number burned out}}{\text{number not burned out}}$ or $\frac{4}{6}$.

The odds in favor of getting a burned-out light bulb are $\frac{4}{6}$ or 4 to 6.

The odds against getting a burned-out light bulb are 6 to 4 or $\frac{6}{4}$.

1. 8 light bulbs; 3 are burned out
   a. odds in favor of choosing a burned-out bulb = _____
   b. odds against choosing a burned-out bulb = _____

2. 20 light bulbs; 8 are burned out
   a. odds in favor of choosing a burned-out bulb = _____
   b. odds against choosing a burned-out bulb = _____

3. 7 light bulbs; 6 are burned out
   a. odds in favor of choosing a burned-out bulb = _____
   b. odds against choosing a burned-out bulb = _____

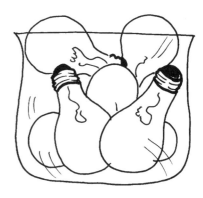

4. 11 light bulbs; 1 is burned out
   a. odds in favor of choosing a burned-out bulb = _____
   b. odds against choosing a burned-out bulb = _____

5. 10 light bulbs; 5 are burned out
   a. odds in favor of choosing a burned-out bulb = _____
   b. odds against choosing a burned-out bulb = _____

Name

THE BIGGEST DROP

Frenchman Jean Francois Gravelet (also known as Charles Blondin) was the first person to walk across Niagara Falls on a tightrope. He accomplished the feat on June 30, 1859.

In one tightrope contest, the competitors rolled two dice to see who would walk the rope first. The person with the highest number was the starter.

When you roll two dice, what are all the possible outcomes of the two events? It is helpful to put the outcomes on a chart. Finish the chart to show all the possibilities.

Use the chart to help solve the probability problems on page 289.

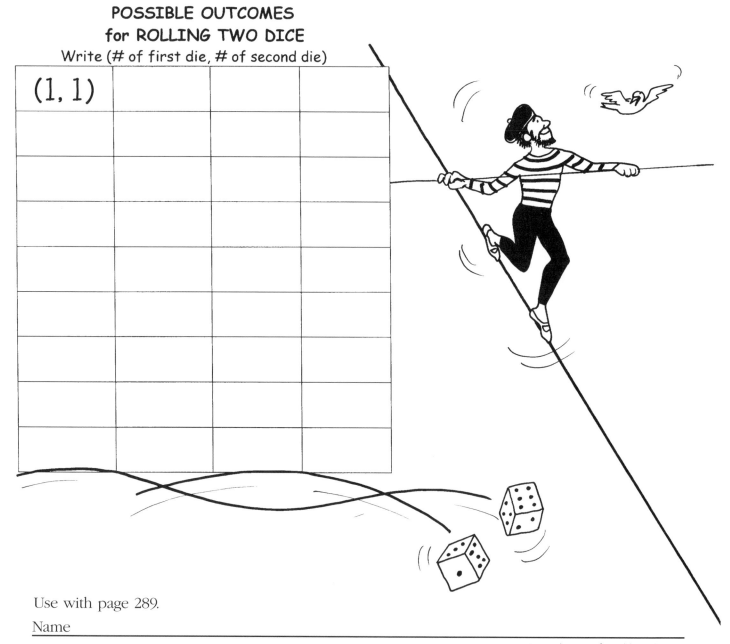

POSSIBLE OUTCOMES for ROLLING TWO DICE

Write (# of first die, # of second die)

(1, 1)			

Use with page 289.

Name _____

THE BIGGEST DROP, CONT.

Use the table you finished on page 288 to help you solve these probability problems. The problems ask about the probability for different outcomes when the tightrope walkers tossed two dice to decide who would walk the rope first.

1. P (1, 3) = _____

2. P (3, 3) = _____

3. P (5, 6) = _____

4. P (6, 7) = _____

5. P (two of same number) = _____

6. P (a 4 and a 3) = _____

7. P (2 even numbers) = _____

8. P (an odd and even number) = _____

9. P (a sum of 2) = _____

10. P (a sum of 4) = _____

11. P (two numbers ≥ 4) = _____

12. P (two numbers < 4) = _____

13. P (two numbers < 6) = _____

14. P (two odd numbers) = _____

15. P (no ones) = _____

16. P (4, 6) = _____

17. P (two numbers < 3) = _____

18. P (a sum of 8) = _____

19. P (a sum of 10) = _____

20. P (a sum of 11) = _____

The longest tightrope walk lasted 205 days. An amazing performer, Jorge Ojeda-Guzman, spent all this time dancing and walking and balancing a chair on the tightrope that was 35 feet above the ground. You can imagine how much fun this was for the spectators!

Use with page 288.

Name _____

CAREFULLY BALANCED EGGS

It is quite a trick to balance one egg on the edge of a table or ledge. Imagine how difficult it must be to balance 1,290 eggs at the same time. This is the record for egg balancing by one person. It was set by Brian Spotts of Colorado, in 2003.

A. When egg balancer Egbert gets ready to practice, he takes several eggs out of his egg bag. Today his bag contains eggs of four colors: red, blue, green, and white.
Egbert chooses two eggs. There are an equal number of all the colors in the bag. What different color combinations are possible for Egbert to choose? (The order of the colors does not matter; for instance, *red and blue* is the same combination as *blue and red*.)

Use the table to show the different combinations.

Combinations of 2 eggs from 4 colors

B. If there are five colors—red, blue, pink, orange, and white—what combinations of two eggs could Egbert possibly choose?

Use the table to show the different combinations.

Combinations of 2 eggs from 5 colors

Name _____

A PUZZLING RECORD

The largest jigsaw puzzle on record that was successfully finished was 551,232 pieces. Imagine how long it took to put this one together!

Patricia wants to figure out how many puzzle pieces of each color are in this bag of 1,200 pieces. She does not have time to count all the pieces, but she can estimate the number of pieces by taking a sample.

She draws 5 puzzle pieces and records the colors. She puts the pieces back and draws another sample of 5. Patricia does this 4 times. Out of her 20 samples, she has found:

    2 white
10 red
    4 purple
    4 black

1. In her sample, what was the probability of white? _____

2. What was the probability of red? _____

3. What was the probability of purple? _____

4. What was the probability of black? _____

5. Can you use these probability fractions to predict the number of each color in the whole bag of 1,200?
    a. white = _____
    b. red = _____
    c. purple = _____
    d. black = _____

6. A bag of snack bars contains 500 bars.
    A sample of 50 gives these results:
        20 chocolate
        25 strawberry
         5 apple

    Predict the total number of each flavor in the bag of 500.
        a. chocolate = _____
        b. strawberry = _____
        c. apple = _____

Name _____

BARROW RACING FOR DOLLARS

The largest wheelbarrow race was by 1,554 people (777 pairs). The record was set in Australia in 2009.

These wheelbarrow racers are hoping to win some prizes. Each race has two competitors. When the race is over, each competitor chooses an envelope. They combine their winnings.

The envelopes contain $10, $20, $50, and $100 bills. Every racer has an equal chance of getting any of the envelopes.

1. How many different possible totals are there? _____ Write them on the table.

$10. #1 $20. #2 $50. #3 $100. #4

Possible Outcomes

OUTCOME	TOTAL $
$10. & $10.	$20.
$10. & $20.	$30.

2. Could Will and Wilma win $100 between the two of them? _____

3. Could they win $250 after one race? _____

4. Could they win $50 total? _____

5. Could they win $70 total? _____

6. What is the probability of winning $200? _____

Name

APPENDIX

CONTENTS

Language Arts Skills Test 294

Social Studies Skills Test 310

Science Skills Test 317

Math Skills Test 320

Skills Test Answer Key 330

Skills Exercises Answer Key 334

LANGUAGE ARTS SKILLS TEST

Part One: Reading Comprehension

I HEAR
by Chloe H., Gr. 6

The cries of eagles awake my peaceful slumber
Snoring floats through the wall and out
into space somewhere, bouncing off walls and trees
The pitter on the window tells me it's raining,
A loud boom sounds as my dog comes running,
toe nails clicking on the hard floor
A flash of light hits the tree outside and cracks
as the tree slowly falls to the ground.

I hear weather crashing crashing,
seashells cracking,
waves roaring
and crabs snapping.
And I hear the yellow sun sparkling.
by Ashley R., Gr. 3

SILENCE
by Christopher B., Gr. 5

I hear silence,
terrible, awful silence,
boring, boring silence.
Trying my patience,
making me mad,
ahhhhhh, I yell.
I break the silence,
but I make happiness.

What I Hear
by Tessah J., Gr. 4

I hear the rumble of the washers in a laundromat.
I hear the crack of lightning during the storm.
I hear the click of the heels on the high school dance floor.
I hear the asteroids flying by Mars.
I hear the whispers as children share secrets.
I hear the recess bell buzzing in my ear.
I hear the scraping of boot nails on the Matterhorn.
I hear Paul Bunyan chopping down trees.

1. What is unusual about the last line of Ashley's poem? _____

2. What things make clicking sounds in the poems? _____

3. What things make cracking sounds in the poems? _____

4. Find three words in the poems that actually sound like the sound they name (examples: "pop" or "hiss")? _____

5. What title would you give the poem that has no title? _____

6. Find a word in one of the poems that is a synonym for "angry." _____

7. Find a word that means the opposite of "interesting." _____

8. Which things are heard in Tessah's poem that are rather fantastic? _____

_____

9. What words does Christopher use to describe silence? _____

10. What is the unusual use of repetition in Tessah's poem? _____

Name _____

Read the poem and the sentences below. Next to each one, write the code letters of the literary devices that have been used. There may be more than one.

P = personification	**I** = idiom	**M** = metaphor
A = alliteration	**S** = simile	**E** = exaggeration

_____ 11. Read the poem *The Wind* and and write the code letters.

_____ 12. *The queen is quite quick at quilting!*

_____ 13. *You are driving me up a wall with your constant complaining!*

_____ 14. **Today the clouds are dragons breathing fires of stinging raindrops.**

_____ 15. A sneaky fog stretched out its long, silvery fingers, reaching for me.

_____ 16. My calculator is like an annoying little brother.

_____ 17. **It was so hot that the chickens laid scrambled eggs.**

The Wind
by Joseph Z., Gr. 4

The wind is a crystal clear icy breeze.
It is a strong giant, a gentle child,
a furious volcano,
a steady moving thing.
　　It has feelings like us,
　　like a rushing person,
　　like a curious child,
　　like a patient waving person.
Sometimes it dies,
Sometimes it's alive—faster than you and me.
The wind shakes us, calms us, freezes us,
It's a dirty job
　　　　but <u>something</u> has to do it.

18. The limerick is out of order! Number the lines in the right order.

_____ *Of the dragons so near,*

_____ *It's just that his suit was too tight!*

_____ *For months kept refusing to fight.*

_____ *He didn't have fear*

_____ *It's strange that Sir Guilford, the Knight*

19. Read the poem. Write two more lines with the same form the writer has used.

What I WAS and What I AM
by Sophie D., Gr. 2
I was a tree but now I'm paper
I was wheat but now I'm bread
I was a stream but now I'm a river
I was a chick but now I'm a chicken
I was a sprout but now I'm the biggest tree in the world
I was nothing but now I am something
I was a loaf of bread but now I'm a crumb

I was _____ but now I'm _____

I was _____ but now I'm _____

Name _____

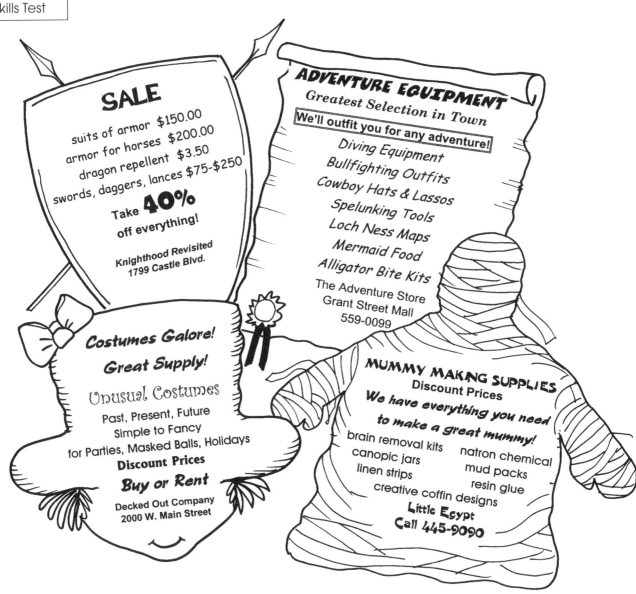

SALE

suits of armor $150.00
armor for horses $200.00
dragon repellent $3.50
swords, daggers, lances $75-$250

Take **40%** off everything!

Knighthood Revisited
1799 Castle Blvd.

ADVENTURE EQUIPMENT
Greatest Selection in Town

We'll outfit you for any adventure!

Diving Equipment
Bullfighting Outfits
Cowboy Hats & Lassos
Spelunking Tools
Loch Ness Maps
Mermaid Food
Alligator Bite Kits

The Adventure Store
Grant Street Mall
559-0099

Costumes Galore!
Great Supply!
Unusual Costumes

Past, Present, Future
Simple to Fancy
for Parties, Masked Balls, Holidays
Discount Prices
Buy or Rent

Decked Out Company
2000 W. Main Street

MUMMY MAKING SUPPLIES
Discount Prices
We have everything you need to make a great mummy!

brain removal kits
canopic jars
linen strips
creative coffin designs

natron chemical
mud packs
resin glue

Little Egypt
Call 445-9090

20. Might you find a costume for a Stone Age Ball at one of these shops? _____

21. How many stores give a discount? _____

22. Which store is on Castle Blvd? _____

23. Where could you get a matador's cape? _____

24. Where would you shop for an Elvis costume? _____

25. Where would you shop for leprechaun-hunting supplies? _____

26. Can you rent a costume at the Decked Out Company? _____

27. How much would you pay for a horse suit of armor? _____

28. Which stores list phone numbers in their ads? _____

29. Does Little Egypt supply all the things needed for mummy-making? _____

30. What is the chemical that's needed for preserving a mummy? _____

Name _____

Are You Ready?

If you ever plan to do any adventuring in space, you will need to know how astronauts get along. When you head into space, the ordinary environment of life is gone. There is no air, sunshine, day or night, or gravity. When your shuttle takes off, your body will feel squished and squashed. Everything in the world of the astronaut is without gravity. You will have to sleep, move, eat, and stay healthy in a place where everything floats around.

Fortunately, you'll have a space suit made of many layers that supplies you with oxygen and removes carbon dioxide and other waste products. The suit keeps the atmospheric pressure right for your body and keeps you warm. It has a special drink bag and a camera for sending pictures to the cockpit. You'll also have to be hooked up to a portable lavatory to take care of body wastes!

Living without gravity is quite a bit different from your normal life! You'll have to be tied to your bunk at night or use a sleeping suit. Your dinner would float away if it were not securely wrapped in a package. Living without day and night is strange, too. Someone will have to tell you when it's time for you to sleep.

So, what do you think? Sounds thrilling, doesn't it? Do you still want to head off into space?

31. Find one statement that is opinion rather than fact. Circle it.
32. Find two statements that give details to support the idea that living without gravity is strange. Underline them.
33. The main idea is
   a. Space travel is dangerous.
   b. Astronauts need special equipment to deal with different life in space.
   c. Space travel is great fun.

Part Two: Words & Vocabulary

Write the letter of the word on the right that matches each definition.

_____ 34. whirlpool

_____ 35. odor

_____ 36. to lie

_____ 37. friendly

_____ 38. on time

_____ 39. scold

_____ 40. very hungry

_____ 41. dictionary

_____ 42. puppet

_____ 43. enemy

_____ 44. fear of germs

_____ 45. gloomy

a. annual
b. minuscule
c. chide
d. microphobia
e. morose
f. scoundrel
g. prevaricate
h. famished
i. shriek
j. maelstrom
k. aroma
l. foe
m. martinet
n. cordial
o. lexicon
p. punctual
q. claustrophobia
r. aggravate

Name _____

297

Circle the word that best fits the blank in each sentence.

46. Amy's _____ remarks hurt everyone's feelings.

   courteous   crude   careful   creative

47. Jake was _____ when he saw how close the shark was to his surfboard.

   horrific   satisfied   terrified   horrible

48. I was surprised by the _____ of a lifeguard on this crowded beach.

   presence   hairdo   tan   absence

49. We laughed when the crab _____ Josie's sunglasses.

   disappeared   snatched   returned   crawled

Tell what you think the words in bold mean as they are used in these sentences.

50. I had never seen a bathing suit quite like the **peculiar** one she wore yesterday.

   I think this word means _____.

51. The **ambidextrous** girl wrote one letter with her left hand and one with her right hand.

   I think this word means _____.

Write the letter of the word on the right that matches each definition.

_____ 52. to make friends	a. hoping	l. phobophobia
_____ 53. a creature with five feet	b. hopeless	m. aquaphobia
_____ 54. to read wrong	c. reread	n. frightful
_____ 55. full of fear	d. misread	o. frighten
_____ 56. one who sails	e. dangerous	p. sharpness
_____ 57. to cause terror	f. friendly	q. sharply
_____ 58. state of being sharp	g. befriend	r. sharper
_____ 59. to make afraid	h. pentapod	s. terrify
_____ 60. fear of water	i. octopod	t. sailor
_____ 61. without hope	j. fearless	u. terrible
_____ 62. full of danger	k. fearful	v. hopeful

Write the letter of the word that has a root that means . . .

_____ 63. flee	a. dynamic	f. fugitive
_____ 64. burn	b. flammable	g. visible
_____ 65. carry	c. transport	h. telegram
_____ 66. act or do	d. descend	i. defend
_____ 67. climb	e. action	j. minivan
_____ 68. see		

Name _____

Write the letter of a synonym for each word below.

_____ 69. novice

_____ 70. cease

_____ 71. foible

_____ 72. valiant

_____ 73. conceal

_____ 74. stationary

_____ 75. tremulous

_____ 76. chide

_____ 77. obstinate

a. scold
b. stop
c. victory
d. stubborn
e. flaw
f. tremendous
g. fearful
h. shriek
i. immovable
j. brave
k. hide
l. beginner

Write the letter of an antonym for each word below.

_____ 78. temporary

_____ 79. sturdy

_____ 80. careless

_____ 81. accelerated

_____ 82. cordial

a. permanent
b. flimsy
c. rude
d. speedy
e. friendly
f. heavy
g. cautious
h. agony
i. slowed

Answer the following questions about denotations and connotations.

83. Circle the connotation of the word **pirate.**
    a. one who robs ships at sea
    b. a mean, ruthless man with a patched eye and a wooden leg who makes people walk the plank

84. Circle the denotation of the word **surf.**
    a. the foamy, breaking waves that are such fun for swimming and jumping
    b. the swelling of the sea that breaks on the shore

85. Read the denotation and connotation. Tell what the word is. _____
    Denotation: the breaking up of a sea-going vessel
    Connotation: crashing into rocks on a wild sea and splitting apart

86. Read the denotation and connotation. Tell what the word is. _____
    Denotation: irritation or blistering caused by exposure to the sun
    Connotation: miserable, painful, red skin that you can't stand to touch

Choose three of these words. Write two meanings for each word you choose.

fly   trunk   pen   quarter   date   fence   run   light   down   saw   spot   box   fire

word   *meaning 1*   *meaning 2*

87. _____ _____ _____

88. _____ _____ _____

89. _____ _____ _____

Name

Write the letter of the figurative language expression that matches each meaning below.

_____ 90. calm down

_____ 91. make you mad

_____ 92. give away a secret

_____ 93. take a chance

_____ 94. start too soon

_____ 95. say something embarrassing

_____ 96. fool around

_____ 97. an argument to have

_____ 98. a bad deal, full of problems

_____ 99. is very expensive

a. spill the beans
b. go bananas
c. cost an arm and a leg
d. red-letter day
e. the last straw
f. a bone to pick
g. drive you up a wall
h. go out on a limb
i. scream bloody murder
j. put a lid on it
k. put your foot in your mouth
l. ham it up
m. jump the gun
n. a real lemon

Below is a description of the history and origin of three words. Write the word that matches each one. Choose from the words below.

frankfurter   Frisbee®
omelette   cologne
comet   cabbage
sardine   tortilla
lasagna   leotard

_____ 100. from a Greek word meaning "head with long hair"

_____ 101. a Latin word meaning "head"

_____ 102. named after a pie company owner

Finish these analogies.

103. legs : crab *as* _____ : octopus

104. motorcycle : motorcycles *as* _____ : geese

105. melt : _____ *as* compliment : criticize

106. _____ : blizzard *as* rain : monsoon

107. argue : _____ *as* excite : excitement

108. calculator : mathematician *as* surfboard : _____

Name _____

Part Three: Spelling

Which words on Freddy's poster do NOT have silent letters? Write them below.

stalk	bridge
ghost	honest
envy	sword
combing	erupt
wriggle	knife

shhhhh

109. _____

Which words on Pierre's poster are NOT correct? Write them on the lines correctly.

firecracker	celery	enerjy
couffed	surprice	phone
skuba	sider	babisitter

110. _____

111. _____

112. _____

113. _____

114. _____

115. _____

Are these words spelled correctly? Write yes or no next to each word.

_____ 116. tommorrow   _____ 120. terrible

_____ 117. Tennessee   _____ 121. annimal

_____ 118. memmory   _____ 122. syllable

_____ 119. bannana

Write each word in its PAST tense.

123. worry   _____

124. wish   _____

125. argue   _____

126. freeze   _____

127. forget   _____

Circle the correctly spelled word in each group.

128. Atlantic, Antartica, Brasil

129. Lincon, Warshington, Jupiter

130. Checago, Michigan, Las Angelas

131. Wednesday, Tuseday, Saterday

132. Chrissmas, Haloween, Thanksgiving

Circle the word in each group that is NOT spelled correctly.

133. tomatoes	136. completely	139. arithmatic
torpedoes	magecal	caterpillar
pianoes	favorable	Pennsylvania
volcanoes	accidental	hippopotamus
solos	dentist	
134. wierd	137. subbmarine	140. stubborn
ancient	transport	elegent
their	exclude	comical
height	semicircle	curious
beige	antiwar	
135. homework	138. terrifick	141. galaxy
bookkeeper	agreement	astronot
roommate	dangerous	rotation
notbook	explosion	atmosphere
somebody	tropical	

Name _____

Which words on the chef's shopping list are spelled INCORRECTLY? Write them correctly below.

SHOPPING LIST

- vegtables
- custard
- suger
- macaroni
- spaghetti
- chocolate
- lettuse
- onions
- sausage
- tomatos
- noodels

142. _____

_____

These words are all misspelled. Write them correctly.

143. pilat _____

144. peopel _____

145. cought _____

146. molacule _____

147. lama _____

148. lafter _____

149. agin _____

150. appeer _____

151. enugh _____

Which word is spelled correctly? Circle the correct spelling.

152. separate, seperate   155. wheather, weather

153. absence, abcense   156. autamatic, automatic

154. criticize, criticise   157. license, lisence

Write these misspelled words correctly.

158. toung _____

159. mosquitoe _____

160. oder _____

161. oppisite _____

162. lonleyness _____

163. lenth _____

164. pleeze _____

165. allmost _____

166. nesessary _____

167. **Circle the correctly spelled words on Sheriff Frog's poster.**

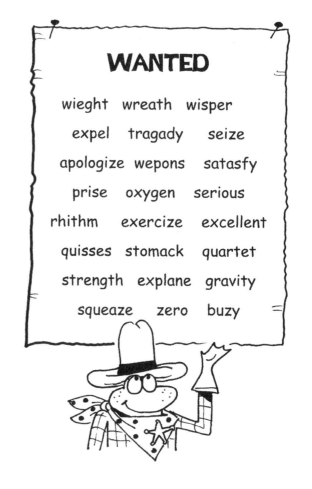

WANTED

wieght   wreath   wisper

expel   tragady   seize

apologize   wepons   satasfy

prise   oxygen   serious

rhithm   exercize   excellent

quisses   stomack   quartet

strength   explane   gravity

squeaze   zero   buzy

Name _____

Circle the correct spelling of each of these confusing words.

168. suprice   surprize   surprise

169. baloon   balloon   ballon

170. marshmellow   marshmalow   marshmallow

171. calender   calendar   callendar

Write the correct word to finish each sentence.

172. _____ (Adopt, Adept) a pet today!

173. I _____ (except, accept) your apology.

174. Count the _____ (angels, angles) in your rectangle.

175. Did you do a _____ (through, though, thorough) job of cleaning?

176. I write in my _____ (dairy, diary) every day.

177. For breakfast, I ate bran _____ (cereal, serial) today.

178. My library book has been _____ (overdue, overdo) for a week.

179. My cat actually _____ (pried, pride) open the cat food box!

180. My _____ (hoarse, horse) is too old to ride anymore.

181. Don't _____ (break, brake) any bones!

Re-write each headline, spelling all the words correctly.

FRIEK AXIDENTS REPORTTED ON PUBLIK BEECHES

182. _____

DOCTER DOES SUPRIZE OPARATION

183. _____

SKI SESON CANCELLED DUE TO DANGROUS ICE STORM

184. _____

TWO HUNRERD HOMES LOST IN TORNADOE

185. _____

ELAPHANT RECIEVES GOLD MEDDLE

186. _____

Part Four: Grammar & Usage

Questions 187 through 271 are worth 1 point each. Question 272 is worth 5 points.

Identify the following sentences by writing . . .

D for **declarative sentence**   **EX** for **exclamatory sentence**

IM for **imperative sentence**   **I** for **interrogative sentence**

_____ 187. How do we get to Camp Lookout?   _____ 190. Please don't feed the bears.

_____ 188. Watch out for scorpions!   _____ 191. It's time to put up the tent.

_____ 189. Did you put the frogs in the boys' bunks?

Identify the following sentences by writing . . .

S for **simple sentence**   **R** for **run-on sentence**

C for **compound sentence**   **F** for **sentence fragment**

_____ 192. Going over the waterfall.

_____ 193. Eat your breakfast, and clean your cabins.

_____ 194. Turn left at the stump take three steps north enter the cave.

_____ 195. What a cute squirrel in your tent!

_____ 196. Did you step in the poison ivy?

Write the simple subject for each sentence on the line.

_____ 197. Sam raced us to the diving board.

_____ 198. Were the bears eating your marshmallows?

_____ 199. The biggest chipmunk took my backpack.

Write the simple predicate for each sentence on the line.

_____ 200. Falling rocks crashed into the campsite.

_____ 201. Could crafty coyotes catch cunning campers?

_____ 202. We watched while the wind blew our tent away.

Identify the parts of speech in the sentence below by writing . . .

N for **noun**   **ADJ** for **adjective**   **V** for **verb**   **ADV** for **adverb**

Three hungry campers gobbled pancakes greedily.

_____ 203. Three   _____ 205. campers   _____ 207. pancakes

_____ 204. hungry   _____ 206. gobbled   _____ 208. greedily

Read the following sentence and look for the nouns. Decide if the nouns are singular or plural.

Last Friday, Billy put spiders in the beds and hot peppers in the meatballs.

_____ 209. Write the singular nouns from the sentence.

_____ 210. Write the plural nouns from the sentence.

Name _____

Write the plural form of each word below.

_____ 211. compass

_____ 212. knife

_____ 213. tomato

_____ 214. deer

_____ 215. family

Write the singular form of each word below.

_____ 216. mice

_____ 217. children

_____ 218. cities

Write a possessive noun phrase (two words) to fit each description.

_____ 219. teeth belonging to one wolf

_____ 220. teeth belonging to more than one wolf

_____ 221. shirts belonging to three campers

_____ 222. tail of one skunk

Write the subject pronoun from each sentence.

_____ 223. They couldn't decide where to pitch their tent.

_____ 224. She said that the task was too hard.

Write the object pronoun from each sentence.

_____ 225. Don't ask him for help.

_____ 226. We gave them a ride on the donkey.

Write the correct form (tense) of the verb needed in the sentence. Find the verb at the end of each sentence.

_____ 227. Yesterday, Carl _____ boats for a contest. (row)

_____ 228. This morning, Lisa _____ away from the sinking boat. (swim)

_____ 229. Oh, no! Matt _____ off his raft into the river! (fall)

_____ 230. Tomorrow our cabin _____ kites. (fly)

_____ 231. Who _____ my green pajamas last night? (wear)

_____ 232. How many campers _____ to their parents this week? (write)

_____ 233. She _____ when she saw the lizard in her shoe. (faint)

_____ 234. Last night we _____ to replace the cook. (vote)

Write the action verb from each sentence.

_____ 235. Lisa screamed at the top of her lungs!

_____ 236. She was there when Maria jumped out of the closet.

_____ 237. Lisa crept underneath the covers.

Name _____

Write the helping verb from each sentence.

_____ 238. He is playing with matches.

_____ 239. Tom should start getting wood for the campfire.

_____ 240. Bigfoot is coming!

_____ 241. Is it true that you have seen a spaceship?

Identify each part of speech shown at the end of the sentence by writing . . .

N for **noun**   **V** for **verb**   **ADJ** for **adjective**   **ADV** for **adverb**

_____ 242. Eat your grilled cheese sandwich. (Eat)

_____ 243. Watch the song leader closely. (closely)

_____ 244. Don't you just love the beautiful camp theme song? (beautiful)

_____ 245. Who won the frog jumping contest? (contest)

_____ 246. Counselor Wacky fell out of the canoe. (fell)

_____ 247. That meat loaf was the most terrible food yet! (terrible)

_____ 248. Back away slowly from the rattlesnake. (slowly)

Write the correct form of the adjective that should be placed in the blank. The adjectives are shown at the end of the sentence.

_____ 249. Karl's race was _____ than Isaac's. (fast)

_____ 250. Whose frog jumped the _____ ? (farther)

_____ 251. This is the _____ lunch meat I've ever seen! (slimy)

Write the adjective form that will correctly fill in the blank.

_____ 252. This is the _____ pizza I have ever eaten. (better, best)

_____ 253. I have eaten a lot, but it is still ____ than you've eaten. (less, least)

_____ 254. My score was the _____ of all the runners. (worse, worst)

Write the adverb form that will correctly fill in the blank.

_____ 255. Billy gets up _____ than the other campers. (early)

_____ 256. He plays pranks _____ than the other campers. (often)

_____ 257. Nick can climb the flagpole the _____ of all of the campers. (quickly)

Choose the word that will show the correct use of a negative.

_____ 258. No one (would, wouldn't) want to miss the shooting stars.

_____ 259. The campers have not gotten (any, no) mail today.

_____ 260. Won't (anyone, no one) come to the haunted cabin with me?

_____ 261. We don't (never, ever) want to go there again.

Write the direct object from each sentence.

_____ 262. The campers ate lunch by the river.

_____ 263. Grab your towels and run!

_____ 264. After dinner, we'll play some good pranks on the boys.

Name _____

Write the correct homophone in each blank.

_____ 265. I've gotten a little (horse, hoarse) from yelling so much.

_____ 266. Watch out! Don't step in that (hole, whole)!

_____ 267. Let's (meet, meat) behind the horse stables at midnight.

_____ 268. That just doesn't make any (cents, sense).

Find the misspelled words in the sentences, and write them correctly on the line.

The cook at are camp allways creats the most delichus meels.
We have our faverite pizza wunce a weak and marshmellows every day for desert!

269. _____

_____

Add quotation marks where needed in each sentence.

270. Camp begins on Sunday and ends on Friday each week in July, said the counselor.

271. Counselor Joe told Lisa, Write to your parents.

Add the missing punctuation to the letter below.

272.

Dear Mom and Dad   July 15

I am having the best time at this camp You won't believe how
well Im doing We have terrible food lots of mosquitoes and grumpy
counselors Doesn't it sound great I think I saw an alien and I fell
out of the canoe three times How much longer can I stay

                                        Your loving son
                                        Manuel

Part Five: Writing

For questions 273–274, circle the letter of the most precise word for each blank.

273. The elephant _____ along heavily in the parade.
   a. pranced   c. slid   e. walked
   b. skipped   d. lumbered

274. Jana's best friend was _____ by her sudden and mysterious disappearance.
   a. amused   c. troubled
   b. bored   d. satisfied

275. Which mood would these words help to set? *hurry, scurry, fast, zip, bustle, quick, dart, dash, race*
   a. curious   c. quiet
   b. playful   d. rushing

276. Which would be a **persuasive** piece of writing?
   a. advertisement convincing someone to buy a new basketball shoe
   b. wild imaginative tale about the future
   c. description of an unusual character
   d. directions for building a kite

277. Which sentence does NOT contain personification?
   a. The vacuum cleaner will chase you until it gobbles the socks off your feet!
   b. I'm sure that doughnut is calling me!
   c. Trees flutter in the soft spring wind.

Name

For each writing task below, follow the directions given. (Worth 5 points each.)

Task 1: Number these sentences (1–7) in an order that makes sense.

_____ When it was over, we found our car in the neighbor's swimming pool.

_____ Our car was hurled across the street like a plastic toy.

_____ The tornado struck at dawn.

_____ Suddenly the roar stopped and everything was still.

_____ Slowly, we crept out of the shelter.

_____ We hurried into the shelter.

_____ A whirling, black funnel headed straight for our house.

Task 2: Replace each ordinary word with a more colorful or interesting word. Write a new word above the underlined word.

It was a <u>bad</u> idea to ride the roller coaster when I was feeling <u>sick</u>. The Triple Loop looked <u>scary</u>. Once I got on, my stomach hurt as the roller coaster <u>moved</u> up and down and <u>went</u> from side to side. I have never felt so <u>awful!</u>

Task 3: Rewrite the following sentences to make the meaning clear.

1. Sitting on the top shelf of the closet, I found an old sandwich.

   _____

   _____

2. We heard about the robber who was caught on the radio.

   _____

   _____

Task 4: Write a strong beginning for one of these topics.

- learning to tame a lion
- a dog who can read
- a strange disappearance
- lizards who can dance
- a visit with Bigfoot
- a shocking letter
- an accident
- a terrible flood
- a memory

_____

_____

_____

Task 5: Write a strong ending for one of these topics.

- an earthquake
- a person to avoid
- a place never to go
- a wild hockey game
- a mystery
- a case of green earlobes
- a person to meet
- an embarrassing moment

_____

_____

_____

Task 6: Write a clear, complete, interesting sentence about one of these topics.

- a bothersome bumblebee
- a wild thunderstorm
- a dark, spooky night
- a slithery snake
- a disappointment
- a tough science test

_____

_____

_____

Task 7: Choose one of the people below, and write two good questions that you would ask him or her.

- your favorite author
- a heart surgeon
- a gorilla trainer
- a Supreme Court justice
- someone who climbed Mt. Everest
- someone who rode a roller coaster for 14 days straight

1. _____

   _____

   _____

2. _____

   _____

   _____

Name _____

Task 8: Write a good headline for this news article.

_____

_____

_____

A man was found wandering on Main Street last night wearing tattered socks and no shoes. He was also missing his shirt, hat, glasses, the left leg of his pants, and his memory. He did not remember anything after seeing an approaching tornado. Police are searching for his family. Anyone having information about his possible identity, call the city police at 555-2222.

Task 9: Rewrite the conversation from the cartoon. Write it in a paragraph that includes dialogue. Use correct punctuation for the dialogue.

Georgia, what time is it when a gorilla knocks on your door?

It's time to run out the back door, Dan!

_____
_____
_____
_____

Editing task 10 is worth 10 points.
Task 10: Correct the spelling, punctuation, capitalization, and grammar in the following letter. Also, eliminate excess words or phrases. Cross out the errors and write the corrections above each line.

Dear editor

In my opinion, I beleeve that the new minature golf corse which the city has built owned by the city should change its rules.

It does not make sens not to allow kids under 18 to come unless they are with adults I thought the city bilt this corse to atract kids and give them something good to do in the evenings. this is a wunderful activity for kids, but you are keeping them away. Most teenagers want to go out for an activity with their friends, not their parents Whose bad idea was this! I protest I hope this rule will be changed soon

Sincerely,
Adam

Writing task 11 is worth 15 points.
Task 11: Write a description, story, or tall tale to go along with the picture. Make sure your piece of writing has:

- a good title
- a strong beginning
- a strong middle
- a strong ending
- details to explain the main idea

SOCIAL STUDIES SKILLS TEST

Part One: U.S. History, Government, & Citizenship

Each correct answer is worth 1 point.
For each headline shown below, write the event.

1. _____   2. _____

3. _____   4. _____

5. _____   _____

```
1  Tribune 1865
   IT'S OVER AT LAST!

2  Sun Times 1920
   Women Celebrate!

3  Gazette 1776
   WE DECLARE!

4  Missouri Gazette 1843
   WAGONS HEAD WEST

5  Morning News July 1969
   BIG STEP IS CHEERED
```

Match the key persons in U.S. history with the correct descriptions.

_____ 6. first man to fly across the Atlantic alone

_____ 7. president during the Iran Hostage Crisis

_____ 8. president during the Civil War

_____ 9. president during World War I

_____ 10. explorer who found the Mississippi River

_____ 11. one of the writers of the Declaration of Independence

_____ 12. explorers of the Louisiana Purchase

_____ 13. general who led the Confederate army

_____ 14. first female candidate for vice president

_____ 15. built a fortune in steel; gave money to start libraries

_____ 16. refused to give up her bus seat, beginning the Montgomery Bus Boycott

_____ 17. Quaker founder of Pennsylvania

_____ 18. Sioux Indian Chief at the Battle of Little Bighorn

_____ 19. became president after Kennedy was shot

_____ 20. first woman appointed to the Supreme Court

_____ 21. president during the Cuban Missile Crisis

_____ 22. former slave who helped other slaves escape through the Underground Railroad

A. Rosa Parks
B. Robert E. Lee
C. Henry de Soto
D. Harriet Tubman
E. Crazy Horse
F. Charles Lindbergh
G. Abraham Lincoln
H. Lyndon Johnson
I. John F. Kennedy
J. Woodrow Wilson
K. Thomas Jefferson
L. Sandra Day O'Connor
M. Jimmy Carter
N. Lewis & Clark
O. William Penn
P. Geraldine Ferraro
Q. Andrew Carnegie
R. Franklin D. Roosevelt
S. Richard Nixon

Name _____

Match each document with its correct description.

_____ 23. first 10 amendments to the Constitution; guarantees rights for all citizens

_____ 24. main document establishing the U.S. government

_____ 25. the beginning of the Constitution

_____ 26. changes added to the Constitution

_____ 27. document that stated the U.S. was free from Great Britain

A. the Constitution
B. amendments
C. Bill of Rights
D. Declaration of Independence
E. Preamble

Write the letter from the map that shows the location where each event took place.

_____ 28. assassination of John F. Kennedy

_____ 29. Statue of Liberty arrives

_____ 30. start of Revolutionary War

_____ 31. Abraham Lincoln's birthplace

_____ 32. purchased for $7.2 million

_____ 33. 1849 Gold Rush

_____ 34. Battle of Little Bighorn

_____ 35. Constitution written

_____ 36. Transcontinental Railroad finished

_____ 37. launch of space shuttle *Challenger*

Write the letter of the correct answer on the blank.

_____ 38. Which war did the U.S. fight against Britain for independence?
a. Revolutionary War   b. Civil War   c. War of 1812

_____ 39. What was the rebuilding period after the Civil War?
a. the Renaissance   b. the Cold War   c. Reconstruction

_____ 40. The earliest European explorers of the North American continent were
a. Austrian   b. French, Spanish, and Italian   c. English

_____ 41. Which was NOT one of the original 13 colonies?
a. Virginia   b. Massachusetts   c. Ohio   d. Pennsylvania   e. Maryland

_____ 42. What was the first permanent English settlement in America?
a. Philadelphia   b. Boston   c. Jamestown   d. Plymouth

_____ 43. When was the Constitution written?
a. before the Revolutionary War   b. after the Revolutionary War   c. during the Civil War

_____ 44. Which did NOT happen during the Revolutionary War period?
a. Paul Revere warned that the British were approaching
b. The Battle of Bunker Hill
c. the British passed the Sugar Act, Tea Act, and Stamp Acts
d. the colonies argued over slavery

Name _____

_____ 45. Which event did NOT happen during the Civil War and Reconstruction period?
  a. Lincoln was assassinated
  b. General Lee surrendered at Appomattox
  c. General Eisenhower led the Union Troops
  d. the Underground Railroad helped slaves escape to Canada
  e. *Uncle Tom's Cabin* was written

_____ 46. What 1803 land purchase nearly doubled the size of the United States?
  a. purchase of Alaska
  b. Louisiana Purchase
  c. purchase of Texas

_____ 47. What event connected the eastern U.S. with the west?
  a. the Mexican War
  b. the election of Roosevelt
  c. the building of the Panama Canal
  d. the completion of the Transcontinental Railroad

_____ 48. Why was the Bill of Rights added to the Constitution?
  a. Thomas Jefferson suggested it
  b. Washington would not be president without it
  c. the citizens of the new states demanded it

Write the correct answers to each of these questions.

49. How are Supreme Court justices chosen? _____

50. Who is the head of the armed forces? _____

51. Name the three branches of the U.S. government. _____

52. How long is a representative's term? _____

53. How long is a president's term? _____

54. Who interprets the laws? _____

55. Who makes the laws? _____

56. A senator's term lasts how long? _____

57. The number of representatives a state has depends upon what? _____

58. How many senators are in the Senate? _____

59. What does the Cabinet do? _____

60. What can a president do to stop a bill after it's approved by Congress? _____

Write the letter from the timeline that matches each event.

_____ 61. Assassinations of Martin Luther King, Jr., & Robert Kennedy

_____ 62. Gulf War

_____ 63. Terrorist attacks on the World Trade Center and Pentagon buildings

_____ 64. Opening of the Panama Canal

_____ 65. Stock Market crash

_____ 66. Atomic bombs dropped on Japan

_____ 67. Korean War begins

_____ 68. U.S. enters World War I

_____ 69. Iran Hostage Crisis

_____ 70. Bombing of Pearl Harbor

Name _____

Match each term and event with its description.

_____ 71. period of rebuilding after the Civil War

_____ 72. Native American desert dwellers

_____ 73. people given free land in the West

_____ 74. conflict over Soviet-made missiles being stored 90 miles away from U.S.

_____ 75. scandal that caused President Nixon to resign

_____ 76. white Southerners who remained loyal to the Union during the Civil War

_____ 77. economic plunge that began in 1929

_____ 78. unpopular war in Southeast Asia

_____ 79. site of the high school where the president sent in troops to make sure that nine black students could attend

_____ 80. 66 Americans held in the U.S. Embassy in Tehran

_____ 81. moving to another country

_____ 82. tension that developed between U.S. and U.S.S.R. after World War II

_____ 83. place where the Constitution is kept

_____ 84. presidential order that freed the slaves in the South

_____ 85. cannot be given or taken away

_____ 86. separation of the races

_____ 87. U.S.S.R. space satellite whose launching began the Space Race

_____ 88. wall in Washington, D.C., with the names of 58,000 killed soldiers

_____ 89. home of the U.S. Congress

_____ 90. outlawing of slavery

A. Reconstruction

B. Iran Hostage Crisis

C. immigration

D. abolition

E. scalawags

F. Cold War

G. Navajo Shepherds

H. inalienable

I. Emancipation Proclamation

J. segregation

K. homesteaders

L. Cuban Missile Crisis

M. Watergate

N. Capitol Building

O. Great Depression

P. Vietnam War

Q. Sputnik

R. Little Rock, Arkansas

S. National Archives

T. Vietnam War Memorial

U. White House

Write the letter of the correct answer on the blank.

___ 91. Which happened first?
a. Gulf War
b. Revolutionary War
c. Civil War

___ 92. Which happened first?
a. 1929 Stock Market Crash
b. World War II
c. Oklahoma City bombing

___ 93. Which happened first?
a. Women got to vote
b. Cuban Missile Crisis
c. Nixon resigned

___ 94. Which happened first?
a. Alaska became a state
b. George Washington inaugurated
c. Korean War

___ 95. Who was president first?
a. Abraham Lincoln
b. George Bush
c. John F. Kennedy

___ 96. Which happened last?
a. Panama Canal built
b. Pilgrims landed at Plymouth
c. Kennedy assassinated

___ 97. Which happened last?
a. Cold War
b. Gulf War
c. World War II

___ 98. Which happened last?
a. Atomic bombs were dropped
b. First moon walk
c. Louisiana Purchase

___ 99. Who lived most recently?
a. Martin Luther King, Jr.
b. Thomas Jefferson
c. Daniel Boone

___100. Which happened last?
a. Boston Tea Party
b. Declaration of Independence
c. California Gold Rush

Name

Part Two: Map Skills & Geography

Answer the questions. Each question is worth 1 point.

Write the letter of the location on the world map that matches each of these countries.

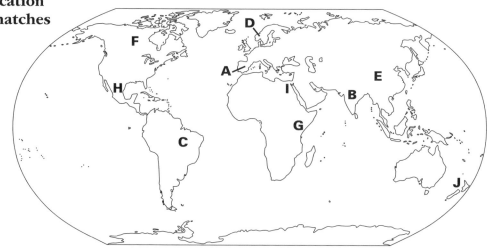

_____ 101. Egypt

_____ 102. Mexico

_____ 103. Brazil

_____ 104. Spain

_____ 105. India

_____ 106. Canada

_____ 107. New Zealand

_____ 108. Norway

_____ 109. Kenya

_____ 110. China

Write the letter of the map term that matches each description.

_____ 111. tells what the map is about

_____ 112. shows amount of rainfall

_____ 113. explains map symbols

_____ 114. shows height of landforms

_____ 115. gives directions on the map

_____ 116. shows cities, states, and countries

_____ 117. shows rivers, lakes, and mountains

_____ 118. tells about distances on a map

_____ 119. shows things a country produces

_____ 120. shows rooms in a building

a. title
b. population map
c. political map
d. elevation map
e. scale
f. product map
g. floor plan
h. physical map
i. weather map
j. road map
k. map key
l. time zone map
m. compass rose

Circle the correct answer or answers.

121. If the scale of a park map is 1 inch = 20 feet, a measurement on the map of 6 inches stands for how much distance in the actual park?
    a. 3.5 feet   b. 12 feet   c. 120 feet   d. 1,200 feet   e. 12,000 feet

122. An island that is 60 miles long is 3 inches long on a map. The map's scale is
    a. 1 in. = 10 miles   b. 1 in. = 3 miles   c. 1 in. = 600 miles   d. 1 in. = 20 miles

123. Which continents does the equator pass through?
    a. Europe   b. South America   c. North America   d. Africa   e. Australia

224. Which continent is entirely south of the equator?
    a. Australia   b. Africa   c. Asia   d. South America

125. Which continents are entirely north of the equator?
    a. Europe   b. South America   c. Asia   d. North America

Name

Circle the correct answer or answers.

126. Which continents are primarily in the Eastern Hemisphere?
    a. Asia   b. North America
    c. Europe   d. Africa   e. Australia

127. Which continents are entirely in the Western Hemisphere?
    a. Europe   b. North America
    c. South America   d. Antarctica

128. Which country does the Tropic of Cancer pass through?
    a. Greenland   b. Brazil
    c. South Africa   d. Mexico

129. Which countries does the Arctic Circle pass through?
    a. Spain   b. Norway
    c. India   d. United States

130. Lines of latitude tell
    a. the distance east or west of the prime meridian
    b. the distance north or south of the equator
    c. the distance east or west of the International Date Line

What can be found at each of these locations? Write the answers.

_____ 131. 0° latitude

_____ 132. 23° 30' north latitude

_____ 133. 90° south latitude

_____ 134. 0° longitude

_____ 135. 66° 30' south latitude

_____ 136. 23° 30' south latitude

_____ 137. 66° 30' north latitude

_____ 138. 90° north latitude

139. Circle the oceans that touch South America.
    a. Atlantic   b. Arctic
    c. Indian   d. Pacific

140. Circle the countries that touch the Arctic Ocean.
    a. Russia   b. Canada   c. Norway
    d. France   e. Mexico

141. Which one is NOT in the Southern Hemisphere? Circle it.
    a. Indian Ocean   b. Africa
    c. Australia   d. Great Lakes

Use the Computer County map (and a metric ruler) to answer these questions.

_____ 142. About how far is Hard Drive City from Floppy Town?

_____ 143. About how far is it from the railroad crossing to the railroad bridge?

_____ 144. Which highway crosses Interstate 95?

_____ 145. Which direction is Laptop Lake from CD Junction?

_____ 146. Which direction is Web Site Peak from Hard Drive City?

_____ 147. Can you drive to Fax Farm on Rom Drive?

_____ 148. Which road runs from northeast to southwest?

_____ 149. How far north of Hard Drive City does Interstate 95 cross Ram Way?

_____ 150. Which direction is the Internet Range from Laptop Lake?

_____ 151. How wide is the lake (east to west)?

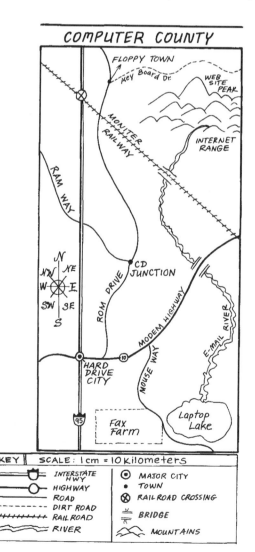

Name _____

Fantasy Village

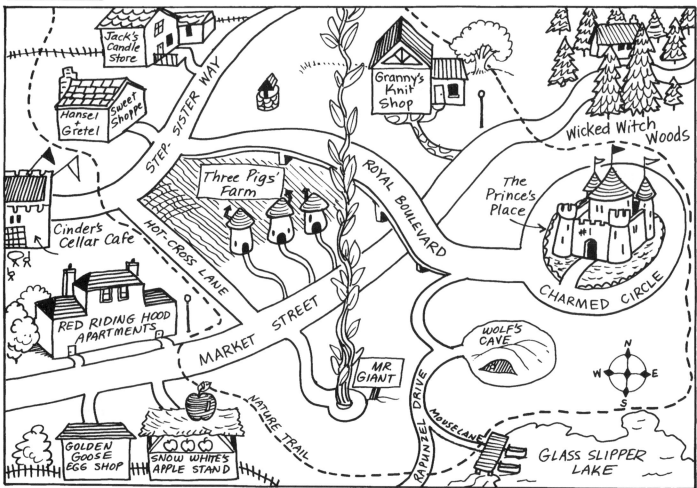

Use the Fantasy Village map (and a ruler) to answer these questions.   Scale 1 inch = 500 feet

_____ 152. Which street does the nature trail cross twice?

_____ 153. Wicked Witch Woods is what direction from Mr. Giant's home?

_____ 154. How tall is Mr. Giant's beanstalk (as much as is shown on the map)?

_____ 155. How far apart are the pigs' driveways?

_____ 156. What direction is Jack's Candle Store from the castle?

_____ 157. How long is Royal Boulevard?

_____ 158. How many streets border the pigs' farm?

_____ 159. Does the wolf live closer to Granny, the pigs, or Red Riding Hood?

_____ 160. What direction is Snow White's Apple Stand from the Sweet Shoppe?

161. Describe the shortest route (on streets and trails) the wolf could take to get to Granny's shop.

_____

_____

Write the letter of the term that matches each definition.

_____ 162. a deep, narrow valley with steep sides

_____ 163. narrow strip of land that connects two larger pieces of land and is bordered on both sides by water

_____ 164. a high, flat landform that rises steeply above surrounding land

_____ 165. an area of very low precipitation

_____ 166. a body of land mostly surrounded by water

_____ 167. place where a river empties into a large body of water

_____ 168. the study of Earth's surface and everything on it

_____ 169. an area of low land between mountains or hills

_____ 170. part of an ocean or sea that extends into land; larger than a bay

a. geography
b. gulf
c. mouth
d. plateau
e. desert
f. valley
g. canyon
h. isthmus
i. peninsula
j. source

Name _____

SCIENCE SKILLS TEST

For each body part or system, write the letter of the correct description.

_____ 1. tendons
_____ 2. esophagus
_____ 3. femur
_____ 4. joint
_____ 5. gastrocnemius
_____ 6. radius
_____ 7. scapula
_____ 8. diaphragm
_____ 9. cornea
_____ 10. stirrup
_____ 11. digestive

A. calf muscle
B. covering of the eye
C. tube from mouth to stomach
D. a bone of the upper arm
E. system for using food in the body
F. largest bone in the human body
G. collarbone
H. bands of fiber that attach muscles to bones
I. place where bones come together
J. a bone of the middle ear
K. a bone of the lower arm
L. large muscle that helps move air in & out of body
M. shoulder blade
N. system for using air in the body

Write the answer on the line.

_____ 12. What kind of exercise strengthens the heart muscle?
_____ 13. What is increased by lifting weights?
_____ 14. What gains flexibility with stretching exercises?

15. In the diagrams at the right, circle the picture that shows the molecules in a liquid.

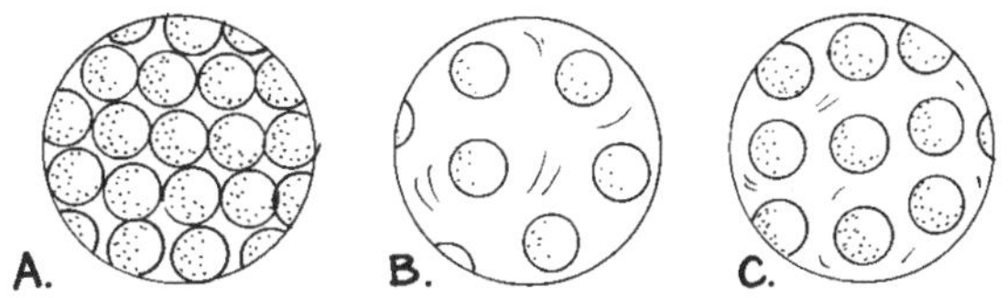

A.   B.   C.

_____ 16. Circle the part of an atom that has a negative electrical charge.
     a. nucleus   b. electron   c. proton   d. neutron

_____ 17. Circle the word that describes the change in state from a liquid to a gas.
     a. evaporation   b. melting   c. freezing   d. condensation

_____ 18. Change in matter that results in a different substance is
     a. a physical change   b. a mixture
     c. condensation   d. a chemical change

_____ 19. A substance that contains atoms of two or more elements chemically combined is
     a. a liquid   b. a compound   c. an element   d. a solid

_____ 20. At which temperatures does water change to ice?
     a. 100 °C and 32 °F   b. 200 °F and 100 °C
     c. 0 °C and 32 °F   d. 0 °F and 32 °C

Write the chemical formula for each compound shown below.

_____ 21.
_____ 22.
_____ 23.
_____ 24.

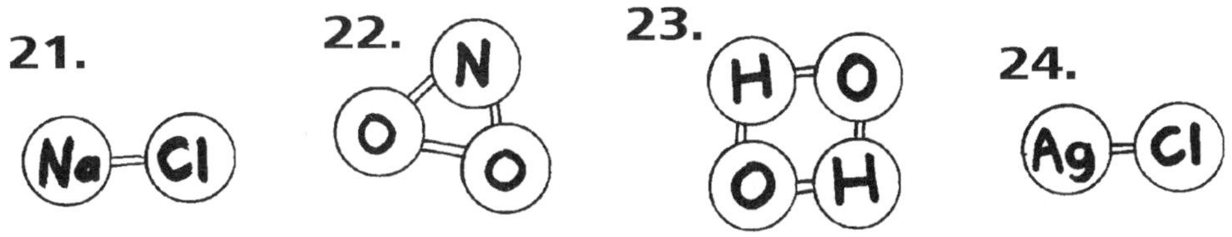

21. Na—Cl

22. N, O, O

23. H—O, O—H

24. Ag—Cl

For each event below, write P for physical change or C for chemical change.

_____ 25. burning toast   _____ 26. a rusting bicycle _____ 27. mixing lemonade and sugar
_____ 28. whipping cream   _____ 29. spoiling food

Name _____

Write the letters of the matching definitions.

_____ 30. the movement of electrons along a path

_____ 31. highness or lowness of a sound

_____ 32. change from one position to another

_____ 33. the force of attraction between two objects

_____ 34. area of force around ends of a magnet

_____ 35. transfer of heat by waves

_____ 36. cause sounds

_____ 37. device used to open or close a circuit

_____ 38. amount of force applied to an area

_____ 39. amount of matter that is in an object

_____ 40. material that heat or electricity can travel through easily

A. vibrations
B. convection
C. field
D. gravity
E. volume
F. conductor
G. radiation
H. switch
I. current
J. friction
K. motion
L. mass
M. pressure
N. pitch

Write the letter of the correct answer.

_____ 41. Sound travels fastest through

    a. a vacuum   b. solids   c. liquids   d. gases

_____ 42. The transfer of heat by movement of heated gases or liquids is

    a. conduction   b. convection   c. radiation   d. insulation

_____ 43. People can hear sounds caused by objects vibrating at

    a. less than 10 times per second

    b. more than 200,000 times per second

    c. 20 to 20,000 times per second

_____ 44. The unit used to measure the rate of electron flow through a circuit is

    a. degree   b. volt   c. inch   d. kilogram

_____ 45. The measure of how far an object moves during a certain period of time

    a. energy   b. watts   c. speed   d. inertia

_____ 46. The result of a force moving an object over a distance is

    a. speed   b. work   c. power   d. pressure

Write the answer on the line.

_____ 47. the force that slows or stops moving objects when they move across each other

_____ 48. the tendency for an object at rest to remain at rest

_____ 49. what like poles of magnets do to each other

_____ 50. the loudness or softness of a sound

Write the letter of the correct answer.

_____ 51. A device used to measure the speed of wind is

    a. a barometer   b. a seismograph   c. an anemometer   d. a thermometer

_____ 52. A major storm with high winds that develops over warm, tropical water is a

    a. hurricane   b. blizzard   c. tornado   d. tsunami

_____ 53. The part of the continent that is just below the ocean water is the

    a. continental slope   b. trough   c. continental shelf   d. plain

_____ 54. The planets closest to the sun are

    a. Mercury & Venus   c. Earth & Neptune

    b. Mercury & Mars   d. Jupiter & Mars

Name _____

_____ 55. Water vapor condensing into little drops near the ground that freezes on grass and other objects is   a. fog   b. dew   c. frost   d. snow   e. hail

_____ 56. The length of a planet's year depends on
     a. the time it takes for a complete rotation
     b. the speed that the planet is spinning
     c. the size of the planet
     d. the time it takes the planet to revolve around the sun

_____ 57. Fragments of planet-like matter that float in space are
     a. meteors   b. meteorites   c. meteoroids   d. comets

_____ 58. Comets are usually named after
     a. their discoverers
     b. the planets they are near
     c. famous astronomers

_____ 59. The four major agents of change on the Earth's surface are
     a. gravity, ice, wind, water
     b. air, water, pollution, heat
     c. lightning, glaciers, animals, radiation

_____ 60. Rocks that are formed from volcanic activity are
     a. igneous   b. minerals   c. metamorphic   d. sedimentary

_____ 61. In the diagram below, what is being shown?
     a. a solar eclipse   b. a lunar eclipse   c. Earth's rotation   d. sunspots

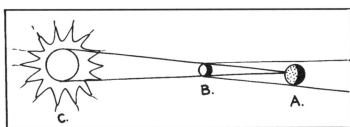

Write the letter of the correct matching definition.

_____ 62. physiology

_____ 63. core

_____ 64. troposphere

_____ 65. barometer

_____ 66. antibody

_____ 67. reflection

_____ 68. caldera

_____ 69. vaccination

_____ 70. translucent

_____ 71. plankton

_____ 72. moraines

_____ 73. front

A. device to measure earthquakes
B. shot that helps the body develop defenses against a disease
C. layer of Earth's atmosphere closest to Earth
D. boundary that separates 2 air masses
E. hole created when the top of a volcano collapses
F. device to measure air pressure
G. bending of a ray of light as it passes through water
H. science that studies human body structure and function
I. innermost layer of Earth
J. deposits left by melting glaciers
K. bouncing of a wave or ray off a surface
L. science that studies Earth's surface
M. a substance in body fluids that kills diseases
N. life found at the ocean bottom
O. can't see through an object, but light can pass through it
P. sea life found floating in waves at ocean surface

Name _____

MATH SKILLS TEST

Part One: Problem Solving

Write the letter of the equation that can be used to solve the problem.

Use the chart to answer questions 1–4.
Write the answers on the lines.

REFRESHING DRINKS	
Fresh Ade	$1.00
Thirst Quencher	$2.00
Gallon O' Gulp	$4.50
Squelch	$ .75
Big Swallow	$1.75
Ener-G	$2.50
Drench	$1.25
Lemon Drench	$2.50
Re-Vive	$3.00
Orange Dunk	$2.10

_____ 1. Which 2 drinks together would cost $7.50?

_____ 2. Could an athlete buy 2 Lemon Drenches and 2 Squelches for $5.00?

_____ 3. What would it cost to buy 2 Ener-Gs and 1 Big Swallow?

_____ 4. What drink costs $0.85 less than an Orange Dunk?

_____ 5. The Grizzlies spent $500 on travel and $350 on food and lodging on their trip to the state championship. Their fund started out with $1,000. How much money was left after the trip?

      a. $500 – $350 + $1,000 = n   b. $500 x $350 x $1,000 = n
      c. $1,000 + $500 + $350 = n   d. $1,000 – $500 – $350 = n

_____ 6. What is the answer to the problem in #5?

Use the chart to answer questions 7–10.

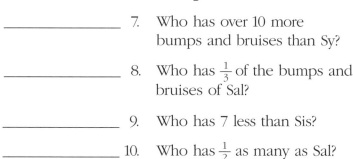

_____ 7. Who has over 10 more bumps and bruises than Sy?

_____ 8. Who has $\frac{1}{3}$ of the bumps and bruises of Sal?

_____ 9. Who has 7 less than Sis?

_____ 10. Who has $\frac{1}{2}$ as many as Sal?

Choose the correct operations for the problems. Write +, –, x, or ÷ in each space.

11. 16 _____ 8 _____ 5 = 10

12. 1,000 _____ 10 = 100

13. 950 _____ 900 _____ 17 = 67

14. 80 _____ 80 _____ 80 = 80

15. 5,000 _____ 2 _____ 5,002 = 0

Name _____

Use the table to answer questions 16–19.

_____16. Which year was a bad one for Matt?

_____17. Who had the best years from 2013 through 2015?

_____18. Whose worst year had $\frac{1}{3}$ of the wins of his or her best year?

_____19. Whose best year had 6 wins less than Max's best year?

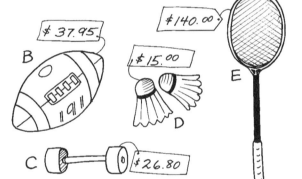

Player	2011	2012	2013	2014	2015	Totals
MAX	24	17	14	18	16	89
MATT	18	2	7	12	21	60
MOE	3	8	14	17	21	63
MUSA	7	18	10	15	21	71
MELODY	18	14	13	16	15	76
TOTALS	70	69	58	79	94	359

WINNING MATCHES

Choose the letter of the percentage that shows each of these amounts.

a. 50%   c. 60%   e. 80%

b. 30%   d. 40%

_____ 20. The team won 40 out of 50 games.

_____ 21. Su Lin had perfect scores on 3 of his 5 dives.

_____ 22. Koki knocked over 12 of the 24 hurdles he jumped.

Choose the letter of the fraction that shows each of these amounts.

a. $\frac{2}{5}$ c. $\frac{1}{10}$ e. $\frac{1}{4}$

b. $\frac{3}{5}$ d. $\frac{1}{5}$ f. $\frac{4}{5}$

_____ 23. 60% of the tickets are sold.

_____ 24. Team A ate 20% of the pizza.

_____ 25. Georgia won 25% of her tennis matches.

Use the picture and prices below to answer questions 26–30.

_____ 26. What would 5% tax on item D be?

_____ 27. On which item would a 5% tax come to $7.00?

_____ 28. With a 10% discount, what would item C cost?

_____ 29. Which item would cost about $19.00 with a 50% discount?

_____ 30. On which item would a 5% tax come to $4.50?

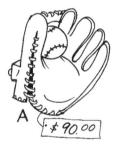

$37.95

$140.00

$15.00

B

$90.00

A

C $26.80

D

E

For each problem 31–34, write YES or NO to tell if the answer is accurate.

_____ 31. The springs on Natasha's trampoline cost $2.50 each. How much would it cost to replace all 90? *Answer: $185.00.*

_____ 32. Tasha's scuba diving equipment weighs $\frac{1}{20}$ of her body weight. Her equipment weighs 6 pounds. How much does Tasha weigh? *Answer: 120 pounds.*

_____ 33. Jamin did 32 pushups on Friday, 25 on Saturday, 40 on Sunday, and 13 on Tuesday. He did a total of 130 on the five days from Friday to Tuesday. How many did he do on Monday? *Answer: 20 pushups.*

_____ 34. Abby runs 4.5 miles a day. She has run 360.5 miles so far this year. How many days has she run? *Answer: 85 days.*

Name _____

Part Two: Computation & Numbers

Answer the questions. Each question is worth 1 point. Write these numerals in words.

_____ 35. 35,100

_____ 36. 1,008

_____ 37. 2,600,000

Write the numerals to match these words.

_____ 38. ten thousand five hundred

_____ 39. three billion

_____ 40. fifty-five thousand nine hundred twenty

_____ 41. six hundred thousand six hundred

_____ 42. eight thousand thirty

_____ 43. Round this number to the nearest ten: 5,976

_____ 44. Round this number to the nearest thousand: 24,130

_____ 45. Round this number to the nearest ten thousand: 278,166

_____ 46. Round this number to the nearest hundred: 555

_____ 47. Write the factors of 24.

_____ 48. Write the factors of 49.

_____ 49. Write the common factors of 12 and 32.

_____ 50. Write the greatest common factor of 50 and 15.

Solve these problems. Write the answer on the line.

_____ 51. $8 \overline{)709}$

56. $5,500 \div 100 =$ _____

_____ 52. $\begin{array}{r} 5,961 \\ + 288 \end{array}$

57. $65 \times 100 =$ _____

58. $900 \times 1,000 =$ _____

_____ 53. $\begin{array}{r} 710,621 \\ - 25,009 \end{array}$

59. $2,400 \div 10 =$ _____

_____ 54. $\begin{array}{r} 279 \\ \times 18 \end{array}$

60. $(75 + 5) \div 2 - 20 =$ _____

_____ 55. $648 \div 2$

61. $10 \times 10 \div 5 - 15 =$ _____

Write the letter of the property used for each example below.

C = Commutative Property of Addition or Multiplication
Z = Zero Property for Addition or Subtraction
ZM = Zero Property for Multiplication
P = Property of 1

_____ 62. $12 \times 6 = 6 \times 12$　　_____ 64. $62 + 17 = 17 + 62$

_____ 63. $75 - 0 = 75$　　_____ 65. $432 \times 0 = 0$　　_____ 66. $550 \times 1 = 550$

Name _____

Write a fraction in each blank.

_____ 67. How many of the athletes are jumping?

_____ 68. How many of the athletes are riding something?

_____ 69. How many of the athletes are using some equipment?

70. Circle the largest fraction: $\frac{2}{3}$ $\frac{7}{8}$

71. Circle the largest fraction: $\frac{2}{12}$ $\frac{3}{9}$

72. Write the fractions in order from smallest to largest. $\frac{14}{16}$ $\frac{7}{12}$ $\frac{2}{3}$ $\frac{6}{8}$

_____

73. Circle the fractions that are equivalent to $\frac{3}{4}$. $\frac{12}{16}$ $\frac{9}{12}$ $\frac{6}{12}$ $\frac{2}{3}$ $\frac{6}{8}$

74. Circle the fractions that are in lowest terms. $\frac{7}{9}$ $\frac{12}{15}$ $\frac{6}{12}$ $\frac{2}{3}$ $\frac{6}{8}$

_____ 75. Write this fraction in lowest terms: $\frac{18}{24}$

_____ 76. Write this fraction in lowest terms: $\frac{12}{16}$

_____ 77. Write this fraction as a mixed numeral: $\frac{50}{20}$

_____ 78. Write this fraction as a mixed numeral: $\frac{37}{5}$

_____ 79. Write this fraction as a mixed numeral: $\frac{44}{10}$

80. Circle the largest decimal numeral. 0.555 0.5 0.05 0.5005

Solve these problems.

81. $\frac{7}{8} - \frac{2}{4} =$ _____

82. $\frac{6}{12} + \frac{2}{3} =$ _____

83. $\frac{7}{10} - \frac{4}{10} =$ _____

84. $\frac{3}{4} \div \frac{2}{5} =$ _____

85. $\frac{5}{12} \div \frac{5}{6} =$ _____

86. $2\frac{1}{2} + 5\frac{1}{2} =$ _____

87. $\frac{12}{5} - \frac{4}{3} =$ _____

88. $ 200.40
     − 15.80

89. $ 1,600.99
     + 743.86

90. $ 29.50
     x 7

91. 3)$75.00

_____ 92. Change $\frac{3}{4}$ to a decimal.

_____ 93. Write 0.60 as a fraction.

_____ 94. Change $\frac{2}{5}$ to a percent.

_____ 95. Change 80% to a fraction.

Solve these problems:

96. − 60 + 15 = _____

97. 13 − 7 + 4 + − 8 = _____

98. 2 5 + 5 + −18 = _____

Name _____

Part Three: Geometry & Measurement

(You will need a protractor and centimeter/inch ruler.)

Use this diagram for questions 99-104.

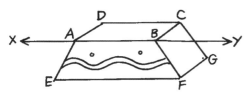

99. $\overleftrightarrow{XY}$ is: a line segment   a ray
    a line   a plane

100. Which ones of these are line segments?
    $\overline{AB}$ $\overline{BF}$ $\overline{EA}$
    $\overline{AC}$ $\overline{FY}$ $\overline{CG}$

101. $\overrightarrow{AY}$ is: a line segment   an angle
    a line   a ray

102. B is: a line   a point   a ray

103. EAB is: a plane   a line
    an angle   a line segment

104. BCGF is: a line segment   an angle
    a plane   a line

Use these angles for questions 105–110.

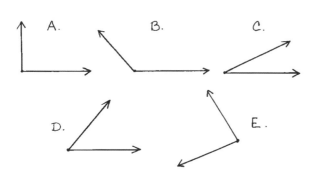

105. Which angles are right angles?

_____

106. Which angles are obtuse angles?

_____

107. Which angles are acute angles?

_____

108. Angle C is about:
    30°   130°   95°   50°

109. Write the measurement of angle B.

_____

110. Which angle is about 80°?

_____

Use the diagram below for questions 111-116.

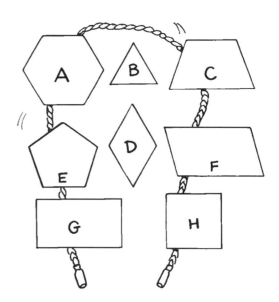

_____ 111. How many figures are rhombuses?

_____ 112. Which figure is a hexagon?

_____ 113. Which figures are parallelograms but not rectangles?

_____ 114. Which figure is a pentagon?

_____ 115. Which figure is a trapezoid?

_____ 116. Which figures are rectangles?

Name _____

Use the signs below for questions 117–121.

Use these diagrams for questions 122–124.

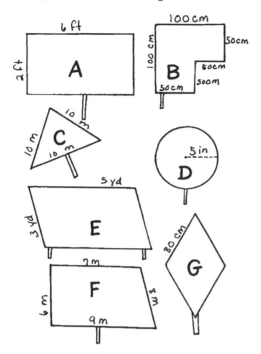

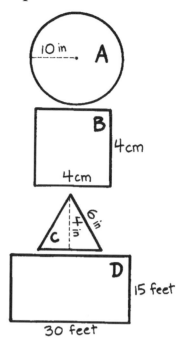

_____ 117. Find the perimeter of E.

_____ 118. Find the perimeter of G.

_____ 119. Is the perimeter of F > the perimeter of C?

_____ 120. Find the circumference of D.

_____ 121. Which has a perimeter of 400 cm?

_____ 122. Find the area of figure A.

_____ 123. Which figure has an area of ≤ 12 in?

_____ 124. Find the area of figure D.

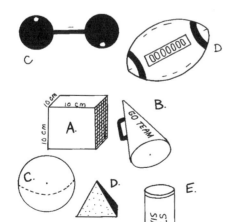

_____ 125.

Which of these figures are symmetrical?

Use these figures for questions 126–128.

_____ 126. Which figure is a cylinder?

_____ 127. Find the volume of the cube.

_____ 128. Find the volume of the rectangular prism.

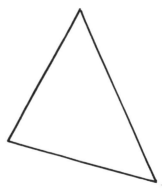

_____ 129. Measure to find the perimeter of this figure in centimeters. Round to the nearest whole centimeter.

Name

_____ 130. Measure with centimeters to find the area of this figure.

Use these figures to answer questions 131–132.

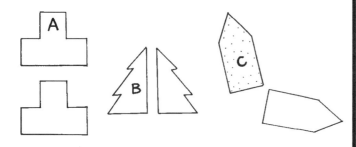

_____ 131. Which figure has been flipped?

_____ 132. Does A show a slide, flip, or turn?

Fill in each blank with the correct amount.

133. 2 minutes = _____ seconds.

134. 1 pound = _____ ounces.

135. _____ yards = 360 inches.

136. 10 hours = _____ minutes.

137. 6 weeks = _____ days.

For each blank, write >, <, or =.

138. 10 qt _____ 2 gal.

139. 1000 mg _____ 1 g.

140. 1 T _____ 3,000 pounds

141. 2 months _____ 12 weeks.

142. 10,000 m _____ 1 km.

Part Four: Graphing, Statistics, & Probability

Choose the matching term for each definition. Write the letter on the line.

a. median

b. statistics

c. frequency

d. mode

e. mean

f. range

_____ 143. the number of times an item appears in a set of data

_____ 144. the average of a number of data items

_____ 145. the collection, organization, and use of sets of numerical data

_____ 146. the number that appears most often in a set of data

_____ 147. the difference between the least and greatest numbers in a set of data

_____ 148. the number that falls in the middle of a set of data arranged in order

Use this frequency table for questions 149-153.

Frequency of Leapfrog Scores

Scores: # of Leaps	Round 1	Round 2
1-10	16	20
11-20	25	20
21-30	30	20
31-40	15	24
41-50	10	21
over 50	4	5

Name _____

149. What group of scores had the greatest frequency for round 1? _____

150. What group of scores had the greatest frequency for round 2? _____

151. What group of scores had the smallest frequency for round 1? _____

152. What group of scores had the smallest frequency for round 2? _____

153. Did more competitors get higher or lower scores in round 2 than they did in round 1? _____

Use this graph for questions 154–158.

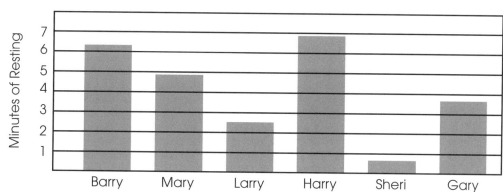

REST STOPS
20-mile Lawnmower Race

154. Who rested about 4.9 minutes during the race? _____

155. Who rested longer than Barry? _____

156. Who rested about 45 seconds? _____

157. Who rested about 2.5 minutes? _____

158. Who rested about 3.8 minutes? _____

Use this table for questions 159–163.

STRANGE JOURNEYS
Approximate Distances for Record

Journey	Miles
taxi ride	21,691
polar sled ride	3,750
lawnmower ride	3,366
backwards walk	8,000
snowmobile ride	10,252
wheelchair ride	24,901
backwards run	3,100
walk	32,202
walk on stilts	3,008
unicycle ride	3,261
leapfrog trip	996

159. Which record is about twice as long as the snowmobile ride?

_____

160. Which record is about 100 miles less than the lawn mower ride?

_____

161. Which is longer: the wheelchair ride or the polar sled ride?

_____

162. Which is longer: the backwards walk or the backwards run?

_____

163. How much farther was the walking record than the walk on stilts?

_____

Name _____

Use this graph for questions 164–168.

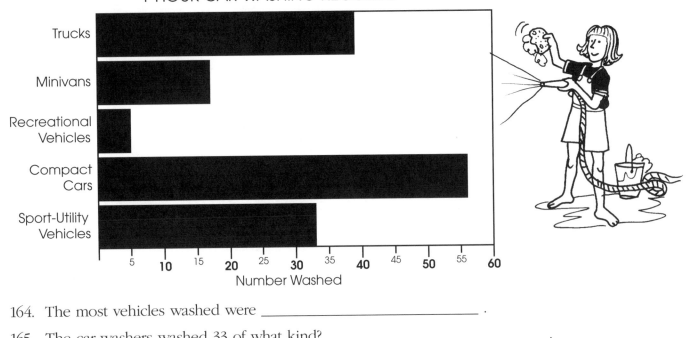

1-HOUR CAR-WASHING RECORDS

Number Washed

164. The most vehicles washed were _____ .

165. The car-washers washed 33 of what kind? _____ .

166. They washed 17 _____ .

167. They washed about 20 more _____ than minivans.

168. They washed about 50 fewer recreational vehicles than _____

Write the number of possible outcomes for each of the following:

_____ 169. flip of a coin

_____ 170. toss of one die

_____ 171. you'll be sick one day next week

_____ 172. flip a coin twice

173. The hot-air balloonists flip a coin twice to see who will start first. What are the possible outcomes of this coin flip? Write them all:

_____

_____

174. What is the probability of 2 heads? _____

Four skydivers get ready for a jump. Their names are Jan, Fran, Stan, and Nan. They want to jump in pairs.

175. Write the possible pairs:

_____

_____

_____

_____

_____

176. How many possible pairs are there? _____

Name _____

177. There are 10,000 light bulbs in boxes in a room. Sam took 100 and tried them out. Out of the 100, twenty were burned out. Predict the number of burned-out light bulbs in the entire room.
_____

178. 10 light bulbs; 4 are burned out. You choose a bulb. What are the odds in favor of getting a burned-out bulb?
_____

179. 8 envelopes contain prize money. 6 contain $100 bills. The rest hold one $20 bill each. You pick an envelope. What are the odds in favor of getting a $100 bill? _____

Hal wants to break the world record for the number of miles hitch-hiked. He is looking for some good shoes to wear.

His closet contains:
    4 black shoes (B)
    7 red shoes (R)
    9 gray shoes (G)
He reaches into the dark closet and grabs a shoe. Tell the probabilities:

180. P (B) = _____

181. P (R) = _____

182. P (G) = _____

183. P (not G) = _____

Hal chooses some socks for his long trip. His drawer contains these:
    5 red socks (R)
    3 blue socks (B)
    2 purple socks (P)
    4 orange socks (O)
    10 white socks (W)
Tell the probability for these:

184. P (P or O) = _____

185. P (W) = _____

186. P (not W) = _____

187. P (R, P, or B) = _____

188. P (P) = _____

Name _____

SKILLS TEST ANSWER KEY

Language Arts
Skills Test

1. You usually do not think of "hearing" sun.
2. dog's toenails, heels on dance floor
3. lightning, seashells
4. 3 of these: crashing, cracking, click, snapping, buzzing, boom, scraping, pitter, cracks, whispers, rumble, roar, chopping
5. Answers will vary.
6. mad
7. boring
8. asteroids, boots on Matterhorn, Paul Bunyan chopping
9. terrible, awful, boring
10. Every line begins with "I hear."
11. S, M, A
12. A
13. I
14. M, P
15. P, A
16. S
17. E
18. 4, 5, 2, 3, 1
19. Answers will vary. See that student follows the pattern accurately.
20. yes
21. 3
22. Knighthood Revisited
23. The Adventure Store or Decked Out Company
24. Decked Out Company
25. The Adventure Store
26. yes
27. $200
28. The Adventure Store, Little Egypt
29. yes
30. natron
31. Sounds thrilling, doesn't it?
32. You'll have to be tied . . .
   and
   Your dinner will float . . .
33. b
34. j
35. k
36. g
37. n
38. p
39. c
40. h
41. o
42. m
43. l
44. d
45. e
46. crude
47. terrified
48. absence
49. snatched
50-51. Answers will vary.
52. g
53. h
54. d
55. k
56. t
57. s
58. p
59. o
60. m
61. b
62. e
63. f
64. b
65. c
66. e
67. d
68. g
69. l
70. b
71. e
72. j
73. k
74. i
75. g
76. a
77. d
78. a
79. b
80. g
81. i
82. c
83. b
84. b
85. shipwreck
86. sunburn
87–89. Answers will vary. See that student writes 2 correct meanings for each word chosen.
90. j
91. g (or b)
92. a
93. h
94. m
95. k
96. l
97. f
98. n
99. c
100. comet
101. cabbage
102. Frisbee®
103. tentacles
104. goose
105. freeze
106. snow
107. argument
108. surfer
109. erupt
110–115. energy, coughed, surprise, scuba, cider, babysitter
116. no
117. yes
118. no
119. no
120. yes
121. no
122. yes
123. worried
124. wished
125. argued
126. froze
127. forgot
128. Atlantic
129. Jupiter
130. Michigan
131. Wednesday
132. Thanksgiving
133. pianoes
134. wierd
135. notbook
136. magecal
137. subbmarine
138. terrifick
139. arithmatic
140. elegent
141. astronot
142. vegetables, sugar, lettuce, tomatoes, noodles
143. pilot
144. people
145. caught
146. molecule
147. llama
148. laughter
149. again
150. appear
151. enough
152. separate
153. absence
154. criticize
155. weather
156. automatic
157. license
158. tongue
159. mosquito

160. odor
161. opposite
162. loneliness
163. length
164. please
165. almost
166. necessary
167. Circle: wreath, expel, seize, apologize, oxygen, serious, excellent, quartet, strength, gravity, zero
168. surprise
169. balloon
170. marshmallow
171. calendar
172. Adopt
173. accept
174. angles
175. thorough
176. diary
177. cereal
178. overdue
179. pried
180. horse
181. break
182. Freak Accidents Reported on Public Beaches
183. Doctor Does Surprise Operation
184. Ski Season Canceled due to Dangerous Ice Storm
185. Two Hundred Homes Lost in Tornado
186. Elephant Receives Gold Medal
187. I
188. EX
189. I
190. IM
191. D
192. F
193. C
194. R
195. F
196. S
197. Sam
198. bears
199. chipmunk
200. crashed
201. could catch
202. watched
203. ADJ
204. ADJ
205. N
206. V
207. N
208. ADV
209. Friday, Billy
210. spiders, beds, pepper, meatballs
211. compasses
212. knives
213. tomatoes
214. deer
215. families

216. mouse
217. child
218. city
219. wolf's teeth
220. wolves' teeth
221. campers' shirts
222. skunk's tail
223. They
224. She
225. him
226. them
227. rowed
228. swam
229. fell or is falling
230. will fly
231. wore
232. wrote or will write or are writing
233. fainted
234. voted
235. screamed
236. jumped
237. crept
238. is
239. should
240. is
241. have
242. V
243. ADV
244. ADJ
245. N
246. V
247. ADJ
248. ADV
249. faster
250. farthest
251. slimiest
252. best
253. less
254. worst
255. earlier
256. more often
257. most quickly
258. would
259. any
260. anyone
261. ever
262. lunch
263. towels
264. pranks
265. hoarse
266. hole
267. meet
268. sense
269. our, always, creates, delicious, meals, favorite, once, week, marshmallows, dessert
270. quotation marks should be placed before Camp and after July
271. quotation marks should be placed before Write and after parents

272.

July 15

Dear Mom and Dad,

I am having the best time at this camp! You won't believe how well I'm doing. We have terrible food, lots of mosquitoes, and grumpy counselors. Doesn't it sound great? I think I saw an alien, and I fell out of the canoe three times. How much longer can I stay?

Your loving son,
Manuel

273. d
274. c
275. d
276. a
277. c

Writing Tasks

Answers will vary on most of the writing tasks. There are no right or wrong answers for Tasks 2, 4, 5, 6, 7, 8, 9, and 11. Answers may vary some on Tasks 3 and 10.

Award points to students based on:
- how thoroughly they completed the task
- if they followed directions
- the mechanical correctness of their writing

Task 1: order—7, 4, 1, 5, 6, 3, 2

Task 3: Answers may vary.
1. I found an old sandwich sitting on top of the shelf in the closet.
2. On the radio, we heard about the robber who was caught.

Task 10: Words that students eliminate may vary. Statements or words in ( ) are not necessary and should be deleted. Corrected paragraph should read:

Dear Editor:

(In my opinion,) I believe that the new miniature golf course (which the city has built) owned by the city should change its rules. It does not make sense not to allow kids under 18 to come unless they are with adults. I thought the city built this course to attract kids and give them something good to do in the evenings. This is a wonderful activity for kids, but you are keeping them away. Most teenagers want to go out (for an activity) with their friends, not their parents! Whose bad idea was this? (I protest!) I hope this rule will be changed soon.

Sincerely,
Adam

Social Studies Skills Test

1. end of Civil War
2. Nineteenth Amendment gives women the right to vote
3. Declaration of Independence
4. first large groups begin traveling the Oregon Trail
5. first steps on the moon
6. F
7. M
8. G
9. J
10. C
11. K
12. N
13. B
14. P
15. Q
16. A
17. O
18. E
19. H
20. L
21. I
22. D
23. C
24. A
25. E
26. B
27. D
28. A
29. E
30. C
31. H
32. J
33. F
34. B
35. G
36. D
37. I
38. a
39. c
40. b
41. c
42. c
43. b
44. d
45. c
46. b
47. d
48. c
49. the president appoints them; confirmed by Senate
50. president
51. Executive, Legislative, Judicial

52. 2 years
53. 4 years
54. Supreme Court/courts
55. Congress/legislatures
56. 6 years
57. the state's population
58. 100
59. advises the president
60. veto it
61. C
62. F
63. A
64. J
65. G
66. D
67. I
68. B
69. E
70. H
71. A
72. G
73. K
74. L
75. M
76. E
77. O
78. P
79. R
80. B
81. C
82. F
83. S
84. I
85. H
86. J
87. Q
88. T
89. N
90. D
91. b
92. a
93. a
94. b
95. a
96. c
97. b
98. b
99. a
100. c
101. I
102. H
103. C
104. A
105. B
106. F
107. J
108. D
109. G
110. E
111. a
112. i
113. k

114. d
115. m
116. c
117. h
118. e
119. f
120. g
121. c
122. d
123. b & d
124. a
125. a & d
126. a, c, d, e
127. b & c
128. d
129. b & d (Alaska)
130. b
131. equator
132. Tropic of Cancer
133. South Pole
134. prime meridian
135. Antarctic Circle
136. Tropic of Capricorn
137. Arctic Circle
138. North Pole
139. a & d
140. a, b, c
141. d
142. 80 kilometers (Answers may vary.)
143. 30 kilometers
144. Hwy 10—Modem Highway
145. SE
146. NE
147. no
148. Modem Highway
149. 40 kilometers
150. N
151. 20 kilometers
152. Market
153. NE
154. about 2,000 feet
155. about 125 feet
156. NW
157. about 1,500 feet
158. 4 (3 or 4)
159. pigs
160. SE
161. Rapunzel Drive to Nature Trail to Market Street to Granny's
162. g
163. h
164. d
165. e
166. i
167. c
168. a
169. f
170. b

Science Skills Test

1. H
2. C
3. F
4. I
5. A
6. K
7. M
8. L
9. B
10. J
11. E
12. aerobic
13. muscle strength
14. muscles
15. C
16. b
17. a
18. d
19. b
20. c
21. NaCl
22. NO_2
23. H_2O_2
24. AgCl
25. C
26. C
27. P
28. P
29. C
30. I
31. N
32. K
33. D
34. C
35. G
36. A
37. H
38. M
39. L
40. F
41. b
42. b
43. c
44. b
45. c
46. b
47. friction
48. inertia
49. repel
50. volume
51. c
52. a
53. c
54. a
55. c
56. d
57. c
58. a
59. a
60. a
61. a

62. H
63. I
64. C
65. F
66. M
67. K
68. E
69. B
70. O
71. P
72. J
73. D

Math Skills Test

1. Gallon O'Gulp & Re-Vive
2. no
3. $6.75
4. Drench
5. d
6. $150
7. Sam
8. Sly
9. Sue
10. Sara
11. $16 \div 8 \times 5 = 10$
12. $1,000 \div 10 = 100$
13. $950 - 900 + 17 = 67$
14. $80 + 80 - 80 = 80$
15. $5,000 + 2 - 5,002 = 0$
16. 2012
17. Moe
18. Musa
19. Melody
20. e
21. c
22. a
23. b
24. d
25. e
26. $0.75
27. E
28. $24.12
29. B
30. A
31. no
32. yes
33. yes
34. no
35. thirty-five thousand one hundred
36. one thousand eight
37. two million six hundred thousand
38. 10,500
39. 3,000,000,000
40. 55,920
41. 600,600
42. 8,030
43. 5,980
44. 24,000
45. 280,000

46. 600
47. 1, 2, 3, 4, 6, 8, 12, 24
48. 1, 7, 49
49. 1, 2, 4
50. 5
51. 88 R5
52. 6,249
53. 685,612
54. 5,022
55. 324
56. 55
57. 6,500
58. 900,000
59. 240
60. 20
61. 5
62. C
63. Z
64. C
65. ZM
66. P
67. $\frac{1}{5}$
68. $\frac{2}{5}$
69. $\frac{4}{5}$
70. $\frac{7}{8}$
71. $\frac{3}{9}$
72. $\frac{7}{12}, \frac{2}{3}, \frac{6}{8}, \frac{14}{16}$
73. $\frac{12}{16}; \frac{9}{12}; \frac{6}{8}$
74. $\frac{7}{9}; \frac{2}{3}$
75. $\frac{3}{4}$
76. $\frac{3}{4}$
77. $2\frac{10}{20}$ or $2\frac{1}{2}$
78. $7\frac{2}{5}$
79. $4\frac{4}{10}$ or $4\frac{2}{5}$
80. 0.555
81. $\frac{3}{8}$
82. $\frac{14}{12}$ or $1\frac{2}{12}$ or $1\frac{1}{6}$
83. $\frac{3}{10}$
84. $\frac{15}{8}$ or $1\frac{7}{8}$
85. $\frac{1}{2}$
86. 8
87. $\frac{16}{15}$ or $1\frac{1}{15}$
88. $184.60
89. $2,344.85
90. $206.50
91. $25.00
92. 0.75
93. $\frac{6}{10}$ or $\frac{3}{5}$
94. 40%

95. $\frac{80}{100}$ or $\frac{4}{5}$
96. -45
97. 2
98. 12
99. a line
100. $\overline{AB}, \overline{BF}, \overline{EA}, \overline{CG}$
101. a ray
102. a point
103. an angle
104. a plane
105. A
106. B
107. C, D, E
108. 50°
109. 130°
110. E
111. 2
112. A
113. D, F
114. E
115. C
116. G, H
117. 16 yds
118. 320 cm
119. no
120. 31.4 in
121. B
122. 314 in²
123. C
124. 450 ft²
125. A, C, D
126. E
127. 1,000 cm³
128. 480 in³
129. 13 cm
130. 9 cm²
131. B
132. slide
133. 120
134. 16
135. 10
136. 600
137. 42
138. >
139. =
140. <
141. <
142. >
143. c
144. e
145. b
146. d
147. f
148. a
149. 21–30

150. 31–40
151. over 50
152. over 50
153. higher
154. Mary
155. Harry
156. Sheri
157. Larry
158. Gary
159. taxi ride
160. unicycle ride
161. wheelchair ride
162. backwards walk
163. 29,194 miles
164. compact cars
165. sport-utility vehicles
166. minivans
167. trucks
168. compact cars
169. 2
170. 6
171. 7
172. 4
173. 4; Outcomes are: H, H; T, T; H, T; T, H
174. $\frac{1}{4}$
175. Possible pairs:
    Jan & Fran
    Jan & Stan
    Jan & Nan
    Fran & Stan
    Fran & Nan
    Stan & Nan
176. 6
177. 2,000
178. $\frac{4}{6}$ or $\frac{2}{3}$
179. $\frac{6}{2}$
180. $\frac{4}{20}$ or $\frac{1}{5}$
181. $\frac{7}{20}$
182. $\frac{9}{20}$
183. $\frac{11}{20}$
184. $\frac{6}{24}$ or $\frac{1}{4}$
185. $\frac{10}{24}$ or $\frac{5}{12}$
186. $\frac{14}{24}$ or $\frac{7}{12}$
187. $\frac{10}{24}$ or $\frac{5}{12}$
188. $\frac{2}{24}$ or $\frac{1}{12}$

SKILLS EXERCISES ANSWER KEY

Pages 20–21

1. escapade
2. soar
3. antics
4. fraternize
5. scrutinize
6. endeavor
7. venture
8. probe; comb
9. fantasy or mythical
10. great
11. culinary
12. scale
13. treacherous
14. mythical or fantasy
15. ancient
16. foreboding
17. colossal
18. lavish
19. unfathomable
20. future
21. elusive
22. legendary
23. ruins
24. bargain
25. engage
26. gander
27. remote
28. fiercest

Page 22

1. ridiculous
2. thrilled
3. cave
4. reached
5. regret
6. damp
7. dangerous
8. break, rest
9. stop
10. complaining
11. upset, bothered
12. evil, scary
Predictions will vary.

Page 23

Answers may vary somewhat from those listed below, but generally should have the same meaning.
   1. certify—prove
   2. render—make inoperable—unworkable
   3. submit—obey
   4. deploy—use
   5. ingesting—drinking
   6. lardaceous—fatty or greasy
   7. refuse—trash
   8. precluded—forbidden
   9. attend—pay attention to disseminated—given out
  10. banned—not allowed
  11. tamper—interfere
  12. excessive—too much chastened—scolded
  13. citations—tickets
  14. promptly—right away termination—end

Page 24

Facts are:
Visit the International Space Station
Travel to the International Space Station by space shuttle
Orbit Earth—see fantastic sights!
See Dextre, the space station robot.
Explore the living and working spaces.
Get fitted with your own space suit.
Walk in space.
All food and equipment are provided.
We provide training!
STAY 5, 10, or 15 days
We won't keep you as long as we kept Cosmonaut Valeri Polyakov. He stayed 438 days!
The first module of the International Space Station was launched in 1998.
Schedule
See your Adventure Company Representative
Health examination required.
Must be at least 25 years of age.

Opinions are:
You'll be so glad you did this!
Astronauts will enjoy your visit!
You'll have fun feeling weightless!
You'll love the food!
No dangers or accidents will occur.
You can afford it!
All astronauts & cosmonauts want a chance to live on the International Space Station.

Page 25

1. halfpipe (snowboarding), aerial skiing, ski jumping
2. to fly farther
3. halfpipe (snowboarding)
4. 30%
5. downhill racing
6. ski jumping
7. aerial skiing and halfpipe (snowboarding)
8. NA
9. 2013
10. a U-shaped structure covered in ice and snow
11. 66 yards

Page 26

1. b   2. a   3. c

Page 27

1. 107 inches
2. his ox, Babe
3. 47
4–9. Answers will vary.

Page 28

Answers will vary.

Page 29

1. The Paleo-Lyths
2. Till the Volcano Blows
3. Be a Little Boulder, Honey
4. I Dino If I Love You Anymore
5. You're As Cuddly As A Woolly Mammoth
6. The Cave Dudes
7. I've Cried Pebbles Over You
8. Terri Dactyl
9. The Cro-Magnon Crooners
10. The Petro Cliff Trio
11. The Hard Rock Arena
12. 5
13. Tommy Shale
14. after dark
15. The Standing Stones

Page 30

Students' predictions will vary.

Page 31

1. Answers will vary some. These may be noted.
You begin to imagine . . .
You are nervous, excited, impatient . . .
You trust this roller coaster . . .
You are sure it will be safe . . .
You don't really care how it works . . .
You just want to get on!
You feel like you are flying . . .
You enjoyed every minute . . .
Your stomach feels great . . .
You want to ride again . . .

2–4. Answers will vary.

Page 32

Students' judgments will vary. Check the reasonableness of answers.

Page 33

Students' questions will vary. Check to see that the questions fit the character.

Copyright © 2016 World Book, Inc./
Incentive Publications, Chicago, IL

Page 34

Summaries will vary. Check to see that students have a complete, brief summary that contains the main ideas.

Page 35

Incorrect details are:
- caught in the depths of a terrible dungeon
- It seems he will have no chance of escape.
- wingless dragon
- back inside the castle
- a worried damsel
- chained to a pillar
- She is waiting for Sir Prance-a-lot.
- Here comes the dashing knight to the rescue!

Rewrite of story will vary. See that students have correct details.

Page 36

Order of numbers for line placement.
1. 3, 1, 6, 5, 2, 4
2. 2, 5, 4, 3, 8, 1, 7, 6
3. 2, 4, 7, 1, 3, 5, 6

Page 37

Look at student graphs to see that they show the following amounts.
1. Isabella II—35 years
2. Maria Theresa—40 years
3. Wu Chao—50 years
4. Victoria—64 years
5. Salote—47 years
6. Suiko—35 years
7. Elizabeth I—45 years
8. Elizabeth II—64 years as of 2016
9. Joanna I—39 years
10. Maria I—39 years
11. Wilhelmina—58 years

Page 38

Examine student drawings to see that they have followed directions accurately, or have students examine one another's drawings.

Page 39

Answers will vary.

Page 40

1. business or busyness
2. twelfth
3. surprise
4. cafeteria
5. calendar
6. balloon
7. embarrass
8. license
9. memory
10. banana
11. memorize
12. necessary
13. Florida
14. restaurant
15. marshmallow
16. recognize
17. receive
18. advertisement
19. trouble
20. vegetable

Page 41

Frannie has these correct:
1, 4, 5, 6, 8, 9, 10, 12, 14, 16, 17, 18, 19
Frankie has these correct:
2, 3, 4, 7, 8, 10, 11, 13, 15, 17, 20
A. Frannie
B. words # 4, 8, 10, 17

Page 42

Words to be corrected: (correct spelling)
2. carrot
4. pilot
5. molecule
6. volcano
8. doctor
9. opposite
12. memory
13. gorilla (or guerrilla)
12. octopus
13. October
15. scorpion
16. cocoon
18. mosquito
19. abdomen
20. dinosaur
23. odor

Page 43

1. unique
2. inquire
3. conquer
4. squash
5. banquet
6. equator
7. quickly
8. quiet
9. sequel
10. quilt
11. quartet
12. quizzes
13. aquarium
14. quarrel
15. frequently
16. question
17. equipment

Page 44

1. yummy
2. envy
3. magnify
4. rhythm
5. yolk
6. rhyme
7. guilty
8. yesterday
9. gravity
10. hyphen
11. chewy
12. synonym
13. oxygen
14. yogurt
15. mystery

Page 45

1. expel
2. saxophone
3. extinct
4. Mexico
5. flex
6. excellent
7. examine
8. exist
9. hexagon
10. maximum
11. exclaim
12. exciting
13. next
14. foxes
15. extreme
16. oxygen
17. excuse
18. exercise
19. exterior
20. flexible
21. mixture
22. exit
23. expect
24. explode
25. expressway

Page 46

Correct phrases:
adopt a pet
Eat your celery!
That's no excuse!
cute cartoons on TV
a custard pie
an inspiring story
I accept your present.
walking on crutches
Write in your diary.
my red and white striped socks
art hanging in galleries

Page 47

Across
1. prize
3. zipper
5. buzz
7. apologize
9. freezer
11. zero
13. blizzard
16. fizzle
17. jazz
18. cozy
Down
2. organize
4. squeeze
6. hazard
8. dozen
10. realize
12. lazy
14. dizzy
15. fizzy

Page 48

1. submarine
2. microphone
3. extraordinary
4. rewrite
5. unicycle
6. hexagon
7. impossible
8. international
9. mislabel
10. transport
11. exclude
12. pregame
13. postholiday
14. antibacterial
15. semicircle
16. unfriendly

Page 49

Words spelled correctly are:
tragic
scary
generally
completely
explosion
dangerous
terrific
agreement
hardship
disappointment
different
actor

Page 50

1. ocean, D,C
2. iceberg, C,D
3. swim, C,D
4. octopus, D,C
5. lifeboat, D,C
6. vacation, C,D
7. money, D,C

Page 51

Answers will vary depending upon
what information student can find about
the words.
1. named after G. W. G. Ferris, an
   American engineer
2. named after William Frisbie, a pie
   company owner
3. named after Mars, the Roman god
   of war
4. means "day of the moon"
5. Greek word meaning "messenger"
6. named after R. J. L. Guppy, a British
   scientist who introduced the fish to
   aquariums in England in the 1800's
7. named after the city of Cologne,
   Germany, where this type of
   perfume was first made; means
   "water of Cologne"
8. named after French botanist Pierre
   Magnol

9. named after President Theodore
   (Teddy) Roosevelt, who rescued a
   bear cub
10. from a French word that means
    "crane's foot"
11. named after a French acrobat, Jules
    Léotard, who wore such a garment
    for his acts
12. from a Greek word meaning "head
    with long hair"
13. from a Greek word for a plant that
    people used as a writing surface
14. named after Sardinia, an island off
    Italy
15. named after a state in Mexico
16. named after the explorer Amerigo
    Vespucci

Page 52

Answers will vary slightly.
1. best
2. good
3. expensive
4. Aunt
5. crooked
6. buy; beautiful; new
7. heavy
8. permanent
9. generous
10. sturdy
11. unusual
12. strong

Page 53

1. exciting
2. novice
3. deed
4. unbelievable
5. peril
6. amaze
7. huge
8. answer
9. drool
10. real
11. movement
12. mob
13. terror
14. diary
15. punish

Page 54

1. carn
2. phobia
3. fug
4. mon
5. vis
6. aqua
7. act
8. flam
9. scend
10. dynam
11. dorm

12. tele
13. port
14. labor
15. phobia
16. port
17. phobia
18. scend

Page 55

Top answers:
1–2. a lead or important person;
shape with 5 points
Other answers will vary. Check to see that
student has accurately illustrated 2 or more
meanings of the three words chosen.

Page 56

Answers may vary.
Check to see that student's definitions are
similar and that items are correctly
colored in the picture.
vessel—a ship or other floating vehicle—
   boat—blue
lunar—having to do with the moon—
   moon—yellow
luminous—shiny—moon, stars, or fire—
   orange
biped—an animal with two legs—any of
   the persons—red
savory—tasty—marshmallows—white
merriment—celebration—any of the
   dancers—green
pentapod—something with five feet or
   limbs—starfish—pink
gritty—sandy—sand—beige
murky—dark—water—gray
kindling—something used to start a fire—
   wood—brown

Page 57

There are 24 examples of figurative
language.
cost me an arm and a leg;
sun beating on me;
pounding like drums;
squawking as loud as a choir;
chip off the old block;
pretty as a picture;
faster than greased lightning;
dry as dust;
dull as a doorknob;
red-letter day;
go bananas;
blow her top;
off her rocker;
take the cake;
breaking up ships like toothpicks;
scared stiff;
screaming bloody murder;
last straw;
Out of sight, out of mind;
absence makes the heart grow fonder;
quick as a wink;

make no bones about it;
wipeout;
deader than a doornail

Pages 58–69, 71, 74–77, 79

Answers will vary. Check to see that students have completed the tasks with reasonable responses that fit the directions given.

Page 70

There may be more than one sequence of sentences that would make a clear report. Here is one possibility:

Farmer McCully called 911 at noon to report a loud roaring sound that was shaking the earth near his farm. I was in the area, so I raced to the farm. When I arrived, I found Farmer McCully's pigs looking shocked. Just then, I heard terrible screaming in addition to the loud roaring sound. I looked up in the sky toward the terrible noise. Unbelievably, a bathtub was whirling through the air. A young man in the tub was screaming for his life. Fortunately, the tub landed safely in the pig pen. No one was hurt, not even the pigs.

Pages 72–73

Unrelated details are:
1. Judge Laws had just had a turkey club sandwich for lunch when the case began. Judge Laws coughed from a bad cold.
2. Anthony was wearing a suit and tie in court today.
3. Mrs. Grundy lives in a pink house on Blossom Street. She told the judge that her grandchildren visit her every Saturday. Mrs. Grundy has a cat.
4. He also buys a dozen sticky buns and two pumpkin pies.
5. Arthur Rush makes his living designing socks for the Shoes & Socks Emporium. Mr. Rush drives a Mustang and Judge Law drives a Volkswagen.
6. The city has a population of 21,000. Her house has three stories.

Page 78

Answers will vary, but students should include details similar to the following examples:

Sahara—Catch a glimpse of a mirage. Enjoy cool drinks in a green oasis. Find out what it's really like to ride on a camel. Find plants and animals that survive on very little water. Watch the wind create dunes and patterns in the sand.

Amazon—Enjoy some unusually fine fishing. Get some close-up photos of big crocodiles. See some of the most beautiful tropical birds in the world.

You might catch a glimpse of a cheetah or an anaconda. Experience a lush tropical rain forest first hand.

Antarctica—See for yourself the most mammoth ice shelf in the world. The sun will shine until midnight! Spend a whole day watching playful penguins. Climb on glaciers and photograph icebergs.

Page 80

Answers may vary slightly, as a choice between exclamatory and imperative statements is sometimes subjective.
1. I (?)
2. IM (.)
3. D (.)
4. D (.)
5. IM (.) or E (!)
6. IM (.)
7. E (!)
8. I (?)
9. I (?)
10. E (.) or IM (!)
11. D (.)
12. E (!)
13. D (.)
Camp Lookout is in Washington.
Sentence examples will vary.

Page 81

10. tree house; is reached
9. coyote; howls
8. owl; hoots
7. Squirrels; jump
6. rope; hangs
5. Birds; have built
4. Moss; is growing
3. some; are falling
2. tree house; looks
1. ladder; shakes

Page 82

S, C, S, C, S, C
S, S, S, S, S
Carl needs to do this:
Take the chipmunk across the lake and leave it. Go back, pick up the owl, take it across the lake, and leave it. Then pick up the chipmunk and bring it back across. Leave the chipmunk and take the marshmallows across the lake. Go back alone to pick up the chipmunk and bring it across the lake.

Page 83

Answers will vary when students expand fragments into sentences on numbers 2, 3, 4, 6, 8, and 9.
1. The boulders rolled slowly at first. They gathered speed soon after.
5. The boulders crushed plants. Animals scampered away quickly.

7. They gained speed. Over and over they rolled.
10. The boulders are approaching Camp Lookout. Will they stop in time?

Page 84

1. marshes
2. cities
3. compasses
4. holidays
5. songs
6. foxes
7. bushes
8. poles
9. bunches
10. branches
11. marshmallows
12. campers; bags

Page 85

1. sheep
2. mice
3. Echoes
4. children
5. potatoes
6. teeth
7. loaves; knives
8. trout
9. tomatoes
10. radios
11. feet
12. lives
13. moose

Page 86

Answers may vary some. Allow anything that makes sense.
1. tent's poles
2. skunk's babies
3. camper's compass
4. tree house's door
5. rabbit's ears
6. counselor's T-shirt
7. Bigfoot's footprints
8. wolf's teeth
Sentences will vary.

Page 87

1. flowers' petals
2. children's treasure map
3. cooks' aprons
4. mice's food
5. campers' sleeping bags
6. deer's tails
7. boats' sails
8. counselors' caps

Page 88

These sentences have subject pronouns:
2. It
4. They
6. She

8. She
9. I
12. You
Sentences for bottom:
3. They were packing for their trip.
5. She had forgotten to include a flashlight.
7. She had packed too much.
10. She couldn't decide where to put her fishing gear.
11. It would not fit in the trunk of Maria's father's car.

Page 89

1. us
2. him
3. her
4. them
5. us
6. it
7. us
8. them
9. me
10. them
11. him
12. us
Sentences at bottom will vary.

Page 90

1. will go
2. will study
3. will bring
4. will try
5. will take
6. will be
7. will find
8. will fly
9. will look
10. will eat
11. will care
12. will hope
Stories at bottom will vary.

Page 91

1. thought
2. saw
3. hid
4. grew
5. came
6. wore
7. ate
8. went
9. ran
10. flew
11. told
12. wrote
Sentences at bottom will vary.

Page 92

Action verbs are:
noticed, appeared, scratched, wiggled, were playing, heard, whisper, crawled, sat, tried, was coming, noticed, did seem, attached, listened, creaked, opened, moved, hid, got, give, hid, heard, Give
Sentences at bottom will vary.

Page 93

1. is
2. were
3. will
4. is
5. has
6. had
7. has
8. am
9. should
10. will
11. should
12. are; will
Check to see that student drawing follows maze accurately.

Page 94

1. tiniest
2. larger
3. biggest
4. wettest
5. latest
6. slimiest
7. smallest
8. farthest
9. fattest
10. highest
11. longest
12. faster
13. slowest
14. fastest
Bottom: 1st—Maria
          2nd—Nick
          3rd—Isaac
          4th—Ann
          5th—Carl

Page 95

1. most
2. more
3. worst
4. best
5. most
6. most
7. worst
8. most
9. most
10. more
11. most
12. worst (or best)
Sentences at bottom will vary.

Page 96

1. more firmly
2. earliest
3. more cleverly
4. fastest
5. more skillfully
6. More often
7. more eagerly
8. more loudly
9. more busily
10. more quietly
11. longer
12. more harshly

Page 97

1. would
2. ever
3. anything
4. anybody
5. anything
6. nowhere
7. anything
8. nothing
9. no one
10. anything
11. anywhere
12. anything

Page 98

1. worms
2. lunches
3. cabins
4. creek
5. deer
6. hole
7. line
8. cap
9. water
10. rock
11. fish
12. friends
Check puzzles to see that students have circled all the above words.

Page 99

1. their, to
2. to, there
3. two, four
4. their, by
5. You're, too, to
6. too, to
7. You're, your
8. buy, by
9. There, their
10. their (or two)
11. two (or four)
12. They're (or You're)
13. their
14. You're
15. there, to
16. your
17. their, for (or to), their, to

Pages 100-101

Look at student art to see that they have crossed out the following words and replaced them as shown:

plain = plane
son = sun
pare = pair
sale = sail
meet = meat
bare = bear
whole = hole
dear = deer
hair = hare
pale = pail
I = eye
tow = toe
night = knight
be = bee
hoarse = horse
flour = flower

Original sentences will vary.

Page 102

"Tonight we'll raid the garbage cans outside the mess hall. Are you ready?" asked Freddy.

"You bet!" exclaimed Moe.

"There's a gold mine in this can! There's even a book. Have you ever read Monster Madness?" asked Moe.

"No! Why are you messing with books? I hear a noise. Grab your stuff and run," said Freddy.

"I got corn cobs, potato peels, apple cores, bread crusts, and some mozzarella cheese. Yummm. What did you get?" questioned Freddy.

Moe answered cheerfully, "It looks like I got everything but the kitchen sink."

Page 103

Check student papers for proper punctuation.

Page 104

Check student papers for accurate editing.

Page 105

Check student papers for accurate editing.

Page 106

Check student pages for accurate punctuation, capitalization, and spelling. The treasure is hidden by the horse riding stables.

Pages 112–113

1. Panama Canal opens
2. Golden Spike hammered in to finish the Transcontinental Railroad
3. U.S. enters World War I
4. Charles Lindbergh is first person to fly solo across the Atlantic Ocean
5. The Nineteenth Amendment gives women the right to vote
6. Cold War begins
7. Stock market crashes
8. World War II begins
9. Eisenhower elected to a second term
10. Alaska & Hawaii become states

11. Cuban Missile Crisis
12. First trip on the Oregon Trail
13. Declaration of Independence
14. Watergate Scandal
15. Civil War ends
16. Boston Massacre
17. Boston Tea Party
18. California Gold Rush
19. Louisiana Purchase
20. First person to walk on moon
21. Jamestown settlement established
22. Lewis & Clark expedition
23. George Washington becomes first president
24. Twenty-Sixth Amendment lowers voting age to 18

Pages 114–115

Examine student map to see that all bodies of water are correctly labeled and all 8 nation areas are accurately colored.

Page 116

Answers may vary somewhat, depending on sources student uses.
1. East Coast; Italy
2. Florida; Spain
3. France; Great Lakes area
4. Florida; Spain
5. England; Hudson River
6. France; St. Lawrence River
7. Spain; New Mexico
8. Mississippi River; Spain
9. the Southwest; Spain

Page 117

Across
2. Manhattan
4. Georgia
5. Delaware
8. New Netherland
10. Penn
11. Virginian
12. Quakers

Down
1. Philadelphia
2. Maryland
3. New Sweden
5. debt
6. thirteen
7. Mayflower
9. religious

Page 118

Answers may vary somewhat.
1. American colonists
2. Great Britain (or England)
3. all people have the same basic rights
4. can't be taken away, sold, or transferred
5. All people are born with rights that can't be taken away.
6. life, liberty, the pursuit of happiness

Page 119

6, 13, 10, 9, 12,
8, 2, 7, 3, 1,
11, 14, 15, 5, 4

1—1764—The British Parliament passes the Sugar Act.
2—1765—The British Parliament passes the Stamp Act.
3—1767—The British Parliament passes the Townshend Acts.
4—1770—The Boston Massacre occurs.
5—December, 1773—The Boston Tea Party takes place.
6—April 18, 1775—Paul Revere rides through the night warning, "The British are coming!"
7—June, 1775—The Battle of Bunker Hill is fought.
8—July, 1776—The Declaration of Independence is completed.
9—1777–1778—Washington's army winters at Valley Forge, Pennsylvania.
10—1778—British General Howe arrives from Britain with 32,000 troops.
11—February, 1778—America signs a treaty for help from France.
12—September, 1778—The Battle of Kings Mountain is fought in North and South Carolina.
13—1781—British General Charles Cornwallis surrenders at Yorktown, Virginia.
14—September, 1783—The final peace treaty is signed in Paris, France.
15—1787—The U.S. Constitution is written.

Page 120

Answers will vary. Check to see that student has expressed the general idea of the Preamble.

Page 121

Across
2. two
8. Constitution
9. laws
12. amend
13. senator

Down
1. Congress
3. Rhode Island
4. judicial
5. president
6. balances
7. population
10. three
11. veto

Page 122

1. Executive Branch
   President & Vice President
   Sees that laws are carried out; appoints officials; heads the armed forces; runs the government; can veto laws passed by Congress

2. Legislative Branch
Congress passes laws; can impeach a president; approves treaties and appointments; can override the president's veto; Senate confirms appointment of justices to the Supreme Court

3. Judicial Branch
Supreme Court interprets and explains laws; can declare a law unconstitutional

Page 123

The vice president is the leader of the Senate.

The Senate has 100 members.

A representative must be at least 25 years old.

No state has less than one representative.

The Senate has 2 members from each state.

The Congress is made up of two houses.

A senator's term is 6 years.

The House of Representatives has 435 members.

A senator must be at least 30 years old.

The number of representatives depends on the state's population.

The leader of the House of Representatives is called the Speaker of the House.

Page 124

1. president & vice president
2. Age—at least 35
   Citizenship—must be a natural-born citizen
   Residency—must have lived in the U.S. for at least 14 years
3. 2 terms, 4 years each
4. Answers may vary somewhat: enforce laws, run government on daily basis, head armed forces, appoint officials
5. conviction of treason, bribery, or other high crimes & misdemeanors
6. Answers will vary (i.e., Secretary of State, Treasury, Justice, etc.)
7. Answers may vary: Commander-in-Chief, Chief of the Party, Mr. President, Chief Executive, etc.
8. A. Vice president
   B. Speaker of the House
   C. President Pro Tem of the Senate
   D. Secretary of State
9. Cabinet gives advice to the president

Page 125

1.	F	7.	T
2.	F	8.	F
3.	T	9.	F
4.	T	10.	F
5.	F	11.	T
6.	T	12.	F

Page 126

1.	J	6.	I
2.	F	7.	B
3.	A	8.	D
4.	G	9.	C
5.	H	10.	E

Page 127

1. Delaware
2. Pennsylvania
3. New Jersey
4. Georgia
5. Connecticut
6. Massachusetts
7. Maryland
8. South Carolina
9. New Hampshire
10. Virginia
11. New York
12. North Carolina
13. Rhode Island

Pages 128–129

Answers may vary somewhat. Adults are encouraged to discuss these with students!

1. No.
2. Yes (if they are not felons).
3. No.
4. No; this is an unreasonable search.
5. Yes.
6. No; no.
7. Yes.
8. No; this is excessive.
9. Yes; their rights are being violated.
10. No.

Page 130

1. ok
2. Pacific Ocean (not Atlantic)
3. $15 million (not $10 million)
4. did not settle together peacefully
5. she was a Shoshone woman (not a chief)
6. Rocky Mountains (not Pacific)
7. ok
8. ok
9. Napoleon (not King Louis XIV)

Page 131

1.	G	7.	D
2.	C	8.	K
3.	I	9.	F
4.	A	10.	J
5.	L	11.	B
6.	E	12.	H

Page 132

1. b
2. d
3. k
4. c
5. a
6. e
7. h
8. i
9. g
10. m
11. f
12. j
13. l

The term is *abolitionists*.

Page 133

1. What was secession?
2. What was Richmond, Virginia?
3. Who was Abraham Lincoln?
4. What happened at Appomattox Courthouse?
5. Who was Robert E. Lee?
6. Who was Jefferson Davis?
7. What was Ford's Theater?
8. What was the Emancipation Proclamation?
9. What was the Thirteenth Amendment?
10. What was the Monitor?
11. What were Missouri, Kentucky, Maryland, and Delaware called during the Civil War? (Some may also add West Virginia.)
12. What were the blockade runners?
13. What was the Army of Northern Virginia?
14. What was Bull Run?
15. Who was Ulysses S. Grant?

Page 134

1.	N	9.	A
2.	E	10.	M
3.	O	11.	L
4.	C	12.	I
5.	F	13.	D
6.	B	14.	J
7.	G	15.	K
8.	H		

Page 135

1.	Congress	7.	spikes
2.	Union Pacific	8.	Rocky Mountains
3.	eastward	9.	Central Pacific
4.	work train	10.	Sierra Nevada
5.	roadbed	11.	Chinese
6.	ties	12.	Promontory

Page 136

1.	G	8.	I
2.	C	9.	D
3.	M	10.	F
4.	Q	11.	L
5.	K	12.	E
6.	A	13.	P
7.	O	14.	H

Page 137

1. gold
2. spike
3. Homesteaders
4. Sioux
5. golden; Promontory
6. Chisholm
7. transcontinental
8. lasso, saddle
9. reservation
10. Pikes Peak
11. bison
12. Nez Perce
13. Central Pacific
14. Little Bighorn
15. Chinese

Pages 138–139

1. 1901–1910
2. Northwestern
3. Eastern
4. Central
5. 1901–1910
6. 8–9 (answers will vary)
7. 1901–1910
8. 3.5 million
9. 1871–1880
10. Northwestern & Central

The Statue of Liberty is in the New York Harbor. It was a gift to the U.S. from France.

Page 140

1. Model T Ford built—1908
2. Panama Canal finished—1914
3. World War I begins—1914
4. First professional radio broadcast—1920
5. Lindbergh crosses the Atlantic—1927
6. Great Stock Market crash—1929
7. The Great Depression—1929
8. Hoover Dam built across Colorado River—1935
9. Pearl Harbor attacked—1941
10. U.S. drops atomic bombs on Japan—1945
11. World War II ends—1945
12. Korean War begins—1950
13. Eisenhower is elected—1952
14. Supreme Court outlaws school segregation—1954
15. First U.S. satellite launched—1958
16. Alaska & Hawaii become states—1959
17. Cuban Missile Crisis—1962
18. Kennedy shot in Dallas—1963
19. Civil Rights Act—1964
20. Martin Luther King, Jr., assassinated—1968
21. First steps on moon—1969
22. U.S. troops leave Vietnam—1973
23. Watergate scandal—(1972-1974)

24. Iran Hostage Crisis—1979
25. First woman appointed to Supreme Court—1981
26. Space shuttle Challenger explodes—1986
27. Persian Gulf War—1991

The first three events—Model T invention, opening of Panama Canal, and beginning of World War I—could not have been broadcast on the radio because widespread radio broadcasts did not yet occur.

Page 141

Across

3. Organization created to keep world peace
6. World's first artificial satellite
8. Soviet-built missiles discovered here caused a crisis in 1962
10. President of Cuba during the 1962 Cuban Missile Crisis
11. U.S. president during the Cuban Missile Crisis

Down

1. Weapons that could carry nuclear warheads
2. Name of conflict between U.S. and U.S.S.R.
4. Abbreviation for North Atlantic Treaty Organization
5. The competition between the U.S. and U.S.S.R. to explore space
7. U.S.S.R. president at the start of the Cold War
9. Place in space both countries wanted to get to first

Pages 142–143

1. Bureau of Engraving & Printing
2. FBI Headquarters
3. Washington Monument
4. White House
5. Library of Congress
6. Smithsonian Institute
7. Lincoln Memorial
8. Supreme Court Building
9. Justice Building
10. National Archives
11. Vietnam Veterans Memorial
12. Capitol Building
13. Department of Treasury
14. Ford's Theater
15. National Mall
16. U.S. Postal Service
17. National Air & Space Museum
18. Government Printing Office

See that student has colored map accurately.

Pages 144–145

A. Check maps for accurate labeling and coloring. The numbers should be in

these states:

1. TX	11. TX	21. CA
2. MA	12. CA	22. IL
3. KY	13. NY	23. WY
4. AL	14. HI	24. AK
5. MT	15. CO	25. NC
6. IL	16. MO	26. NJ
7. GA	17. OR	27. OK
8. WA	18. CT	28. VA
9. NV	19. SD	29. FL
10. UT	20. PA	30. LA

B. Virginia, New Hampshire, Massachusetts, Maryland, Connecticut, Rhode Island, North Carolina, New York, New Jersey, South Carolina, Pennsylvania, Delaware, and Georgia should be colored yellow.

C. Alaska and Hawaii should be colored green.

Pages 146–147

Before 13,000 B.C.—First people cross from Asia into North America

700–1400—Native American cultures spread through North America

1492—Columbus reaches the coast of North America

1565—St. Augustine, Florida, oldest city settled

1607—First English settlement, Jamestown

1620—Pilgrims land at Plymouth Rock

1770—Boston Massacre

1776—Declaration of Independence

1789—George Washington inaugurated

1849—California Gold Rush

1861—Civil War begins

1865—Civil War ends

1869—Transcontinental Railroad finished

1890—Battle at Wounded Knee

1908—Model T car invented

1914—Panama Canal completed

1927—Lindbergh flies across the Atlantic

1929—Stock Market Crash & Great Depression

1933—Roosevelt's New Deal

1941—Japanese bomb Pearl Harbor

1945—U.S. drops atomic bombs on Japan (WWII ends)

1950—Korean War

1960—John F. Kennedy elected president

1964—Civil Rights Act

1968—Assassination of Martin Luther King, Jr.

1969—First walk on moon

1973—U.S. troops leave Vietnam

1979—66 Americans taken hostage in Iran

1986—Space shuttle Challenger explodes

1989—San Francisco earthquake

2001—Terrorist attacks on the World Trade Center and Pentagon buildings

2008—Barack Obama elected president

Page 148

1–8. Answers will vary. Check for accuracy.
9. 18
10–13. Answers will vary. Check for accuracy.
14. *In God We Trust*
Check to see that student has drawn the flag and seal accurately.

Page 149

1. Crazy Horse
2. Alexander Graham Bell
3. Lyndon B. Johnson
4. Franklin D. Roosevelt
5. Neil Armstrong
6. Woodrow Wilson
7. Jesse Jackson
8. Sandra Day O'Connor
9. Rosa Parks
10. Clara Barton
11. Paul Revere
12. Harriet Tubman

Page 150

Check students' pictures to see that they are accurately colored.

Page 151

Answers may vary somewhat.
1. map
2. globe or map
3. map, globe, or atlas
4. atlas
5. map (or atlas) and scale
6. map or globe
7. map or globe
8. map, compass rose, and scale
9. map (or globe) and compass rose
10. map and compass rose

Page 152

Answers may vary somewhat. Check to see that:
1. Peevish Peak is by black triangle.
2. Maniac Mountains label is by mountains.
3. Moody City label is by large city symbol.
4. Mad River is at X beside river symbol.
5. Lake Grumpy label is by lake.
6. HWY 66 is at X beside double line symbol.
7. Route 86 is at X beside solid black line.
8. Cranky Village is beside small town dot.
9. Whiny Ranger Station is by station symbol.
10. Blubbering Buttes is near the two buttes.

Page 153

Check map key to see that student has drawn symbols accurately.
1. Lost Moon
2. Sierra Padre National Park
3. Check student maps
4. 2
5. 5
6. Windy Pines Rd., Last Chance Rd.
7. no
8. before
9. Death Valley
10. HWY 125, Hwy 5, Twin Buttes Rd., Windy Pines Rd., Last Chance Rd. (Answers may vary somewhat.)

Page 154

Answers may vary somewhat.
1. 34 meters
2. 37 meters
3. 100 meters
4. 10 meters
5. 7 meters
6. 4 meters
7. 24 meters
8. 16 meters
9. 34 meters

Page 155

1. S, E
2. N, E
3. N, W
4. N, E
5. S, E, W
6. N, S, E
7. N, E
8. N, W
9. N, E
10. N, S, W
11. S, W

Pages 156–157

Check student's map to see that all states are accurately labeled and that candy symbols are drawn correctly according to the alphabetical labeling.

Page 158

Correct answers are
1, 2, 3, 5, 9, 12, 15, 19
Corrected answers may vary somewhat:
4. measure of distance on a map
6. part that explains the symbols used on the map
7. farthest point north on Earth; at 90°N
8. symbol showing the directions on a map
10. high, flat landform that rises steeply above the surrounding land
11. line of latitude north of the equator
13. 0° line of longitude
14. divisions of Earth used to measure time
16. 90° South Latitude
17. distance north or south of the equator
18. distance east or west of the prime meridian
19. line of latitude at 23°30' south of the equator
20. farthest point south on the Earth; bottom of the Earth; at 66°30' S

Page 159

1. D 3, E 3
2. E 2, F 2
3. C 1– C 6
4. A 2, A 3
5. E 4, E 5
6. B 4, C 4
7. E 2, E 3
8. D 2, E 2
9. A 2, B 2, C 2
10. A 5, B 5, C 5
11. D 4, D 5
12. A 3, B 3
13. F 4, F 5, F 6
14. C 4, D 4, E 4, F 4
15. E 2, E 3
16. C 1, D 1

Page 160

1. South Pole
2. 30° N
3. Mexico
4. Nuuk, Fort Yukon
5. Quito
6. south
7. Boston
8. 60° S approximately

Page 161

Check student maps for accurate placement of tea bags. Placement on numbers 3, 4, 5, 7, 9, and 10 may be on any reasonable place along the specified line of longitude.

Pages 162–163

1. approximately 39° N, 98° W
2. Answers will vary.
Check map to see that cities noted on Page 38 are accurately located.

Page 164

Answers may vary somewhat according to decisions student makes about the deliveries.
1. 8
2. Lower Level
3. 1
4. 9

5. Shop #4 should be pink.
6. Shop #17 should be green.
7. 18
8. 2
9. Upper Level
10. 6
11. 10
12. 3

Page 165

1. Check student's map for accuracy.
2. Check to see that northernmost New Zealand island is colored red.
3. NE
4. Sydney
5. earthquakes, storms
6. volcanoes, earthquakes, tsunamis, storms
7. Southern Ocean
8. Check to see that the desert areas are colored yellow.

Pages 166–167

1. 5:00 A.M. Eastern Time
2. It's only 8:10 A.M. in Hawaii!
3. perhaps 3:00 P.M. Mountain Time
4. 7:00 A.M. Central Time
5. No
6. 9:00 A.M. Central Time
7. NO_2
8. 12:30 A.M. Central Time

Pages 168–169

Maps will vary. Check to see that student has included several items on the map, and that a key, scale, and compass rose have been added.
A sarcophagus is a type of casket.

Page 173

These words should be circled in the puzzle.
1. sleep
2. water
3. aerobic
4. strength
5. no
6. heart
7. flexibility
8. pulse
9. diet
10. muscles
11. frequently
12. health
13. posture
14. fitness
15. checkups
16. exercise
17. nutrition

Page 174

True statements are 1, 2, 3, 5, 8, 10, 11, 12.
See that students color these spaceships green and cross out others.

Page 175

True statements are 2, 3, 5, 8, 10, 11, 12, 13, 15.
See that these sections of the suit are colored red.

False statements are 1, 4, 6, 7, 9, 14, 16, 17, 18.
See that these sections of the suit are colored black.

Pages 176–177

1. HCl
2. CO_2
3. P_2O_5
4. H_2O
5. H_2O_2
6. SiO_2
7. CO
8. NaCl
9. PbO
10. HBr
11. $AgNO_3$
12. Na_2O_2
13. HF
14. AgCl
15. NO_2
16. Make sure student shows 1 calcium atom, 1 carbon atom, and 3 oxygen atoms.

Page 178

1. P
2. P
3. C
4. C
5. P
6. P
7. C
8. P
9. P
10. C
11. C
12. C
13. C
14. C
15. P
16. C
17. P
18. C
19. C
20. P

Page 179

red	yellow	red	yellow	yellow	green
L	S	L	S	S	G

yellow	green	green	yellow	red	yellow
S	G	G	S	L	S

red	yellow	yellow	green	red	yellow
L	S	S	G	L	S

red	red	red	green	yellow	green
L	L	L	G	S	G

green	red	green	red	yellow	green
G	L	G	L	S	G

Page 180

1. energy
2. degree
3. Hot; cold
4. radiation
5. Convection
6. thermometer
7. conductor
8. transfer
9. boiling
10. current
11. insulation
12. conduction
Joke answer: Hot! You can easily catch cold!

Page 181

Wrong answers to be corrected.
1. I   11. L
2. H   12. K
4. D   13. M
7. B   14. N
9. J

Page 182

Student clues should be similar to these.
1. material that absorbs light
2. bending of a light ray
3. object that bends light twice and shows a spectrum
4. light passes through, cannot be seen through
5. bouncing a light ray off a surface
6. colored material that absorbs certain light colors and reflects others
7. something you can see through
8. all the colors that make up light
9. absence of light
10. all colors combined
11. instrument using light to see things far away, make things larger
12. visible parts of the spectrum
13. visible colors of the spectrum
14. name of Northern lights
15. shafts or streaks of light

Page 183

1. motion
2. speed
3. acceleration
4. force
5. gravity
6. pressure
7. weight
8. mass
9. energy
10. work
11. inertia
12. friction

Page 184–185

Features given may vary, depending on sources students use.

Inner Planets:

1. Mercury/ 0 moons/ 2nd smallest, heavily cratered, dark color
2. Venus/ 0 moons/ cloud cover/ yellow color
3. Earth/ 1 moon/ water vapor atmosphere, sustains life
4. Mars/ 2 moons/ polar caps, craters, clouds & fog, appears red

Outer Planets:

5. Jupiter/ 67 known satellites/ largest planet, gaseous, reddish-brown & white cloud bands, large red spot
6. Saturn/ 62 satellites/ gaseous, many rings
7. Uranus/ 27 satellites/ gaseous, dark rings
8. Neptune/ 14 satellites/ gaseous, rings

Pages 186–187

A. 8 black hole
B. 1 nova
C. 10 sun
D. 4 comet
E. 7 supergiant
F. 9 star cluster
G. 6 solar flare
H. 2 asteroid belt
I. 11 double stars (or binary star)
J. 5 comet tail
K. 3 meteors (or meteoroids)
L. 12 vacuum
M. 17 orbit
N. 16 astronaut
O. 13 spaceship
P. 21 white dwarf
Q. 20 worm hole
R. 19 satellite
S. 15 planet
T. 14 moon
U. 18 galaxy
V. 23 meteoroid
W. 22 asteroid

Page 188

1. volcano
2. sinkhole
3. earthquake
4. aftershock
5. epicenter
6. tsunami or tidal wave
7. caldera or crater
8. seismograph
9. geyser
10. fault

Page 189

1. I
2. S
3. S
4. S
5. I
6. M
7. S
8. M
9. I
10. M
11. S
12. M
13. M
14. I
15. S
16. S
17. S
18. I
19. M
20. M or I

Pages 190–191

1. tornado warning
2. windy
3. dew
4. ice storm
5. drought
6. front
7. rain
8. fog
9. sunshine
10. blizzard
11. tornado
12. sleet
13. lightning
14. clouds
15. frost
16. hurricane
17. thunder
18. heat wave
19. snow
20. hail

Page 192

1. waves
2. crest
3. trough
4. current
5. dissolved salts
6. tides
7. Earth, moon, sun
8. nutrients
9. continental slope
10. rift zones
11. benthos
12. plankton

Page 193

1. c
2. b
3. c
4. a
5. a
6. b
7. c
8. b
9. a
10. b
11. b
12. a
13. a
14. b
15. b
16. c
17. b
18. b

Pages 194–195

SCIENCE CHALLENGE

LIFE SCIENCE

1. mollusks
2. extinct
3. camouflage or protective coloration
4. desert
5. photosynthesis

EARTH & SPACE SCIENCE

1. rotation
2. Mercury
3. 365
4. igneous, metamorphic, sedimentary
5. water

PHYSICAL SCIENCE

1. mass
2. evaporation
3. condensation
4. motion
5. energy

Possible points: 5,500

SUPER SCIENCE CHALLENGE

LIFE SCIENCE

1. warm-blooded or mammal
2. acid rain
3. arachnids
4. drugs
5. skin

EARTH & SPACE SCIENCE

1. mantle
2. when it hits Earth's surface (or another surface)
3. rocks
4. Uranus & Neptune
5. minerals

PHYSICAL SCIENCE

1. weight
2. work
3. chemical change
4. volume
5. newton-meter or joule

Possible points: 10,600

Possible points for pages 194 and 195 together: 16,100

Page 196

1. drought
2. They are both conductors.
3. no
4. no
5. orbiting the Earth
6. gravity
7. no
8. in a wave
9. hanging from a ceiling in a cave
10. standing on ground of a cave
11. Halley's comet
12. no
13. no
14. took a space flight
15. no
16. Answers will vary.
17. yes
18. measure air pressure

Page 197

1. G caldera
2. C geyser
3. A hot springs
4. H mudspots
5. B fumorale
6. I solfataros
7. J batholith
8. F sinkhole
9. D laccolith
10. K dike
11. E volcanic neck

Page 206

Answers may vary somewhat.
1. the speed of the wind at the bottom
2. fraction that are experts or fraction that are intermediate
3. number of times she fell in the third hour
4. number of passes sold last season
5. price of the boots
6. number of days of the trip
7. number of skiers rescued each day
8. number won by Will or Thomas
9. amount of snow before last night
10. number of collisions on Monday or Tuesday

Page 207

1. new $700 snowboard, today is my 14th birthday; *answer is 27*
2. including 3 Flips; *answer is 5*
3. did 3 Backscratchers, 2 Iguana Back Flips, and 5 Nose Rolls; *answer is 3 minutes 20.54 seconds*
4. I've done 200 Ollies; *answer is 4,800*
5. takes 45 minutes to get to the park from home, season pass cost $350; *answer is 3 hours*

6. 1,200 snowboarders, 180 boarders under 12, 70 boarders over 16; *answer is $315*
7. movie tickets cost $6.50 each; *answer is "no"*
8. 37 bruises, 6 cuts, 1 broken finger; *answer is 260*
9. 6 tacos, 2 hot dogs; *answer is 104*

Page 208

1. c; $11\frac{1}{2}$ miles
2. c; 8 hours
3. b; 52
4. c; 8
5. a; 6
6. a; 16

Page 209

Equations may vary in the order in which they are written.
1. n = (42 x 2) + (7 x 3)
   (n = 105)
2. n = 216 ÷ 3
   (n = 72)
3. n = 400 – 195
   (n = 205 miles)
4. n = 96 – 28
   (n = 68 pairs)
5. n = 7 x 20
   (n = 140 quarts)
6. n = 2,224 + 155 + 2,224 – 350
   (n = 4,253)
7. n = $4,500 – $1,850 – $570
   (n = $2,080)
8. n = .5 x 4,788.5 or $\frac{1}{2}$ x 4,788.5
   (n = 2,394.25 ft or 2,394 $\frac{1}{4}$ ft)

Page 210

Jose—3,200
Abby—3,880
Dylan—4,261
Jessica—4,109
Ryan—4,496
Brad—4,323
Lauren—4,975
Andy—3,495
Alexa—5,000
Denise—4,370
1. Alexa
2. yes

Page 211

1. 50%, 6
2. Carla, Josie
3. 9
4. 38
5. Dana, 4
6. 66
7. $\frac{38}{66}$ or $\frac{19}{33}$
8. Josie
9. $\frac{11}{13}$
10. Dana

11. Josie & Carla
12. Patti & Carla

Page 212

Matching pairs are:
5,280 feet — 1 mile
20 qt — 5 gal
54 in. — $1\frac{1}{2}$ yd
108 in. — 3 yd
4 cups — 2 pints
$3\frac{1}{2}$ lb — 56 oz
3,000 lb — $1\frac{1}{2}$ tons
2 qt — 8 cups
10 gal — 80 pints
12 feet — 4 yards

Page 213

Answers may vary somewhat depending on exactly where students measure. Allow answers in these ranges:
1. 24–30 cm
2. 18 cm
3. 36 cm
4. 30–36 cm
5. 21–24 cm
6. 24–27 cm
7. 15–18 cm
8. 21–24 cm
9. 48 cm
10. 27 cm
11. 60 cm

Page 214

Recipe for 8
  6 cups milk
  12 eggs
  5 bananas
  $1\frac{1}{2}$ teaspoons vanilla
  $1\frac{1}{3}$ cups protein powder

Recipe for 2
  $1\frac{1}{2}$ cups milk
  3 eggs
  $1\frac{1}{4}$ bananas
  $\frac{3}{8}$ teaspoon vanilla
  $\frac{1}{3}$ cup protein powder

Recipe for 12
  9 cups milk
  18 eggs
  $7\frac{1}{2}$ bananas
  $2\frac{1}{4}$ teaspoons vanilla
  2 cups protein powder

Page 215

1. Red 7.1
2. Blue 6.35
3. Pink 0.6

4. Black........ 100.12
5. Yellow 0.36
6. Purple.......... 0.09
7. Tan 9.1
8. Orange....... 14.2
9. Brown.......... 2.05
10. Tan 0.9
11. Silver........... 0.24
12. Green.......... 0.99
13. Red 10.12
14. Blue 8.08
15. Green........... 9.9
16. Pink 8.8
17. Purple.......... 2.4
18. Red 0.009
19. Orange 0.22
20. Yellow 3.6
21. Blue 0.5
22. Green......... 50.5
23. Silver.......... 20.5
24. Purple 100.2

Page 216

Annie Ace—$5.19
Movin' Marika—$5.55
Daring Donna—$5.45
Suzie Spiker—$4.94
Jumpin' Julie—$9.15
Colleen Cool—$4.34
Towering Tara—$6.04
No-Foul Fran—$8.27
Sally Smasher—$4.95
Nellie Net—$4.70
Sara Server—$8.05
Power Pam—$5.45

Page 217

1. D; $25,000
2. S; 351
3. D; 5
4. M; 156
5. A & S (or just S); 35
6. M, A, & S or (M & S); 9
7. A & M; 20
8. A; 8

Page 218

1. P = 39 in
2. V = 27 in³
3. V = 87.92 in³
4. V = 180 in³
5. V = 1,024 in³
6. V = 75.36 in³
7. V = 48 in³
8. A = 54 in²
9. P = 6 in
10. A = 957 in²
11. A = 4,900 in²

Page 219

1. baseball—8,100 ft²
2. tennis—2,808 ft²
3. boxing—256 ft²
4. swimming—11,108 ft²
5. archery—1,125 ft²
6. wrestling—452.16 ft²
7. track—151,400 ft²
8. sailboat—138 ft²

Page 220

1.	75%	11.	55%
2.	10%	12.	15%
3.	20%	13.	90%
4.	90%	14.	75%
5.	25%	15.	10%
6.	80%	16.	25%
7.	50%	17.	30%
8.	40%	18.	40%
9.	5%	19.	80%
10.	30%	20.	50%

Page 221

1.	8	6.	3
2.	72	7.	960
3.	1	8.	24
4.	54	9.	72
5.	18	10.	9

Page 222

1. 1 hour 5 minutes
2. 9:50 A.M.
3. 11:10 A.M.
4. 1:40 P.M.
5. 20 minutes
6. 5:05 P.M.
7. 30 minutes
8. 7:35 P.M.
9. 10:55 P.M.
10. 8 hours 55 minutes

Page 223

1. $24.08
2. sleeveless T-shirt
   (for $19.80)
3. $51.94
4. $85.12
5. $52.43
6. $33.07
7. no
8. $2.10
9. yes
10. $48.16

Page 224

1. 30 gal
2. 160 towels
3. 80 cups
4. 40 sticks
5. 3
6. $90
7. 75 pairs

8. $2,800
9. 660

Page 225

1. from left to right:
   Tony, Toby, Timothy, Terence, Tiny;
   Tiny finished first.
Drawings on 2–5 may vary.
2. Iron Arms
3. Grizzlies
4. Serena
5. Ramon

Page 226

Paths should follow these numbers:
1. 1—8—160—80—trophy 92
2. 2—26—106—212—trophy 200
3. 3—45—5—55—trophy 11
4. 4—84—74—174—trophy 0

Page 227

Sunday 10
Monday 440
Tuesday 42
Wednesday 24
Thursday 75 (or 25)
Friday 100
Saturday 56

Page 228

Top: The cheese is in Carla's locker.
Bottom: R. J. could not open his locker.

Page 229

Problem 1—Jamie is the fourth person
   from the front of the line.
Problem 2—One is the man with the
   Tiger's flag, and the other is the girl
   second from the end.

Pages 230–231

Answers will vary. Check student
equations to make sure they add up to
correct score and to make sure they are
methods that are actually possible for
football scores.

Page 232

Answers may vary somewhat.
1. yes, b
2. Ted, b
3. 30, b
4. 11, c
5. 66, a
6. 144 square meters, b

Page 233

Answers may vary as to strategies chosen.
1. yes; mental math or estimate
2. 480 feet; write equation, estimate, or
   mental math
3. 180; write equation

4. 5:40 P.M.; draw a diagram or write equation
5. Lucy; draw a diagram
6. 5, 11, 17; trial and error or write equation

Pages 234–235

Explanations of problem solutions will vary.
1. 11
2. Seth
3. $86
4. 864 ft³
5. 15, 18, 9

Page 236

Correct answers are
2, 3, 4, 8, 9, 10, 13, 15

Pages 237–238

1. ten thousand three hundred
2. one billion six hundred million
3. two million
4. forty thousand
5. three thousand
6. forty million one hundred thousand
7. one thousand nine hundred twenty-nine
8. eighty-five thousand
9. seven thousand one hundred thirty-seven
10. three hundred fifty thousand
11. 35,000,000,000
12. 95,000
13. 4,104
14. $30,000,000
15. 9,356
16. $1,500,000,000
17. 28,065
18. 1,300,000
19. 200,000
20. 2,176
21. $394,000
22. 10,500

Page 239

1. 56
2. 312
3. 522
4. 940
5. 113
6. 111
7. 1,254
8. 189
9. 515
10. 873
11. 125,649
12. 11,038
13. 7,495
14. 2,062
15. 2,892
16. 7,358

Page 240

1. 5,493
2. 1,339
3. Hungary
4. 1,377
5. Spain
6. Italy
7. 376
8. 266
9. 955
10. 7,308
11. 23
12. 101

Page 241

Accept any four correct factors.
1. 1, 2, 3, 6, 9, 18
2. 1, 2, 5, 10
3. 1, 3, 5, 15
4. 1, 3, 5, 9, 15, 45
5. 1, 2, 3, 6
6. 1, 2, 3, 6, 9, 10, 15, 30, 45, 90
7. 1, 3, 7, 21
8. 1, 3, 11, 33
9. 1, 2, 3, 4, 6, 8, 12, 24
10. 1, 2, 4, 7, 8, 14, 28, 56
11. 1, 2, 4, 8, 16, 32
12. 1, 3, 9, 27
13. 1, 2, 3, 6, 7, 14, 21, 42
14. 1, 2, 4, 5, 8, 10, 20, 40
15. 1, 3, 13, 39

Page 242

1.	2	10.	12	19.	4
2.	3	11.	3	20.	7
3.	11	12.	4	21.	4
4.	14	13.	2	22.	10
5.	15	14.	2	23.	5
6.	6	15.	2	24.	10
7.	4	16.	10	25.	2
8.	3	17.	5	26.	3
9.	10	18.	5	27.	3

The driver dragged a garden rake to stop the sled.

Page 243

Check to see that students have colored picture correctly, according to answers given in color code.

Page 244

1. 700
2. 300
3. 950
4. 200
5. 1,460
6. 1,000
7. 1,700
8. 200
9. 4,000

10. 1,300
11. 910
12. 409
13. 1,589
14. 5,791

Page 245

Hurdle problem: 100
1. 161
2. 6
3. 2,002
4. 888
5. 1
6. 202
7. 1,000
8. 0

Page 246

1. divide; 1,089
2. multiply; $1,972,886.00
3. multiply; 15,600
4. add; 265.03 km
5. multiply; 2,000
6. divide; $22.90
7. multiply; $300,000,000
8. multiply and add; $3,944.00

Page 247

1. commutative property of mult.
2. property of 1
3. zero property of mult.
4. commutative property of mult.
5. property of 1
6. commutative property of mult.
7. commutative property of addition
8. zero property of subtraction
9. opposites property of addition
10. zero property of addition
11. commutative property of mult.
12. zero property of mult.

Page 248

1. $\frac{2}{6}$ or $\frac{1}{3}$
2. $\frac{3}{6}$ or $\frac{1}{2}$
3. $\frac{3}{9}$ or $\frac{1}{3}$
4. $\frac{1}{9}$
5. $\frac{6}{9}$ or $\frac{2}{3}$
6. $\frac{5}{6}$
7. $\frac{2}{8}$ or $\frac{1}{4}$
8. $\frac{1}{8}$
9. $\frac{2}{6}$ or $\frac{1}{3}$
10. $\frac{4}{12}$ or $\frac{1}{3}$
11. $\frac{1}{6}$
12. $\frac{4}{6}$ or $\frac{2}{3}$
13. $\frac{4}{12}$ or $\frac{1}{3}$

14. $\frac{11}{12}$

15. $\frac{2}{6}$ or $\frac{1}{3}$

16. $\frac{2}{6}$ or $\frac{1}{3}$

17. $\frac{1}{4}$

18. $\frac{1}{6}$

19. $\frac{4}{10}$ or $\frac{2}{5}$

Page 249

1. $\frac{2}{4}$

2. $\frac{5}{7}$

3. both

4. $\frac{1}{3}$

5. $\frac{1}{3}$

6. $\frac{5}{6}$

7. $\frac{7}{8}$

8. both

9. $\frac{2}{3}$

10. $\frac{11}{12}$

11. $\frac{5}{6}$

12. both

13. $\frac{1}{4}$; $\frac{2}{5}$; $\frac{1}{2}$

14. $\frac{3}{18}$; $\frac{2}{3}$; $\frac{5}{6}$

15. $\frac{2}{5}$; $\frac{5}{9}$; $\frac{6}{7}$

Page 250

Path follows these equations:

$\frac{8}{12} = \frac{2}{3}$

$\frac{2}{4} = \frac{5}{10}$

$\frac{6}{3} = \frac{8}{4}$

$\frac{8}{4} = \frac{12}{6}$

$\frac{20}{25} = \frac{4}{5}$

$\frac{7}{12} = \frac{14}{24}$

$\frac{0}{2} = \frac{0}{4}$

$\frac{2}{3} = \frac{4}{6}$

Page 251

1. C
2. B
3. B
4. A
5. C
6. B
7. A
8. A
9. B
10. C

Page 252

1. $28\frac{1}{2}$

2. $9\frac{3}{6}$ or $9\frac{1}{2}$

3. $24\frac{1}{4}$

4. $23\frac{1}{2}$

5. $6\frac{2}{5}$

6. $10\frac{5}{8}$

7. $29\frac{1}{3}$

8. $20\frac{3}{4}$

9. $12\frac{1}{4}$

10. $27\frac{1}{4}$

11. $23\frac{2}{3}$

12. $15\frac{3}{4}$

13. $27\frac{3}{6}$ or $27\frac{1}{2}$

14. $10\frac{9}{12}$ or $10\frac{3}{4}$

15. $25\frac{1}{4}$

16. $4\frac{2}{3}$

Page 253

a. $1\frac{1}{4}$

b. $2\frac{1}{7}$

c. $1\frac{6}{7}$

d. $1\frac{1}{5}$

e. $8\frac{8}{10}$ or $8\frac{4}{5}$

f. $3\frac{1}{3}$

g. $1\frac{1}{2}$

h. $1\frac{4}{14}$ or $1\frac{1}{4}$

i. $1\frac{6}{10}$ or $1\frac{3}{5}$

j. $1\frac{4}{11}$

k. $4\frac{6}{8}$ or $4\frac{3}{4}$

l. $4\frac{2}{4}$ or $4\frac{1}{2}$

m. $4\frac{5}{10}$ or $4\frac{1}{2}$

n. $1\frac{3}{4}$

o. $13\frac{2}{6}$ or $13\frac{1}{3}$

p. $5\frac{2}{3}$

q. $8\frac{4}{6}$ or $8\frac{2}{3}$

r. $1\frac{2}{9}$

s. $6\frac{3}{5}$

t. $5\frac{1}{20}$

u. $10\frac{3}{6}$ or $10\frac{1}{2}$

v. $1\frac{1}{5}$

w. $2\frac{5}{7}$

x. $1\frac{1}{3}$

Page 254

See that fractions are circled with correct colors.

1. $\frac{5}{6}$

2. $\frac{3}{10}$

3. $\frac{1}{12}$

4. $\frac{1}{8}$

5. $\frac{1}{2}$

6. $\frac{4}{5}$

7. $\frac{1}{6}$

8. $\frac{13}{22}$

9. $\frac{1}{3}$

10. $\frac{4}{9}$

11. $\frac{7}{9}$

12. $\frac{19}{21}$

13. $\frac{1}{2}$

14. $\frac{19}{24}$

Page 255

1. $\frac{24}{28}$ or $\frac{6}{7}$

2. $\frac{8}{7}$ or $1\frac{1}{7}$

3. $\frac{27}{22}$ or $1\frac{5}{22}$

4. $\frac{10}{3}$ or $3\frac{1}{3}$

5. $\frac{20}{60}$ or $\frac{1}{3}$

6. $\frac{10}{36}$ or $\frac{5}{18}$

7. $\frac{42}{40}$ or $1\frac{1}{20}$

8. $\frac{100}{121}$

9. $\frac{1}{4}$

10. $\frac{36}{5}$ or $7\frac{1}{5}$

11. $\frac{15}{12}$ or $1\frac{3}{12}$ or $1\frac{1}{4}$

12. $\frac{32}{27}$ or $1\frac{5}{27}$

13. $\frac{5}{12}$

14. $\frac{12}{12}$ or 1

15. $\frac{4}{25}$

Page 256

1. .1
2. .9
3. 10.1
4. .3
5. 1.6
6. 4.9
7. 2.2
8. .1
9. .1
10. 4.8
11. .18
12. 2.81
13. .78
14. .06
15. 6.00
16. 100.48
17. .94

18. 1.37
19. 4.60
20. 3.67
21. .469
22. 4.679
23. 7.090
24. .056
25. 41.523
26. .199
27. 5.011
28. .022
29. .7478
30. .1999
31. .7400
32. 15.0289
33. 1.1515
34. 4.3337
35. .5902

Page 257

Karin	39.479	4th
Sofia	39.272	5th
Elena	37.901	11th
Kim	38.464	9th
Kerri	38.886	6th
Tatiana	39.928	1st
Nina	38.562	7th
Larissa	38.545	8th
Svetlana	39.738	2nd
Olga	37.063	12th
Kathy	39.482	3rd
Tamara	38.289	10th

gold—Tatiana
silver—Svetlana
bronze—Kathy

Page 258

1. $3.00
2. $2.60
3. $945.00
4. $210.00
5. $120.00
6. $26.80
7. $360.00
8. approx $133
9. $2,085.00
10. $26.83
11. $143.00
12. $725.00

Page 259

1. 0.78
2. 0.80
3. 0.74
4. 0.72
5. 0.77
6. 0.81
7. 0.75
8. 0.73
9. 0.71
10. 0.75

Page 260

Earvin	90
Tony	90
Christian	90
Clyde	80
Alan	95
David	80
Rimas	83
Charles	94
Aramis	80
Karls	75
Gintaros	67
Patrick	78
Larry	83
John	86
Sergejus	83
Stojko	80
Chris	87
Scottie	93

1. Gintaros
2. Sergejus
3. Alan, Charles, and Scottie
4. Alan

Page 261

1. 25°
2. 11°
3. 24°
4. 21°
5. −12°
6. 0°
7. −11
8. +5
9. −2
10. −5
11. −16
12. +24
13. 0
14. +17

Page 262

1. Plane ABCD
2. Ray AB
3. Line Segment AB
4. Point B
5. Line AB
6. Angle ABC
7. Angle CBD
8. Angle ACB
9. Line Segment BC
10. Angle DCE

Page 263

A. octagon
B. hexagon
C. pentagon
D. trapezoid
E. square
F. rectangle (or square)
G. parallelogram
   (or square or rectangle)
H. quadrilateral
I. obtuse triangle
J. equilateral triangle
K. right triangle
L. scalene triangle
M. triangle
N. polygon
O. isosceles triangle
P. rhombus (or square)

Page 264

1. P = 14 in
2. P = 160 cm
   A = 1500 cm²
3. P = 48 in
   A = 140 in²
4. V = 180 in³
5. C = 25.12 in
6. V = 254.34 in³
7. V = 27 in³
8. V = 3014.4 cm³

Page 265

CHART:
   Monday: 4 hours, 15 minutes
   Tuesday: 4 hours, 25 minutes
   Wednesday: 5 hours, 55 minutes
   Thursday: 3 hours
   Friday: 5 hours, 20 minutes
   Saturday: 3 hours. 40 minutes
   Sunday: 1 hour, 40 minutes
1. 2 hours, 25 minutes
2. 3 hours, 55 minutes
3. 9 hours, 45 minutes
4. 8:35 a.m.
5. 2:05 p.m.

Page 266

1. Rae Rectangle
2. Tru Trapezoid
3. Helen Hexagon
4. Tish Triangle
5. Dee Decagon
6. Suki Square
7. Olive Octagon
8. Pat Pentagon
9. Rosa Rhombus
10. Pam Parallelogram

Page 267

Top
1. rectangle
2. trapezoid
3. square
4. parallelogram
5. square or rhombus
6. rhombus
Bottom
1. T
2. T
3. T
4. F
5. F
6. T
7. T
8. T
9. F
10. F

Page 268

The symmetrical figures are: A, B, D, F, G, and H. These should be colored. Also, check to see that student has drawn a correct line of symmetry in each of these figures.

At the bottom of the page, check to see that student has completed each figure to look symmetrical.

Page 269

The pairs of items should be labeled:

ping pong paddles:	T
Pennants:	S and F
gloves:	F
black shoes:	F
football helmets	F
skis:	F
ping pong balls:	S
footballs:	S
boxing gloves:	S
tennis racquets:	T or F or both
ballet slippers:	T
oars:	F

Figures at bottom: check to see that student has followed instructions accurately in drawing new figures.

Page 270

1.	=	11.	>
2.	=	12.	>
3.	>	13.	>
4.	=	14.	>
5.	=	15.	<
6.	<	16.	<
7.	=	17.	>
8.	>	18.	<
9.	=	19.	=
10.	=	20.	=

Page 271

Paths students draw will vary in length. Check student's path to see that it is measured correctly, and has been correctly converted into meters, according to the scale.

Page 272

1. 62.8 in
2. 9.42 in
3. 4.71 in
4. 28.26 in
5. 4.71 in
6. 7.85 in
7. 6.28 in
8. 9.42 ft
9. 25.12 in
10. 12.56 in
11. 18.84 cm
12. 31.4 in
13. 37.68 ft

Page 273

1. 400 in^2
2. 12 ft^2
3. 14 m^2

4. 3,600 in^2
5. 50 ft^2
6. 100,000 cm^2
7. 30 m^2
8. 24 yds^2

Page 274

1. P = 58 in
   A = 125 in^2
2. P = 10 ft
   A = 4 ft^2
3. P = 136 in
   A = 987 in^2
4. P = 96 in
   A = 576 in^2
5. P = 6.5 ft
   A = 1.5 ft^2
6. P = 120 in
   A = 900 in^2
7. P = 60 in
   A = 221 in^2
8. 3
9. 3

Page 275

1. 1,500 cm^3
2. 2,250 cm^3
3. 2,500 cm^3
4. 4,000 cm^3
5. 1,500 cm^3
6. 3,750 cm^3
7. 1,344 cm^3
A. Maria and Val
B. Sal

Pages 276–277

1.	D	5.	B
2.	E	6.	A
3.	H	7.	F
4.	C	8.	G

The hockey uniforms need the largest box.

Page 278

1.	F	8.	F
2.	T	9.	T
3.	T	10.	F
4.	F	11.	T
5.	F	12.	F
6.	F	13.	T
7.	F	14.	T

Page 279

Check to see that students have drawn bars on graphs to these heights:

0–1,000	 1
1,000–2,000	 6
2,000–3,000	 17
3,000–4,000	 12
4,000–5,000	 11
5,000–6,000	 3

Page 280

A. 27–66

B. 42
C. 42
1. a. 1–9
   b. 2
   c. 5
2. a. 72–92%
   b. 72%
   c. 84%
3. a. 6–23
   b. 9
   c. 10
4. a. 4%–80%
   b. 16%
   c. 12%
5. a. 119–221 mi
   b. 121 mi
   c. 121 mi

Page 281

1. 12
2. 9
3. 12
4. 9
5. Castle Quartet
6. Sand Wizards
7. Builders Four
8. Sculptors
9. Sand Wizards, Sculptors
10. Saturday

Page 282

1. 32
2. 13
3. 21
4. 8 (or leapfrogging)
5. 2
6. 22
7. egg balancing (or 9)
8. leapfrogging (or 8)

Page 283

A.	(-6, 5)	J.	(6, 1)
B.	(-2, 2)	K.	(-5, -4)
C.	(3, 4)	L.	(1, -6)
D.	(-6, -2)	M.	(-2, -6)
E.	(-4, 4)	N.	(-2, 5)
F.	(4, -2)	O.	(1, 3)
G.	(-4, -6)	P.	(5, -3)
H.	(3, -5)	Q.	(4, 0)
I.	(5, 3)		

Page 284

A. 1. $\frac{3}{7}$
   2. $\frac{1}{7}$
   3. $\frac{2}{7}$
   4. $\frac{1}{7}$

B. 1. $\frac{6}{14}$ or $\frac{3}{7}$
   2. $\frac{3}{14}$
   3. $\frac{3}{14}$